COLORADO'S
BEST FISHING WATERS™

Detailed Maps for Anglers of over 70 of the Best Waters

Wilderness
Adventures
Press, Inc.™

Belgrade, Montana

Wilderness Adventures Press is dedicated to making these angling maps as accurate as possible. Please contact us at books@wildadv.com to let us know about any information in this book that you feel needs to be corrected. We appreciate your help.

Special thanks to Chuck Rizuto at Rizuto's San Juan River Lodge, for detailed map information on the special trout water of the San Juan River (map 7 of 7, page 139).

Rizuto's San Juan River Lodge
PO Box 6309
Navajo Dam, NM 87419
505-632-3893 or 505-632-1411

TABLE OF CONTENTS

Colorado's Best Fishing Waters, Rivers...........iv
Colorado's Best Fishing Waters, Lakes...........v
Introduction...vi

RIVERS

Animas River 1
Arkansas River 8
Big Thompson River 19
Blue River...24
Cache La Poudre River 29
Cochetopa Creek.....................................35
Colorado River 39
Conejos River 48
Crystal River 53
Dolores River 56
Eagle River..64
East River 70
Elk River 74
Fryingpan River 78
Gunnison River 83
Lake Fork of the Gunnison River.....................92
Laramie River..97
Los Pinos River 100
North Platte River 105
Piedra River 109
Rio Grande River.................................... 113
Roaring Fork River...................................123
Rocky Mountain National Park 130
San Juan River 132
San Miguel River 140
South Platte River 143
St. Vrain Creek...................................... 151
Taylor River...156
Uncompahgre River 160
White River..164
Yampa River..169

LAKES

Aurora Reservoir.....................................176
Blue Mesa Reservoir 177
Bonny Reservoir 178
Chambers Lake 179
Chatfield Reservoir 180
Cherry Creek Reservoir 181
Delaney Butte Lakes 182
Elevenmile Reservoir 183
Grand Lake and Shadow Mountain Lake.................184
Grand Mesa Lakes, East..............................185
Grand Mesa Lakes, West.............................. 186
Green Mountain Reservoir 187
Hohnholz Lakes 188
Horseshoe Lake and Martin Lake......................189
Horsetooth Reservoir.................................190
Jackson Reservoir.................................... 191
John Martin Reservoir 192
Lake Granby..193
Lake John..194
Lon Hagler Reservoir 195
McPhee Reservoir 196
Neenoshe, Neegronda, and Queens Reservoirs....197
North Sterling Reservoir.............................198
Pearl Lake...199
Pueblo Reservoir 200
Quincy Reservoir 201
Red Feather Lakes 202
Sanchez Reservoir 203
Spinney Mountain Reservoir 204
Stagecoach Reservoir 205
Steamboat Lake.......................................206
Taylor Park Reservoir 207
Trappers Lake 208
Turquoise Lake.......................................209
Vallecito Reservoir..................................210
Vega Reservoir....................................... 211
Williams Fork Reservoir..............................212
Wolford Mountain Reservoir 213

Fly & Tackle Shops,
Guides & Sporting Good Stores 214

RIVERS

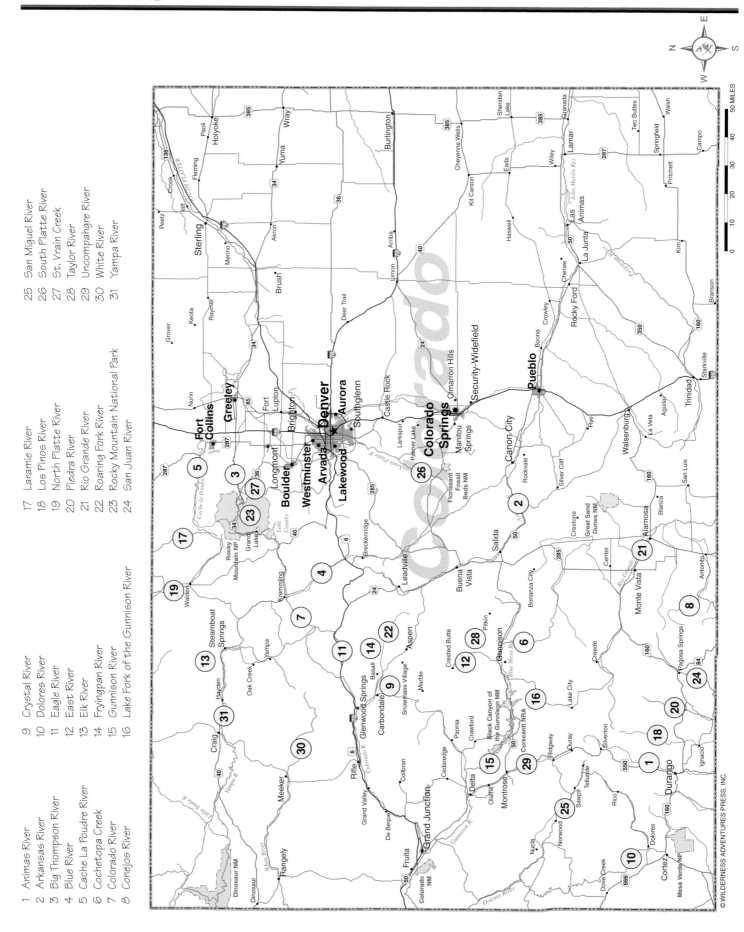

1 Animas River
2 Arkansas River
3 Big Thompson River
4 Blue River
5 Cache La Poudre River
6 Cochetopa Creek
7 Colorado River
8 Conejos River

9 Crystal River
10 Dolores River
11 Eagle River
12 East River
13 Elk River
14 Fryingpan River
15 Gunnison River
16 Lake Fork of the Gunnison River

17 Laramie River
18 Los Pinos River
19 North Platte River
20 Piedra River
21 Rio Grande River
22 Roaring Fork River
23 Rocky Mountain National Park
24 San Juan River

25 San Miguel River
26 South Platte River
27 St. Vrain Creek
28 Taylor River
29 Uncompahgre River
30 White River
31 Yampa River

LAKES

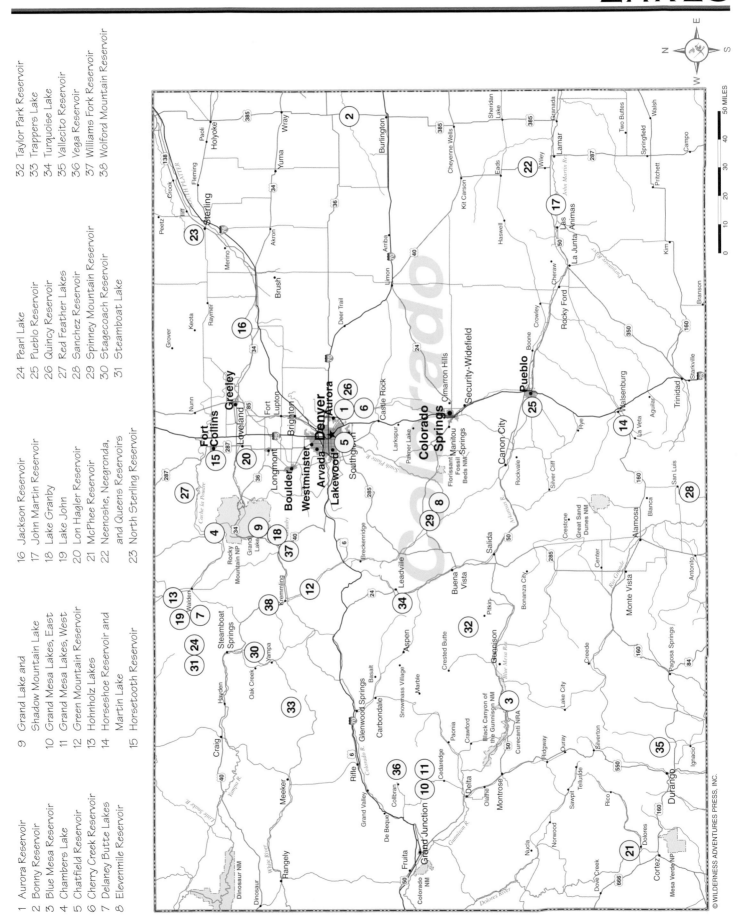

1   Aurora Reservoir
2   Bonny Reservoir
3   Blue Mesa Reservoir
4   Chambers Lake
5   Chatfield Reservoir
6   Cherry Creek Reservoir
7   Delaney Butte Lakes
8   Elevenmile Reservoir

9   Grand Lake and
    Shadow Mountain Lake
10 Grand Mesa Lakes, East
11 Grand Mesa Lakes, West
12 Green Mountain Reservoir
13 Hohnholz Lakes
14 Horseshoe Reservoir and
    Martin Lake
15 Horsetooth Reservoir

16 Jackson Reservoir
17 John Martin Reservoir
18 Lake Granby
19 Lake John
20 Lon Hagler Reservoir
21 McPhee Reservoir
22 Neenoshe, Neegronda,
    and Queens Reservoirs
23 North Sterling Reservoir

24 Pearl Lake
25 Pueblo Reservoir
26 Quincy Reservoir
27 Red Feather Lakes
28 Sanchez Reservoir
29 Spinney Mountain Reservoir
30 Stagecoach Reservoir
31 Steamboat Lake

32 Taylor Park Reservoir
33 Trappers Lake
34 Turquoise Lake
35 Vallecito Reservoir
36 Vega Reservoir
37 Williams Fork Reservoir
38 Wolford Mountain Reservoir

© WILDERNESS ADVENTURES PRESS, INC.

INTRODUCTION

The state of Colorado has long been famous for its fishing. From tiny high-country lakes and creeks to world-renowned rivers like the South Platte and Colorado Rivers to massive reservoirs like Blue Mesa or Pueblo, anglers of all types will find water here that suits them. Rainbow, brown, cutthroat, lake, and brook trout are available, as are kokanee salmon, arctic grayling, and hybrid trout like splake. Many warmwater species are present too, such as northern pike, largemouth and smallmouth bass, walleye, wipers, tiger muskie, and crappie, among others.

Much has been written about the state's amazing fisheries over the years, but good maps that anglers can actually use to pinpoint key areas are a rarity. This book changes all of that. The maps herein are based on U.S. Geological Survey maps, and a wealth of useful angling information is included on each one, along with an overview of the fishing.

The land along Colorado's most popular waters is usually a mix of private and public land and heavy fishing pressure in the most popular public areas can detract from the overall angling experience. So it pays to know every out-of-the-way access that casual anglers might overlook. The Department of Wildlife has worked hard to provide anglers with good access to their favorite waters through state wildlife areas and easements, and BLM and Forest Service lands also border many fisheries. The angler who can quickly identify all of these areas will find a whole new world of fishing opportunities.

The waters are listed in alphabetical order for easy reference without the need to consult an index for specific page numbers. Please note: Lake depths are shown on some of the reservoirs but these are approximations only, as siltation and drought can affect depths and water levels over time.

For the best information on up-to-the-minute water conditions for all of the rivers and lakes covered here, contact outdoor stores and fly shops near the water you're planning to fish. And it's always a good idea to acquire a copy of the latest fishing regulations. These are free for the asking by contacting:

Colorado Department of Wildlife
6060 Broadway
Denver, CO 80216
303-297-1192
www.wildlife.state.co.us

LEGEND

▬▬▬	Interstate	▬	BLM - Public Land	⚲	Picnic Area
═══	Primary Highway	▬	State - Public Land	✈	Airport
────	Road or Street	▬	Indian Reservation	〰	Rapids
·········	Trails	▬	National Forest	▬▬	Dam
70	Interstate Route	🐟	Fishing Access	▪ ▪ ▪ ▪	Continental Divide
131	State Route	⬭	Boat Launch	┼──┼	Railroad
192	U.S. Route	▲	Campsite		

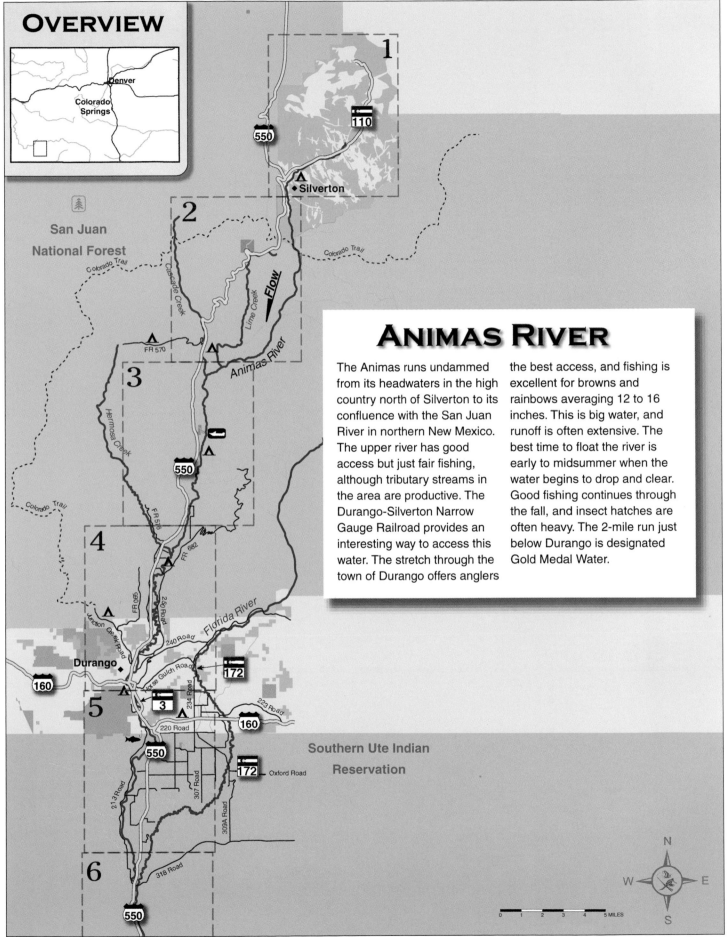

OVERVIEW

Denver

Colorado Springs

San Juan National Forest

Colorado Trail

Cascade Creek

Lime Creek

Flow

Colorado Trail

Animas River

Silverton

Hermosa Creek

Colorado Trail

Florida River

Junction Creek Road

Durango

Lightner Gulch Road

Oxford Road

Southern Ute Indian Reservation

FR 570

FR 576

FR 682

FR 065

250 Road

240 Road

234 Road

223 Road

220 Road

307 Road

309A Road

213 Road

318 Road

1 · 2 · 3 · 4 · 5 · 6

550 · 110 · 550 · 172 · 3 · 160 · 550 · 172 · 160

ANIMAS RIVER

The Animas runs undammed from its headwaters in the high country north of Silverton to its confluence with the San Juan River in northern New Mexico. The upper river has good access but just fair fishing, although tributary streams in the area are productive. The Durango-Silverton Narrow Gauge Railroad provides an interesting way to access this water. The stretch through the town of Durango offers anglers the best access, and fishing is excellent for browns and rainbows averaging 12 to 16 inches. This is big water, and runoff is often extensive. The best time to float the river is early to midsummer when the water begins to drop and clear. Good fishing continues through the fall, and insect hatches are often heavy. The 2-mile run just below Durango is designated Gold Medal Water.

N
W   E
S

0 1 2 3 4 5 MILES

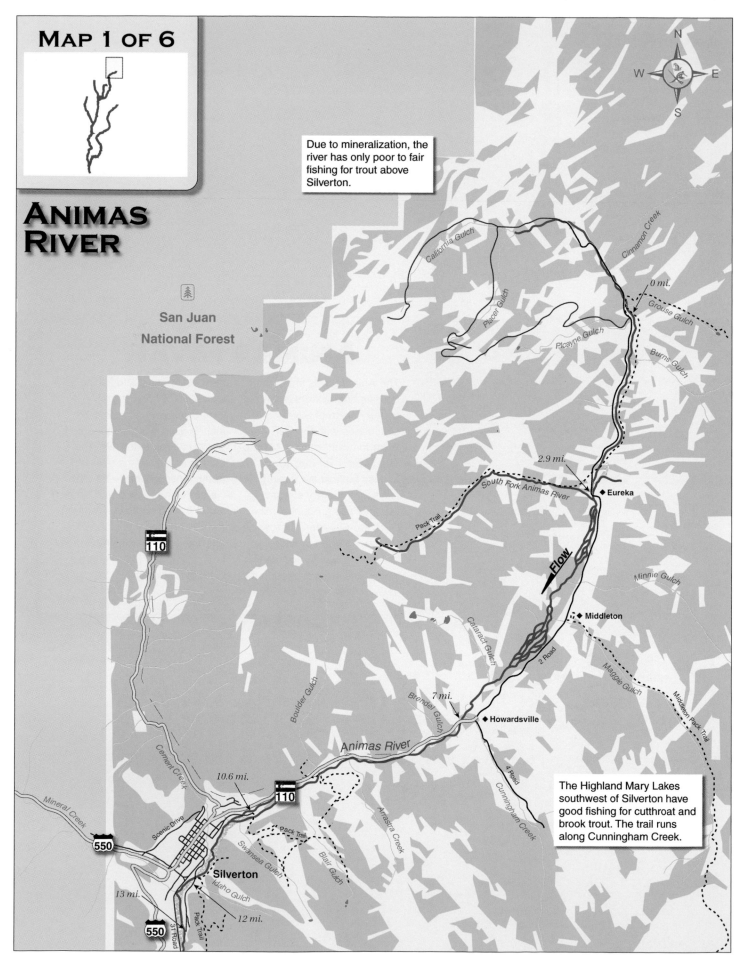

MAP 1 OF 6

ANIMAS RIVER

San Juan
National Forest

Due to mineralization, the river has only poor to fair fishing for trout above Silverton.

The Highland Mary Lakes southwest of Silverton have good fishing for cutthroat and brook trout. The trail runs along Cunningham Creek.

California Gulch

Cinnamon Creek

Placer Gulch

Picayne Gulch

Grouse Gulch

Burns Gulch

0 mi.

2.9 mi.

South Fork Animas River

Pack Trail

◆ Eureka

Flow

Minnie Gulch

Cataract Gulch

Middleton

2 Road

◆ Middleton

Maggie Gulch

Boulder Gulch

Brender Gulch

7 mi.

◆ Howardsville

Middleton Pack Trail

Animas River

4 Road

Cement Creek

10.6 mi.

Arrastra Creek

Cunningham Creek

Mineral Creek

Scenic Drive

Pack Trail

Swansea Gulch

Blair Gulch

Silverton

Idaho Gulch

13 mi.

12 mi.

31 Road

Pack Trail

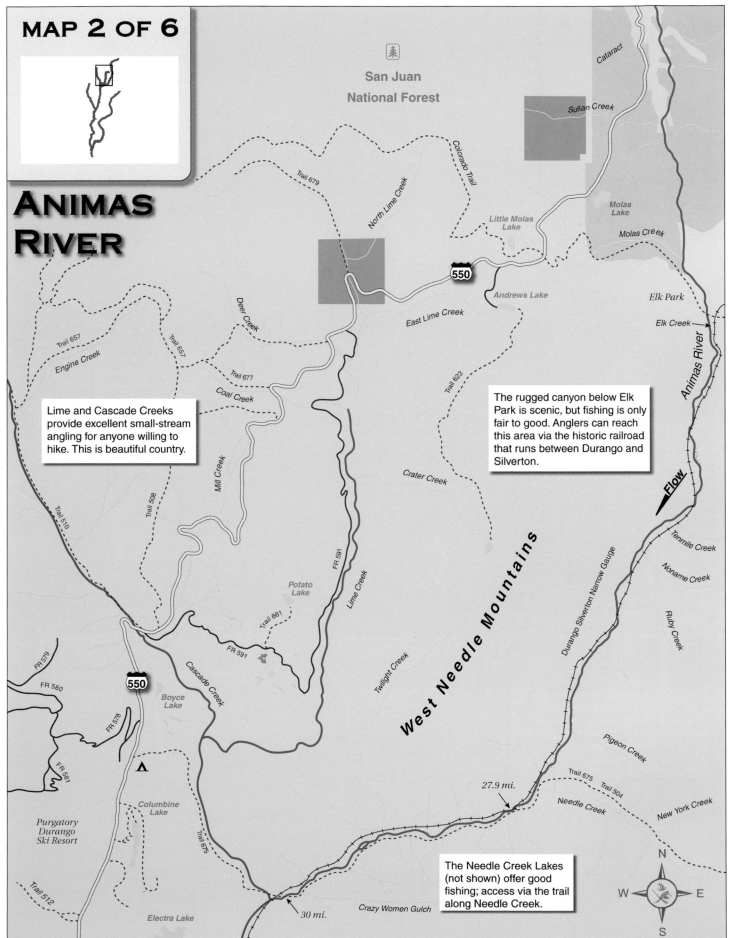

MAP 2 OF 6

ANIMAS RIVER

San Juan
National Forest

Trail 679

North Lime Creek

Colorado Trail

Cataract

Sullan Creek

Molas
Lake

Little Molas
Lake

Molas Creek

550

East Lime Creek

Andrews Lake

Elk Park

Elk Creek

Deer Creek

Trail 657

Trail 657

Engine Creek

Trail 677

Coal Creek

Trail 623

Animas River

Lime and Cascade Creeks provide excellent small-stream angling for anyone willing to hike. This is beautiful country.

The rugged canyon below Elk Park is scenic, but fishing is only fair to good. Anglers can reach this area via the historic railroad that runs between Durango and Silverton.

Mill Creek

Trail 510

Trail 508

Crater Creek

Flow

Tenmile Creek

Noname Creek

FR 591

Potato
Lake

Lime Creek

Ruby Creek

Trail 661

FR 579

FR 580

FR 591

Twilight Creek

West Needle Mountains

Durango Silverton Narrow Gauge

550

FR 578

Boyce
Lake

Cascade Creek

Pigeon Creek

FR 581

27.9 mi.

Trail 675

Trail 504

Columbine
Lake

Needle Creek

New York Creek

Purgatory
Durango
Ski Resort

Trail 675

N

Trail 512

The Needle Creek Lakes (not shown) offer good fishing; access via the trail along Needle Creek.

W   E

Electra Lake

30 mi.

Crazy Women Gulch

S

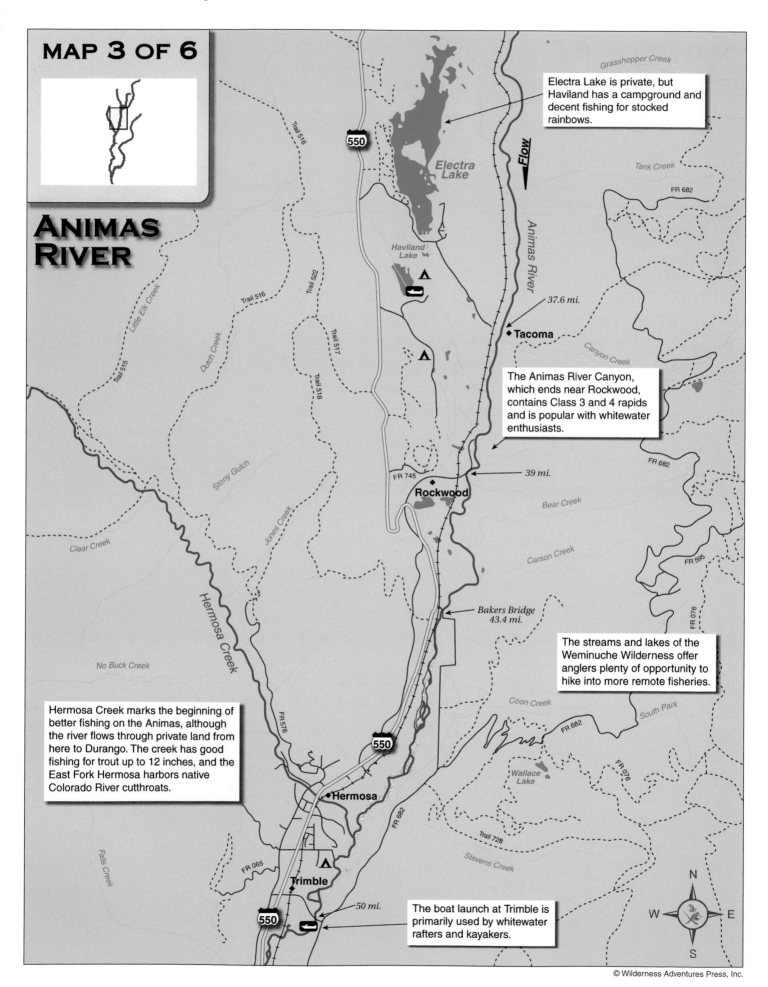

MAP 3 OF 6

ANIMAS RIVER

Grasshopper Creek

Electra Lake is private, but Haviland has a campground and decent fishing for stocked rainbows.

Flow

Tank Creek

Electra Lake

FR 682

Haviland Lake

Animas River

37.6 mi.

◆ **Tacoma**

Canyon Creek

The Animas River Canyon, which ends near Rockwood, contains Class 3 and 4 rapids and is popular with whitewater enthusiasts.

FR 682

FR 745

39 mi.

Rockwood

Bear Creek

Carson Creek

FR 595

Bakers Bridge
43.4 mi.

FR 076

The streams and lakes of the Weminuche Wilderness offer anglers plenty of opportunity to hike into more remote fisheries.

Coon Creek

South Park

Hermosa Creek marks the beginning of better fishing on the Animas, although the river flows through private land from here to Durango. The creek has good fishing for trout up to 12 inches, and the East Fork Hermosa harbors native Colorado River cutthroats.

FR 576

FR 682

FR 076

Wallace Lake

◆ **Hermosa**

Trail 728

Stevens Creek

FR 065

Falls Creek

Trimble

50 mi.

The boat launch at Trimble is primarily used by whitewater rafters and kayakers.

Trail 515
Trail 516
Little Elk Creek
Trail 516
Trail 522
Trail 517
Trail 518
Dutch Creek
Stony Gulch
Jones Creek
Clear Creek
Hermosa Creek
No Buck Creek

N
W · E
S

© Wilderness Adventures Press, Inc.

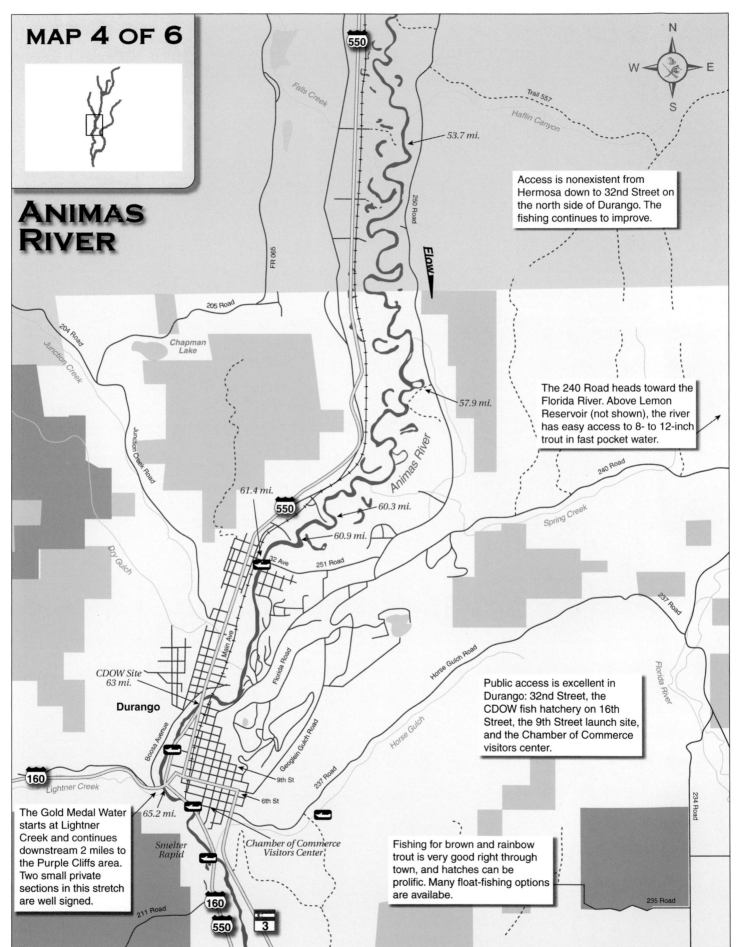

MAP 4 OF 6

ANIMAS RIVER

N W E S

53.7 mi.

Falls Creek

Trail 557

Haflin Canyon

250 Road

Access is nonexistent from Hermosa down to 32nd Street on the north side of Durango. The fishing continues to improve.

Flow

FR 065

205 Road

204 Road

Junction Creek

Chapman Lake

57.9 mi.

Animas River

The 240 Road heads toward the Florida River. Above Lemon Reservoir (not shown), the river has easy access to 8- to 12-inch trout in fast pocket water.

240 Road

61.4 mi.

550

60.3 mi.

60.9 mi.

Spring Creek

Junction Creek Road

Dry Gulch

32 Ave

251 Road

237 Road

Florida River

Main Ave

Florida Road

Horse Gulch Road

Public access is excellent in Durango: 32nd Street, the CDOW fish hatchery on 16th Street, the 9th Street launch site, and the Chamber of Commerce visitors center.

CDOW Site 63 mi.

Durango

Boosa Avenue

Geoglein Gulch Road

Horse Gulch

237 Road

160

Lightner Creek

9th St

6th St

234 Road

The Gold Medal Water starts at Lightner Creek and continues downstream 2 miles to the Purple Cliffs area. Two small private sections in this stretch are well signed.

65.2 mi.

Smelter Rapid

Chamber of Commerce Visitors Center

Fishing for brown and rainbow trout is very good right through town, and hatches can be prolific. Many float-fishing options are availabe.

211 Road

160

550

3

235 Road

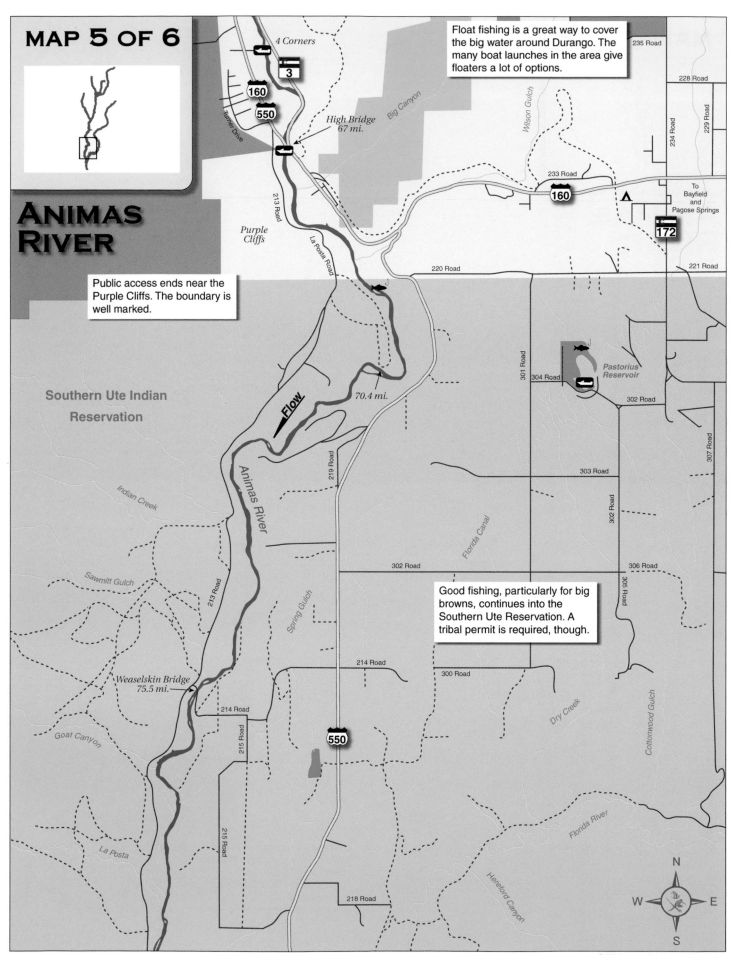

MAP **5** OF **6**

ANIMAS RIVER

Float fishing is a great way to cover the big water around Durango. The many boat launches in the area give floaters a lot of options.

4 Corners

3

160

550

High Bridge 67 mi.

Big Canyon

Wilson Gulch

235 Road

228 Road

229 Road

234 Road

233 Road

160

To Bayfield and Pagose Springs

172

Turner Drive

213 Road

Purple Cliffs

La Posta Road

220 Road

221 Road

Public access ends near the Purple Cliffs. The boundary is well marked.

Southern Ute Indian Reservation

70.4 mi.

Flow

301 Road

304 Road

Pastorius Reservoir

302 Road

303 Road

302 Road

307 Road

Indian Creek

219 Road

Animas River

Florida Canal

306 Road

Sawmitt Gulch

213 Road

Spring Gulch

302 Road

305 Road

Good fishing, particularly for big browns, continues into the Southern Ute Reservation. A tribal permit is required, though.

214 Road

300 Road

Weaselskin Bridge 75.5 mi.

214 Road

215 Road

550

Dry Creek

Cottonwood Gulch

Goat Canyon

215 Road

La Posta

Florida River

218 Road

Hereford Canyon

N
W E
S

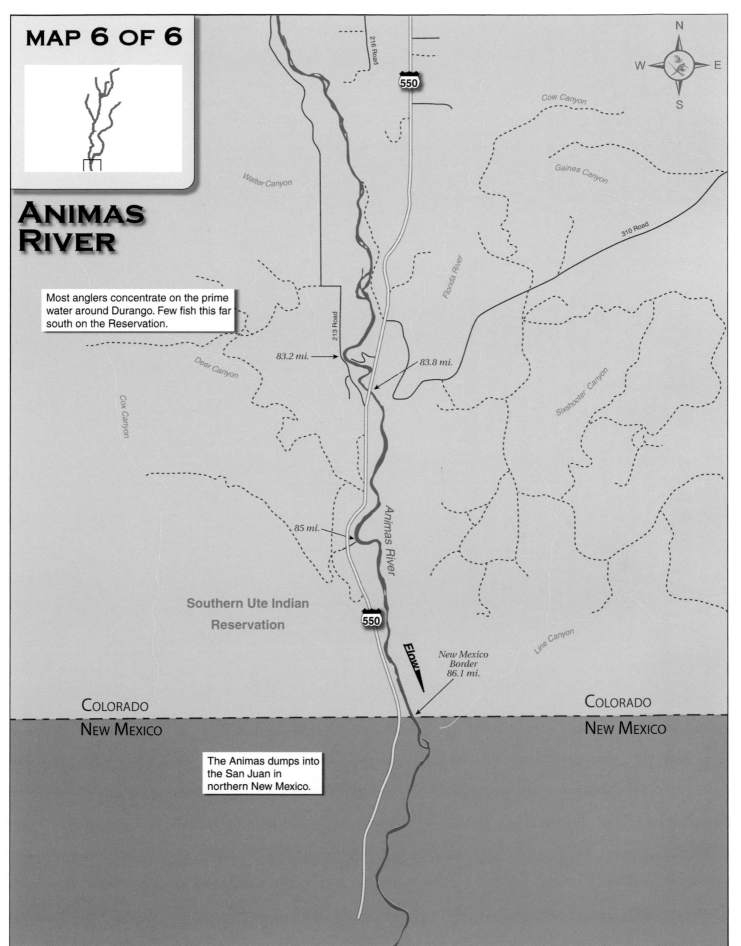

MAP 6 OF 6

ANIMAS RIVER

N

W   E

S

216 Road

550

Cow Canyon

Gaines Canyon

310 Road

Walter Canyon

Florida River

Most anglers concentrate on the prime water around Durango. Few fish this far south on the Reservation.

213 Road

Deer Canyon

83.2 mi.

83.8 mi.

Sixshooter Canyon

Cox Canyon

85 mi.

Animas River

Southern Ute Indian Reservation

550

Flow

Line Canyon

New Mexico Border 86.1 mi.

COLORADO

COLORADO

NEW MEXICO

NEW MEXICO

The Animas dumps into the San Juan in northern New Mexico.

© Wilderness Adventures Press, Inc.

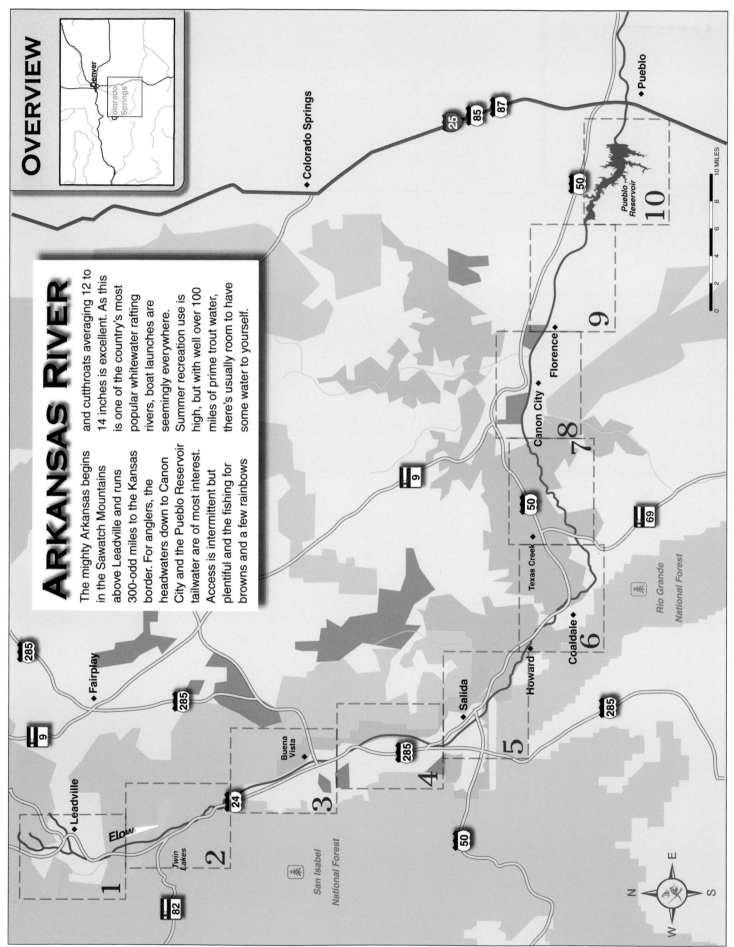

ARKANSAS RIVER

The mighty Arkansas begins in the Sawatch Mountains above Leadville and runs 300-odd miles to the Kansas border. For anglers, the headwaters down to Canon City and the Pueblo Reservoir tailwater are of most interest. Access is intermittent but plentiful and the fishing for browns and a few rainbows and cutthroats averaging 12 to 14 inches is excellent. As this is one of the country's most popular whitewater rafting rivers, boat launches are seemingly everywhere. Summer recreation use is high, but with well over 100 miles of prime trout water, there's usually room to have some water to yourself.

© Wilderness Adventures Press, Inc.

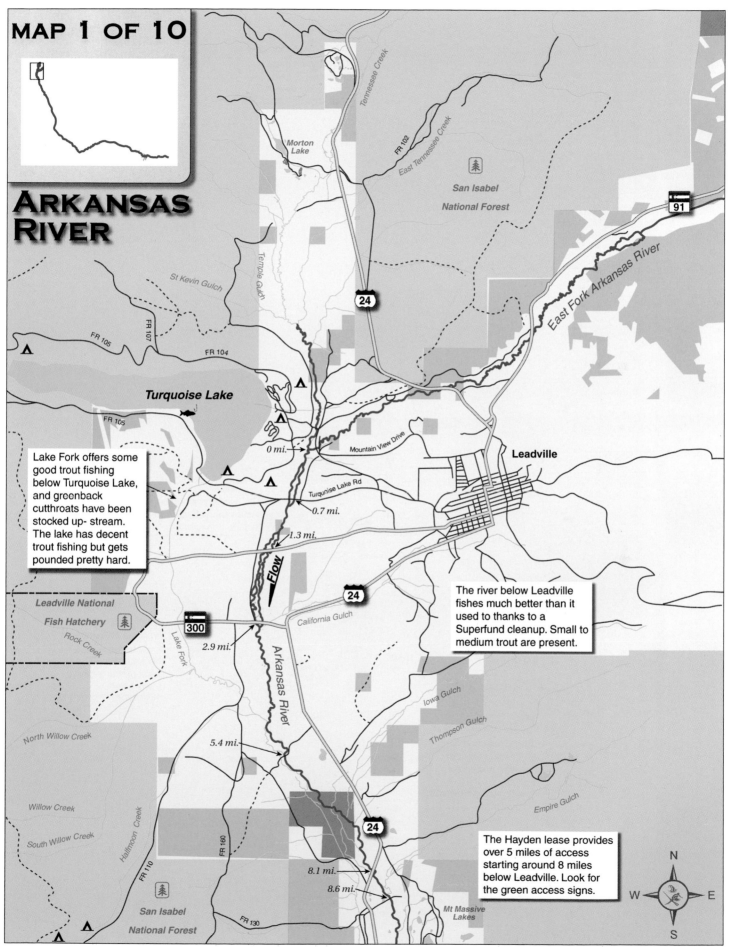

MAP 1 OF 10

ARKANSAS RIVER

Tennessee Creek

Morton Lake

FR 102

East Tennessee Creek

San Isabel National Forest

91

St Kevin Gulch

Temple Gulch

FR 107

FR 105

24

East Fork Arkansas River

FR 104

Turquoise Lake

FR 105

0 mi.

Mountain View Drive

Leadville

Lake Fork offers some good trout fishing below Turquoise Lake, and greenback cutthroats have been stocked up- stream. The lake has decent trout fishing but gets pounded pretty hard.

Turquoise Lake Rd

0.7 mi.

1.3 mi.

Flow

Leadville National Fish Hatchery

Rock Creek

300

Lake Fork

2.9 mi.

California Gulch

24

The river below Leadville fishes much better than it used to thanks to a Superfund cleanup. Small to medium trout are present.

Arkansas River

Iowa Gulch

North Willow Creek

Thompson Gulch

5.4 mi.

Willow Creek

Empire Gulch

Halfmoon Creek

South Willow Creek

FR 110

FR 160

24

8.1 mi.

8.6 mi.

The Hayden lease provides over 5 miles of access starting around 8 miles below Leadville. Look for the green access signs.

San Isabel National Forest

FR 130

Mt Massive Lakes

N

W E

S

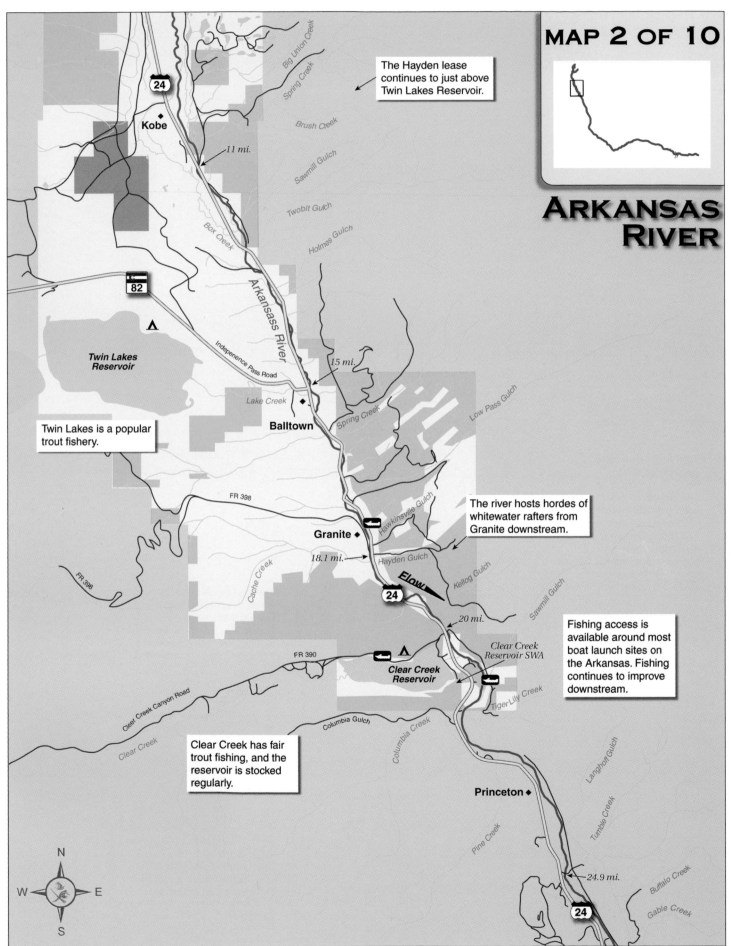

MAP 2 OF 10

ARKANSAS RIVER

The Hayden lease continues to just above Twin Lakes Reservoir.

Kobe

11 mi.

82

Twin Lakes Reservoir

Twin Lakes is a popular trout fishery.

Independence Pass Road

Arkansas River

15 mi.

Lake Creek

Balltown

Spring Creek

Big Union Creek

Spring Creek

Brush Creek

Sawmill Gulch

Twobit Gulch

Holmes Gulch

Low Pass Gulch

FR 398

Cache Creek

FR 398

Hawkinsville Gulch

The river hosts hordes of whitewater rafters from Granite downstream.

Granite

18.1 mi.

Hayden Gulch

Kellog Gulch

Sawmill Gulch

Flow

24

20 mi.

FR 390

Clear Creek Reservoir

Clear Creek Reservoir SWA

Tiger Lily Creek

Fishing access is available around most boat launch sites on the Arkansas. Fishing continues to improve downstream.

Clear Creek Canyon Road

Clear Creek

Columbia Gulch

Columbia Creek

Clear Creek has fair trout fishing, and the reservoir is stocked regularly.

Princeton

Langhoff Gulch

Pine Creek

Tumble Creek

24.9 mi.

Buffalo Creek

Gable Creek

24

N
W E
S

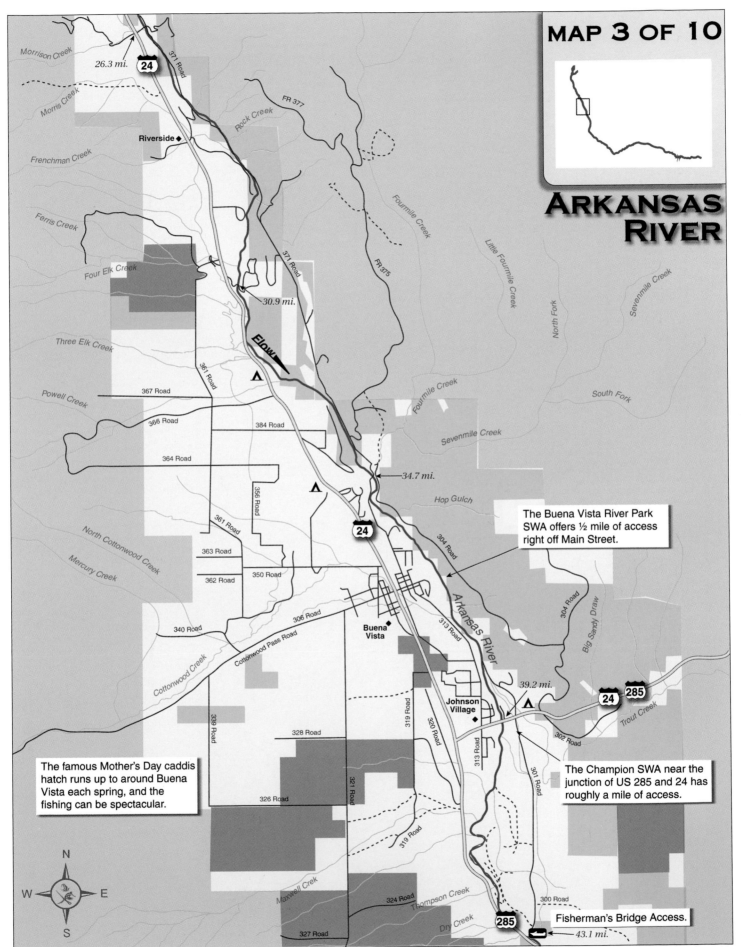

MAP 3 OF 10

ARKANSAS RIVER

Morrison Creek

26.3 mi.

24

371 Road

Morris Creek

FR 377

Rock Creek

Riverside ◆

Frenchman Creek

Fourmile Creek

FR 375

Ferris Creek

Little Fourmile Creek

North Fork

Sevenmile Creek

Four Elk Creek

371 Road

30.9 mi.

Flow

South Fork

Three Elk Creek

361 Road

Fourmile Creek

Powell Creek

367 Road

Sevenmile Creek

366 Road

384 Road

364 Road

356 Road

34.7 mi.

Hop Gulch

The Buena Vista River Park SWA offers ½ mile of access right off Main Street.

361 Road

304 Road

363 Road

North Cottonwood Creek

362 Road

350 Road

Mercury Creek

306 Road

340 Road

Arkansas River

304 Road

Big Sandy Draw

Buena Vista ◆

313 Road

Cottonwood Pass Road

319 Road

320 Road

39.2 mi.

24 285

Johnson Village ◆

302 Road

Trout Creek

339 Road

328 Road

313 Road

301 Road

The Champion SWA near the junction of US 285 and 24 has roughly a mile of access.

Cottonwood Creek

The famous Mother's Day caddis hatch runs up to around Buena Vista each spring, and the fishing can be spectacular.

321 Road

326 Road

319 Road

N
W · E
S

324 Road

Maxwell Creek

Thompson Creek

300 Road

327 Road

Dry Creek

285

Fisherman's Bridge Access.

43.1 mi.

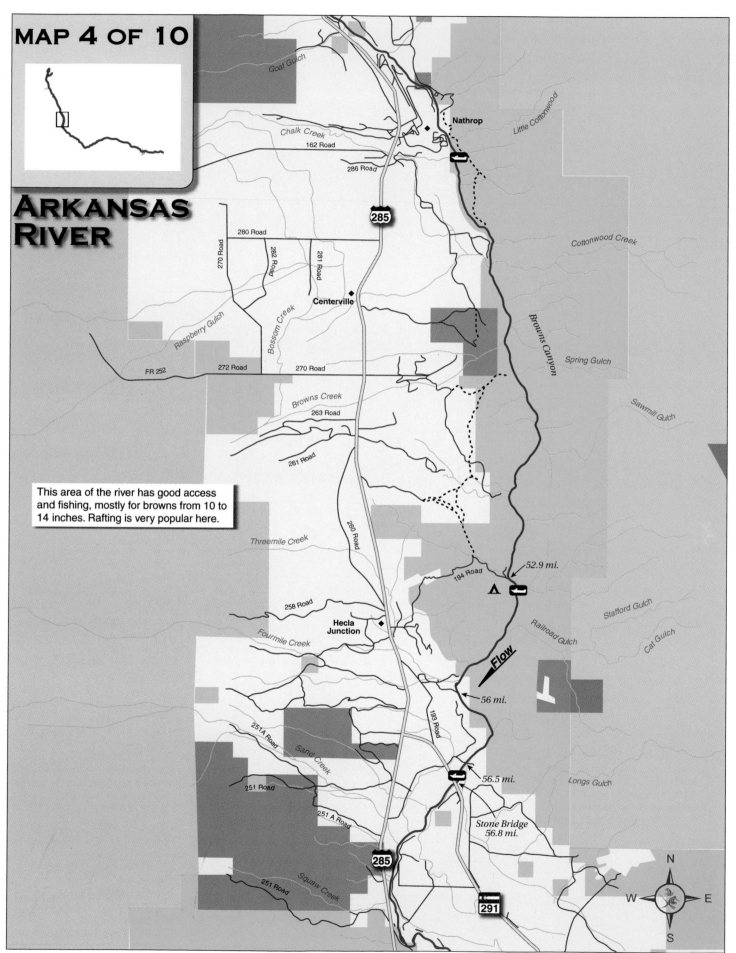

MAP 4 OF 10

ARKANSAS RIVER

This area of the river has good access and fishing, mostly for browns from 10 to 14 inches. Rafting is very popular here.

Nathrop

Goat Gulch

Chalk Creek

162 Road

286 Road

Little Cottonwood

Cottonwood Creek

285

280 Road

270 Road

282 Road

281 Road

Centerville

Browns Canyon

Spring Gulch

Raspberry Gulch

Bossom Creek

FR 252

272 Road

270 Road

Sawmill Gulch

Browns Creek

263 Road

261 Road

260 Road

Threemile Creek

194 Road

52.9 mi.

Stafford Gulch

258 Road

Railroad Gulch

Cat Gulch

Hecla Junction

Fourmile Creek

Flow

56 mi.

193 Road

251 A Road

Sand Creek

56.5 mi.

Longs Gulch

251 Road

251 A Road

Stone Bridge
56.8 mi.

285

Squaw Creek

251 Road

291

N
W   E
S

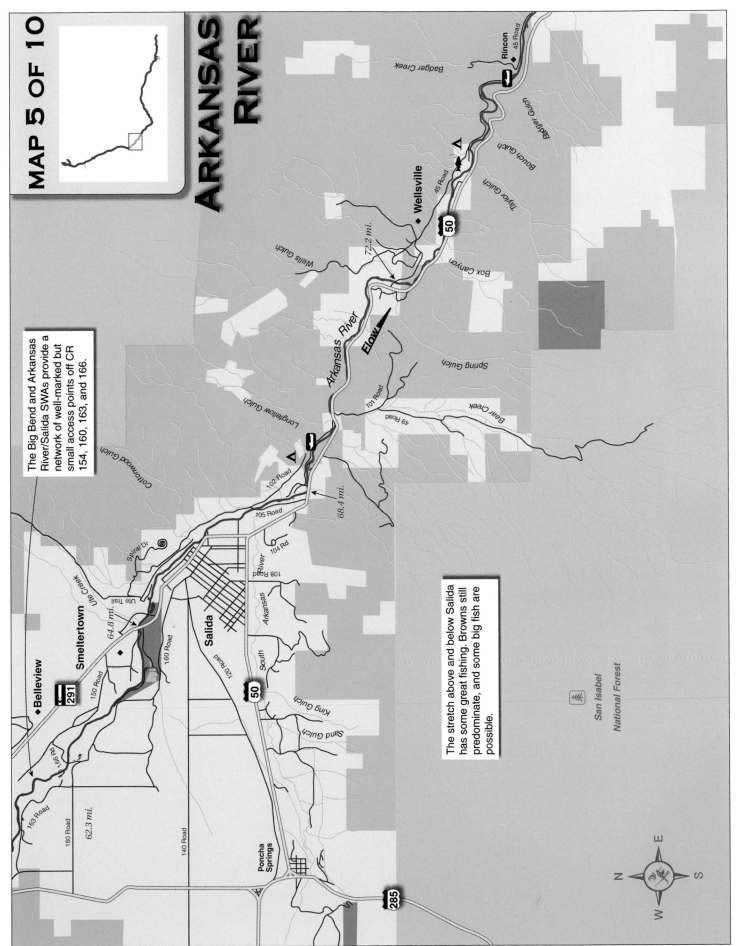

MAP 5 OF 10

ARKANSAS RIVER

The Big Bend and Arkansas River/Salida SWAs provide a network of well-marked but small access points off CR 154, 160, 163, and 166.

The stretch above and below Salida has some great fishing. Browns still predominate, and some big fish are possible.

Rincon

Badger Creek

45 Road

Badger Gulch

Bouch Gulch

Wellsville

Taylor Gulch

45 Road

72.2 mi.

50

Box Canyon

Wells Gulch

Arkansas River

Flow

Spring Gulch

101 Road

Longfellow Gulch

49 Road

Bear Creek

Cottonwood Gulch

102 Road

68.4 mi.

105 Road

104 Rd

108 Road

Spiral Dr

San Isabel National Forest

Ute Creek

Ute Trail

64.8 mi.

Arkansas River

Smeltertown

Salida

120 Road

Belleview

291

160 Road

150 Road

King Gulch

Sand Gulch

South Arkansas

50

166 Rd

163 Road

160 Road

62.3 mi.

140 Road

Poncha Springs

285

N E S W

© Wilderness Adventures Press, Inc.

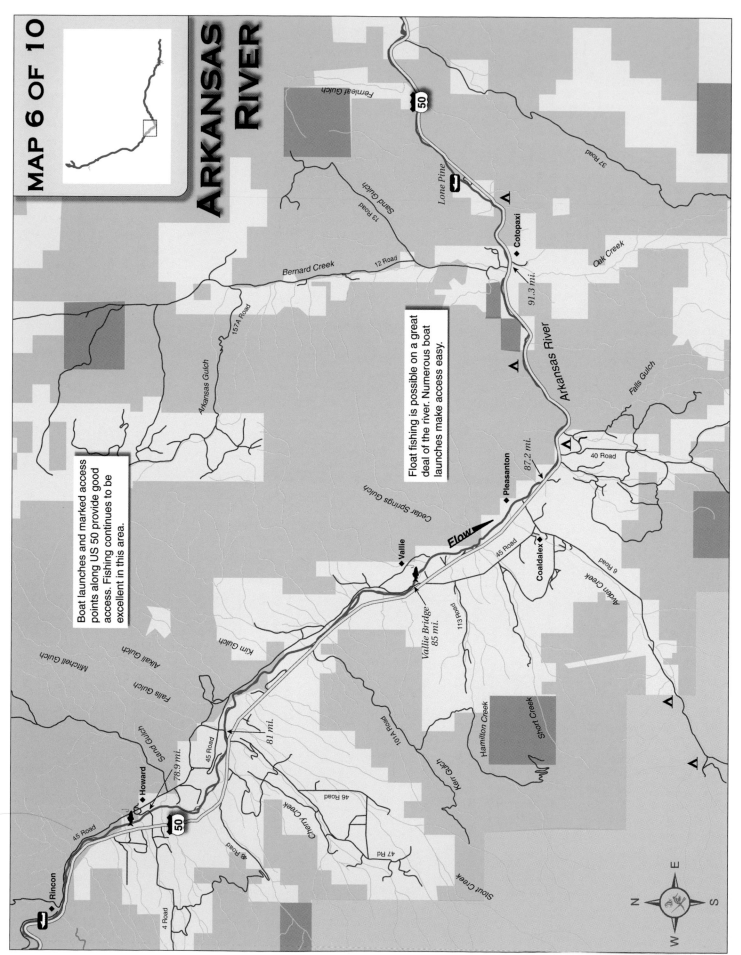

MAP 6 OF 10

ARKANSAS RIVER

Boat launches and marked access points along US 50 provide good access. Fishing continues to be excellent in this area.

Float fishing is possible on a great deal of the river. Numerous boat launches make access easy.

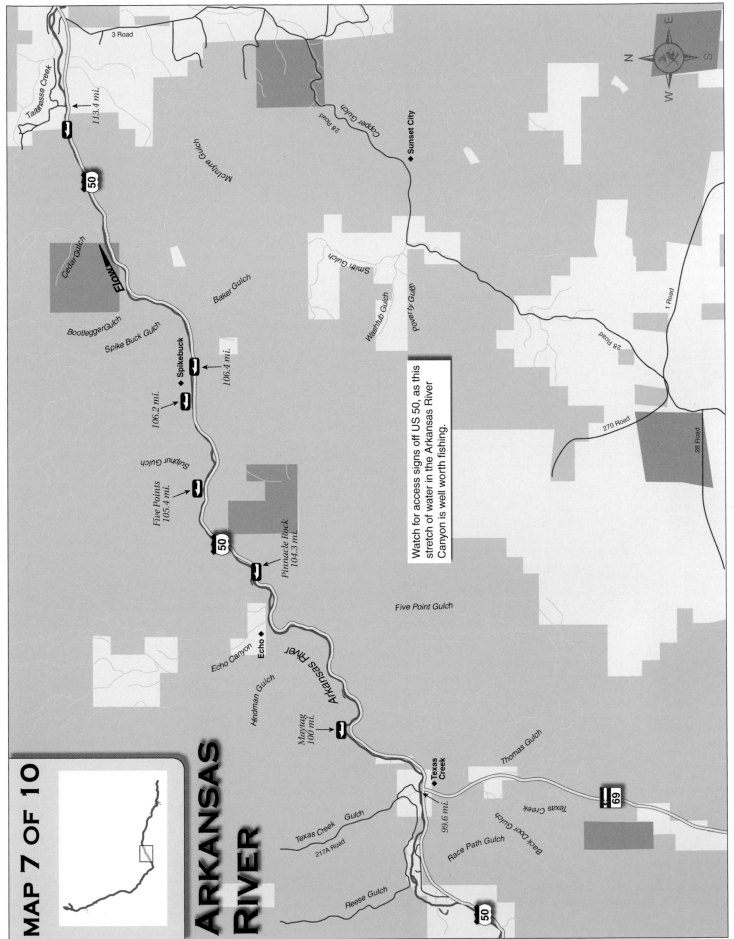

MAP 7 OF 10

ARKANSAS RIVER

Watch for access signs off US 50, as this stretch of water in the Arkansas River Canyon is well worth fishing.

3 Road

Talarasse Creek

113.4 mi.

50

Cedar Gulch

McIntyre Gulch

Copper Gulch

28 Road

Sunset City

Bootlegger Gulch

Baker Gulch

Smith Gulch

Washtub Gulch

Poverty Gulch

1 Road

28 Road

Spike Buck Gulch

Spikebuck

106.4 mi.

106.2 mi.

Sulphur Gulch

270 Road

28 Road

Five Points
105.4 mi.

Pinnacle Rock
104.3 mi.

50

Five Point Gulch

Echo Canyon   Echo

Hindman Gulch

Arkansas River

Maytag
100 mi.

Thomas Gulch

Texas
Creek

69

99.6 mi.

Texas Creek

Texas Creek   Gulch

Back Door Gulch

217A Road

Race Path Gulch

Reese Gulch

50

© Wilderness Adventures Press, Inc.

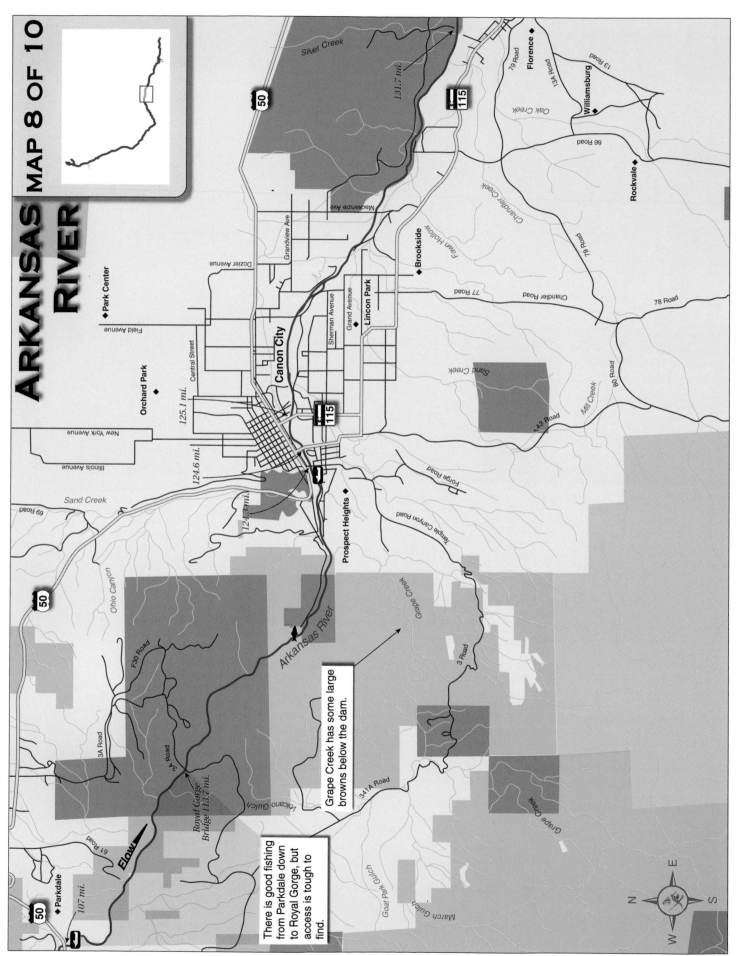

ARKANSAS
MAP 8 OF 10
RIVER

Grape Creek has some large browns below the dam.

There is good fishing from Parkdale down to Royal Gorge, but access is tough to find.

Royal Gorge Bridge 113.7 mi.

131.7 mi.

125.1 mi.

124.6 mi.

124.3 mi.

107 mi.

Flow

Arkansas River

Florence

Williamsburg

Rockvale

Brookside

Lincon Park

Canon City

Park Center

Orchard Park

Prospect Heights

Parkdale

Ohio Canyon

Silver Creek

Sand Creek

Grape Creek

Chandler Creek

Oak Creek

Sand Creek

Mill Creek

Grape Creek

Fern Hollow

Volcano Gulch

Goat Park Gulch

March Gulch

Mackenzie Ave

Grandview Ave

Dozier Avenue

Field Avenue

Central Street

New York Avenue

Illinois Avenue

Sherman Avenue

Grand Avenue

69 Road

3A Road

3 A Road

F30 Road

61 Road

341A Road

3 Road

Forge Road

Temple Canyon Road

1 43 Road

Chandler Road

77 Road

78 Road

80 Road

79 Road

13A Road

13 Road

86 Road

76 Road

N E S W

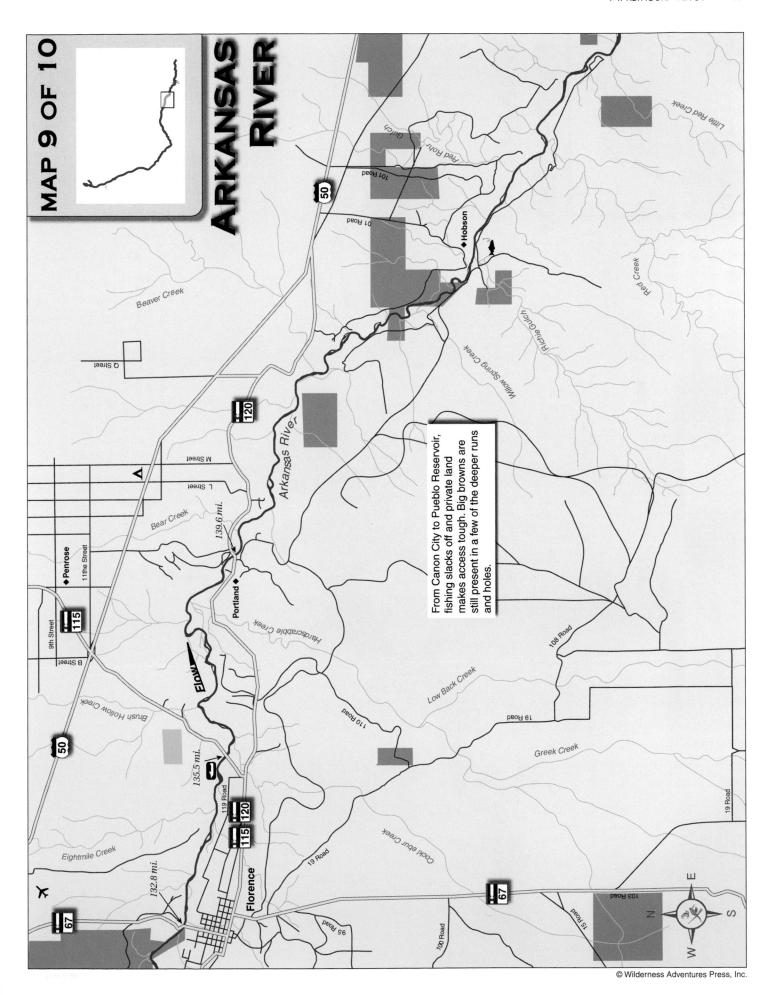

MAP 9 OF 10

ARKANSAS RIVER

Beaver Creek

Q Street

120

M Street

L Street

Bear Creek

139.6 mi.

Penrose ◆

11the Street

115

9th Street

B Street

FLOW

135.5 mi.

50

Brush Hollow Creek

119 Road

120

115

Eightmile Creek

132.8 mi.

67

Florence

95 Road

100 Road

19 Road

Cockl ebur Creek

19 Road

Arkansas River

Portland ◆

Hardscrabble Creek

110 Road

Low Back Creek

19 Road

Greek Creek

108 Road

103 Road

15 Road

19 Road

50

01 Road

Hobson ◆

101 Road

Red Rohr Gulch

Willow Spring Creek

Richie Gulch

Red Creek

Little Red Creek

67

67

From Canon City to Pueblo Reservoir, fishing slacks off and private land makes access tough. Big browns are still present in a few of the deeper runs and holes.

N
W   E
S

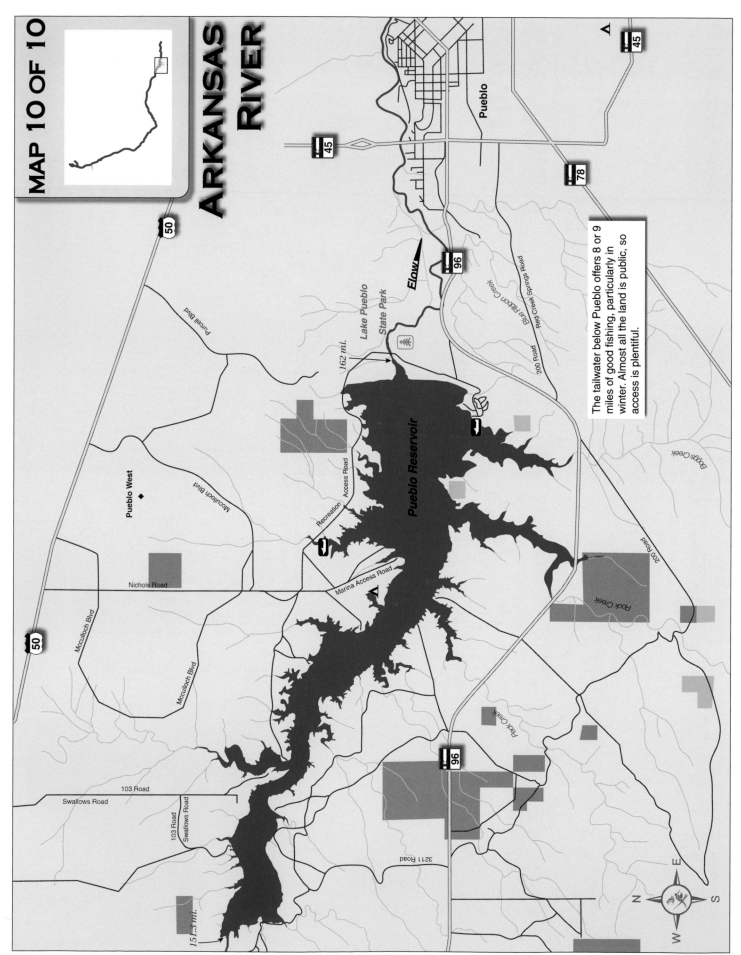

MAP 10 OF 10

ARKANSAS RIVER

Pueblo

Pueblo West

Lake Pueblo State Park

Pueblo Reservoir

The tailwater below Pueblo offers 8 or 9 miles of good fishing, particularly in winter. Almost all the land is public, so access is plentiful.

Purcell Blvd

Mcculloch Blvd

Mcculloch Blvd

Mcculloch Blvd

Nichols Road

Recreation Access Road

Marina Access Road

162 mi.

15.3 mi.

103 Road

Swallows Road

103 Road

Swallows Road

3211 Road

200 Road

200 Road

Rock Creek

Peck Creek

Boggs Creek

Blue Ribbon Creek

Red Creek Springs Road

Flow

N E S W

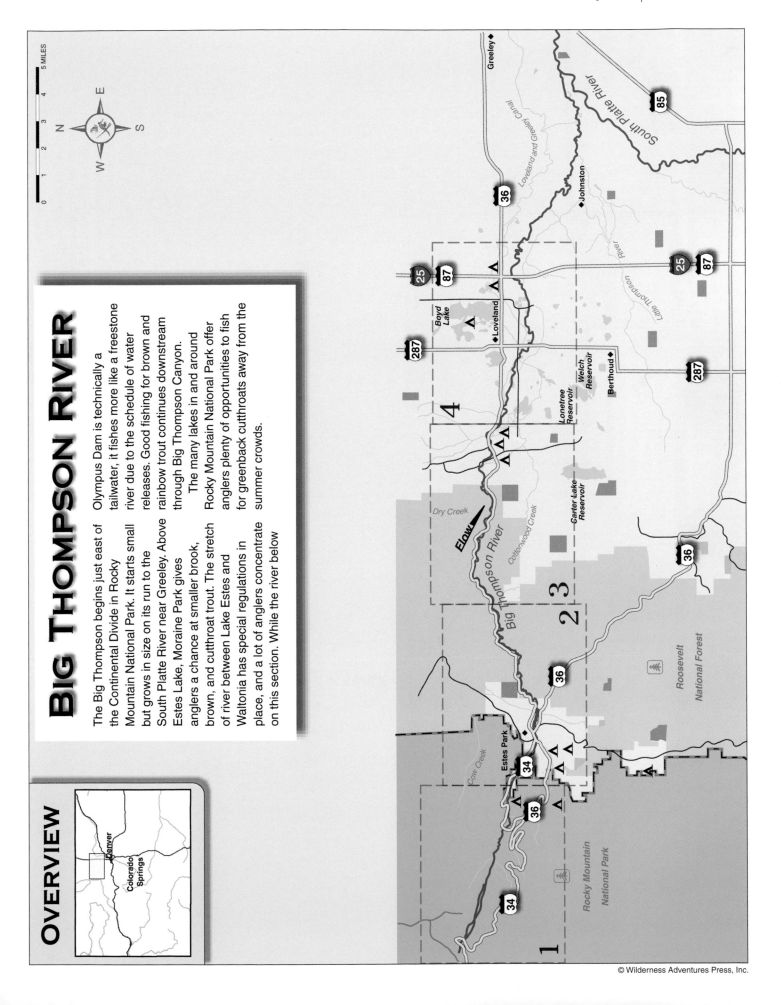

OVERVIEW

Big Thompson River

The Big Thompson begins just east of the Continental Divide in Rocky Mountain National Park. It starts small but grows in size on its run to the South Platte River near Greeley. Above Estes Lake, Moraine Park gives anglers a chance at smaller brook, brown, and cutthroat trout. The stretch of river between Lake Estes and Waltonia has special regulations in place, and a lot of anglers concentrate on this section. While the river below

Olympus Dam is technically a tailwater, it fishes more like a freestone river due to the schedule of water releases. Good fishing for brown and rainbow trout continues downstream through Big Thompson Canyon.

The many lakes in and around Rocky Mountain National Park offer anglers plenty of opportunities to fish for greenback cutthroats away from the summer crowds.

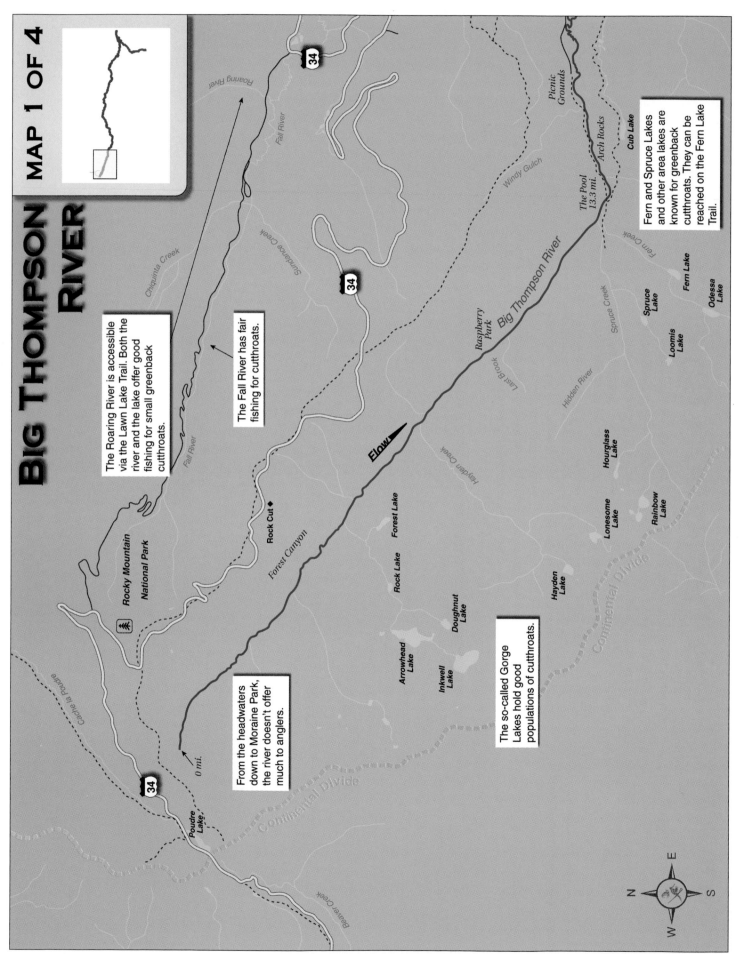

BIG THOMPSON RIVER

MAP 1 OF 4

The Roaring River is accessible via the Lawn Lake Trail. Both the river and the lake offer good fishing for small greenback cutthroats.

The Fall River has fair fishing for cutthroats.

From the headwaters down to Moraine Park, the river doesn't offer much to anglers.

The so-called Gorge Lakes hold good populations of cutthroats.

Fern and Spruce Lakes and other area lakes are known for greenback cutthroats. They can be reached on the Fern Lake Trail.

Rocky Mountain National Park

Cache la Poudre

Poudre Lake

Beaver Creek

Fall River

Roaring River

Chiquita Creek

Sundance Creek

Windy Gulch

Forest Canyon

Rock Cut ◆

Raspberry Park

Big Thompson River

Forest Lake

Rock Lake

Arrowhead Lake

Inkwell Lake

Doughnut Lake

Hayden Lake

Hayden Creek

Hidden River

Last Brook

Lonesome Lake

Hourglass Lake

Rainbow Lake

Continental Divide

Picnic Grounds

Arch Rocks

The Pool 13.3 mi.

Cub Lake

Fern Creek

Spruce Creek

Spruce Lake

Fern Lake

Loomis Lake

Odessa Lake

Flow

0 mi.

34

N E S W

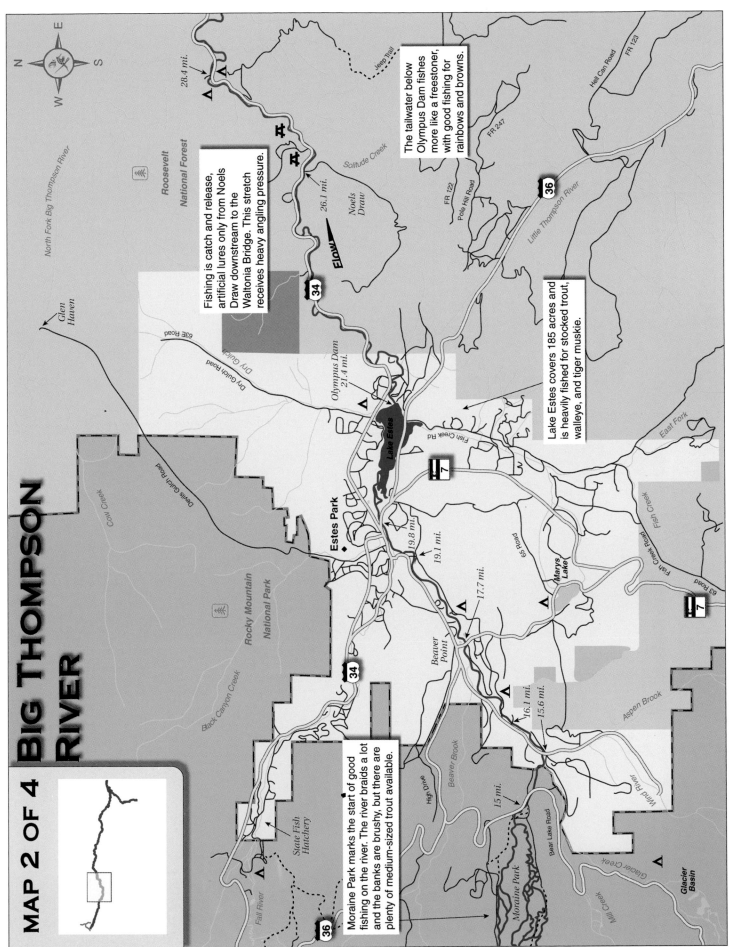

MAP 2 OF 4

BIG THOMPSON RIVER

The tailwater below Olympus Dam fishes more like a freestoner, with good fishing for rainbows and browns.

Fishing is catch and release, artificial lures only from Noels Draw downstream to the Waltonia Bridge. This stretch receives heavy angling pressure.

Lake Estes covers 185 acres and is heavily fished for stocked trout, walleye, and tiger muskie.

Moraine Park marks the start of good fishing on the river. The river braids a lot and the banks are brushy, but there are plenty of medium-sized trout available.

28.4 mi.

26.1 mi.

FLOW

Olympus Dam
21.4 mi.

19.8 mi.

19.1 mi.

17.7 mi.

16.1 mi.

15.6 mi.

15 mi.

Roosevelt
National Forest

North Fork Big Thompson River

Glen
Haven

63E Road

Dry Gulch Road

Dry Gulch

Devils Gulch Road

Cow Creek

Black Canyon Creek

Rocky Mountain
National Park

Estes Park

Lake Estes

Fish Creek Rd

Marys
Lake

65 Road

Beaver
Point

Beaver Brook

High Drive

State Fish
Hatchery

Fall River

Moraine Park

Bear Lake Road

Mill Creek

Glacier Creek

Glacier
Basin

Wind River

Aspen Brook

Fish Creek

Fish Creek Road

63 Road

East Fork

Little Thompson River

FR 247

FR 122

Pole Hill Road

Hell Can Road

FR 123

Jeep Trail

Solitude Creek

Noels
Draw

Noels Draw

36

34

34

36

7

7

N E S W

© Wilderness Adventures Press, Inc.

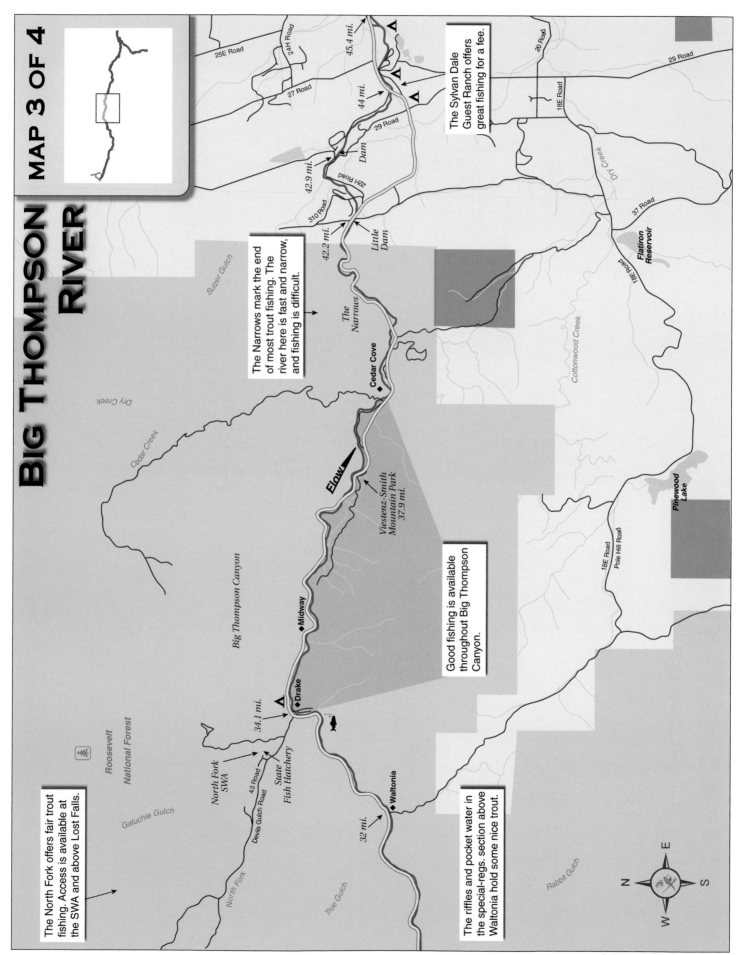

BIG THOMPSON RIVER

MAP 3 OF 4

The North Fork offers fair trout fishing. Access is available at the SWA and above Lost Falls.

The Narrows mark the end of most trout fishing. The river here is fast and narrow, and fishing is difficult.

The Sylvan Dale Guest Ranch offers great fishing for a fee.

Good fishing is available throughout Big Thompson Canyon.

The riffles and pocket water in the special-regs. section above Waltonia hold some nice trout.

Roosevelt National Forest

Big Thompson Canyon

Dry Creek

Cedar Creek

Sulzer Gulch

Galuchie Gulch

North Fork

North Fork SWA

43 Road

Devils Gulch Road

State Fish Hatchery

◆ Drake

34.1 mi.

◆ Midway

Flow

Viestenz-Smith Mountain Park 37.9 mi.

Cedar Cove ◆

The Narrows

42.2 mi.

Little Dam

310 Road

22H Road

42.9 mi.

Dam

29 Road

44 mi.

27 Road

24H Road

25E Road

45.4 mi.

◆ Waltonia

32 mi.

True Gulch

Rabbit Gulch

Cottonwood Creek

Pole Hill Road

18E Road

18E Road

37 Road

Dry Creek

29 Road

18E Road

20 Road

Flatiron Reservoir

Pinewood Lake

N W E S

© Wilderness Adventures Press, Inc.

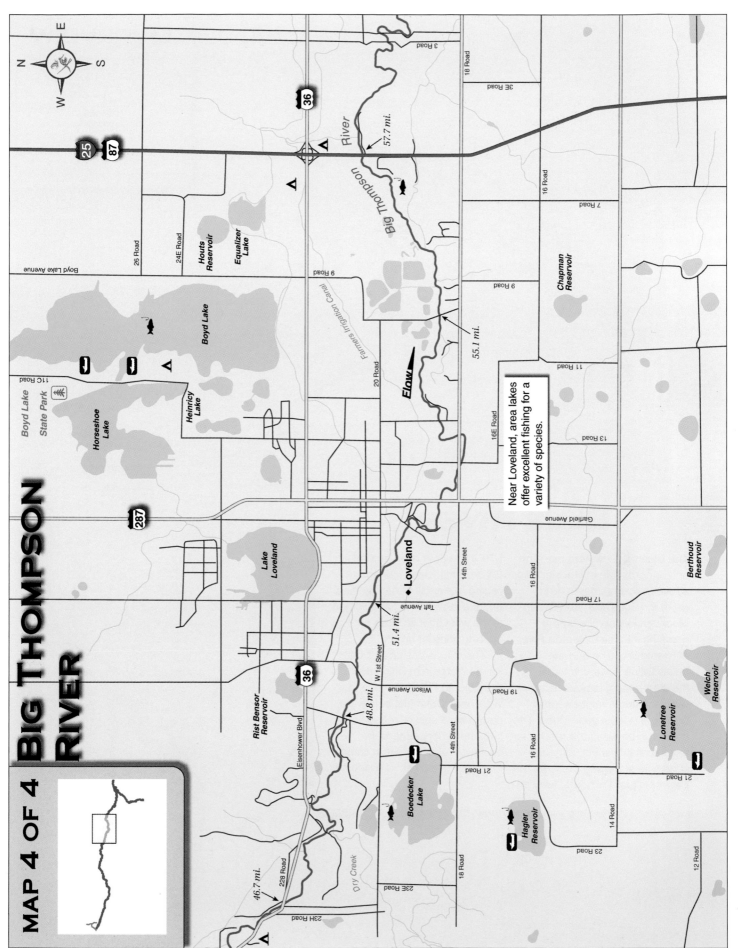

MAP 4 OF 4

BIG THOMPSON RIVER

Near Loveland, area lakes offer excellent fishing for a variety of species.

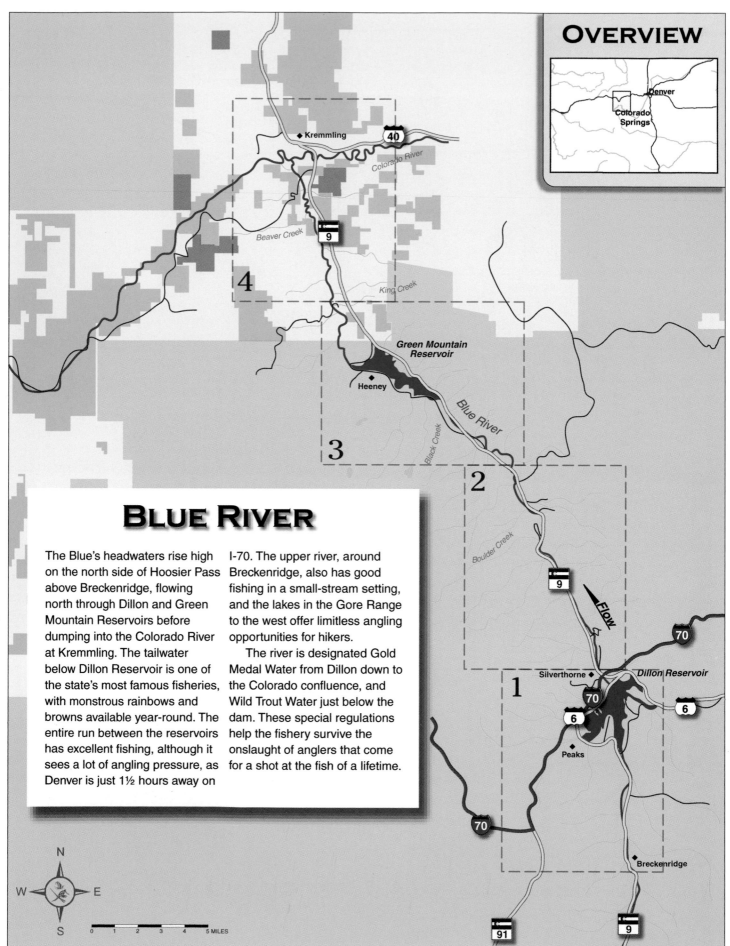

OVERVIEW

BLUE RIVER

The Blue's headwaters rise high on the north side of Hoosier Pass above Breckenridge, flowing north through Dillon and Green Mountain Reservoirs before dumping into the Colorado River at Kremmling. The tailwater below Dillon Reservoir is one of the state's most famous fisheries, with monstrous rainbows and browns available year-round. The entire run between the reservoirs has excellent fishing, although it sees a lot of angling pressure, as Denver is just 1½ hours away on I-70. The upper river, around Breckenridge, also has good fishing in a small-stream setting, and the lakes in the Gore Range to the west offer limitless angling opportunities for hikers.

The river is designated Gold Medal Water from Dillon down to the Colorado confluence, and Wild Trout Water just below the dam. These special regulations help the fishery survive the onslaught of anglers that come for a shot at the fish of a lifetime.

Kremmling

Colorado River

Beaver Creek

King Creek

Green Mountain Reservoir

Heeney

Blue River

Black Creek

Boulder Creek

Flow

Silverthorne

Dillon Reservoir

Peaks

Breckenridge

N
W E
S

0 1 2 3 4 5 MILES

© Wilderness Adventures Press, Inc.

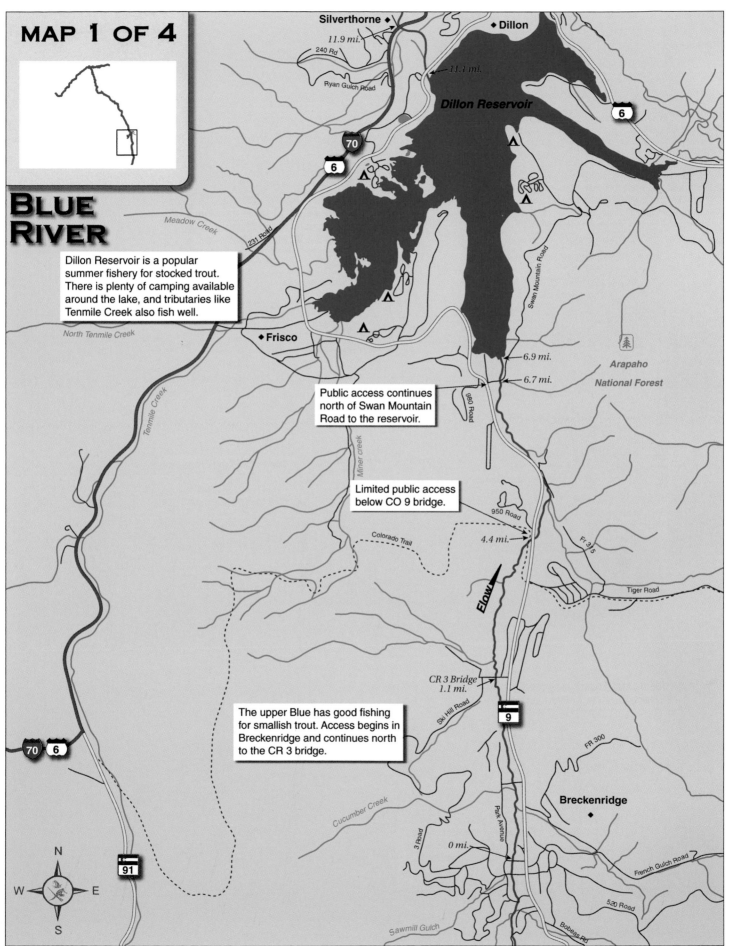

MAP 1 OF 4

BLUE RIVER

Dillon Reservoir is a popular summer fishery for stocked trout. There is plenty of camping available around the lake, and tributaries like Tenmile Creek also fish well.

Public access continues north of Swan Mountain Road to the reservoir.

Limited public access below CO 9 bridge.

The upper Blue has good fishing for smallish trout. Access begins in Breckenridge and continues north to the CR 3 bridge.

Silverthorne ◆
11.9 mi.
Dillon ◆
11.1 mi.
240 Rd
Ryan Gulch Road

Dillon Reservoir

Meadow Creek
231 Road

North Tenmile Creek
◆ Frisco
Tenmile Creek
Miner creek

6.9 mi.
6.7 mi.
980 Road

Arapaho
National Forest

Swan Mountain Road

Colorado Trail
950 Road
4.4 mi.
FR 315
Tiger Road

Flow

CR 3 Bridge
1.1 mi.

Ski Hill Road
9

FR 300

Cucumber Creek
3 Road
Park Avenue
0 mi.

Breckenridge ◆

French Gulch Road

N
W E
S

91
520 Road
Sawmill Gulch
Bobcas Rd

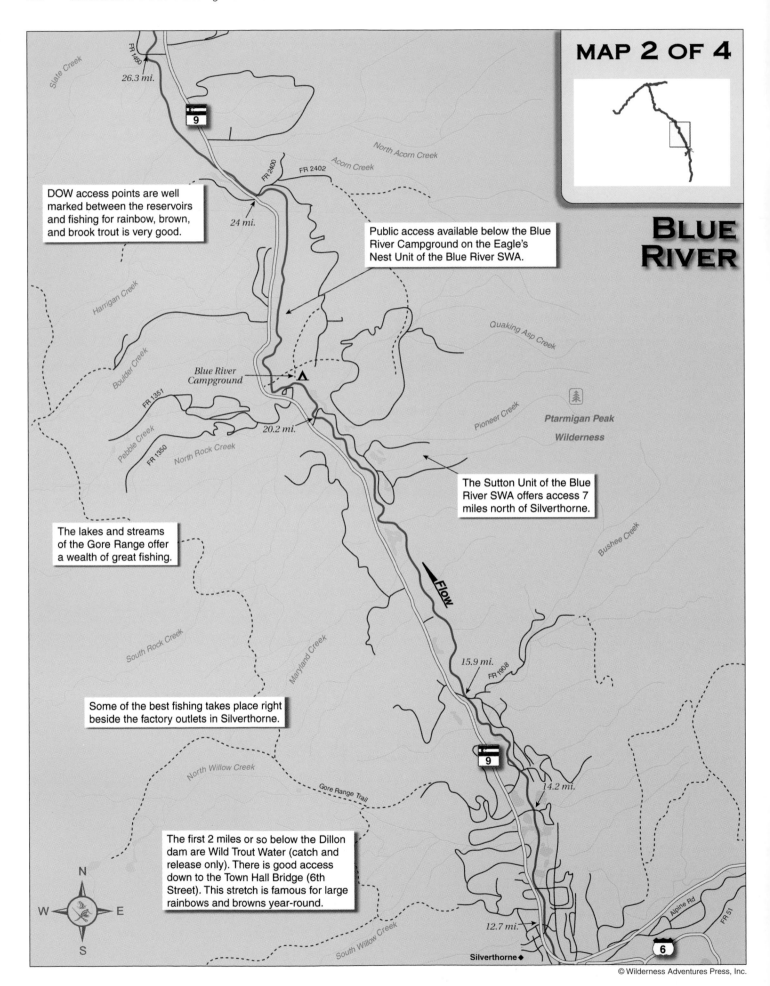

MAP 2 OF 4

BLUE RIVER

FR 1450

26.3 mi.

9

Slate Creek

North Acorn Creek

FR 2400

FR 2402

Acorn Creek

DOW access points are well marked between the reservoirs and fishing for rainbow, brown, and brook trout is very good.

24 mi.

Public access available below the Blue River Campground on the Eagle's Nest Unit of the Blue River SWA.

Harrigan Creek

Quaking Asp Creek

Boulder Creek

Blue River Campground

FR 1351

Pebble Creek

FR 1350

North Rock Creek

Pioneer Creek

Ptarmigan Peak Wilderness

20.2 mi.

The Sutton Unit of the Blue River SWA offers access 7 miles north of Silverthorne.

The lakes and streams of the Gore Range offer a wealth of great fishing.

Bushee Creek

South Rock Creek

Maryland Creek

Flow

Some of the best fishing takes place right beside the factory outlets in Silverthorne.

15.9 mi.

FR 1908

9

North Willow Creek

Gore Range Trail

14.2 mi.

The first 2 miles or so below the Dillon dam are Wild Trout Water (catch and release only). There is good access down to the Town Hall Bridge (6th Street). This stretch is famous for large rainbows and browns year-round.

N
W   E
S

Alpine Rd

FR 51

12.7 mi.

South Willow Creek

Silverthorne

6

© Wilderness Adventures Press, Inc.

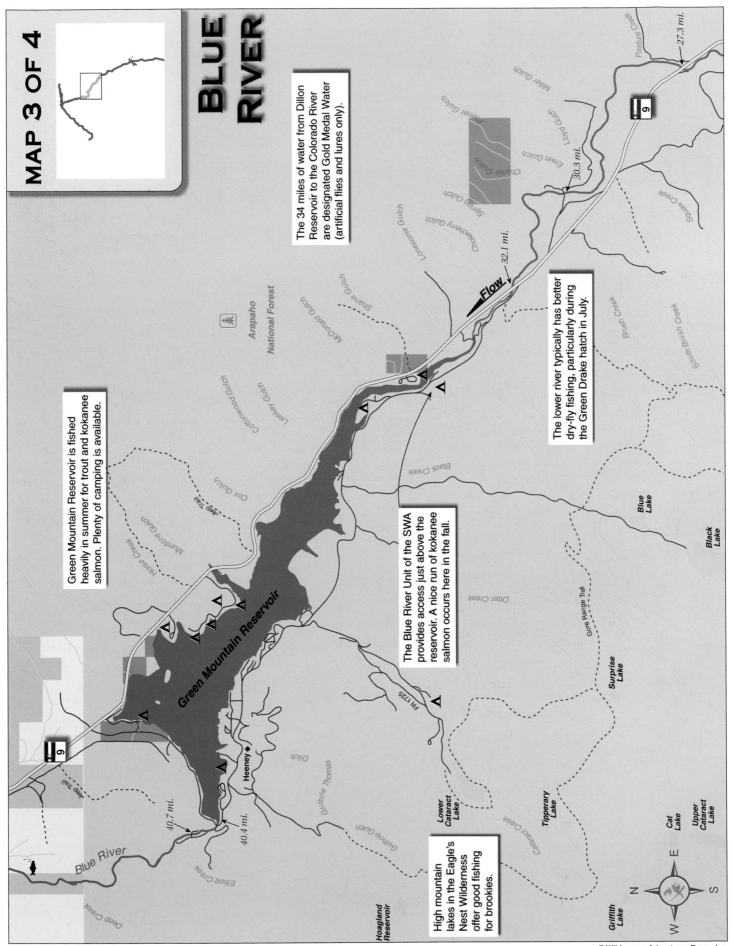

MAP 3 OF 4

BLUE RIVER

The 34 miles of water from Dillon Reservoir to the Colorado River are designated Gold Medal Water (artificial flies and lures only).

The lower river typically has better dry-fly fishing, particularly during the Green Drake hatch in July.

Green Mountain Reservoir is fished heavily in summer for trout and kokanee salmon. Plenty of camping is available.

The Blue River Unit of the SWA provides access just above the reservoir. A nice run of kokanee salmon occurs here in the fall.

High mountain lakes in the Eagle's Nest Wilderness offer good fishing for brookies.

Arapaho National Forest

Green Mountain Reservoir

Heeney

Blue River

Pasture Creek

Spawn Creek

Miller Gulch

Lloyd Gulch

Erwin Gulch

Palmer Gulch

Charlie Gulch

Spring Gulch

Chokecherry Gulch

Lonesome Gulch

Shane Gulch

McDonald Gulch

Leckey Gulch

Cottonwood Gulch

Cox Gulch

Jeep Trail

Munford Gulch

Horse Creek

Brush Creek

South Brush Creek

Black Creek

Otter Creek

Gore Range Trail

Cataract Creek

Guthrie Thomas Ditch

Guthrie Gulch

Elliott Creek

Deep Creek

Jeep Trail

FR 1725

27.3 mi.

30.3 mi.

32.1 mi.

Flow

40.7 mi.

40.4 mi.

Blue Lake

Black Lake

Surprise Lake

Tipperary Lake

Lower Cataract Lake

Hoagland Reservoir

Griffith Lake

Cat Lake

Upper Cataract Lake

N E S W

© Wilderness Adventures Press, Inc.

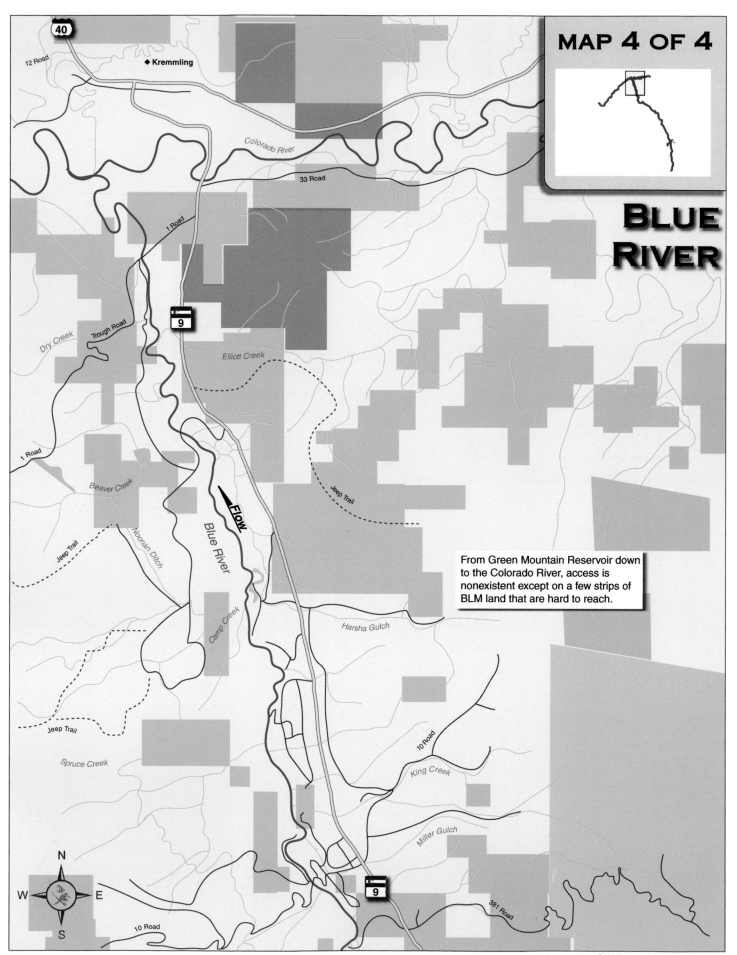

MAP **4** OF **4**

BLUE RIVER

Kremmling

Colorado River

33 Road

1 Road

Dry Creek

Trough Road

Elliott Creek

1 Road

Beaver Creek

Jeep Trail

Flow

Blue River

Noonan Ditch

Jeep Trail

Camp Creek

Spruce Creek

Jeep Trail

Harsha Gulch

10 Road

King Creek

Miller Gulch

10 Road

381 Road

12 Road

From Green Mountain Reservoir down to the Colorado River, access is nonexistent except on a few strips of BLM land that are hard to reach.

N
W E
S

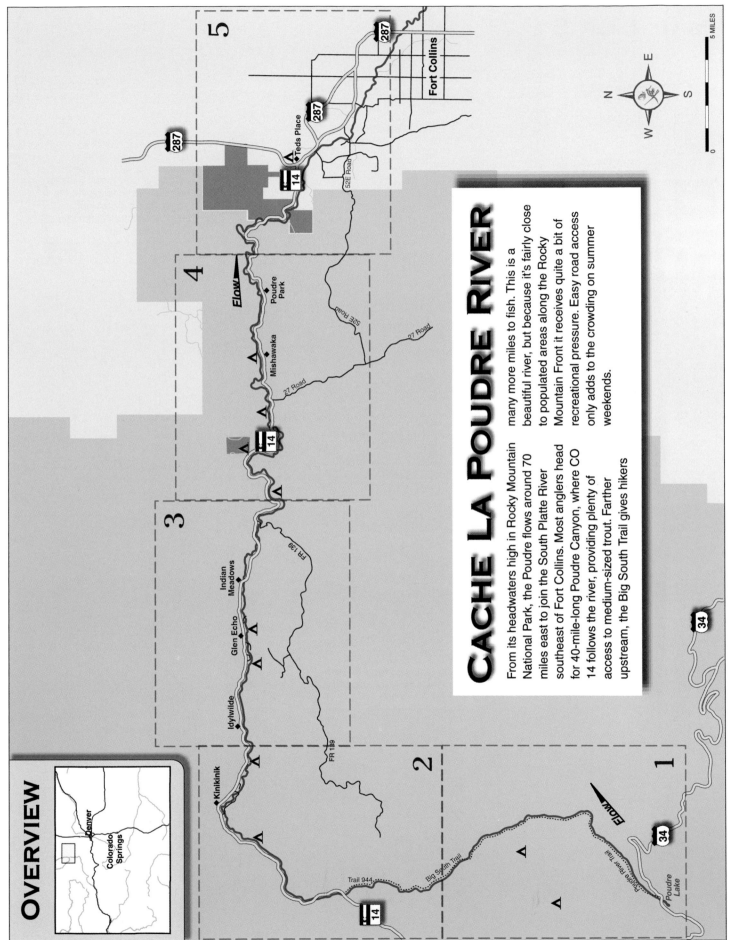

CACHE LA POUDRE RIVER

From its headwaters high in Rocky Mountain National Park, the Poudre flows around 70 miles east to join the South Platte River southeast of Fort Collins. Most anglers head for 40-mile-long Poudre Canyon, where CO 14 follows the river, providing plenty of access to medium-sized trout. Farther upstream, the Big South Trail gives hikers many more miles to fish. This is a beautiful river, but because it's fairly close to populated areas along the Rocky Mountain Front it receives quite a bit of recreational pressure. Easy road access only adds to the crowding on summer weekends.

OVERVIEW

© Wilderness Adventures Press, Inc.

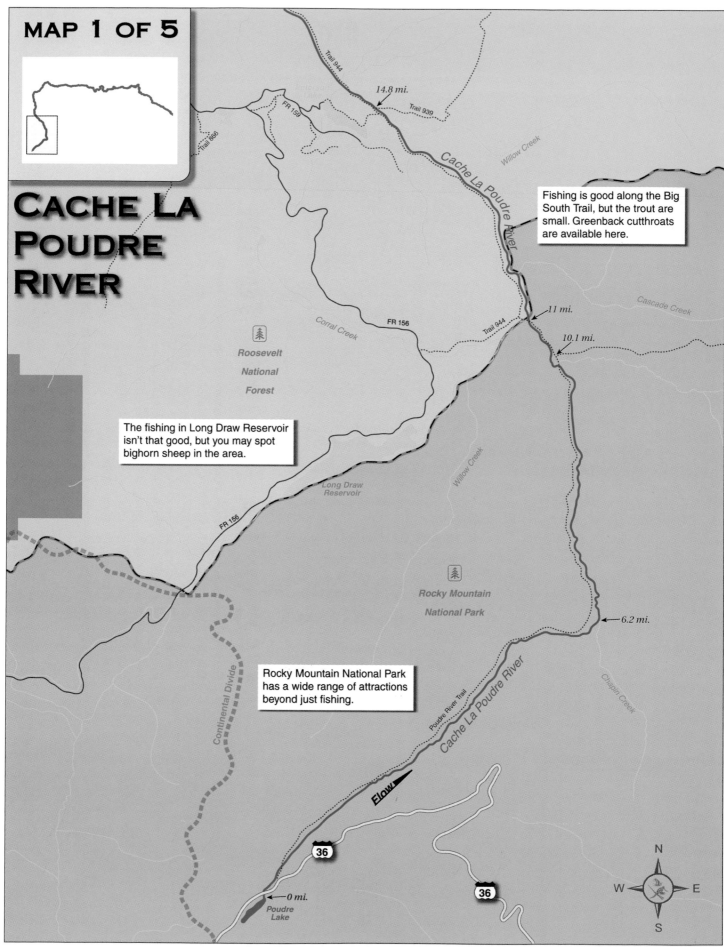

MAP 1 OF 5

CACHE LA POUDRE RIVER

Trail 944

Trail 939

14.8 mi.

FR 159

Trail 866

Cache La Poudre River

Willow Creek

Fishing is good along the Big South Trail, but the trout are small. Greenback cutthroats are available here.

Corral Creek

FR 156

Trail 944

11 mi.

Cascade Creek

10.1 mi.

Roosevelt

National

Forest

The fishing in Long Draw Reservoir isn't that good, but you may spot bighorn sheep in the area.

Long Draw Reservoir

Willow Creek

FR 156

Rocky Mountain

National Park

6.2 mi.

Continental Divide

Rocky Mountain National Park has a wide range of attractions beyond just fishing.

Poudre River Trail

Cache La Poudre River

Chapin Creek

Flow

36

36

N

W

E

S

0 mi.

Poudre Lake

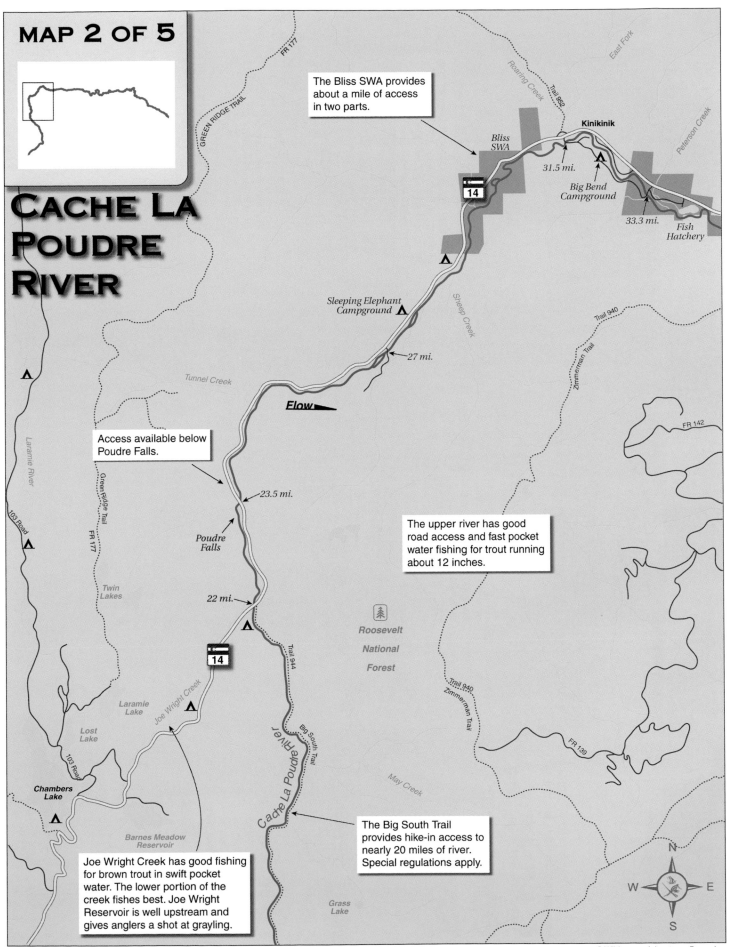

MAP 2 OF 5

CACHE LA POUDRE RIVER

The Bliss SWA provides about a mile of access in two parts.

Bliss SWA

Kinikinik

31.5 mi.

Big Bend Campground

33.3 mi.

Fish Hatchery

Roaring Creek

East Fork

Peterson Creek

Trail 952

14

Sheep Creek

Zimmerman Trail

Trail 940

FR 142

Sleeping Elephant Campground

27 mi.

Tunnel Creek

Flow

Access available below Poudre Falls.

23.5 mi.

Poudre Falls

22 mi.

The upper river has good road access and fast pocket water fishing for trout running about 12 inches.

Trail 940

Zimmerman Trail

FR 139

Laramie River

Green Ridge Trail

FR 177

GREEN RIDGE TRAIL

FR 177

Twin Lakes

103 Road

14

Laramie Lake

Joe Wright Creek

Trail 944

Roosevelt National Forest

Lost Lake

103 Road

Cache La Poudre River

Big South Trail

May Creek

The Big South Trail provides hike-in access to nearly 20 miles of river. Special regulations apply.

Chambers Lake

Barnes Meadow Reservoir

Joe Wright Creek has good fishing for brown trout in swift pocket water. The lower portion of the creek fishes best. Joe Wright Reservoir is well upstream and gives anglers a shot at grayling.

Grass Lake

N
W E
S

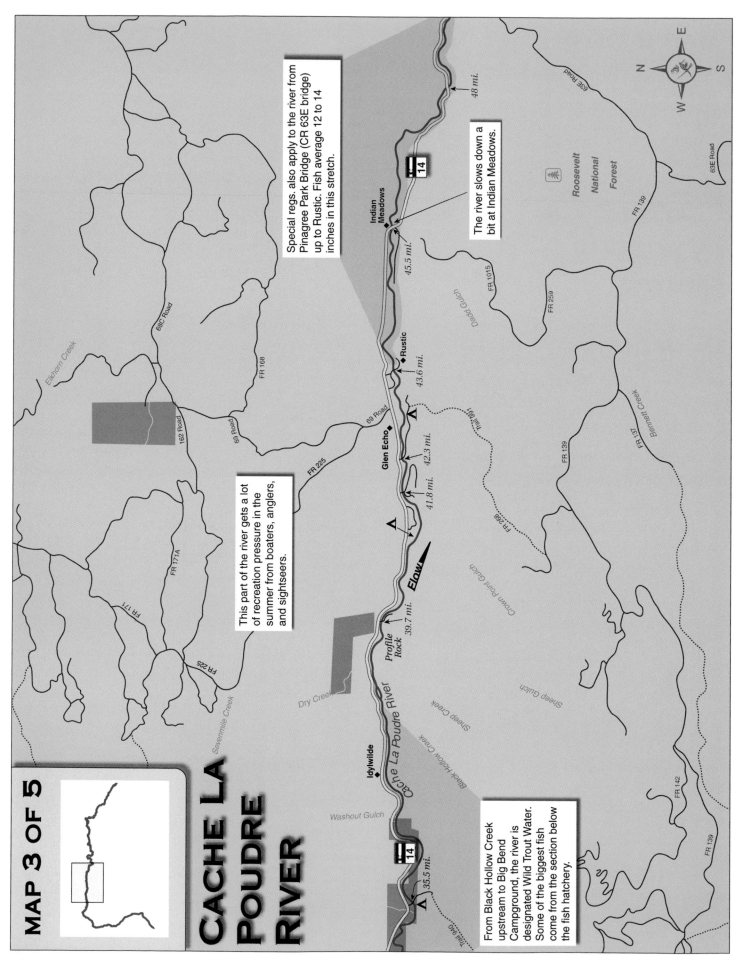

MAP 3 OF 5

CACHE LA POUDRE RIVER

Special regs. also apply to the river from Pinagree Park Bridge (CR 63E bridge) up to Rustic. Fish average 12 to 14 inches in this stretch.

The river slows down a bit at Indian Meadows.

This part of the river gets a lot of recreation pressure in the summer from boaters, anglers, and sightseers.

From Black Hollow Creek upstream to Big Bend Campground, the river is designated Wild Trout Water. Some of the biggest fish come from the section below the fish hatchery.

Roosevelt National Forest

Indian Meadows
48 mi.
45.5 mi.
Rustic
43.6 mi.
Glen Echo
42.3 mi.
41.8 mi.
Flow
39.7 mi.
Profile Rock
Idylwilde
35.5 mi.

Cache La Poudre River

Elkhorn Creek
Seventmile Creek
Dry Creek
Black Hollow Creek
Washout Gulch
Sheep Creek
Crown Point Gulch
Sheep Gulch
Dadd Gulch
Bennett Creek

68C Road
162 Road
69 Road
FR 168
FR 225
FR 171A
FR 171
FR 225
69 Road
Trail 891
FR 288
FR 1015
FR 259
FR 139
FR 137
FR 139
FR 142
FR 139
63E Road
63E Road
Trail 940

© Wilderness Adventures Press, Inc.

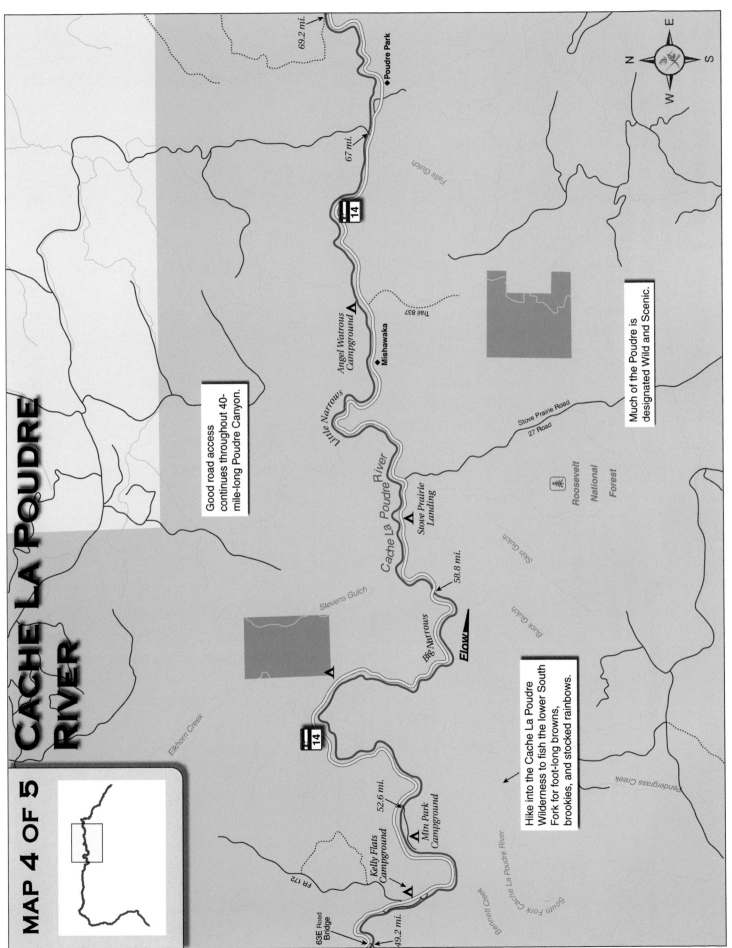

CACHE LA POUDRE RIVER

MAP 4 OF 5

Good road access continues throughout 40-mile-long Poudre Canyon.

Much of the Poudre is designated Wild and Scenic.

Hike into the Cache La Poudre Wilderness to fish the lower South Fork for foot-long browns, brookies, and stocked rainbows.

69.2 mi.

◆ Poudre Park

67 mi.

14

Falls Gulch

Angel Watrous Campground

Trail 837

◆ Mishawaka

Little Narrows

Cache La Poudre River

Stove Prairie Landing

Stove Prairie Road

27 Road

Roosevelt National Forest

58.8 mi.

Big Narrows

Flow

Skin Gulch

Buck Gulch

Stevens Gulch

Elkhorn Creek

14

52.6 mi.

FR 172

Kelly Flats Campground

Mtn Park Campground

63E Road Bridge

49.2 mi.

South Fork Cache La Poudre River

Bennett Creek

Pendergrass Creek

© Wilderness Adventures Press, Inc.

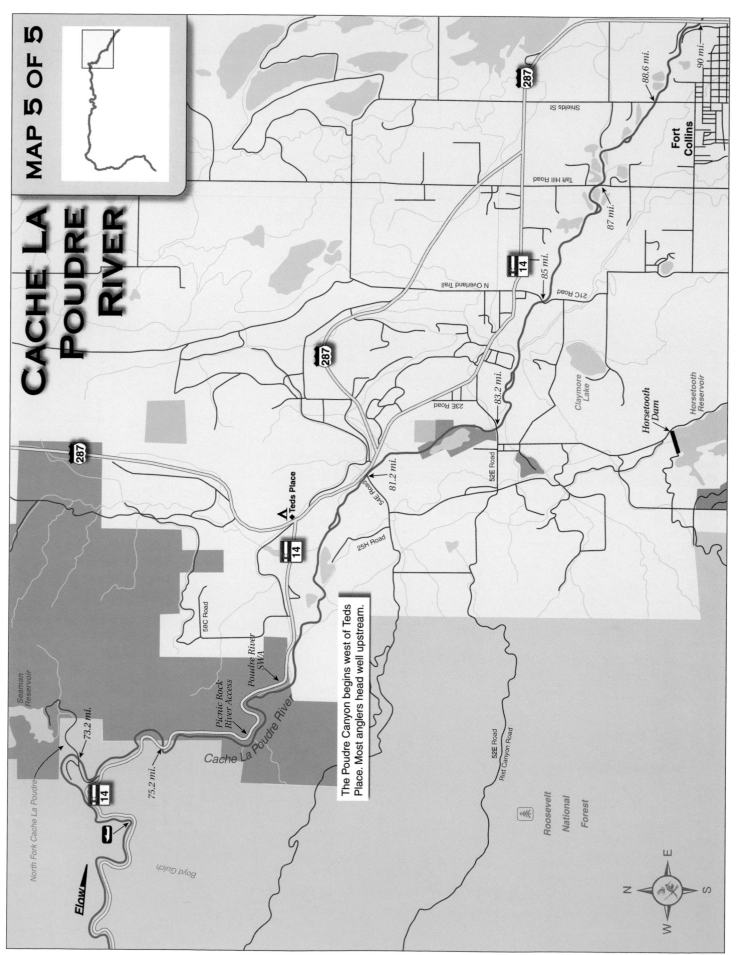

MAP 5 OF 5

CACHE LA POUDRE RIVER

287

Fort Collins

88.6 mi.

90 mi.

Shields St

87 mi.

Taft Hill Road

14

85 mi.

21C Road

N Overland Trail

83.2 mi.

287

23E Road

Claymore Lake

Horsetooth Dam

Horsetooth Reservoir

52E Road

81.2 mi.

54E Road

287

△ Teds Place

25H Road

14

58C Road

Poudre River SWA

52E Road

Rist Canyon Road

The Poudre Canyon begins west of Teds Place. Most anglers head well upstream.

Seaman Reservoir

73.2 mi.

Picnic Rock River Access

Roosevelt National Forest

Cache La Poudre River

75.2 mi.

14

North Fork Cache La Poudre

Flow

Boyd Gulch

N E S W

© Wilderness Adventures Press, Inc.

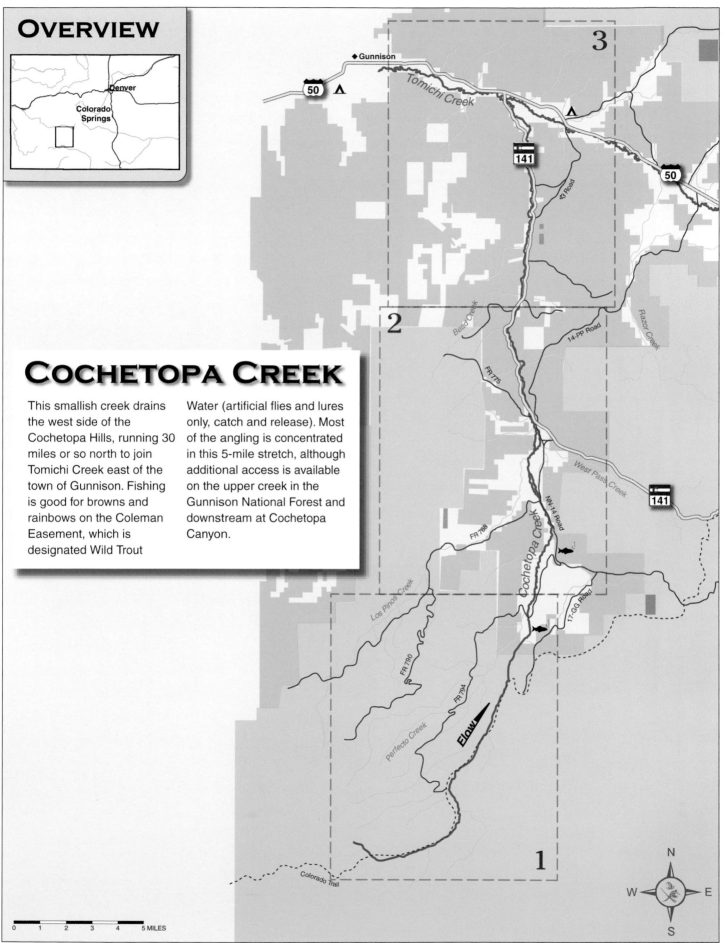

OVERVIEW

COCHETOPA CREEK

This smallish creek drains the west side of the Cochetopa Hills, running 30 miles or so north to join Tomichi Creek east of the town of Gunnison. Fishing is good for browns and rainbows on the Coleman Easement, which is designated Wild Trout Water (artificial flies and lures only, catch and release). Most of the angling is concentrated in this 5-mile stretch, although additional access is available on the upper creek in the Gunnison National Forest and downstream at Cochetopa Canyon.

0 1 2 3 4 5 MILES

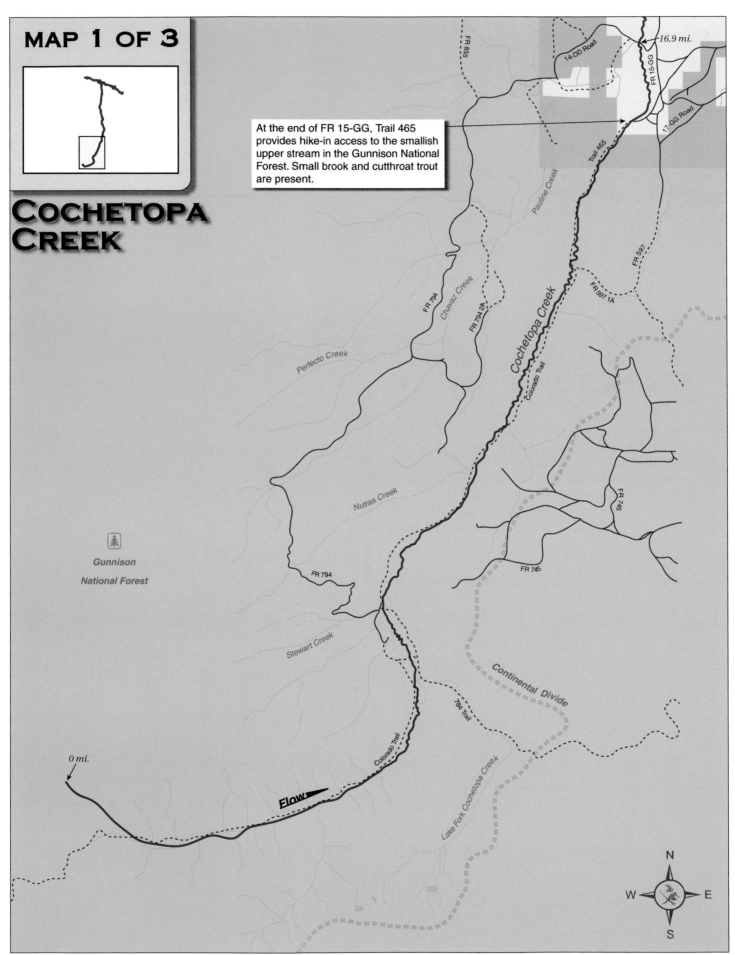

MAP 1 OF 3

COCHETOPA CREEK

At the end of FR 15-GG, Trail 465 provides hike-in access to the smallish upper stream in the Gunnison National Forest. Small brook and cutthroat trout are present.

16.9 mi.

14-DD Road

17-GG Road

FR 855

Trail 465

FR 15-GG

Pauline Creek

FR 597

FR 794

Chavaz Creek

FR 794-2A

FR 597-1A

Perfecto Creek

Cochetopa Creek

Colorado Trail

FR 745

Nutras Creek

FR 745

Gunnison

National Forest

FR 794

Stewart Creek

Continental Divide

784 Trail

Colorado Trail

Lake Fork Cochetopa Creek

0 mi.

Flow

N

W — E

S

© Wilderness Adventures Press, Inc.

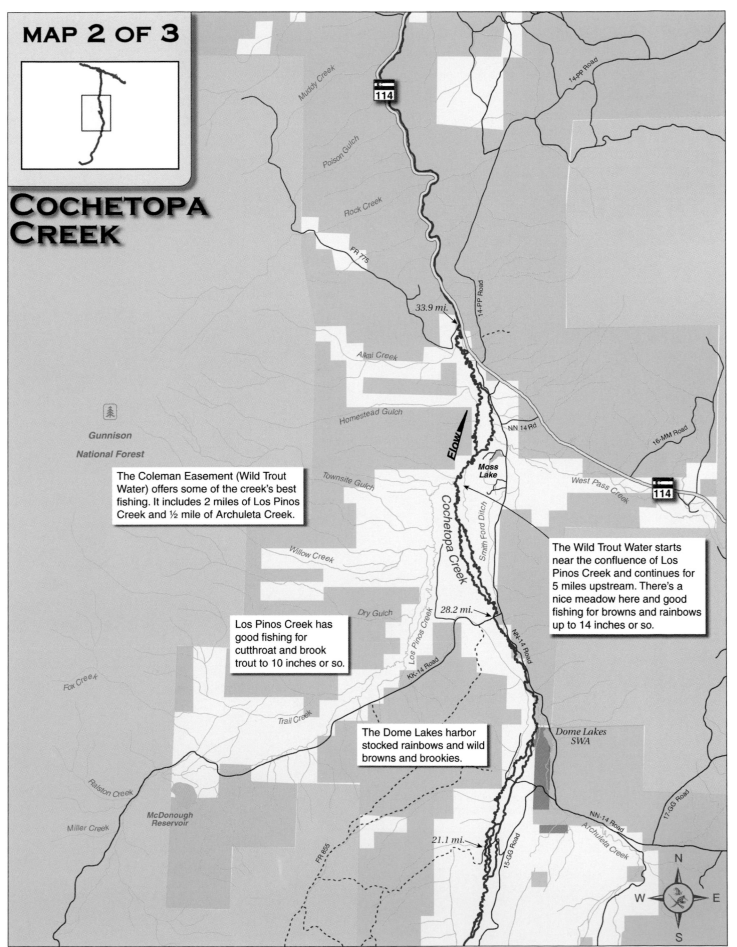

MAP 2 OF 3

COCHETOPA CREEK

Gunnison

National Forest

The Coleman Easement (Wild Trout Water) offers some of the creek's best fishing. It includes 2 miles of Los Pinos Creek and ½ mile of Archuleta Creek.

Los Pinos Creek has good fishing for cutthroat and brook trout to 10 inches or so.

The Dome Lakes harbor stocked rainbows and wild browns and brookies.

The Wild Trout Water starts near the confluence of Los Pinos Creek and continues for 5 miles upstream. There's a nice meadow here and good fishing for browns and rainbows up to 14 inches or so.

Muddy Creek

Poison Gulch

Rock Creek

FR 775

Alkai Creek

Homestead Gulch

Townsite Gulch

Willow Creek

Dry Gulch

Fox Creek

Trail Creek

Ralston Creek

Miller Creek

McDonough Reservoir

33.9 mi.

28.2 mi.

21.1 mi.

Flow

Moss Lake

Cochetopa Creek

Smith Ford Ditch

Los Pinos Creek

Dome Lakes SWA

Archuleta Creek

West Pass Creek

14-PP Road

14-PP Road

NN 14 Rd

16-MM Road

NN-14 Road

NN-14 Road

KK-14 Road

15-GG Road

17-GG Road

FR 855

114

114

N

W   E

S

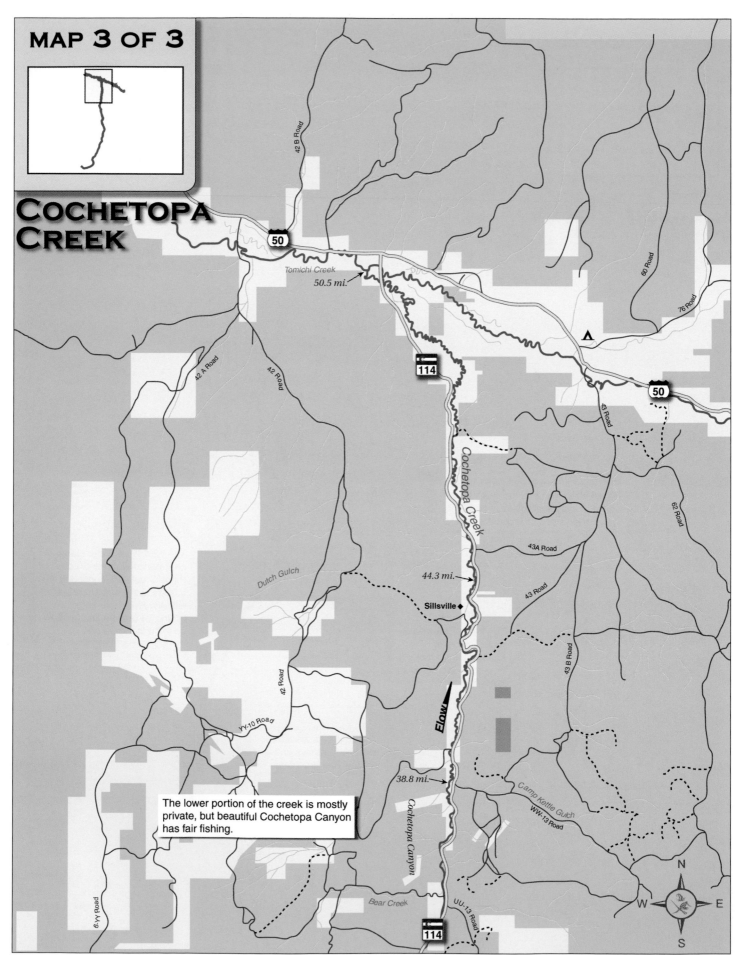

MAP 3 OF 3

COCHETOPA CREEK

Tomichi Creek

50.5 mi.

42 B Road

60 Road

76 Road

42 A Road

42 Road

114

Cochetopa Creek

43 Road

50

62 Road

43A Road

43 Road

44.3 mi.

Dutch Gulch

Sillsville

42 Road

43 B Road

YY-10 Road

Flow

The lower portion of the creek is mostly private, but beautiful Cochetopa Canyon has fair fishing.

38.8 mi.

Camp Kettle Gulch

WW-13 Road

Cochetopa Canyon

6-YY Road

Bear Creek

UU-13 Road

114

N
W   E
S

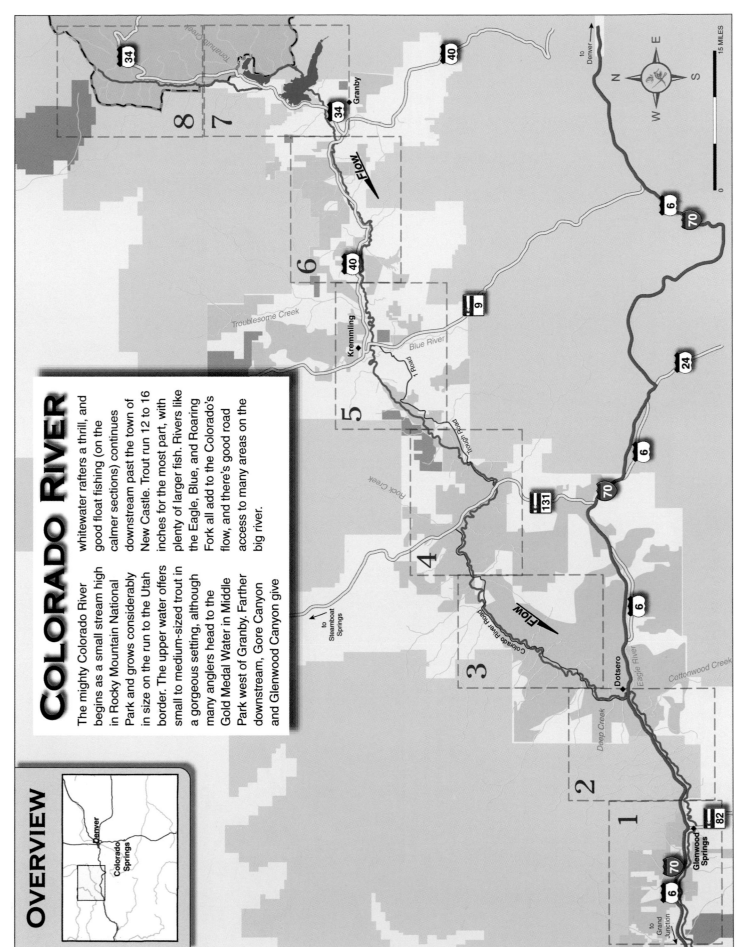

COLORADO RIVER

The mighty Colorado River begins as a small stream high in Rocky Mountain National Park and grows considerably in size on the run to the Utah border. The upper water offers small to medium-sized trout in a gorgeous setting, although many anglers head to the Gold Medal Water in Middle Park west of Granby. Farther downstream, Gore Canyon and Glenwood Canyon give whitewater rafters a thrill, and good float fishing (on the calmer sections) continues downstream past the town of New Castle. Trout run 12 to 16 inches for the most part, with plenty of larger fish. Rivers like the Eagle, Blue, and Roaring Fork all add to the Colorado's flow, and there's good road access to many areas on the big river.

OVERVIEW

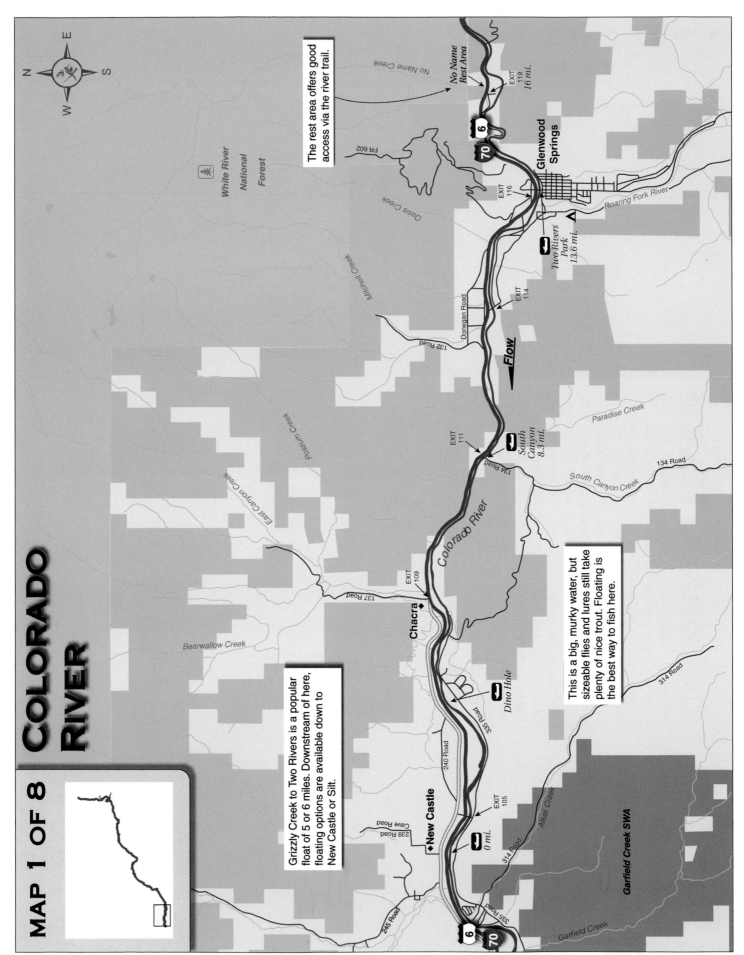

COLORADO RIVER

MAP 1 OF 8

The rest area offers good access via the river trail.

No Name Rest Area

EXIT 119
16 mi.

Glenwood Springs

Roaring Fork River

Two Rivers Park
13.6 mi.

EXIT 116

EXIT 114

Flow

White River National Forest

South Canyon
8.3 mi.

EXIT 111

South Canyon Creek

134 Road

Paradise Creek

Colorado River

EXIT 109

137 Road

Chacra

This is a big, murky water, but sizeable flies and lures still take plenty of nice trout. Floating is the best way to fish here.

314 Road

Dino Hole

335 Road

240 Road

Garfield Creek SWA

Grizzly Creek to Two Rivers is a popular float of 5 or 6 miles. Downstream of here, floating options are available down to New Castle or Silt.

EXIT 105

Alkali Creek

239 Road
Cave Road

Bearwallow Creek

East Canyon Creek

Possum Creek

Mitchell Creek

Oasis Creek

No Name Creek

FR 602

132 Road

Donegan Road

▶ New Castle

0 mi.

314 Road

245 Road

335 Road

Garfield Creek

© Wilderness Adventures Press, Inc.

MAP 2 OF 8

COLORADO RIVER

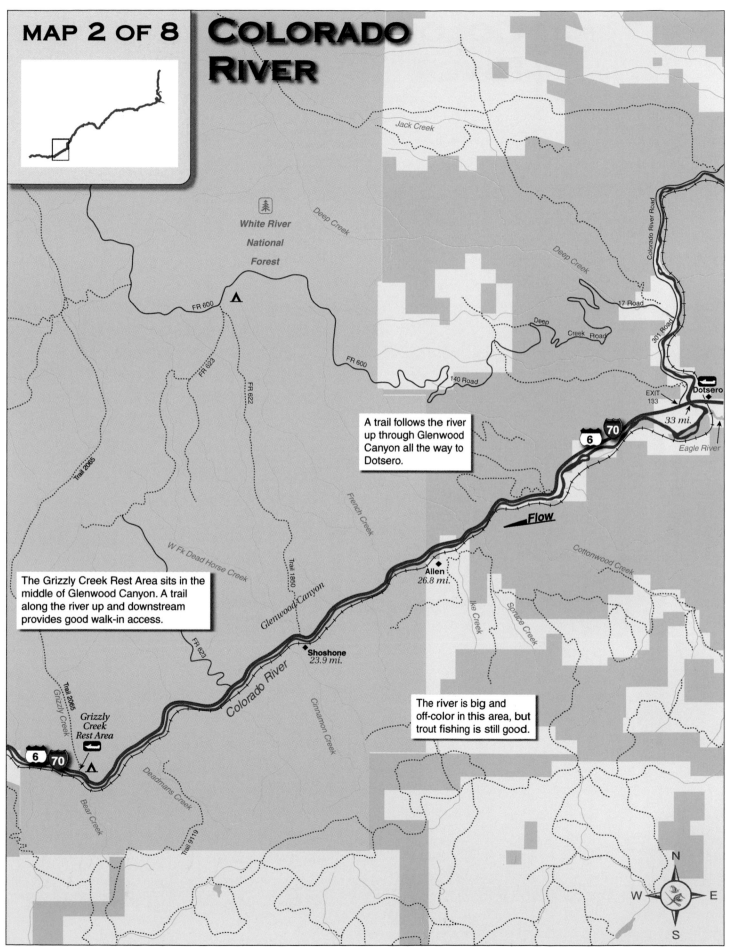

Jack Creek

Deep Creek

White River

National

Forest

Deep Creek

Colorado River Road

FR 600

17 Road

301 Road

FR 600

Deep Creek Road

140 Road

FR 623

FR 622

🏕 Dotsero

EXIT
133

33 mi.

A trail follows the river
up through Glenwood
Canyon all the way to
Dotsero.

6 **70**

Eagle River

Trail 2065

French Creek

Cottonwood Creek

W Fk Dead Horse Creek

Trail 1850

Allen
26.8 mi.

◄ Flow

The Grizzly Creek Rest Area sits in the
middle of Glenwood Canyon. A trail
along the river up and downstream
provides good walk-in access.

Glenwood Canyon

Ike Creek

Spruce Creek

FR 623

Shoshone
23.9 mi.

Colorado River

Cinnamon Creek

The river is big and
off-color in this area, but
trout fishing is still good.

Trail 2065
Grizzly Creek

Grizzly
Creek
Rest Area

6 **70**

Deadmans Creek

Bear Creek

Trail 9119

N

W   E

S

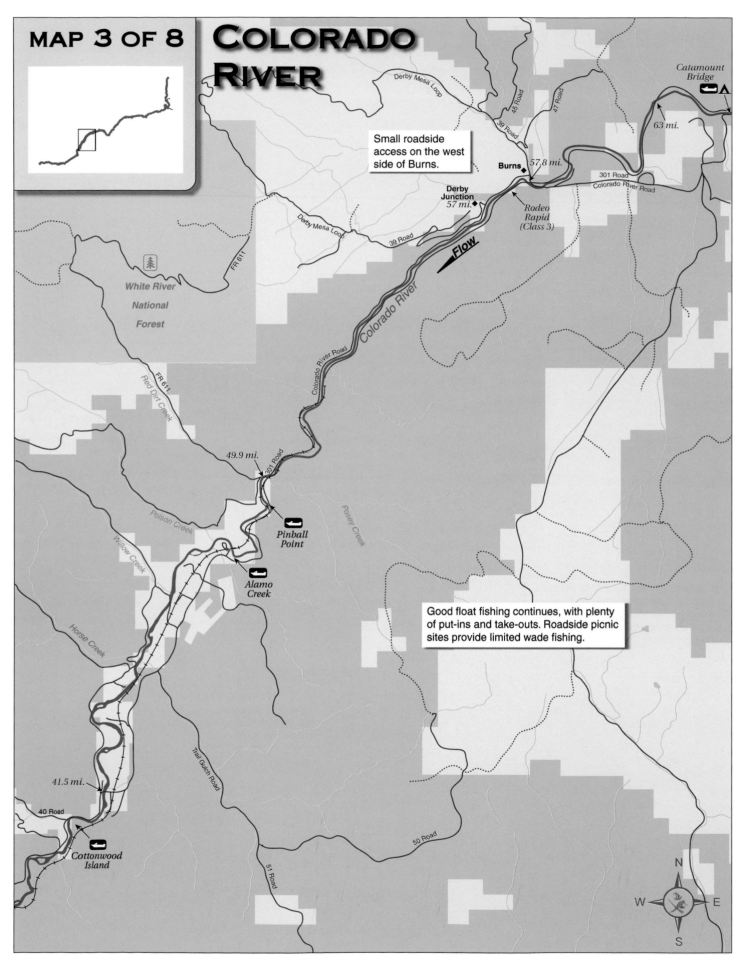

MAP 3 OF 8

COLORADO RIVER

Catamount Bridge

63 mi.

Derby Mesa Loop

45 Road

47 Road

39 Road

Small roadside access on the west side of Burns.

Burns ◆ 57,8 mi.

301 Road
Colorado River Road

Derby Junction 57 mi. ◆

Rodeo Rapid (Class 3)

Derby Mesa Loop

39 Road

Flow

Colorado River

Colorado River Road

White River National Forest

FR 611

FR 611

Red Dirt Creek

49.9 mi.

301 Road

Poison Creek

Posey Creek

Pinball Point

Willow Creek

Alamo Creek

Good float fishing continues, with plenty of put-ins and take-outs. Roadside picnic sites provide limited wade fishing.

Horse Creek

Trail Gulch Road

41.5 mi.

40 Road

50 Road

51 Road

Cottonwood Island

N
W   E
S

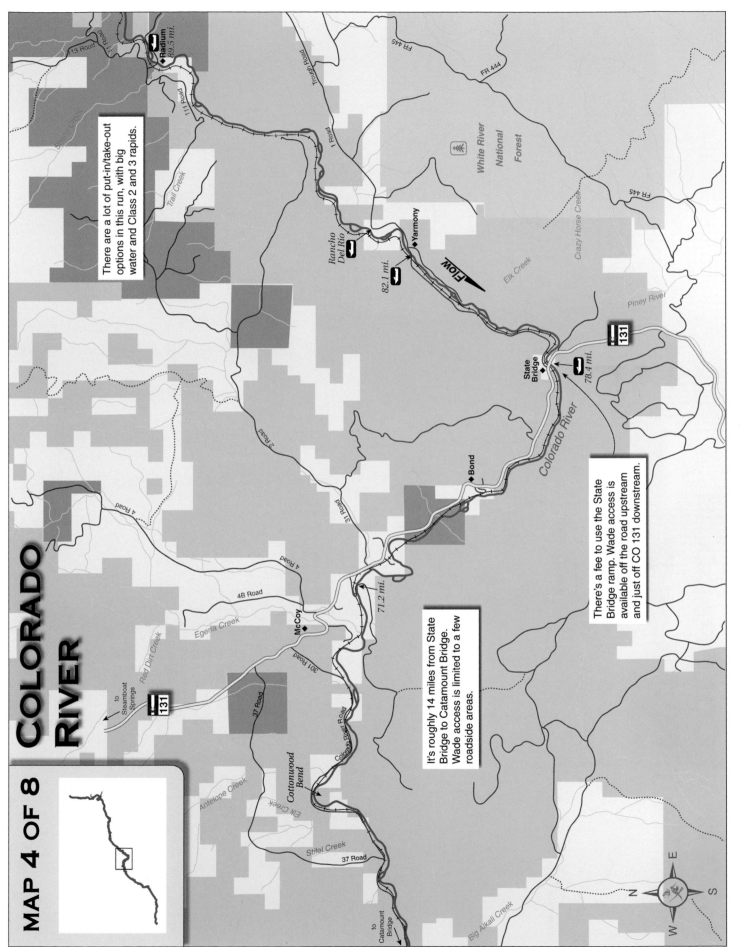

MAP 4 OF 8

COLORADO RIVER

There are a lot of put-in/take-out options in this run, with big water and Class 2 and 3 rapids.

There's a fee to use the State Bridge ramp. Wade access is available off the road upstream and just off CO 131 downstream.

It's roughly 14 miles from State Bridge to Catamount Bridge. Wade access is limited to a few roadside areas.

◆Radium
89.5 mi.

Rancho Del Rio

82.1 mi.

◆Yarmony

Flow

State Bridge

78.4 mi.

131

♦ Bond

Colorado River

71.2 mi.

McCoy

131

to Steamboat Springs

Cottonwood Bend

to Catamount Bridge

White River National Forest

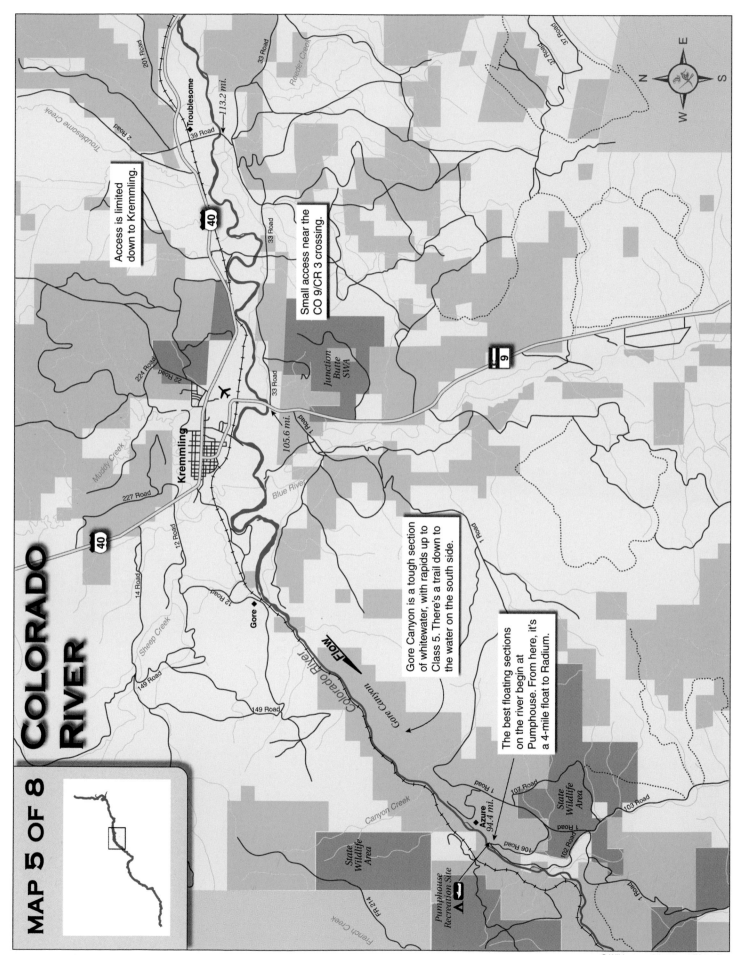

MAP **5** OF 8

COLORADO RIVER

Access is limited down to Kremmling.

Small access near the CO 9/CR 3 crossing.

Gore Canyon is a tough section of whitewater, with rapids up to Class 5. There's a trail down to the water on the south side.

The best floating sections on the river begin at Pumphouse. From here, it's a 4-mile float to Radium.

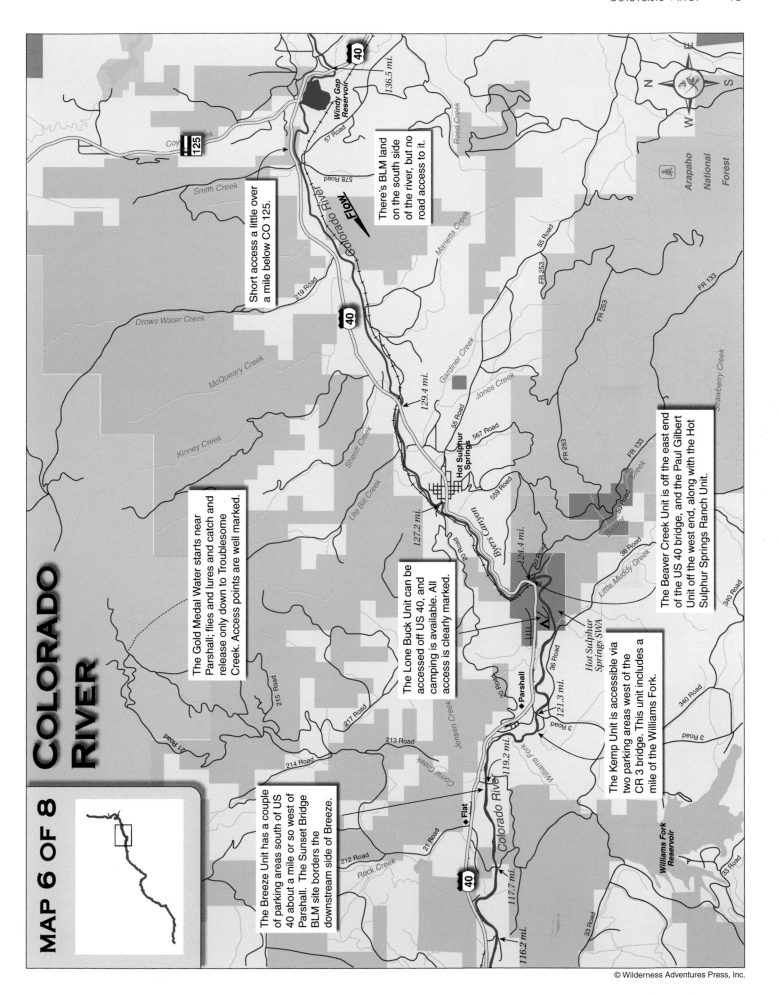

MAP 6 OF 8 | COLORADO RIVER

Short access a little over a mile below CO 125.

There's BLM land on the south side of the river, but no road access to it.

The Gold Medal Water starts near Parshall; flies and lures and catch and release only down to Troublesome Creek. Access points are well marked.

The Lone Buck Unit can be accessed off US 40, and camping is available. All access is clearly marked.

The Breeze Unit has a couple of parking areas south of US 40 about a mile or so west of Parshall. The Sunset Bridge BLM site borders the downstream side of Breeze.

The Kemp Unit is accessible via two parking areas west of the CR 3 bridge. This unit includes a mile of the Williams Fork.

The Beaver Creek Unit is off the east end of the US 40 bridge, and the Paul Gilbert Unit off the west end, along with the Hot Sulphur Springs Ranch Unit.

136.5 mi.

129.4 mi.

127.2 mi.

124.4 mi.

121.3 mi.

119.2 mi.

117.7 mi.

116.2 mi.

Windy Gap Reservoir

Coyote Creek

Smith Creek

Drows Water Creek

McQueary Creek

Kinney Creek

Sheriff Creek

Ute Bill Creek

Reed Creek

Marietta Creek

Gardiner Creek

Jones Creek

Byers Canyon

Strawberry Creek

Hot Sulphur Springs

Parshall

Flat

Hot Sulphur Springs SWA

Jensen Creek

Corral Creek

Rock Creek

Williams Fork

Williams Fork Reservoir

Colorado River

FLOW

Arapaho National Forest

57 Road

578 Road

219 Road

215 Road

217 Road

213 Road

214 Road

212 Road

21 Road

55 Road

FR 253

FR 253

FR 253

FR 133

FR 133

55 Road

567 Road

559 Road

50 Road

36 Road

340 Road

340 Road

33 Road

33 Road

3 Road

3 Road

20 Road

20 Road

21 Road

© Wilderness Adventures Press, Inc.

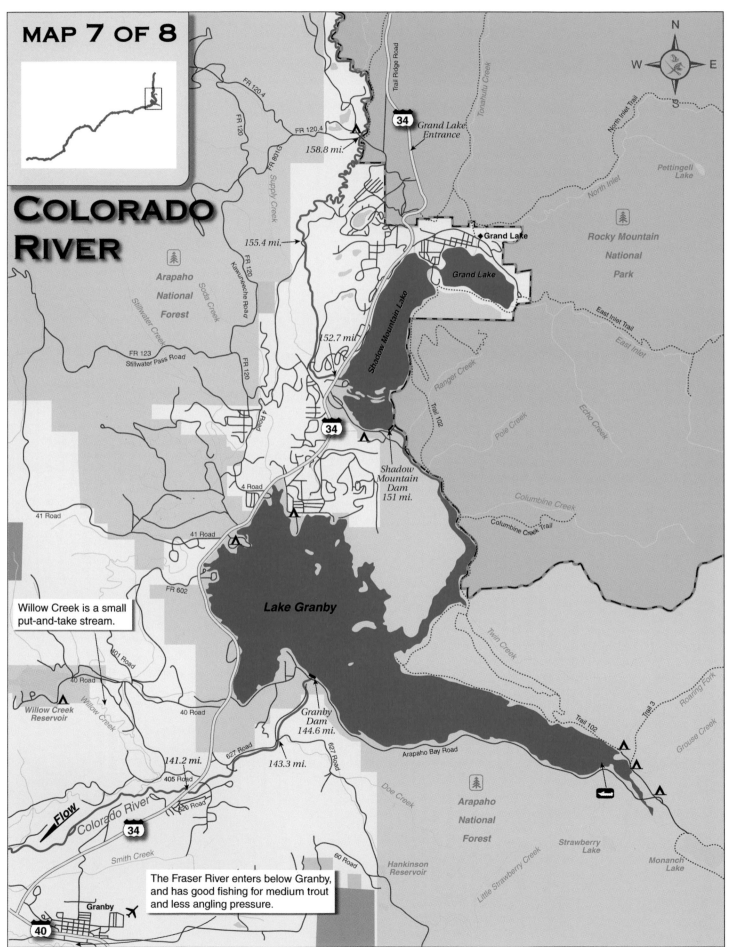

MAP 7 OF 8

COLORADO RIVER

Trail Ridge Road

FR 120.4

FR 120.4

FR 120.4

FR 120

Supply Creek

34 Grand Lake Entrance

158.8 mi.

North Inlet Trail

Pettingell Lake

155.4 mi.

◆ Grand Lake

Rocky Mountain

North Inlet

Arapaho

National

Forest

Grand Lake

National

Park

Stillwater Creek

Soda Creek

Kawuneeche Road

FR 120

Shadow Mountain Lake

East Inlet Trail

East Inlet

152.7 mi.

FR 123
Stillwater Pass Road

FR 120

Ranger Creek

Trail 102

Pole Creek

Echo Creek

4 Road

34

Shadow Mountain Dam 151 mi.

Columbine Creek

Columbine Creek Trail

41 Road

4 Road

41 Road

FR 602

Lake Granby

Twin Creek

Trail 3

Roaring Fork

Willow Creek is a small put-and-take stream.

401 Road

40 Road

Willow Creek Reservoir

Willow Creek

40 Road

Trail 102

Grouse Creek

627 Road

Granby Dam 144.6 mi.

Arapaho Bay Road

141.2 mi.

627 Road

143.3 mi.

405 Road

Doe Creek

Arapaho

420 Road

National

Flow

Colorado River

Forest

Strawberry Lake

34

Smith Creek

60 Road

Little Strawberry Creek

Monarch Lake

The Fraser River enters below Granby, and has good fishing for medium trout and less angling pressure.

Hankinson Reservoir

Granby ✈

40

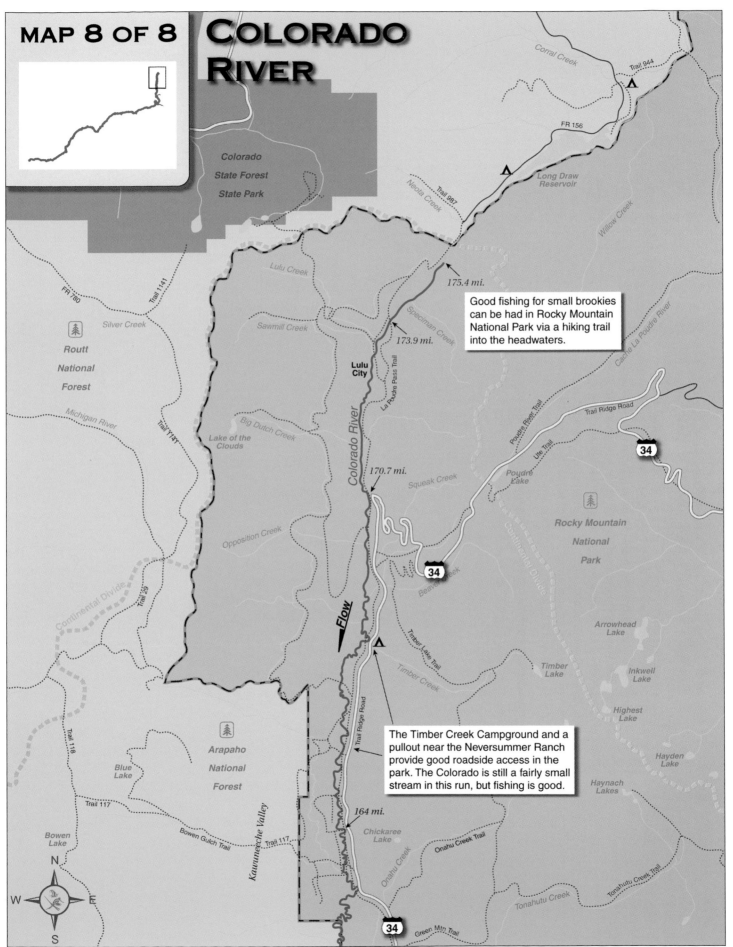

MAP 8 OF 8 COLORADO RIVER

Corral Creek

Trail 944

FR 156

Colorado State Forest State Park

Long Draw Reservoir

Neota Creek

Trail 987

Willow Creek

Lulu Creek

175.4 mi.

Specimen Creek

Good fishing for small brookies can be had in Rocky Mountain National Park via a hiking trail into the headwaters.

173.9 mi.

Sawmill Creek

Cache La Poudre River

FR 780

Trail 1141

Silver Creek

Routt National Forest

Lulu City

La Poudre Pass Trail

Poudre River Trail

Trail Ridge Road

34

Michigan River

Trail 1141

Big Dutch Creek

Lake of the Clouds

Colorado River

170.7 mi.

Squeak Creek

Ute Trail

Poudre Lake

Rocky Mountain National Park

Opposition Creek

Beaver Creek

34

Continental Divide

Arrowhead Lake

Continental Divide

Trail 29

Flow

Timber Lake Trail

Timber Lake

Inkwell Lake

Highest Lake

The Timber Creek Campground and a pullout near the Neversummer Ranch provide good roadside access in the park. The Colorado is still a fairly small stream in this run, but fishing is good.

Trail 118

Arapaho National Forest

Blue Lake

Trail Ridge Road

Timber Creek

Hayden Lake

Haynach Lakes

Trail 117

Bowen Gulch Trail

Kawuneeche Valley

Trail 117

164 mi.

Chickaree Lake

Onahu Creek

Onahu Creek Trail

Bowen Lake

Green Mtn Trail

Tonahutu Creek

Tonahutu Creek Trail

34

N W E S

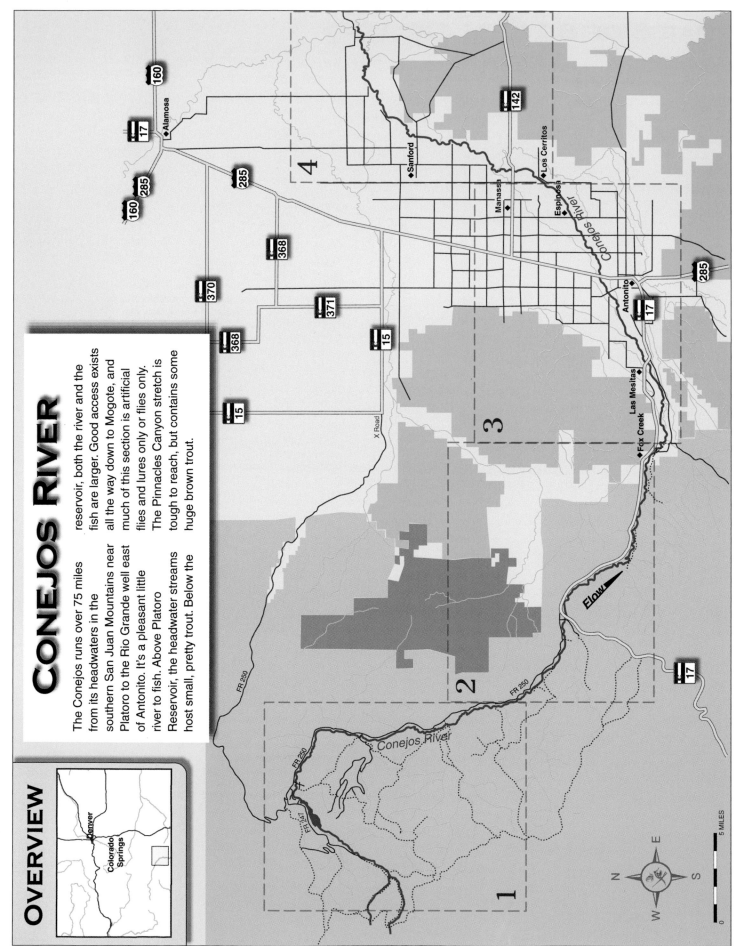

OVERVIEW

CONEJOS RIVER

The Conejos runs over 75 miles from its headwaters in the southern San Juan Mountains near Platoro to the Rio Grande well east of Antonito. It's a pleasant little river to fish. Above Platoro Reservoir, the headwater streams host small, pretty trout. Below the reservoir, both the river and the fish are larger. Good access exists all the way down to Mogote, and much of this section is artificial flies and lures only or flies only. The Pinnacles Canyon stretch is tough to reach, but contains some huge brown trout.

5 MILES

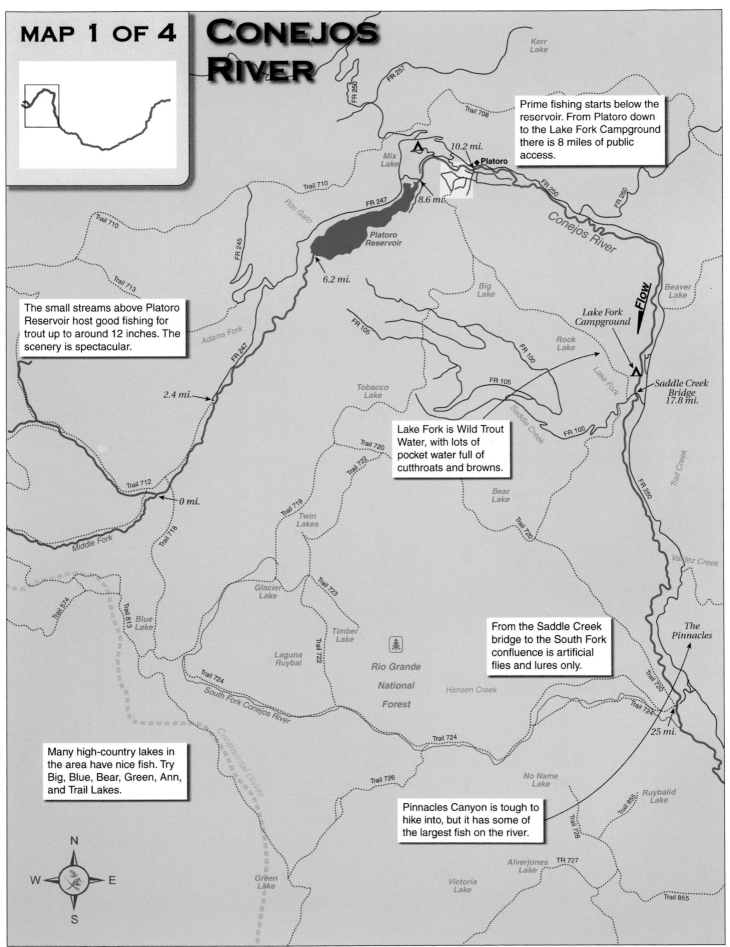

MAP 1 OF 4 CONEJOS RIVER

Kerr Lake

FR 257

FR 250

Trail 708

Prime fishing starts below the reservoir. From Platoro down to the Lake Fork Campground there is 8 miles of public access.

Mix Lake

10.2 mi.

Platoro

FR 250

FR 280

Trail 710

Rito Gato

FR 247

8.6 mi.

Conejos River

Flow

FR 245

Platoro Reservoir

6.2 mi.

Big Lake

Beaver Lake

The small streams above Platoro Reservoir host good fishing for trout up to around 12 inches. The scenery is spectacular.

Trail 713

FR 105

Lake Fork Campground

Lake Fork

Rock Lake

Adams Fork

FR 247

FR 100

Saddle Creek Bridge 17.8 mi.

2.4 mi.

Tobacco Lake

FR 105

Saddle Creek

FR 105

Lake Fork is Wild Trout Water, with lots of pocket water full of cutthroats and browns.

Trail 720

Trail 722

Trail Creek

Trail 712

0 mi.

Trail 719

Bear Lake

Middle Fork

Trail 718

Twin Lakes

Trail 720

FR 250

Valdez Creek

Trail 574

Trail 813

Blue Lake

Glacier Lake

Trail 723

The Pinnacles

Timber Lake

Trail 722

From the Saddle Creek bridge to the South Fork confluence is artificial flies and lures only.

Laguna Ruybal

Rio Grande

National

Forest

Hansen Creek

Trail 724

South Fork Conejos River

Continental Divide

Trail 720

Trail 724

25 mi.

Many high-country lakes in the area have nice fish. Try Big, Blue, Bear, Green, Ann, and Trail Lakes.

Trail 726

No Name Lake

Trail 855

Ruybalid Lake

Pinnacles Canyon is tough to hike into, but it has some of the largest fish on the river.

Trail 728

Green Lake

Alverjones Lake

TR 727

Victoria Lake

Trail 855

N
W E
S

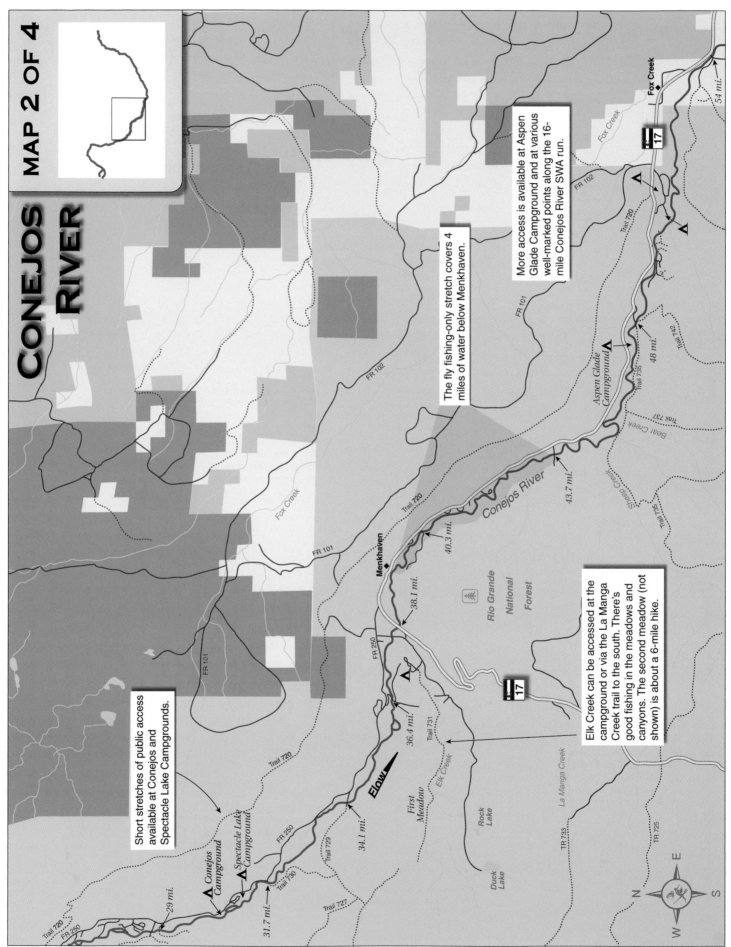

MAP 2 OF 4

CONEJOS RIVER

Short stretches of public access available at Conejos and Spectacle Lake Campgrounds.

The fly fishing-only stretch covers 4 miles of water below Menkhaven.

More access is available at Aspen Glade Campground and at various well-marked points along the 16-mile Conejos River SWA run.

Elk Creek can be accessed at the campground or via the La Manga Creek trail to the south. There's good fishing in the meadows and canyons. The second meadow (not shown) is about a 6-mile hike.

Fox Creek

FR 102

FR 101

FR 102

FR 101

Fox Creek

Conejos River

Menkhaven

Rio Grande National Forest

Aspen Glade Campground

Bear Creek

Sheep Creek

Trail 720

Trail 735

Trail 737

Trail 735

Trail 742

48 mi.

43.7 mi.

40.3 mi.

38.1 mi.

54 mi.

Fox Creek

17

FR 250

Conejos Campground

Spectacle Lake Campground

Trail 720

FR 250

Trail 729

Trail 730

Trail 727

Trail 720

FR 250

Elk Creek

First Meadow

Rock Lake

Duck Lake

La Manga Creek

TR 733

TR 725

17

Flow

29 mi.

31.7 mi.

34.1 mi.

36.4 mi.

Trail 731

N
E
S
W

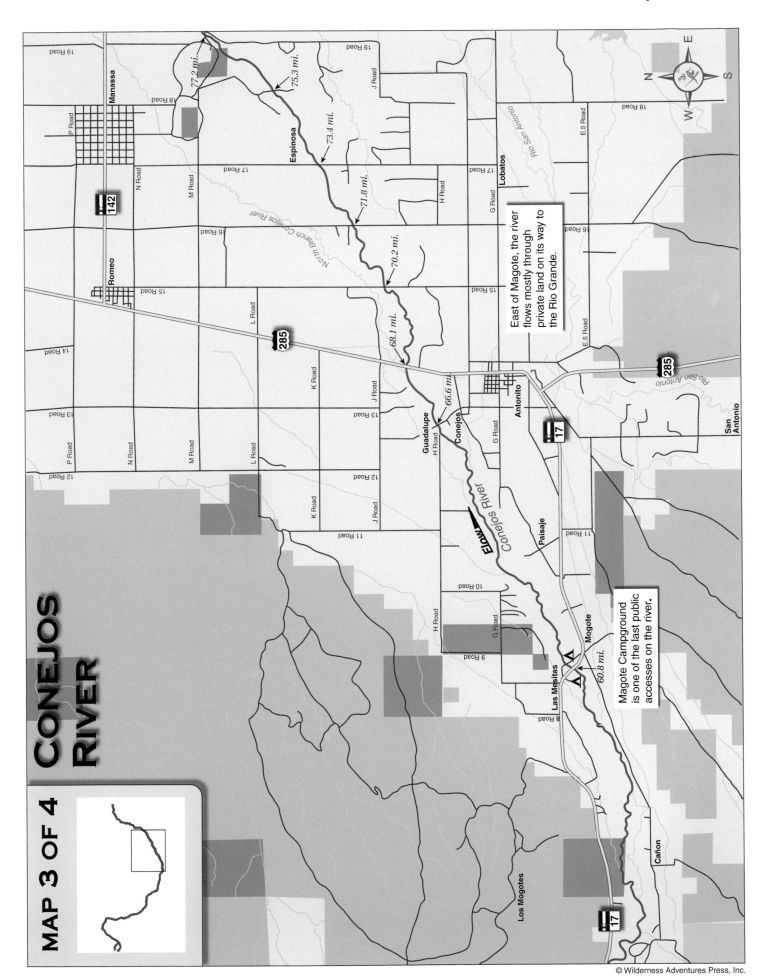

MAP 3 OF 4

CONEJOS
RIVER

East of Magote, the river flows mostly through private land on its way to the Rio Grande.

Magote Campground is one of the last public accesses on the river.

77.2 mi.

75.3 mi.

73.4 mi.

71.8 mi.

70.2 mi.

68.1 mi.

66.6 mi.

60.8 mi.

Manassa

Espinosa

Romeo

Lobatos

Rio San Antonio

Guadalupe

Conejos

Antonito

Paisaje

San Antonio

Rio San Antonio

Mogote

Las Mesitas

Los Mogotes

Cañon

North Branch Conejos River

Conejos River

FLOW

142

285

285

17

17

© Wilderness Adventures Press, Inc.

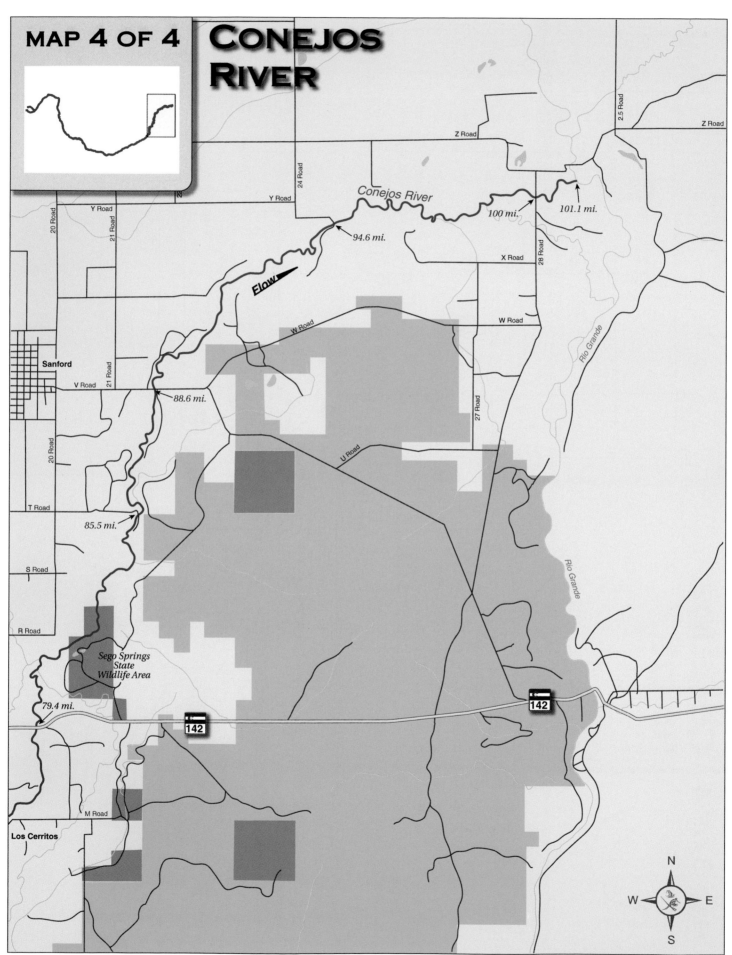

MAP 4 OF 4 **CONEJOS RIVER**

Conejos River

100 mi.

101.1 mi.

94.6 mi.

Z Road

Z Road

2.5 Road

24 Road

Y Road

28 Road

X Road

Rio Grande

W Road

Flow

W Road

27 Road

Y Road

21 Road

20 Road

Sanford

V Road

88.6 mi.

U Road

20 Road

T Road

85.5 mi.

S Road

Rio Grande

R Road

*Sego Springs
State
Wildlife Area*

79.4 mi.

142

142

M Road

Los Cerritos

N
W E
S

© Wilderness Adventures Press, Inc.

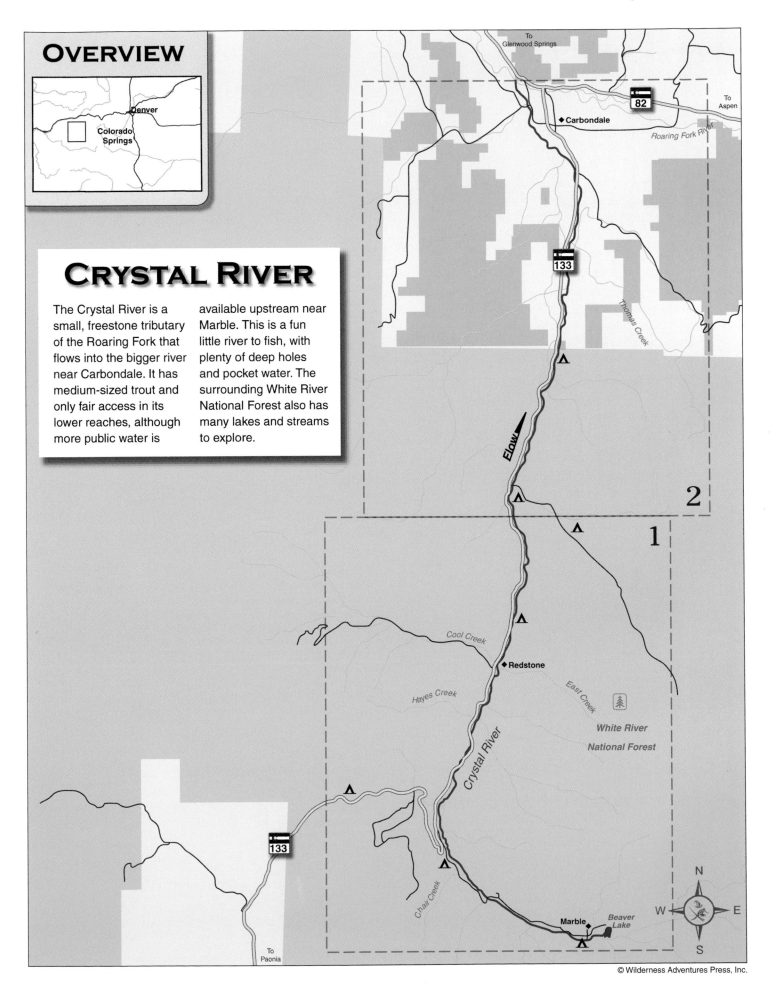

OVERVIEW

CRYSTAL RIVER

The Crystal River is a small, freestone tributary of the Roaring Fork that flows into the bigger river near Carbondale. It has medium-sized trout and only fair access in its lower reaches, although more public water is available upstream near Marble. This is a fun little river to fish, with plenty of deep holes and pocket water. The surrounding White River National Forest also has many lakes and streams to explore.

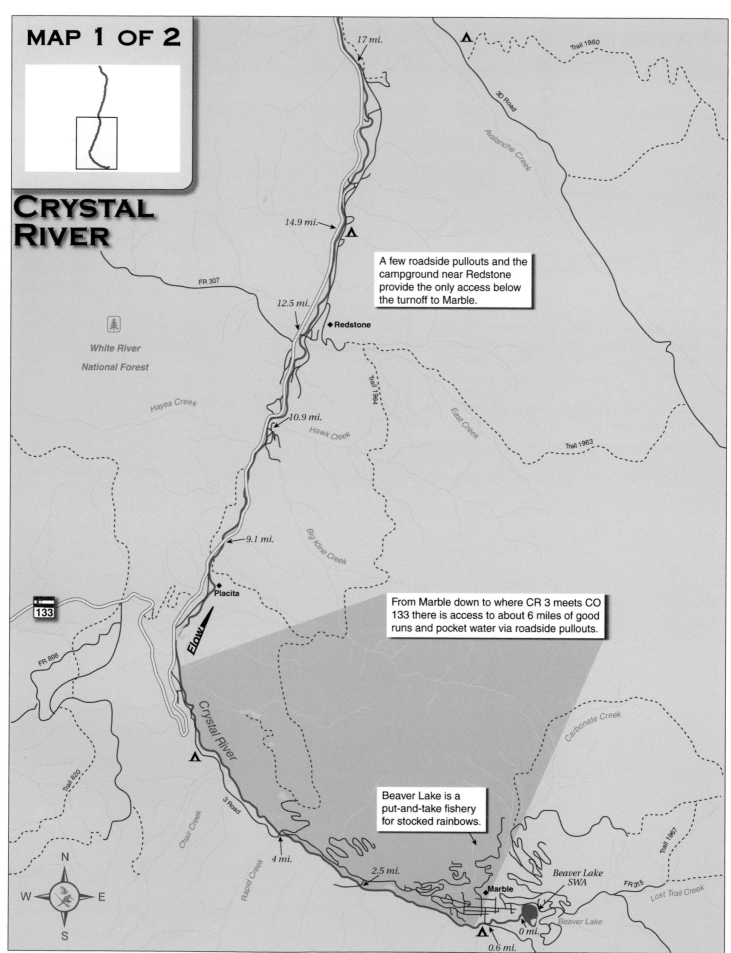

MAP 1 OF 2

CRYSTAL RIVER

17 mi.

Trail 1960

3D Road

Avalanche Creek

14.9 mi.

A few roadside pullouts and the campground near Redstone provide the only access below the turnoff to Marble.

FR 307

12.5 mi.

◆ Redstone

White River

National Forest

Trail 1964

East Creek

Trail 1963

Hayes Creek

10.9 mi.

Hawk Creek

Big Kline Creek

9.1 mi.

133

FR 898

◆ Placita

Flow

From Marble down to where CR 3 meets CO 133 there is access to about 6 miles of good runs and pocket water via roadside pullouts.

Crystal River

Carbonate Creek

Trail 820

3 Road

Beaver Lake is a put-and-take fishery for stocked rainbows.

Chair Creek

4 mi.

2.5 mi.

Trail 1967

Rapid Creek

Beaver Lake SWA

FR 315

Lost Trail Creek

N

W ⊕ E

S

◆ Marble

0 mi.

Beaver Lake

0.6 mi.

© Wilderness Adventures Press, Inc.

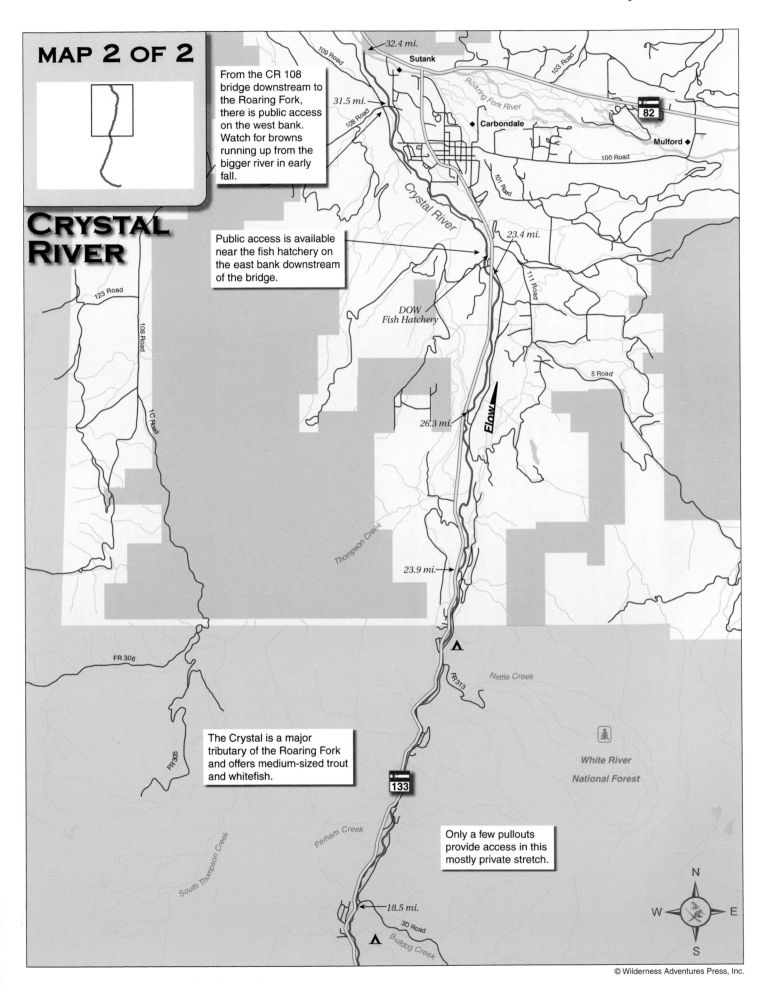

MAP 2 OF 2

CRYSTAL RIVER

From the CR 108 bridge downstream to the Roaring Fork, there is public access on the west bank. Watch for browns running up from the bigger river in early fall.

Public access is available near the fish hatchery on the east bank downstream of the bridge.

The Crystal is a major tributary of the Roaring Fork and offers medium-sized trout and whitefish.

Only a few pullouts provide access in this mostly private stretch.

32.4 mi.

Sutank

109 Road

103 Road

Roaring Fork River

31.5 mi.

108 Road

Carbondale

Mulford

82

100 Road

101 Road

Crystal River

23.4 mi.

111 Road

DOW
Fish Hatchery

5 Road

123 Road

108 Road

1C Road

Flow

26.3 mi.

Thompson Creek

23.9 mi.

FR 306

FR 313

Nettle Creek

FR 305

White River

National Forest

133

Perham Creek

South Thompson Creek

18.5 mi.

3D Road

Bulldog Creek

N

W   E

S

© Wilderness Adventures Press, Inc.

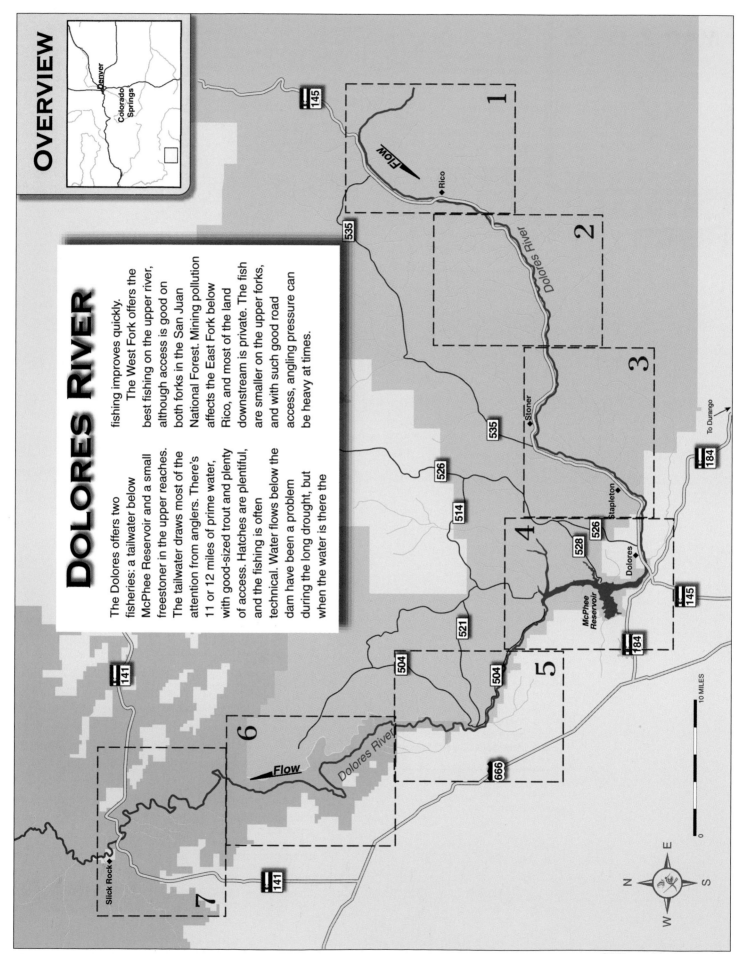

OVERVIEW

DOLORES RIVER

The Dolores offers two fisheries: a tailwater below McPhee Reservoir and a small freestoner in the upper reaches. The tailwater draws most of the attention from anglers. There's 11 or 12 miles of prime water, with good-sized trout and plenty of access. Hatches are plentiful, and the fishing is often technical. Water flows below the dam have been a problem during the long drought, but when the water is there the fishing improves quickly.

The West Fork offers the best fishing on the upper river, although access is good on both forks in the San Juan National Forest. Mining pollution affects the East Fork below Rico, and most of the land downstream is private. The fish are smaller on the upper forks, and with such good road access, angling pressure can be heavy at times.

© Wilderness Adventures Press, Inc.

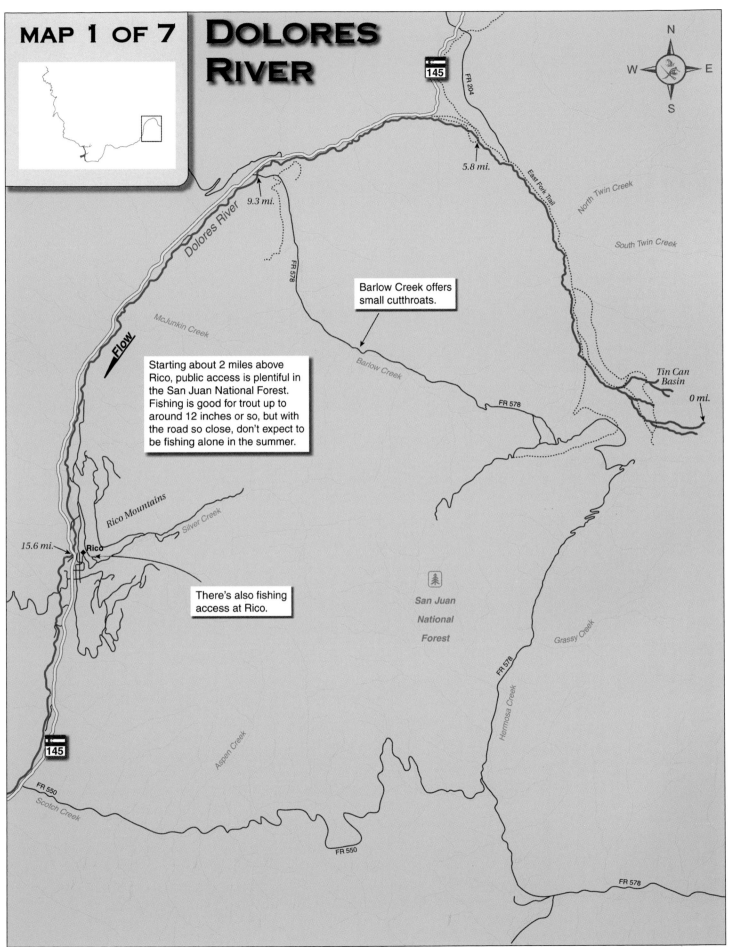

MAP 1 OF 7 DOLORES RIVER

145

FR 204

5.8 mi.

East Fork Trail

North Twin Creek

South Twin Creek

9.3 mi.

Dolores River

FR 578

McJunkin Creek

Barlow Creek offers small cutthroats.

Barlow Creek

Tin Can Basin

0 mi.

FR 578

Flow

Starting about 2 miles above Rico, public access is plentiful in the San Juan National Forest. Fishing is good for trout up to around 12 inches or so, but with the road so close, don't expect to be fishing alone in the summer.

Rico Mountains

Silver Creek

15.6 mi.   ◆ **Rico**

There's also fishing access at Rico.

San Juan National Forest

Grassy Creek

Hermosa Creek

FR 578

145

Aspen Creek

FR 550

Scotch Creek

FR 550

FR 578

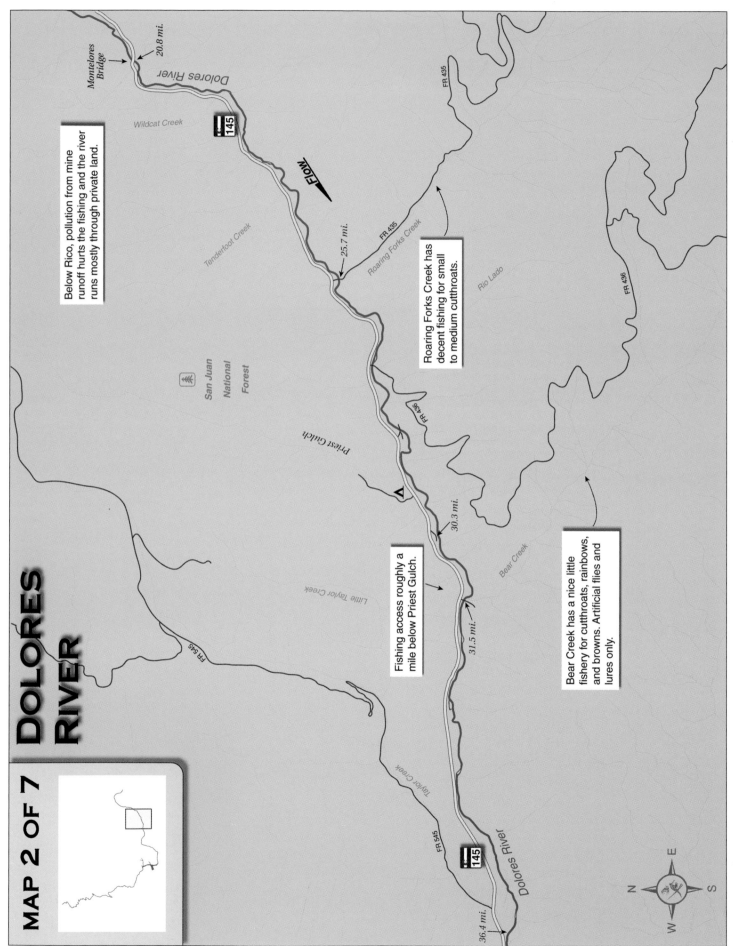

MAP 2 OF 7

DOLORES RIVER

Below Rico, pollution from mine runoff hurts the fishing and the river runs mostly through private land.

Roaring Forks Creek has decent fishing for small to medium cutthroats.

Fishing access roughly a mile below Priest Gulch.

Bear Creek has a nice little fishery for cutthroats, rainbows, and browns. Artificial flies and lures only.

Dolores River

Montelores Bridge

20.8 mi.

Wildcat Creek

145

FLOW

Tenderfoot Creek

FR 435

25.7 mi.

Roaring Forks Creek

FR 435

Rio Lado

FR 436

San Juan National Forest

Priest Gulch

FR 436

30.3 mi.

Bear Creek

Little Taylor Creek

31.5 mi.

FR 545

Taylor Creek

FR 545

145

Dolores River

36.4 mi.

N E S W

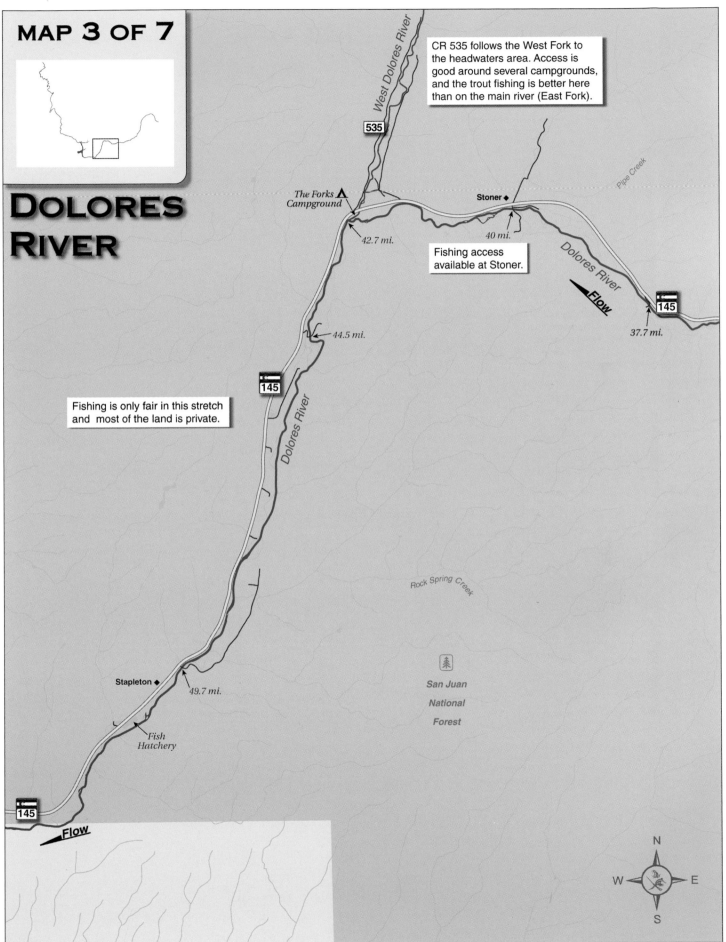

MAP 3 OF 7

DOLORES RIVER

CR 535 follows the West Fork to the headwaters area. Access is good around several campgrounds, and the trout fishing is better here than on the main river (East Fork).

West Dolores River

535

The Forks △
Campground

42.7 mi.

Stoner ◆

40 mi.

Fishing access available at Stoner.

Pipe Creek

Dolores River

Flow

145

37.7 mi.

44.5 mi.

145

Fishing is only fair in this stretch and most of the land is private.

Dolores River

Rock Spring Creek

San Juan

National

Forest

Stapleton ◆

49.7 mi.

*Fish
Hatchery*

145

Flow

N
W ✦ E
S

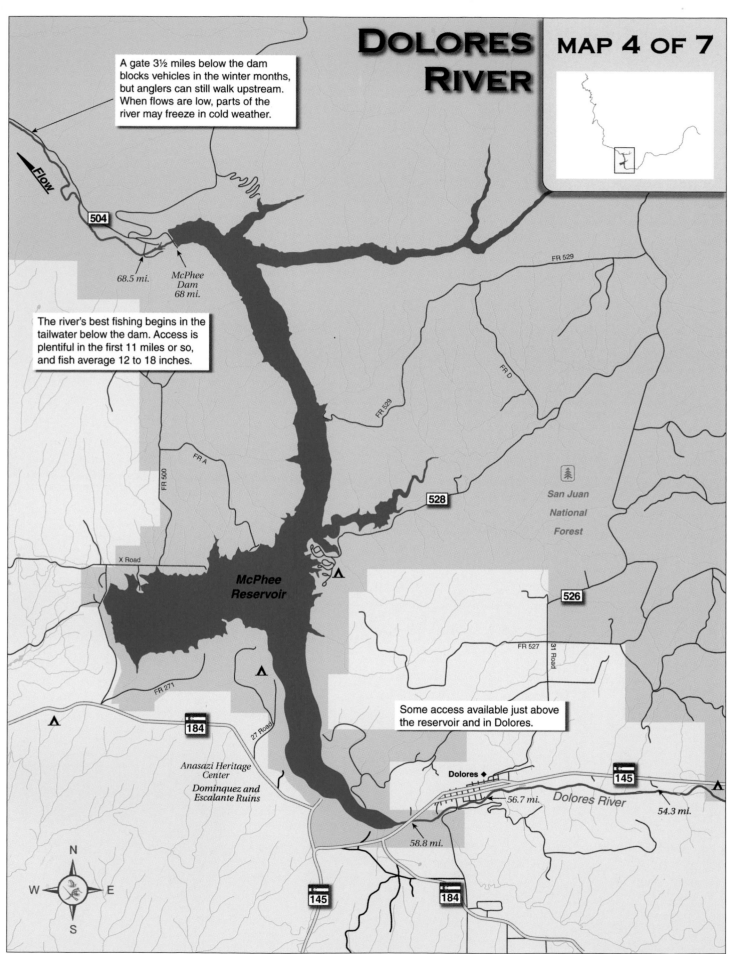

DOLORES RIVER

MAP 4 OF 7

A gate 3½ miles below the dam blocks vehicles in the winter months, but anglers can still walk upstream. When flows are low, parts of the river may freeze in cold weather.

Flow

504

68.5 mi.

McPhee Dam 68 mi.

The river's best fishing begins in the tailwater below the dam. Access is plentiful in the first 11 miles or so, and fish average 12 to 18 inches.

FR 529

FR 529

FR D

FR A

FR 500

528

San Juan National Forest

526

X Road

McPhee Reservoir

FR 527

31 Road

FR 271

Some access available just above the reservoir and in Dolores.

184

27 Road

Anasazi Heritage Center
Dominquez and Escalante Ruins

Dolores ♦

145

56.7 mi.

Dolores River

54.3 mi.

58.8 mi.

N
W   E
S

145

184

© Wilderness Adventures Press, Inc.

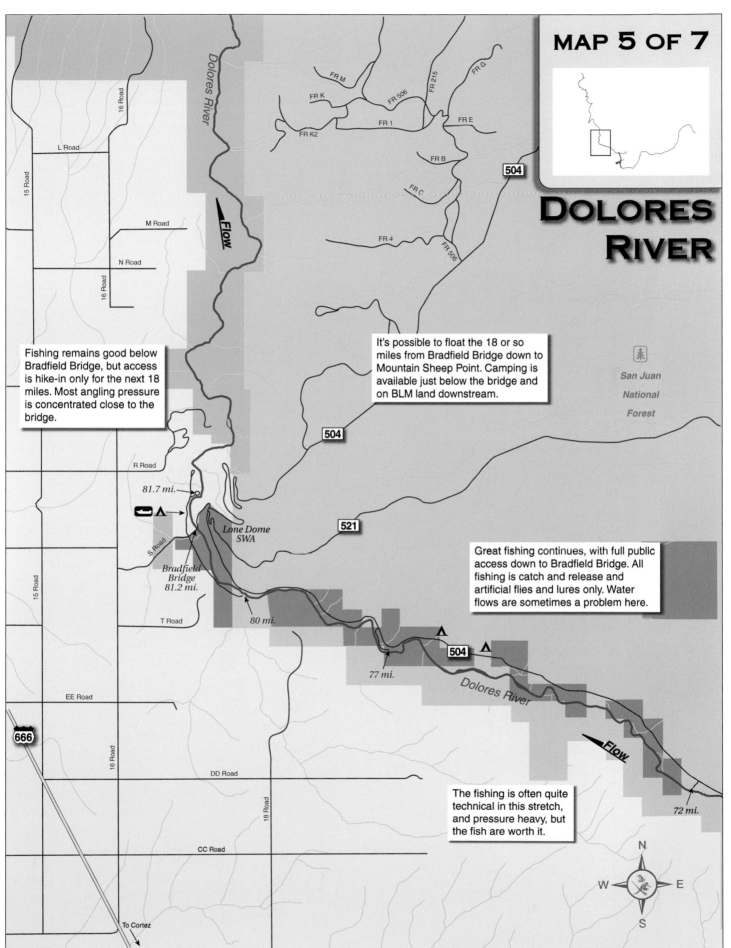

MAP 5 OF 7

DOLORES RIVER

Fishing remains good below Bradfield Bridge, but access is hike-in only for the next 18 miles. Most angling pressure is concentrated close to the bridge.

It's possible to float the 18 or so miles from Bradfield Bridge down to Mountain Sheep Point. Camping is available just below the bridge and on BLM land downstream.

San Juan

National

Forest

Great fishing continues, with full public access down to Bradfield Bridge. All fishing is catch and release and artificial flies and lures only. Water flows are sometimes a problem here.

The fishing is often quite technical in this stretch, and pressure heavy, but the fish are worth it.

Dolores River

Flow

81.7 mi.

Lone Dome SWA

Bradfield Bridge 81.2 mi.

80 mi.

77 mi.

72 mi.

Dolores River

Flow

To Cortez

L Road

M Road

N Road

R Road

S Road

T Road

EE Road

DD Road

CC Road

15 Road

16 Road

18 Road

16 Road

666

504

504

521

504

FR M

FR K

FR K2

FR 1

FR 506

FR 215

FR G

FR E

FR B

FR C

FR 4

FR 506

N
W E
S

MAP 6 OF 7

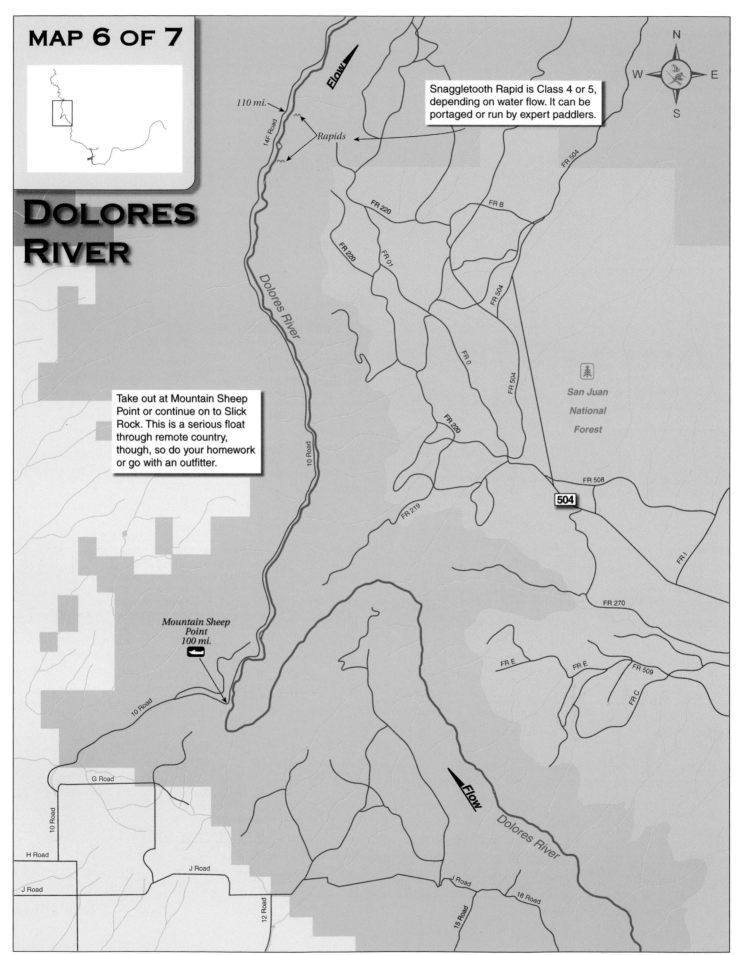

DOLORES RIVER

Flow

110 mi.

14F Road

Rapids

Snaggletooth Rapid is Class 4 or 5, depending on water flow. It can be portaged or run by expert paddlers.

N
W E
S

FR 504

FR 220

FR B

FR 220

FR 01

FR 504

Dolores River

FR 0

FR 504

San Juan National Forest

Take out at Mountain Sheep Point or continue on to Slick Rock. This is a serious float through remote country, though, so do your homework or go with an outfitter.

10 Road

FR 220

FR 508

504

FR 219

FR 1

FR 270

Mountain Sheep Point
100 mi.

10 Road

FR E

FR E

FR 509

FR C

Flow

Dolores River

G Road

10 Road

H Road

J Road

J Road

J Road

12 Road

15 Road

16 Road

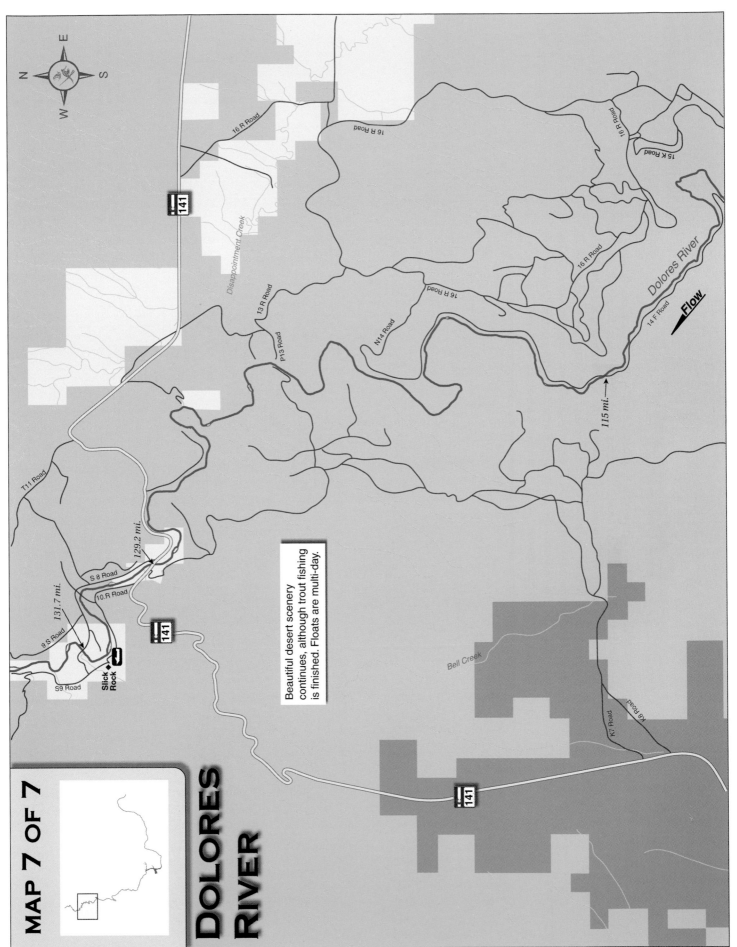

N E S W

16 R Road

16 R Road

16 R Road

15 K Road

141

Disappointment Creek

13 R Road

P13 Road

N14 Road

16 R Road

16 R Road

14 F Road

Dolores River

Flow

115 mi.

T11 Road

129.2 mi.

S 8 Road

131.7 mi.

10.R Road

9 S Road

141

S9 Road

Slick Rock

Beautiful desert scenery continues, although trout fishing is finished. Floats are multi-day.

Bell Creek

K7 Road

K8 Road

141

MAP 7 OF 7

DOLORES RIVER

EAGLE RIVER

Starting along US 24 near the Continental Divide in the White River National Forest, the Eagle River flows roughly 70 miles west to its confluence with the Colorado River near Dotsero. Brown and rainbow trout averaging 12 to 16 inches are the main catch, although cutthroats are present along with a few brookies (in the upper river). From Dowds Junction down to Dotsero, plenty of access is available for wading and floating anglers. Gore Creek, a Gold Medal stream, joins the river at Dowds Junction and provides good fishing for medium-sized fish.

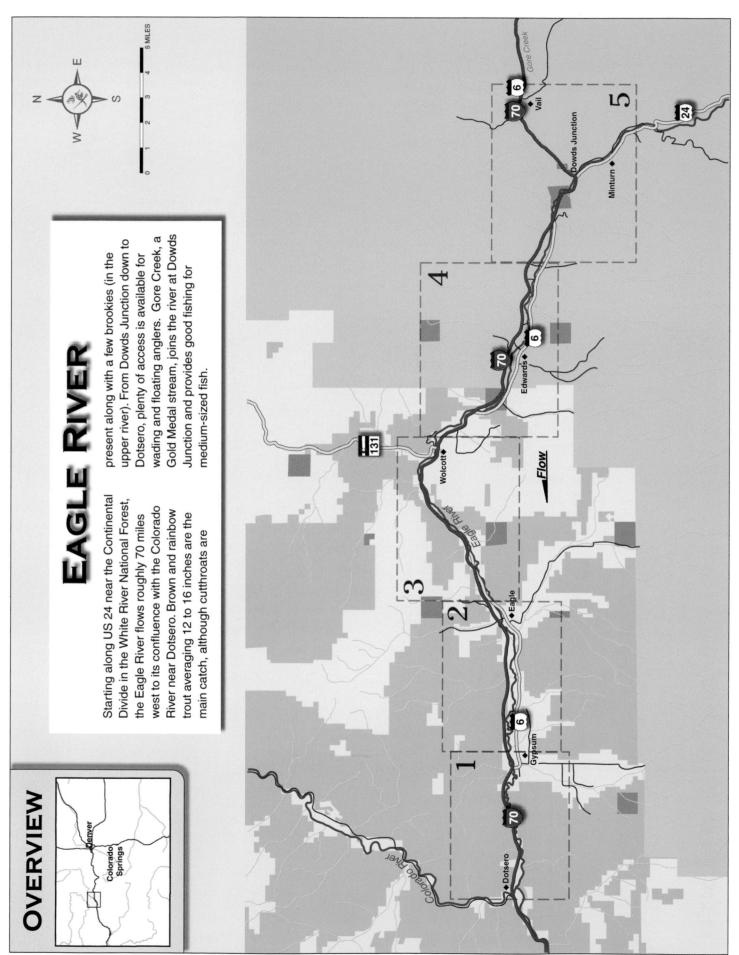

OVERVIEW

© Wilderness Adventures Press, Inc.

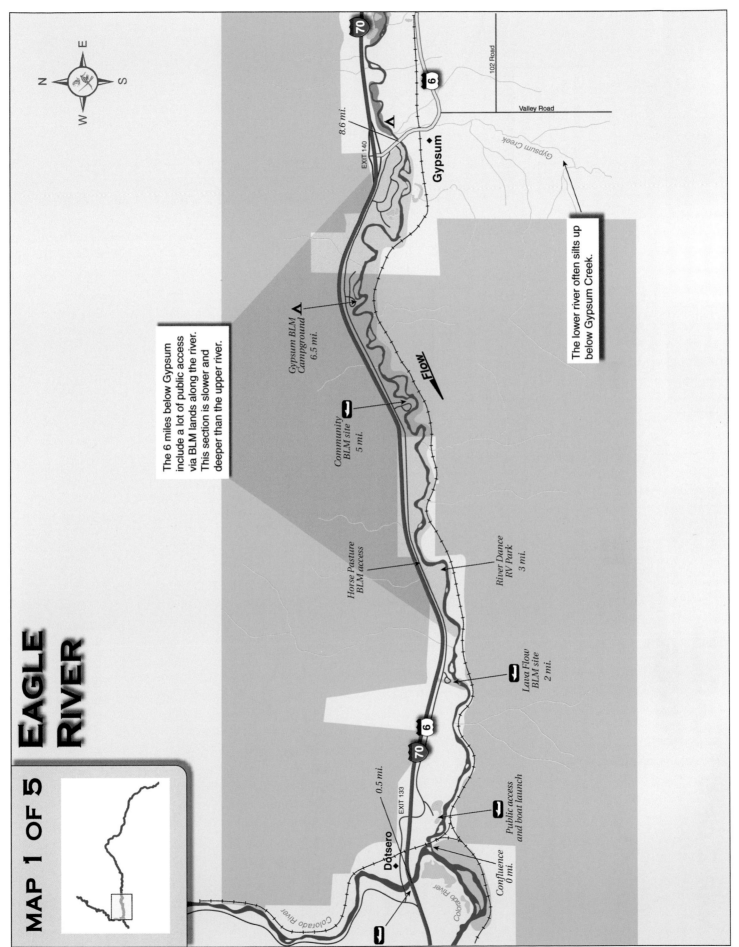

MAP 1 OF 5

EAGLE RIVER

Dotsero

Colorado River

Confluence
0 mi.

Public access
and boat launch

Lava Flow
BLM site
2 mi.

EXIT 133

0.5 mi.

River Dance
RV Park
3 mi.

Horse Pasture
BLM access

Community
BLM site
5 mi.

FLOW

Gypsum BLM
Campground
6.5 mi.

EXIT 140

8.6 mi.

Gypsum

Gypsum Creek

Valley Road

102 Road

The 6 miles below Gypsum include a lot of public access via BLM lands along the river. This section is slower and deeper than the upper river.

The lower river often silts up below Gypsum Creek.

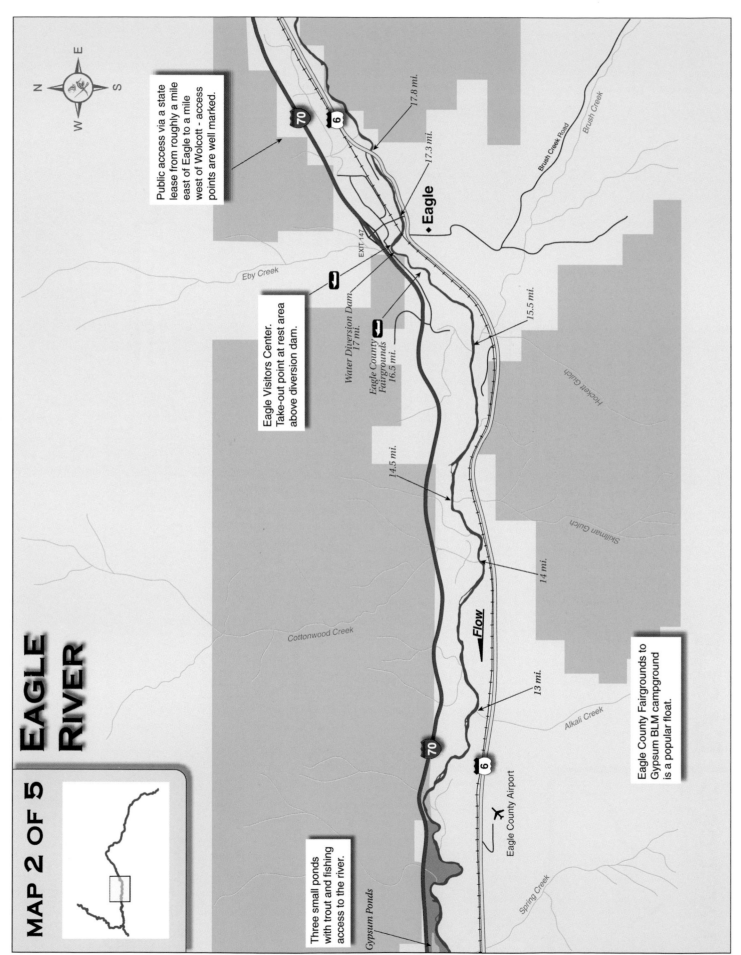

MAP 2 OF 5

EAGLE RIVER

Public access via a state lease from roughly a mile east of Eagle to a mile west of Wolcott - access points are well marked.

Eagle Visitors Center. Take-out point at rest area above diversion dam.

Water Diversion Dam. 17 mi.

Eagle County Fairgrounds 16.5 mi.

Three small ponds with trout and fishing access to the river.

Eagle County Fairgrounds to Gypsum BLM campground is a popular float.

Eby Creek

Cottonwood Creek

Gypsum Ponds

Eagle County Airport

Alkali Creek

Spring Creek

Brush Creek Road

Brush Creek

Hockett Gulch

Skillman Gulch

♦ Eagle

EXIT 147

Flow

17.8 mi.

17.3 mi.

15.5 mi.

14.5 mi.

14 mi.

13 mi.

© Wilderness Adventures Press, Inc.

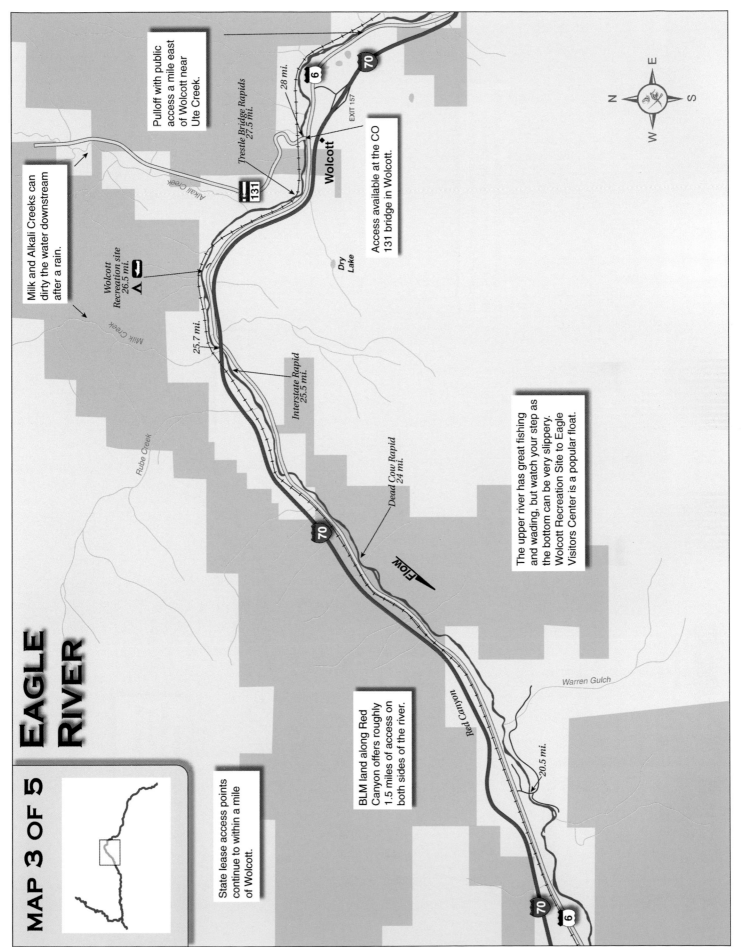

MAP **3** OF **5**

EAGLE RIVER

State lease access points continue to within a mile of Wolcott.

BLM land along Red Canyon offers roughly 1.5 miles of access on both sides of the river.

The upper river has great fishing and wading, but watch your step as the bottom can be very slippery. Wolcott Recreation Site to Eagle Visitors Center is a popular float.

Milk and Alkali Creeks can dirty the water downstream after a rain.

Pulloff with public access a mile east of Wolcott near Ute Creek.

Access available at the CO 131 bridge in Wolcott.

Wolcott Recreation site 26.5 mi.

Trestle Bridge Rapids 27.5 mi.

28 mi.

EXIT 157

Wolcott

Dry Lake

25.7 mi.

Interstate Rapid 25.5 mi.

Dead Cow Rapid 24 mi.

Flow

Warren Gulch

Red Canyon

20.5 mi.

Alkali Creek

Milk Creek

Rube Creek

70

6

131

70

70

6

N E S W

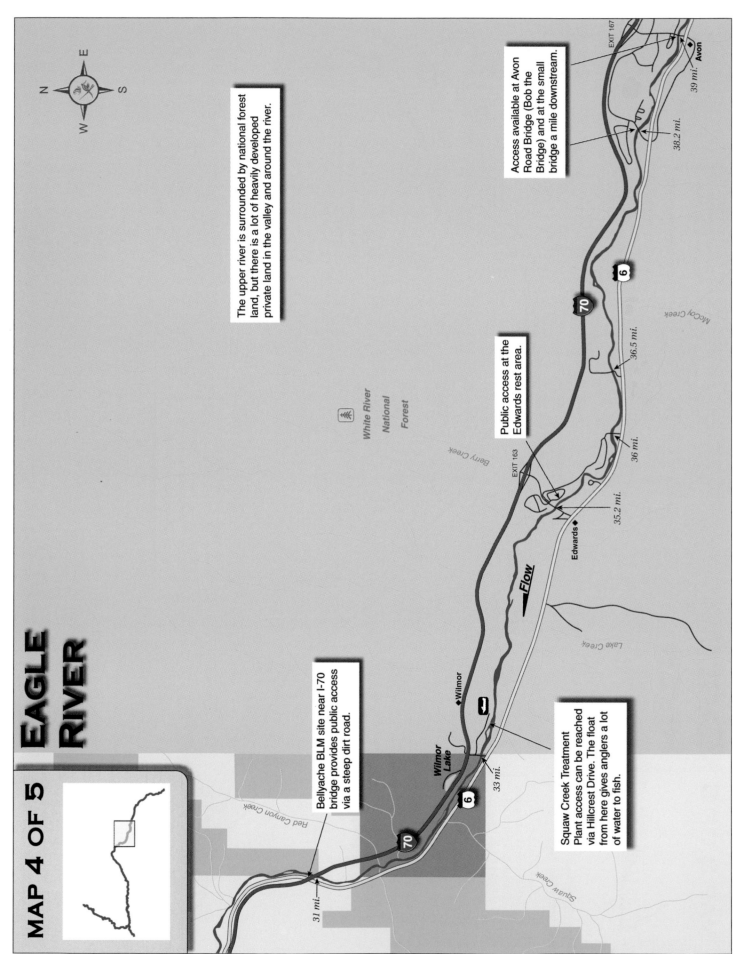

MAP 4 OF 5

EAGLE RIVER

The upper river is surrounded by national forest land, but there is a lot of heavily developed private land in the valley and around the river.

Access available at Avon Road Bridge (Bob the Bridge) and at the small bridge a mile downstream.

Public access at the Edwards rest area.

Bellyache BLM site near I-70 bridge provides public access via a steep dirt road.

Squaw Creek Treatment Plant access can be reached via Hillcrest Drive. The float from here gives anglers a lot of water to fish.

White River National Forest

Flow

EXIT 167
EXIT 163

39 mi.
38.2 mi.
36.5 mi.
36 mi.
35.2 mi.
33 mi.
31 mi.

Avon
Edwards
Wilmor
Wilmor Lake

McCoy Creek
Berry Creek
Lake Creek
Squaw Creek
Red Canyon Creek

© Wilderness Adventures Press, Inc.

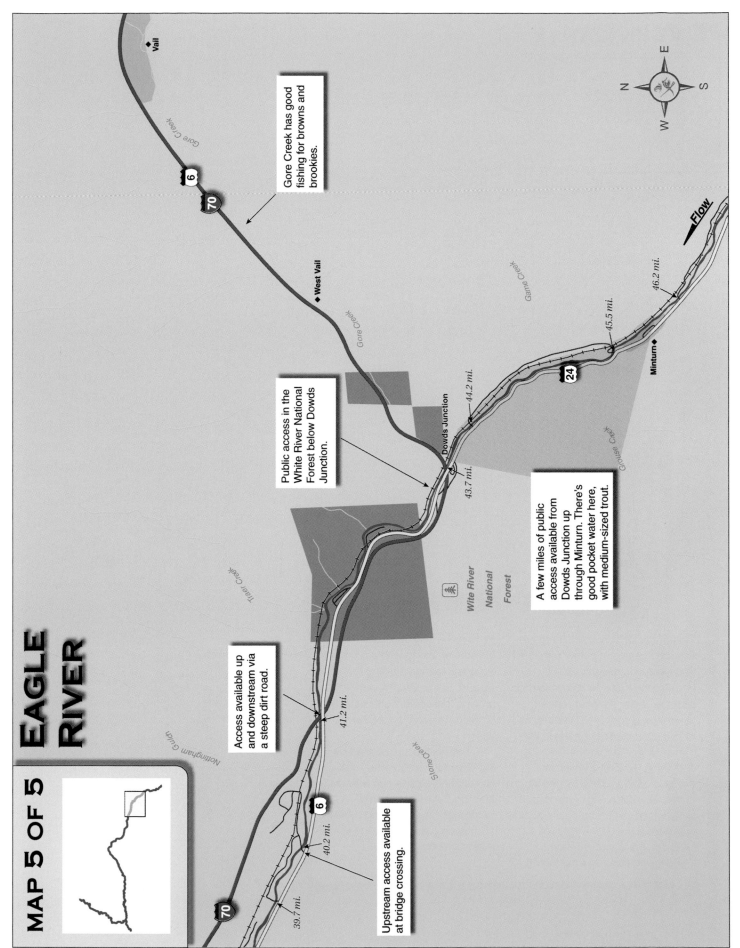

MAP 5 OF 5

EAGLE RIVER

Gore Creek has good fishing for browns and brookies.

Public access in the White River National Forest below Dowds Junction.

A few miles of public access available from Dowds Junction up through Minturn. There's good pocket water here, with medium-sized trout.

Access available up and downstream via a steep dirt road.

Upstream access available at bridge crossing.

Vail

Gore Creek

♦ West Vail

Gore Creek

Game Creek

Dowds Junction

44.2 mi.

43.7 mi.

45.5 mi.

46.2 mi.

Grouse Creek

Minturn ♦

24

Flow

White River National Forest

Traer Creek

Nottingham Gulch

Stone Creek

41.2 mi.

40.2 mi.

39.7 mi.

70

6

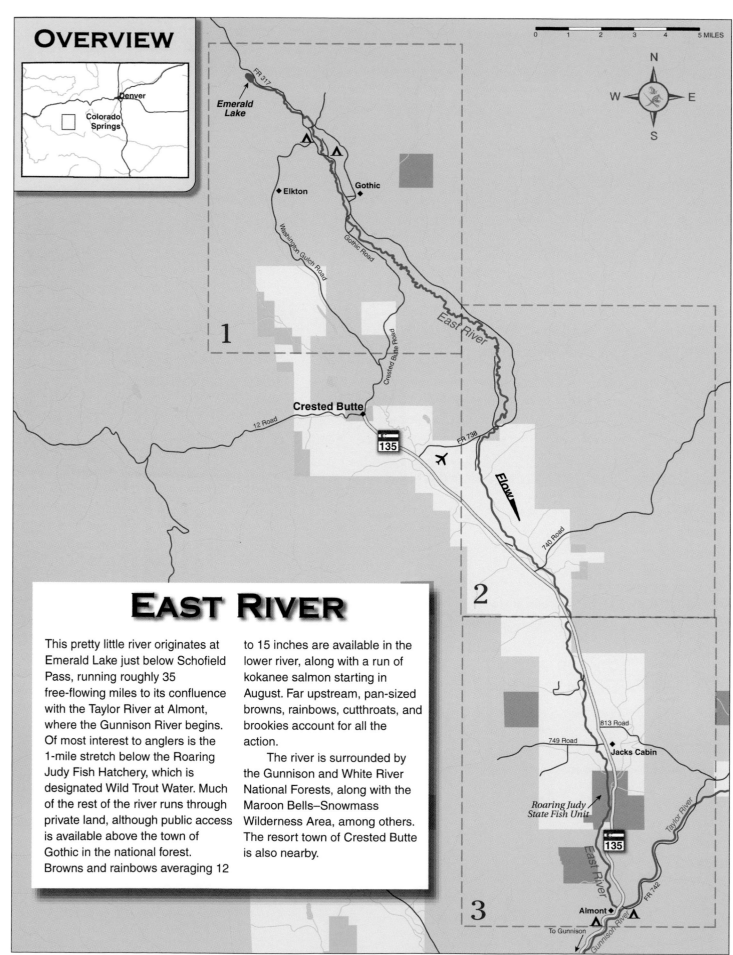

OVERVIEW

Denver
Colorado Springs

Emerald Lake

FR 317

Elkton

Gothic

Washington Gulch Road

Gothic Road

Crested Butte Road

East River

1

Crested Butte

12 Road

135

FR 738

Flow

740 Road

2

813 Road

749 Road

Jacks Cabin

Taylor River

Roaring Judy State Fish Unit

135

East River

3

Almont

Gunnison River

FR 742

To Gunnison

EAST RIVER

This pretty little river originates at Emerald Lake just below Schofield Pass, running roughly 35 free-flowing miles to its confluence with the Taylor River at Almont, where the Gunnison River begins. Of most interest to anglers is the 1-mile stretch below the Roaring Judy Fish Hatchery, which is designated Wild Trout Water. Much of the rest of the river runs through private land, although public access is available above the town of Gothic in the national forest. Browns and rainbows averaging 12 to 15 inches are available in the lower river, along with a run of kokanee salmon starting in August. Far upstream, pan-sized browns, rainbows, cutthroats, and brookies account for all the action.

The river is surrounded by the Gunnison and White River National Forests, along with the Maroon Bells–Snowmass Wilderness Area, among others. The resort town of Crested Butte is also nearby.

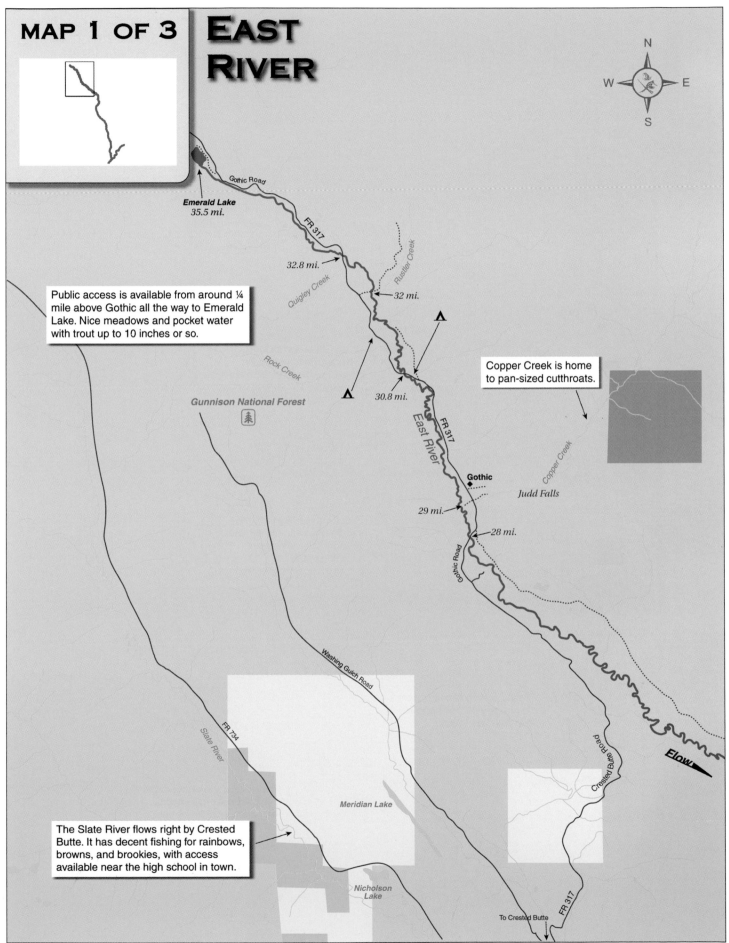

MAP 1 OF 3 EAST RIVER

Emerald Lake
35.5 mi.

Gothic Road

FR 317

Rustler Creek

32.8 mi.

32 mi.

Quigley Creek

Public access is available from around ¼ mile above Gothic all the way to Emerald Lake. Nice meadows and pocket water with trout up to 10 inches or so.

Rock Creek

Copper Creek is home to pan-sized cutthroats.

30.8 mi.

Gunnison National Forest

East River

FR 317

Gothic

Copper Creek

Judd Falls

29 mi.

28 mi.

Gothic Road

Washing Gulch Road

FR 734

Slate River

Crested Butte Road

Flow

Meridian Lake

The Slate River flows right by Crested Butte. It has decent fishing for rainbows, browns, and brookies, with access available near the high school in town.

Nicholson Lake

FR 317

To Crested Butte

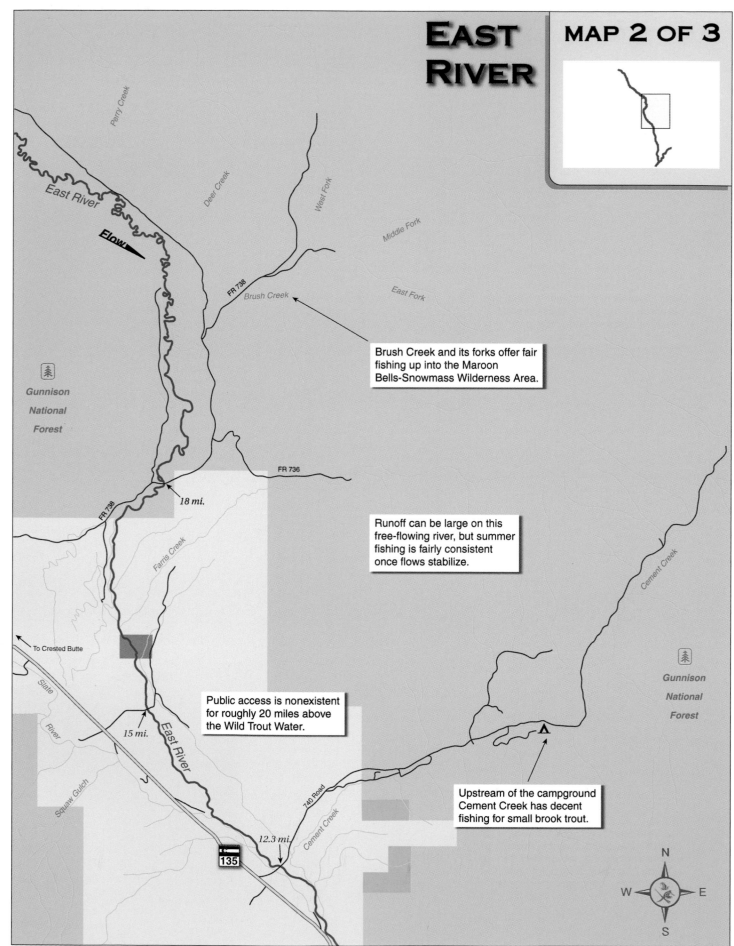

EAST RIVER

MAP 2 OF 3

Perry Creek

Deer Creek

West Fork

Middle Fork

East River

Flow

FR 738

Brush Creek

East Fork

Brush Creek and its forks offer fair fishing up into the Maroon Bells-Snowmass Wilderness Area.

Gunnison National Forest

FR 736

FR 738

18 mi.

Runoff can be large on this free-flowing river, but summer fishing is fairly consistent once flows stabilize.

Farris Creek

Cement Creek

To Crested Butte

Slate

River

Gunnison National Forest

Public access is nonexistent for roughly 20 miles above the Wild Trout Water.

15 mi.

East River

Upstream of the campground Cement Creek has decent fishing for small brook trout.

Squaw Gulch

740 Road

Cement Creek

135

12.3 mi.

N

W E

S

© Wilderness Adventures Press, Inc.

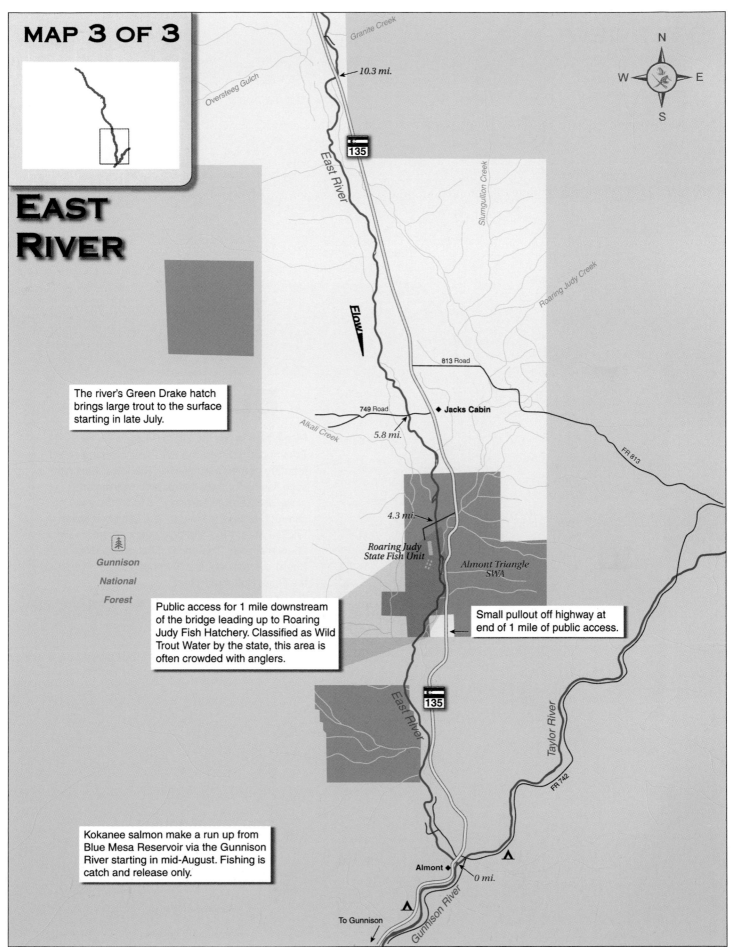

MAP 3 OF 3

EAST RIVER

The river's Green Drake hatch brings large trout to the surface starting in late July.

Public access for 1 mile downstream of the bridge leading up to Roaring Judy Fish Hatchery. Classified as Wild Trout Water by the state, this area is often crowded with anglers.

Kokanee salmon make a run up from Blue Mesa Reservoir via the Gunnison River starting in mid-August. Fishing is catch and release only.

Small pullout off highway at end of 1 mile of public access.

Gunnison

National

Forest

Roaring Judy
State Fish Unit

Almont Triangle
SWA

Granite Creek

Oversteeg Gulch

Slumgullion Creek

Roaring Judy Creek

East River

135

FLOW

813 Road

749 Road

◆ Jacks Cabin

Alkali Creek

FR 813

10.3 mi.

5.8 mi.

4.3 mi.

East River

135

Taylor River

FR 742

Almont ◆

0 mi.

Gunnison River

To Gunnison

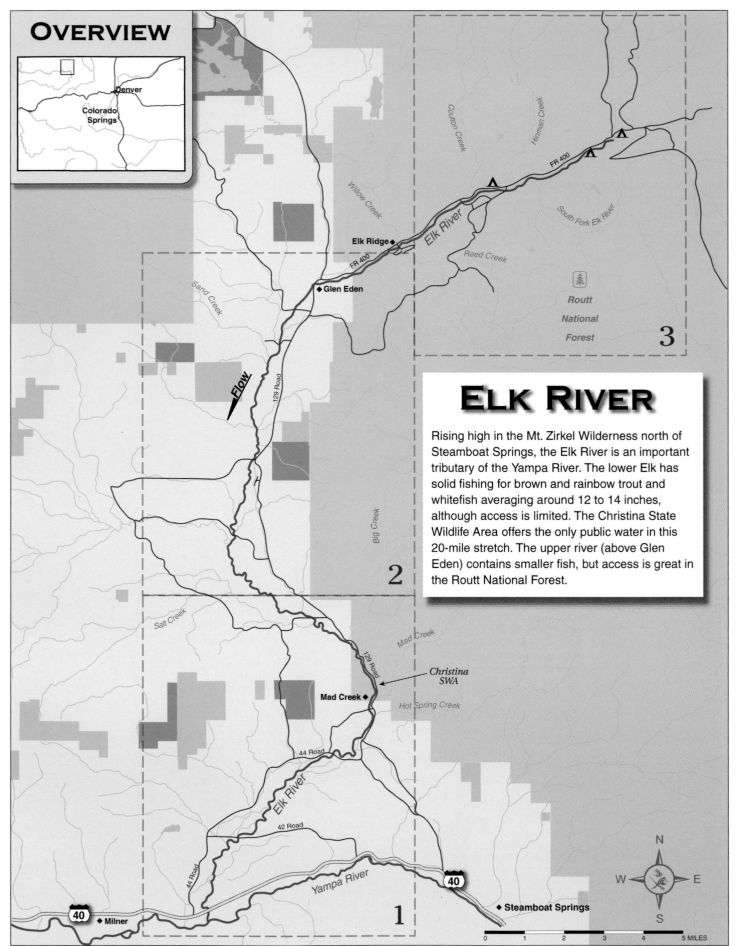

OVERVIEW

Denver

Colorado
Springs

Caution Creek

Hinman Creek

FR 400

Willow Creek

South Fork Elk River

Elk River

Reed Creek

Elk Ridge ◆

FR 400

◆ Glen Eden

Sand Creek

Flow

129 Road

Routt

National

Forest

3

ELK RIVER

Rising high in the Mt. Zirkel Wilderness north of Steamboat Springs, the Elk River is an important tributary of the Yampa River. The lower Elk has solid fishing for brown and rainbow trout and whitefish averaging around 12 to 14 inches, although access is limited. The Christina State Wildlife Area offers the only public water in this 20-mile stretch. The upper river (above Glen Eden) contains smaller fish, but access is great in the Routt National Forest.

Big Creek

2

Salt Creek

Mad Creek

129 Road

Christina SWA

Mad Creek ◆

Hot Spring Creek

44 Road

Elk River

42 Road

44 Road

Yampa River

40

N
W   E
S

40 ◆ Milner

◆ **Steamboat Springs**

0   1   2   3   4   5 MILES

1

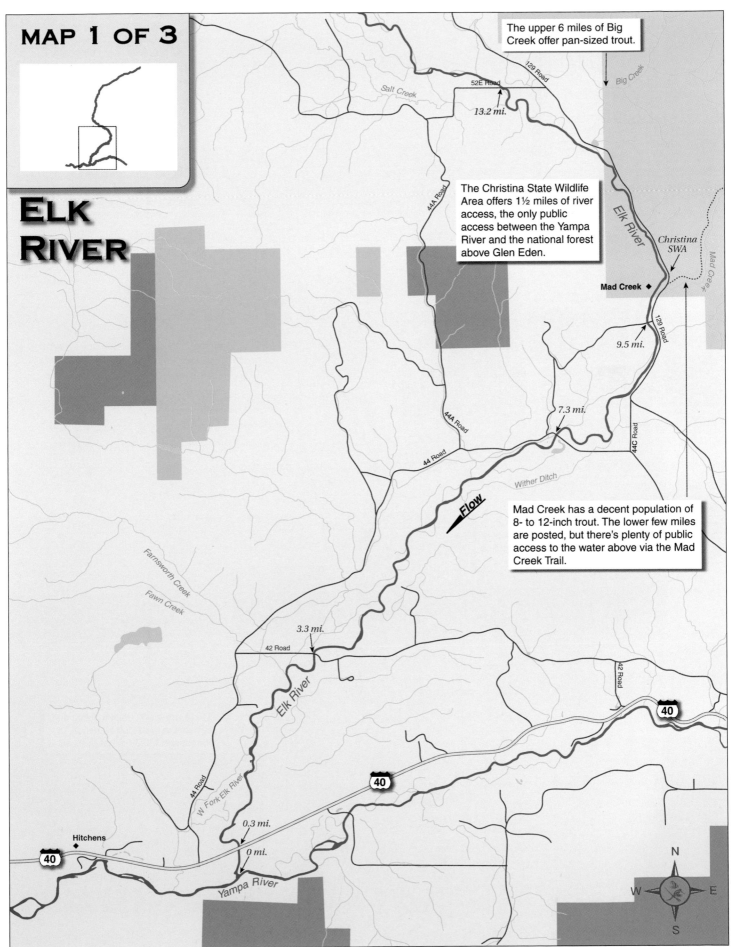

MAP 1 OF 3

ELK RIVER

The upper 6 miles of Big Creek offer pan-sized trout.

The Christina State Wildlife Area offers 1½ miles of river access, the only public access between the Yampa River and the national forest above Glen Eden.

Mad Creek has a decent population of 8- to 12-inch trout. The lower few miles are posted, but there's plenty of public access to the water above via the Mad Creek Trail.

Salt Creek

52E Road

129 Road

Big Creek

13.2 mi.

Elk River

Christina SWA

Mad Creek ◆

Mad Creek

44A Road

129 Road

9.5 mi.

44A Road

7.3 mi.

44C Road

44 Road

Wither Ditch

Flow

Farnsworth Creek

Fawn Creek

3.3 mi.

42 Road

Elk River

42 Road

40

40

44 Road

W Fork Elk River

0.3 mi.

0 mi.

Hitchens

40

Yampa River

N
W   E
S

© Wilderness Adventures Press, Inc.

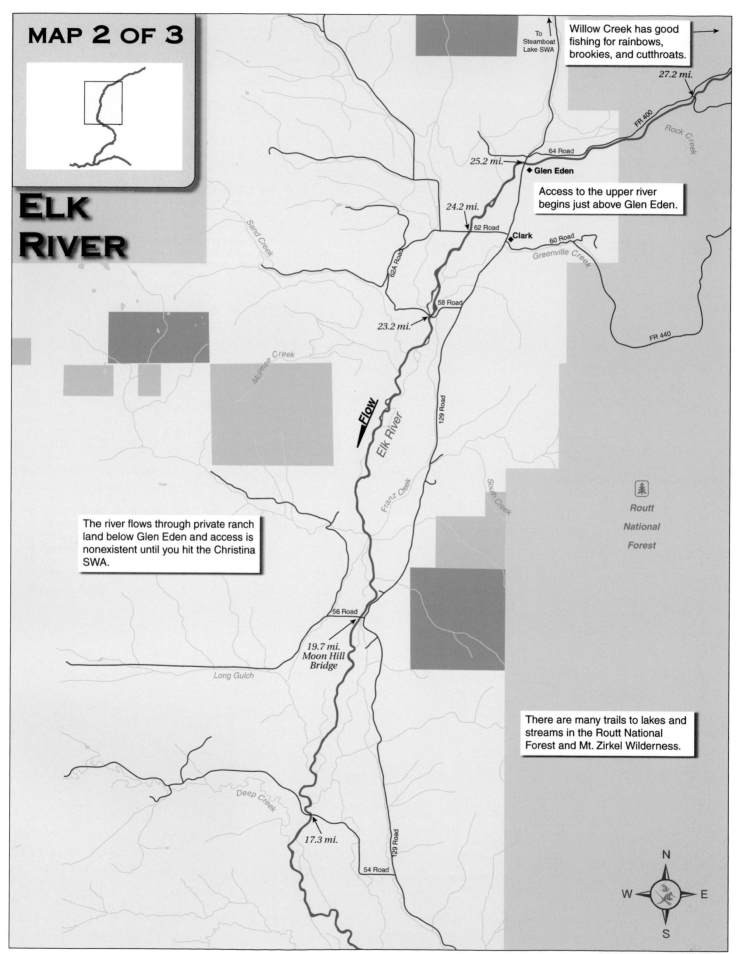

MAP 2 OF 3

ELK RIVER

To Steamboat Lake SWA

Willow Creek has good fishing for rainbows, brookies, and cutthroats.

27.2 mi.

FR 400

Rock Creek

64 Road

25.2 mi.

◆ Glen Eden

Access to the upper river begins just above Glen Eden.

24.2 mi.

62 Road

◆ Clark

60 Road

Greenville Creek

62A Road

58 Road

23.2 mi.

FR 440

Sand Creek

McPhee Creek

Flow

Elk River

129 Road

Franz Creek

South Creek

Routt

National

Forest

The river flows through private ranch land below Glen Eden and access is nonexistent until you hit the Christina SWA.

56 Road

19.7 mi.
Moon Hill
Bridge

Long Gulch

There are many trails to lakes and streams in the Routt National Forest and Mt. Zirkel Wilderness.

Deep Creek

17.3 mi.

129 Road

54 Road

N
W — E
S

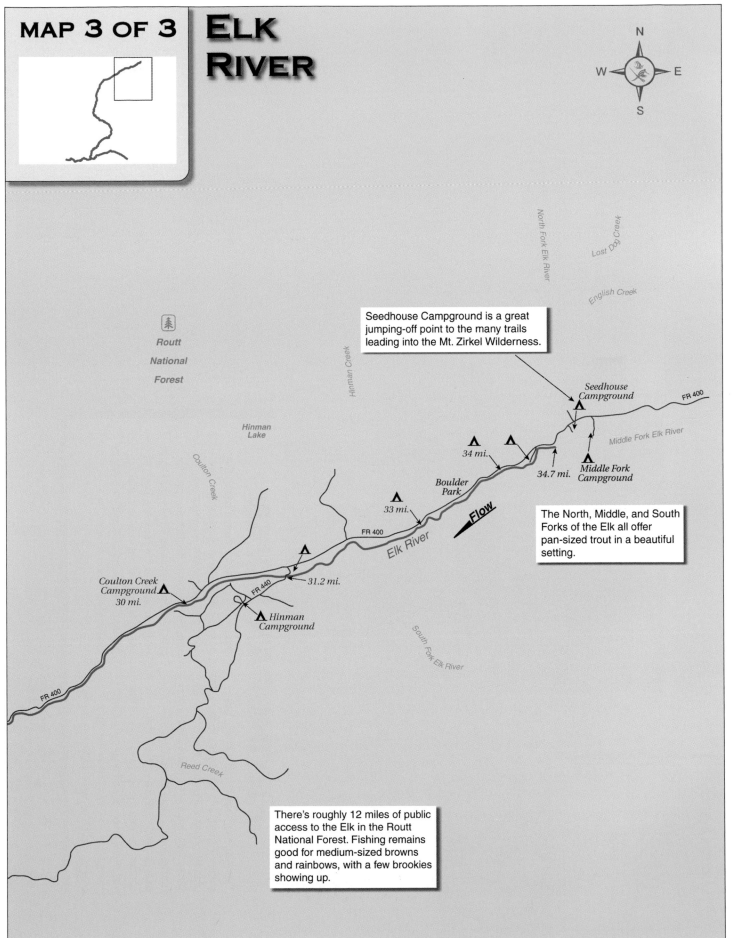

MAP 3 OF 3

ELK RIVER

Routt

National

Forest

North Fork Elk River

Lost Dog Creek

English Creek

Seedhouse Campground is a great jumping-off point to the many trails leading into the Mt. Zirkel Wilderness.

Seedhouse Campground

FR 400

Hinman Creek

Hinman Lake

Middle Fork Elk River

34 mi.

34.7 mi.

Middle Fork Campground

Coulton Creek

Boulder Park

33 mi.

Flow

The North, Middle, and South Forks of the Elk all offer pan-sized trout in a beautiful setting.

FR 400

Elk River

31.2 mi.

Coulton Creek Campground 30 mi.

FR 440

Hinman Campground

South Fork Elk River

There's roughly 12 miles of public access to the Elk in the Routt National Forest. Fishing remains good for medium-sized browns and rainbows, with a few brookies showing up.

FR 400

Reed Creek

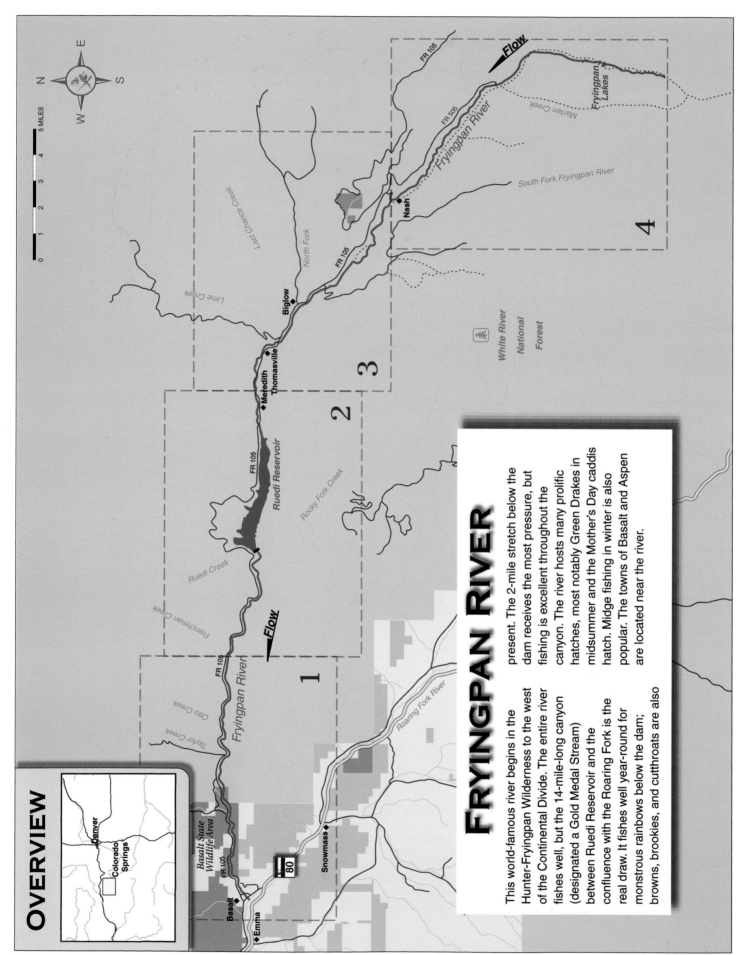

FRYINGPAN RIVER

This world-famous river begins in the Hunter-Fryingpan Wilderness to the west of the Continental Divide. The entire river fishes well, but the 14-mile-long canyon (designated a Gold Medal Stream) between Ruedi Reservoir and the confluence with the Roaring Fork is the real draw. It fishes well year-round for monstrous rainbows below the dam; browns, brookies, and cutthroats are also present. The 2-mile stretch below the dam receives the most pressure, but fishing is excellent throughout the canyon. The river hosts many prolific hatches, most notably Green Drakes in midsummer and the Mother's Day caddis hatch. Midge fishing in winter is also popular. The towns of Basalt and Aspen are located near the river.

OVERVIEW

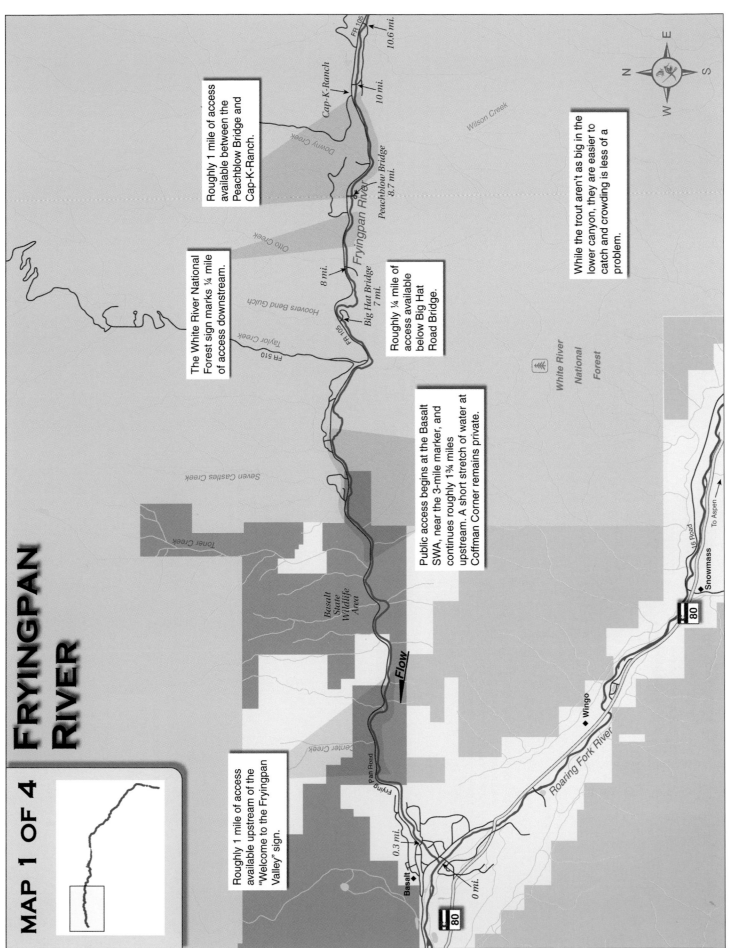

MAP 1 OF 4

FRYINGPAN RIVER

Roughly 1 mile of access available between the Peachblow Bridge and Cap-K-Ranch.

The White River National Forest sign marks ¼ mile of access downstream.

While the trout aren't as big in the lower canyon, they are easier to catch and crowding is less of a problem.

Roughly ¼ mile of access available below Big Hat Road Bridge.

Public access begins at the Basalt SWA, near the 3-mile marker, and continues roughly 1¾ miles upstream. A short stretch of water at Coffman Corner remains private.

Roughly 1 mile of access available upstream of the "Welcome to the Fryingpan Valley" sign.

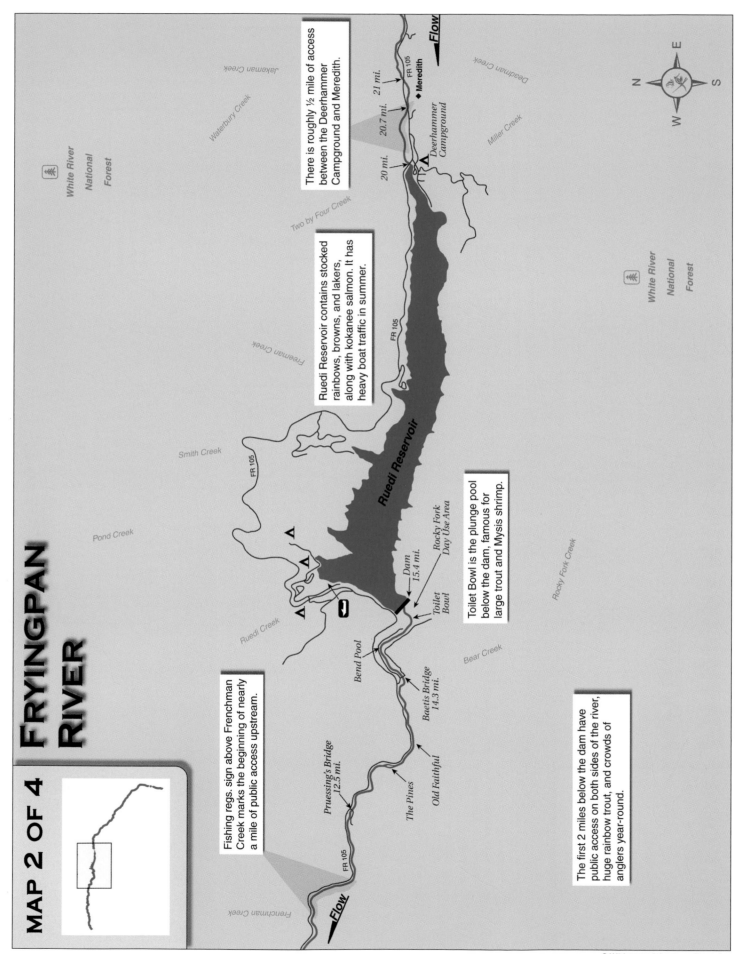

MAP 2 OF 4

FRYINGPAN RIVER

There is roughly ½ mile of access between the Deerhammer Campground and Meredith.

Ruedi Reservoir contains stocked rainbows, browns, and lakers, along with kokanee salmon. It has heavy boat traffic in summer.

Toilet Bowl is the plunge pool below the dam, famous for large trout and Mysis shrimp.

Fishing regs. sign above Frenchman Creek marks the beginning of nearly a mile of public access upstream.

The first 2 miles below the dam have public access on both sides of the river, huge rainbow trout, and crowds of anglers year-round.

White River National Forest

White River National Forest

Jackeman Creek

Waterbury Creek

Two by Four Creek

Freeman Creek

Smith Creek

Pond Creek

FR 105

FR 105

FR 105

FR 105

Ruedi Creek

Ruedi Reservoir

Deadman Creek

Miller Creek

Meredith

Deerhammer Campground

21 mi.

20.7 mi.

20 mi.

Dam
15.4 mi.

Rocky Fork
Day Use Area

Toilet
Bowl

Bear Creek

Rocky Fork Creek

Bend Pool

Baetis Bridge
14.3 mi.

The Pines

Old Faithful

Pruessing's Bridge
12.5 mi.

Frenchman Creek

Flow

Flow

N E S W

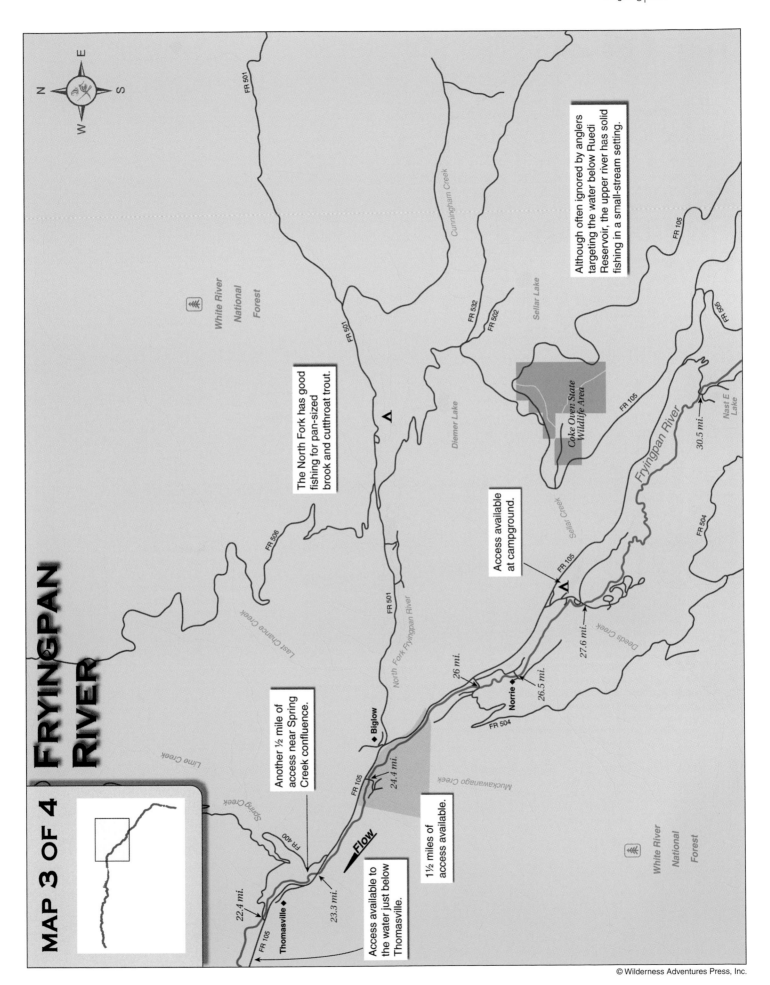

MAP 3 OF 4

FRYINGPAN RIVER

White River National Forest

Lime Creek

Spring Creek

Last Chance Creek

FR 506

FR 501

FR 400

FR 105

Thomasville ◆

22.4 mi.

23.3 mi.

24.4 mi.

◆ Biglow

North Fork Fryingpan River

FR 501

Flow

Cunningham Creek

White River National Forest

Muckawanago Creek

Norrie ◆

FR 504

26 mi.

26.5 mi.

27.6 mi.

Diemer Lake

FR 532

FR 502

Sellar Lake

Sellar Creek

Coke Oven State Wildlife Area

FR 105

Deeds Creek

Fryingpan River

FR 504

FR 105

FR 505

Nast E. Lake

30.5 mi.

The North Fork has good fishing for pan-sized brook and cutthroat trout.

Another ½ mile of access near Spring Creek confluence.

Access available to the water just below Thomasville.

1½ miles of access available.

Access available at campground.

Although often ignored by anglers targeting the water below Ruedi Reservoir, the upper river has solid fishing in a small-stream setting.

© Wilderness Adventures Press, Inc.

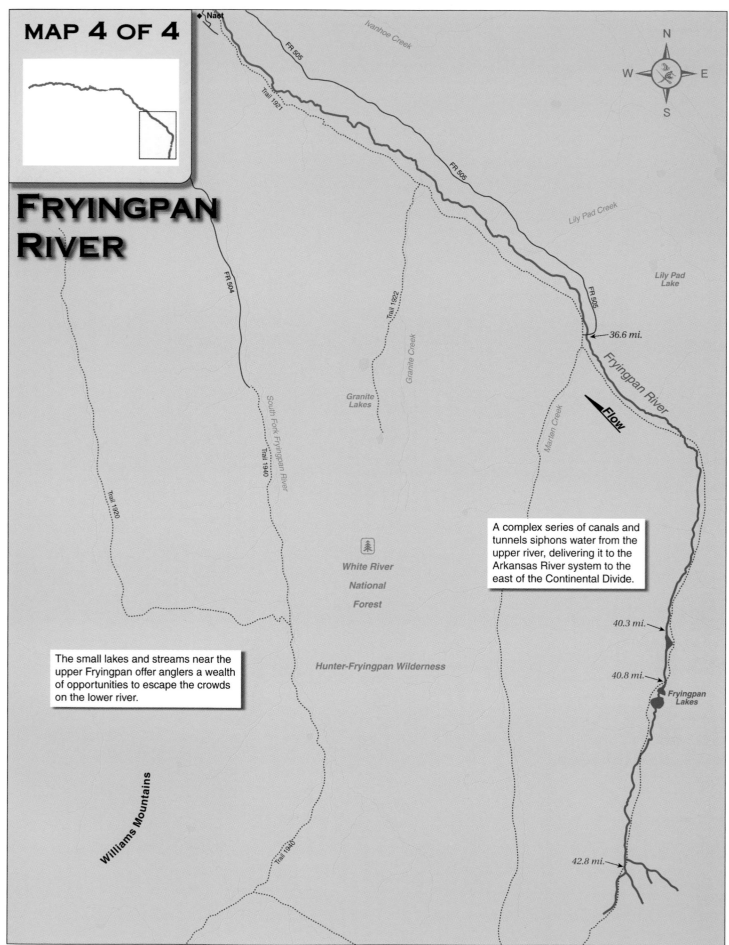

MAP 4 OF 4

FRYINGPAN RIVER

Nast

Ivanhoe Creek

FR 505

Trail 1921

FR 505

Lily Pad Creek

Lily Pad Lake

FR 504

FR 505

Trail 1922

36.6 mi.

Granite Creek

Fryingpan River

South Fork Fryingpan River

Granite Lakes

Flow

Trail 1940

Marten Creek

Trail 1920

White River

National

Forest

A complex series of canals and tunnels siphons water from the upper river, delivering it to the Arkansas River system to the east of the Continental Divide.

Hunter-Fryingpan Wilderness

40.3 mi.

The small lakes and streams near the upper Fryingpan offer anglers a wealth of opportunities to escape the crowds on the lower river.

40.8 mi.

Fryingpan Lakes

Williams Mountains

Trail 1940

42.8 mi.

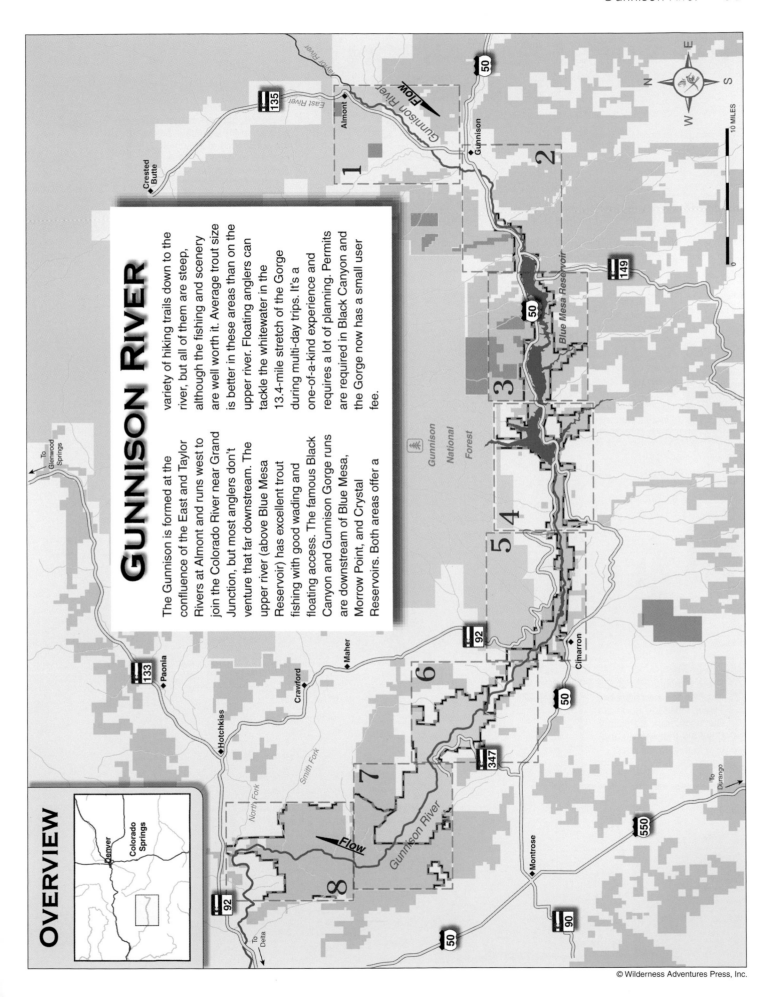

GUNNISON RIVER

The Gunnison is formed at the confluence of the East and Taylor Rivers at Almont and runs west to join the Colorado River near Grand Junction, but most anglers don't venture that far downstream. The upper river (above Blue Mesa Reservoir) has excellent trout fishing with good wading and floating access. The famous Black Canyon and Gunnison Gorge runs are downstream of Blue Mesa, Morrow Point, and Crystal Reservoirs. Both areas offer a variety of hiking trails down to the river, but all of them are steep, although the fishing and scenery are well worth it. Average trout size is better in these areas than on the upper river. Floating anglers can tackle the whitewater in the 13.4-mile stretch of the Gorge during multi-day trips. It's a one-of-a-kind experience and requires a lot of planning. Permits are required in Black Canyon and the Gorge now has a small user fee.

OVERVIEW

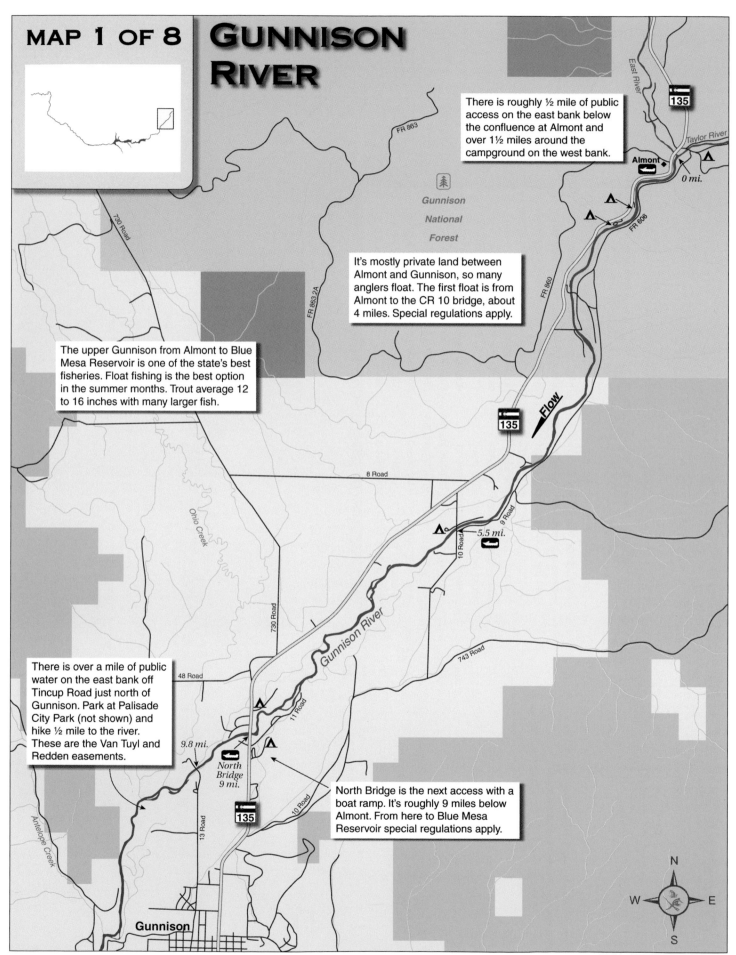

MAP 1 OF 8 GUNNISON RIVER

There is roughly ½ mile of public access on the east bank below the confluence at Almont and over 1½ miles around the campground on the west bank.

It's mostly private land between Almont and Gunnison, so many anglers float. The first float is from Almont to the CR 10 bridge, about 4 miles. Special regulations apply.

The upper Gunnison from Almont to Blue Mesa Reservoir is one of the state's best fisheries. Float fishing is the best option in the summer months. Trout average 12 to 16 inches with many larger fish.

There is over a mile of public water on the east bank off Tincup Road just north of Gunnison. Park at Palisade City Park (not shown) and hike ½ mile to the river. These are the Van Tuyl and Redden easements.

North Bridge is the next access with a boat ramp. It's roughly 9 miles below Almont. From here to Blue Mesa Reservoir special regulations apply.

Gunnison National Forest

Gunnison River

Almont
0 mi.
5.5 mi.
9.8 mi.
North Bridge
9 mi.

Gunnison

East River
Taylor River

FR 863
FR 606
FR 860
730 Road
8 Road
9 Road
10 Road
730 Road
743 Road
48 Road
11 Road
13 Road
10 Road
Ohio Creek
Antelope Creek
FR 863.2A

135

Flow

N
W   E
S

© Wilderness Adventures Press, Inc.

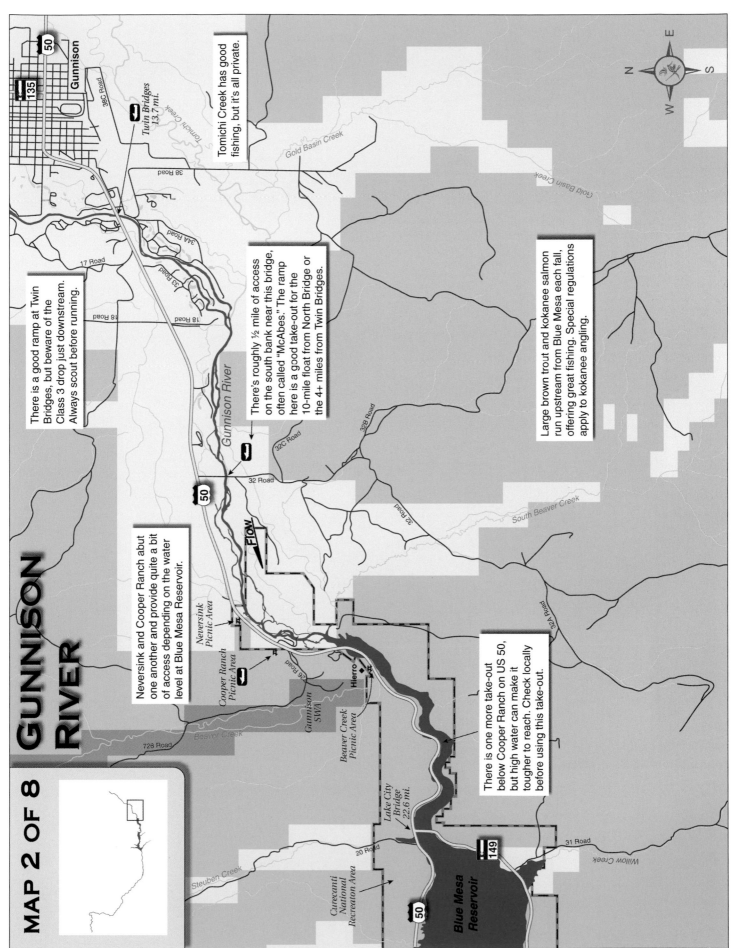

MAP 2 OF 8

GUNNISON RIVER

There is a good ramp at Twin Bridges, but beware of the Class 3 drop just downstream. Always scout before running.

There's roughly ½ mile of access on the south bank near this bridge, often called "McAbes." The ramp here is a good take-out for the 10-mile float from North Bridge or the 4+ miles from Twin Bridges.

Tomichi Creek has good fishing, but it's all private.

Large brown trout and kokanee salmon run upstream from Blue Mesa each fall, offering great fishing. Special regulations apply to kokanee angling.

Neversink and Cooper Ranch abut one another and provide quite a bit of access depending on the water level at Blue Mesa Reservoir.

There is one more take-out below Cooper Ranch on US 50, but high water can make it tougher to reach. Check locally before using this take-out.

Twin Bridges 13.7 mi.

Lake City Bridge 22.6 mi.

Gunnison River

Gunnison

Neversink Picnic Area

Cooper Ranch Picnic Area

Gunnison SWA

Beaver Creek Picnic Area

Hierro

Curecanti National Recreation Area

Blue Mesa Reservoir

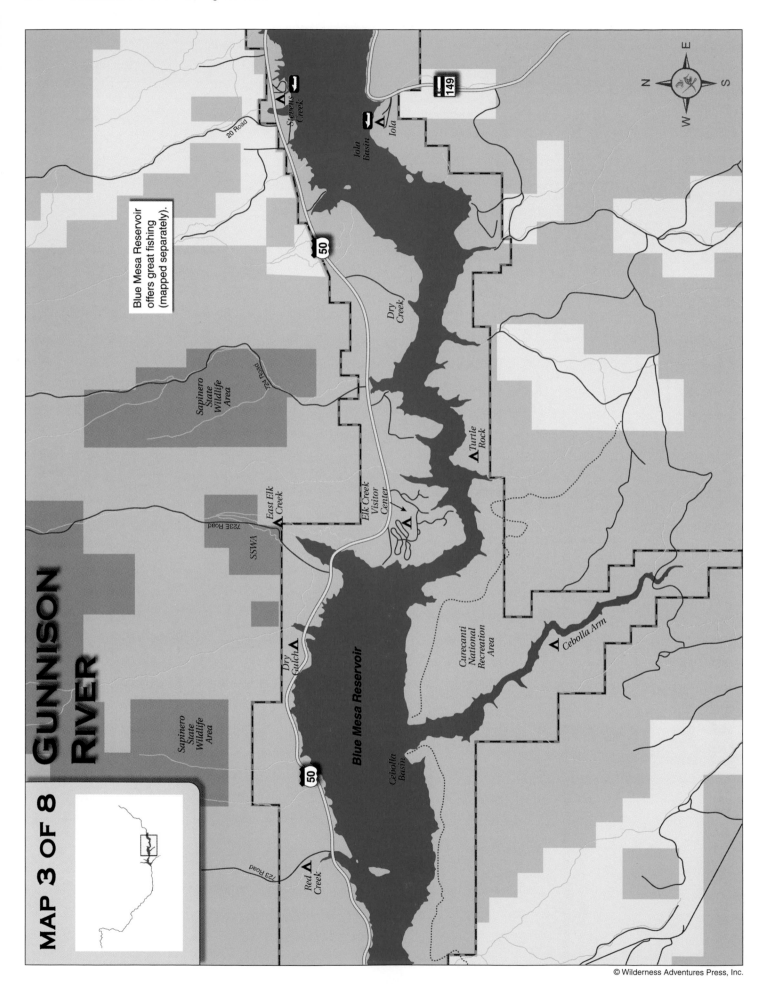

Blue Mesa Reservoir offers great fishing (mapped separately).

MAP 3 OF 8 GUNNISON RIVER

Stevens Creek

20 Road

Iola

Iola Basin

149

50

Dry Creek

Sapinero State Wildlife Area

721 Road

Turtle Rock

East Elk Creek

723E Road

SSWA

Elk Creek Visitor Center

Curecanti National Recreation Area

Cebolla Arm

Dry Gulch Creek

Sapinero State Wildlife Area

Blue Mesa Reservoir

Cebolla Basin

50

Red Creek

723 Road

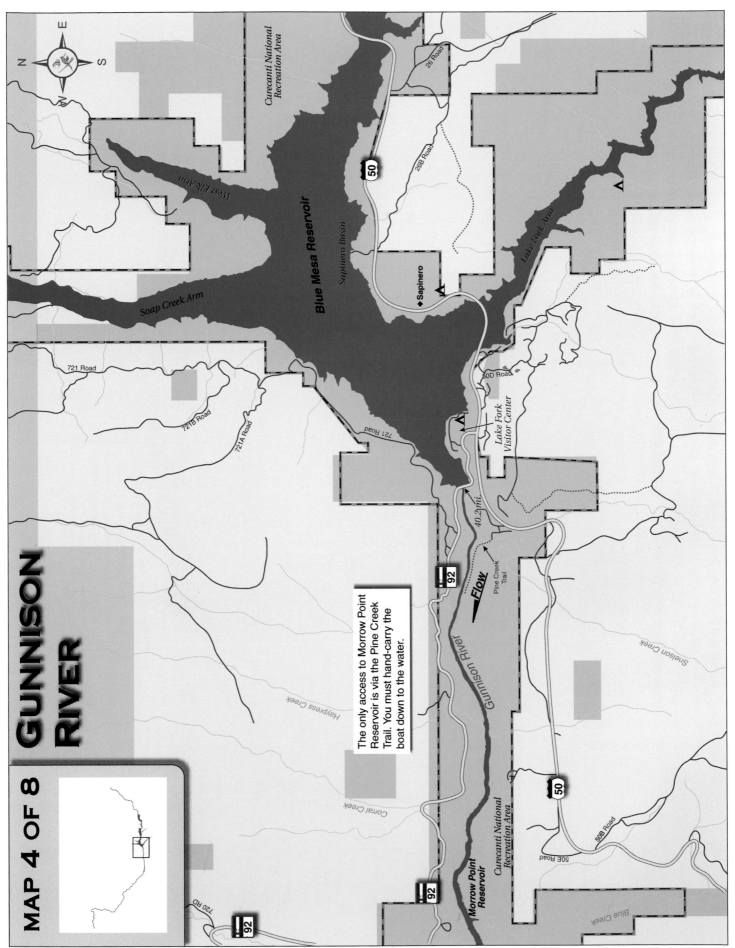

MAP 4 OF 8

GUNNISON RIVER

N E S

Curecanti National Recreation Area

26 Road

26B Road

50

West Elk Arm

Soap Creek Arm

Blue Mesa Reservoir

Sapinero Basin

♦ Sapinero

Lake Fork Arm

30D Road

Lake Fork Visitor Center

721 Road

721B Road

721A Road

721 Road

40.2 mi.

Pine Creek Trail

The only access to Morrow Point Reservoir is via the Pine Creek Trail. You must hand-carry the boat down to the water.

Haypress Creek

92

Flow

Gunnison River

Corral Creek

Snelson Creek

50

50B Road

50E Road

Morrow Point Reservoir

Curecanti National Recreation Area

92

720 RD

92

Blue Creek

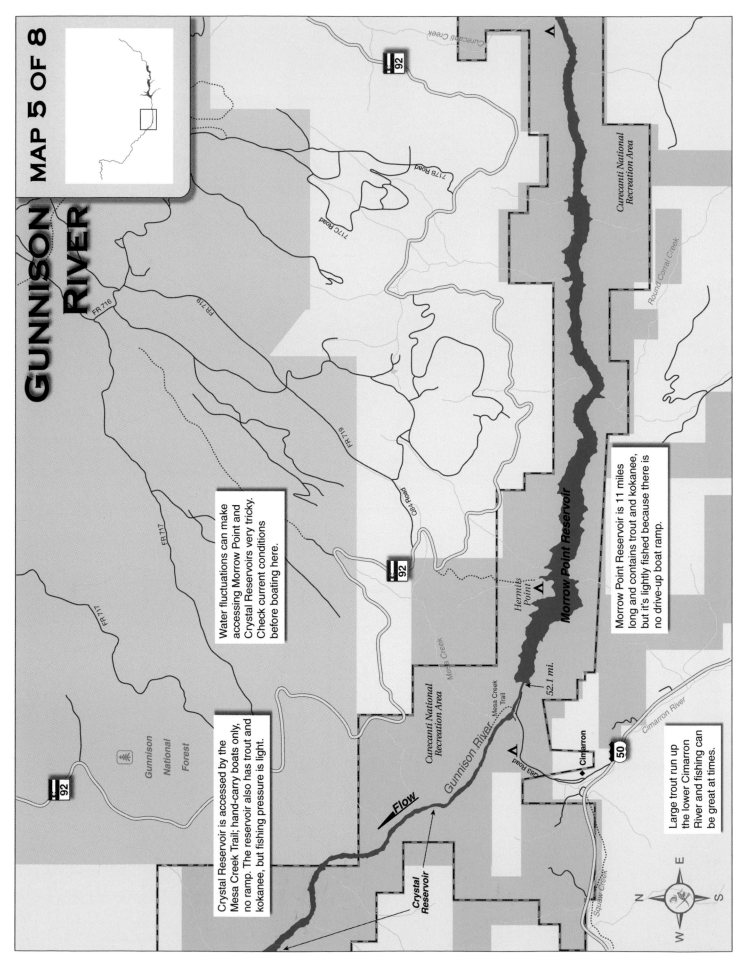

GUNNISON
RIVER

MAP 5 OF 8

FR 716

FR 717

FR 719

FR 719

FR 717

Gunnison
National
Forest

Curecanti Creek

717B Road

717C Road

Q84 Road

92

92

92

92

50

Water fluctuations can make accessing Morrow Point and Crystal Reservoirs very tricky. Check current conditions before boating here.

Crystal Reservoir is accessed by the Mesa Creek Trail; hand-carry boats only, no ramp. The reservoir also has trout and kokanee, but fishing pressure is light.

Morrow Point Reservoir is 11 miles long and contains trout and kokanee, but it's lightly fished because there is no drive-up boat ramp.

Large trout run up the lower Cimarron River and fishing can be great at times.

Curecanti National
Recreation Area

Round Corral Creek

Morrow Point Reservoir

Hermits
Point

Mesa Creek

Mesa Creek Trail

52.1 mi.

Curecanti National
Recreation Area

Gunnison River

283 Road

Cimarron

Cimarron River

Squaw Creek

Flow

Crystal
Reservoir

N
E
W
S

© Wilderness Adventures Press, Inc.

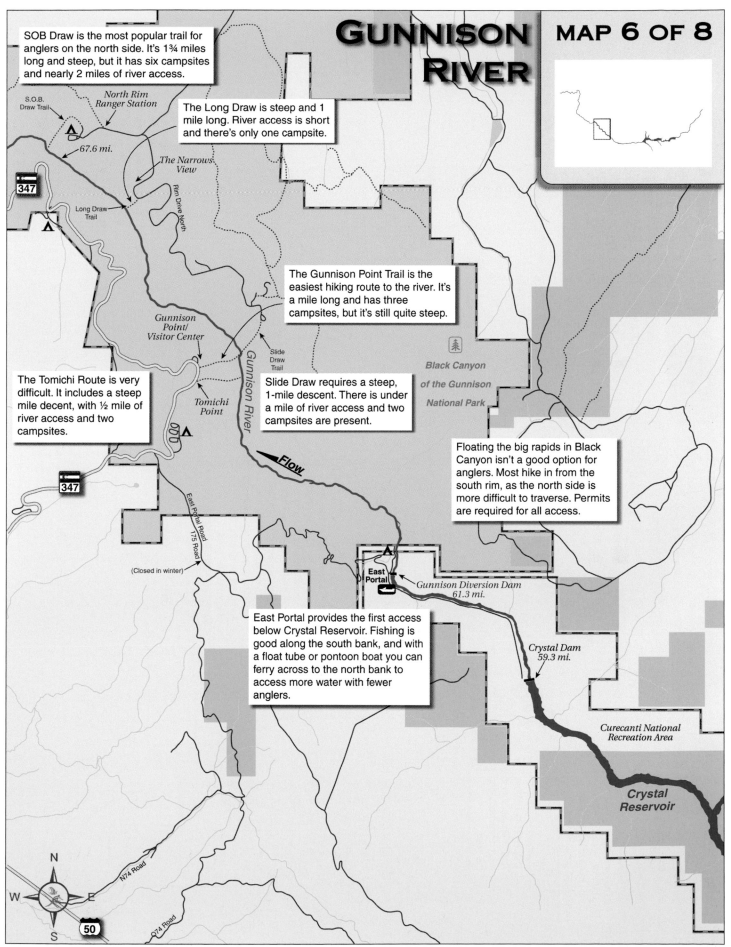

GUNNISON RIVER

MAP 6 OF 8

SOB Draw is the most popular trail for anglers on the north side. It's 1¾ miles long and steep, but it has six campsites and nearly 2 miles of river access.

The Long Draw is steep and 1 mile long. River access is short and there's only one campsite.

S.O.B. Draw Trail

North Rim Ranger Station

—67.6 mi.

347

The Narrows View

Long Draw Trail

Rim Drive North

The Gunnison Point Trail is the easiest hiking route to the river. It's a mile long and has three campsites, but it's still quite steep.

Gunnison Point/ Visitor Center

Slide Draw Trail

Black Canyon

of the Gunnison

National Park

The Tomichi Route is very difficult. It includes a steep mile decent, with ½ mile of river access and two campsites.

Tomichi Point

Gunnison River

Slide Draw requires a steep, 1-mile descent. There is under a mile of river access and two campsites are present.

Floating the big rapids in Black Canyon isn't a good option for anglers. Most hike in from the south rim, as the north side is more difficult to traverse. Permits are required for all access.

Flow

347

East Portal Road

175 Road

(Closed in winter)

East Portal

Gunnison Diversion Dam 61.3 mi.

East Portal provides the first access below Crystal Reservoir. Fishing is good along the south bank, and with a float tube or pontoon boat you can ferry across to the north bank to access more water with fewer anglers.

Crystal Dam 59.3 mi.

Curecanti National Recreation Area

Crystal Reservoir

N74 Road

N
W E
S

50

Q74 Road

© Wilderness Adventures Press, Inc.

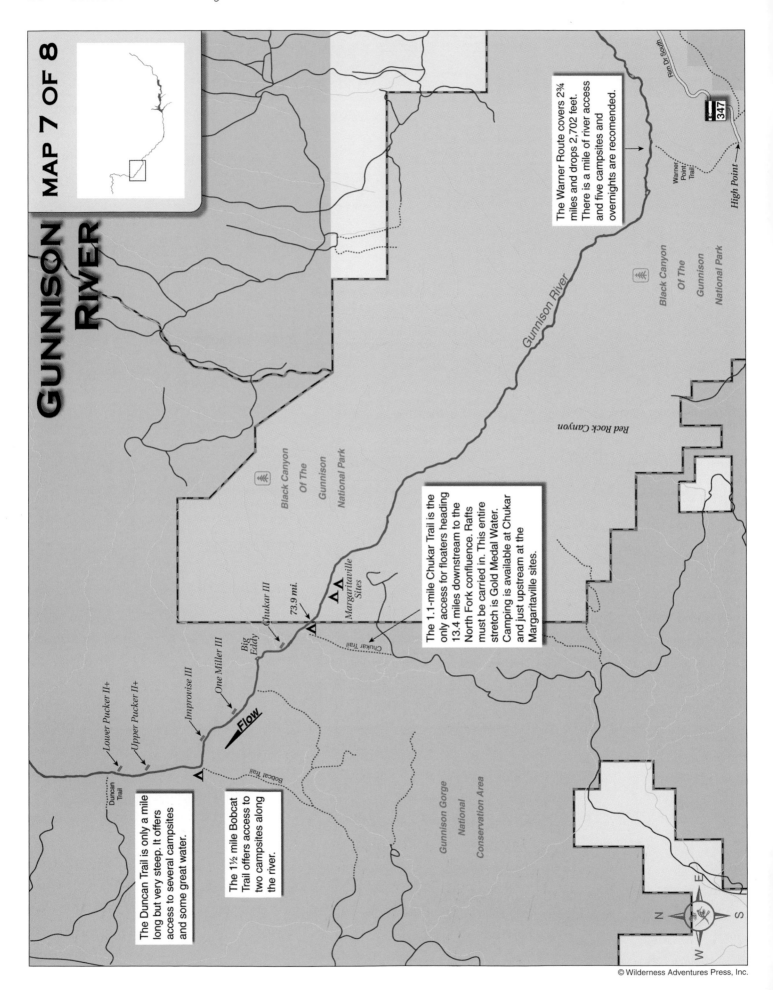

MAP 7 OF 8

GUNNISON RIVER

The Warner Route covers 2¾ miles and drops 2,702 feet. There is a mile of river access and five campsites and overnights are recomended.

The 1.1-mile Chukar Trail is the only access for floaters heading 13.4 miles downstream to the North Fork confluence. Rafts must be carried in. This entire stretch is Gold Medal Water. Camping is available at Chukar and just upstream at the Margaritaville sites.

The Duncan Trail is only a mile long but very steep. It offers access to several campsites and some great water.

The 1½ mile Bobcat Trail offers access to two campsites along the river.

Gunnison River

Black Canyon Of The Gunnison National Park

Red Rock Canyon

Black Canyon Of The Gunnison National Park

Gunnison Gorge National Conservation Area

347

Rim Dr South

Warner Point Trail

High Point

Margaritaville Sites

73.9 mi.

Chukar III

Big Eddy

One Miller III

Improvise III

Upper Pucker II+

Lower Pucker II+

Duncan Trail

Chukar Trail

Bobcat Trail

Flow

N E S W

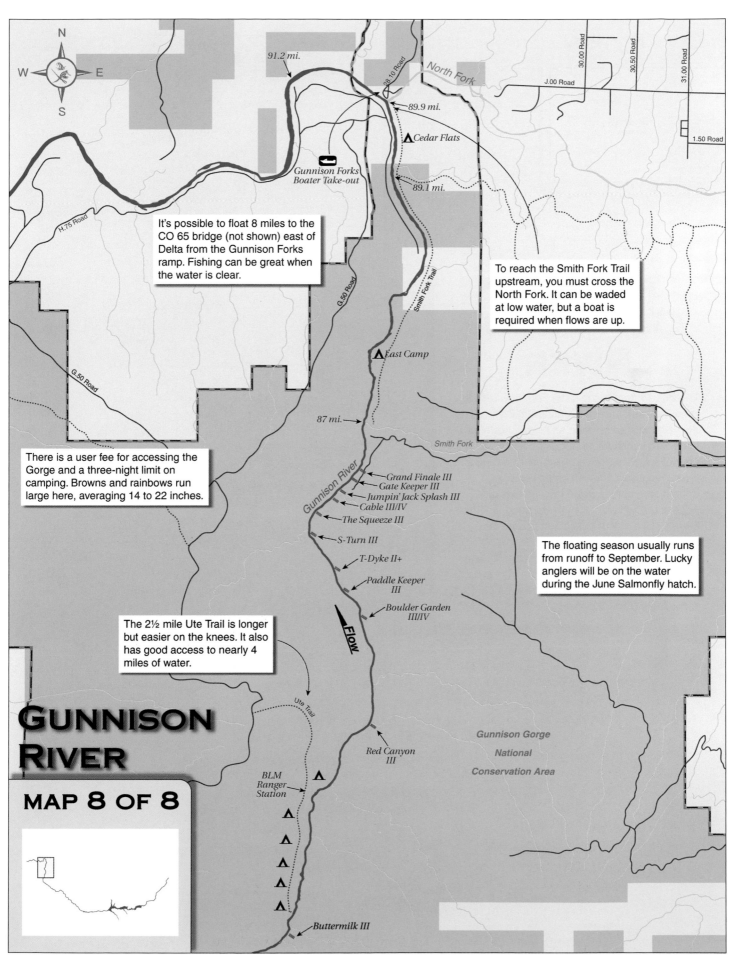

91.2 mi.

North Fork

28.10 Road

30.00 Road
30.50 Road
31.00 Road

J.00 Road

1.50 Road

89.9 mi.

Cedar Flats

Gunnison Forks
Boater Take-out

89.1 mi.

It's possible to float 8 miles to the CO 65 bridge (not shown) east of Delta from the Gunnison Forks ramp. Fishing can be great when the water is clear.

H.75 Road

G.50 Road

To reach the Smith Fork Trail upstream, you must cross the North Fork. It can be waded at low water, but a boat is required when flows are up.

Smith Fork Trail

G.50 Road

East Camp

87 mi.

Smith Fork

There is a user fee for accessing the Gorge and a three-night limit on camping. Browns and rainbows run large here, averaging 14 to 22 inches.

Gunnison River

Grand Finale III
Gate Keeper III
Jumpin' Jack Splash III
Cable III/IV
The Squeeze III

S-Turn III

T-Dyke II+

The floating season usually runs from runoff to September. Lucky anglers will be on the water during the June Salmonfly hatch.

Paddle Keeper III

Boulder Garden III/IV

Flow

The 2½ mile Ute Trail is longer but easier on the knees. It also has good access to nearly 4 miles of water.

Ute Trail

GUNNISON
RIVER

Red Canyon III

Gunnison Gorge

National

Conservation Area

BLM
Ranger
Station

MAP 8 OF 8

Buttermilk III

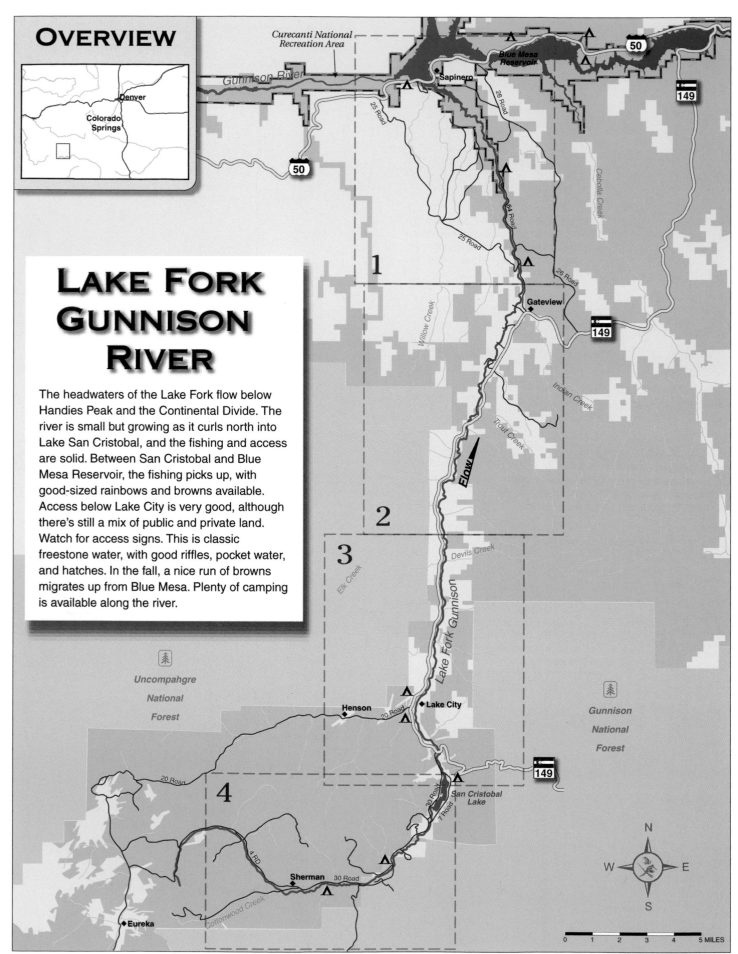

OVERVIEW

Curecanti National Recreation Area

Denver

Colorado Springs

LAKE FORK GUNNISON RIVER

The headwaters of the Lake Fork flow below Handies Peak and the Continental Divide. The river is small but growing as it curls north into Lake San Cristobal, and the fishing and access are solid. Between San Cristobal and Blue Mesa Reservoir, the fishing picks up, with good-sized rainbows and browns available. Access below Lake City is very good, although there's still a mix of public and private land. Watch for access signs. This is classic freestone water, with good riffles, pocket water, and hatches. In the fall, a nice run of browns migrates up from Blue Mesa. Plenty of camping is available along the river.

Gunnison River

Blue Mesa Reservoir

Sapinero

25 Road

64 Road

26 Road

25 Road

Cebolla Creek

Gateview

Willow Creek

Indian Creek

Trout Creek

Flow

Devils Creek

Lake Fork Gunnison

Elk Creek

Uncompahgre National Forest

Henson

20 Road

Lake City

Gunnison National Forest

20 Road

4 RD

30 Road

7 Road

San Cristobal Lake

Sherman

30 Road

Cottonwood Creek

Eureka

N
W   E
S

0 1 2 3 4 5 MILES

© Wilderness Adventures Press, Inc.

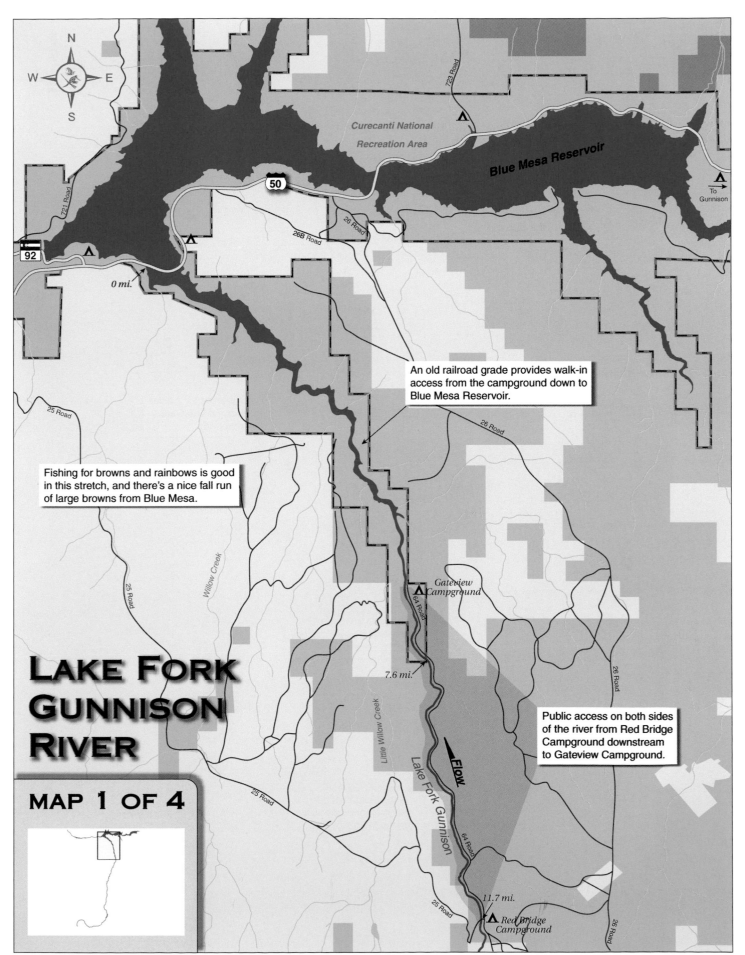

An old railroad grade provides walk-in access from the campground down to Blue Mesa Reservoir.

Fishing for browns and rainbows is good in this stretch, and there's a nice fall run of large browns from Blue Mesa.

Public access on both sides of the river from Red Bridge Campground downstream to Gateview Campground.

LAKE FORK
GUNNISON
RIVER

MAP 1 OF 4

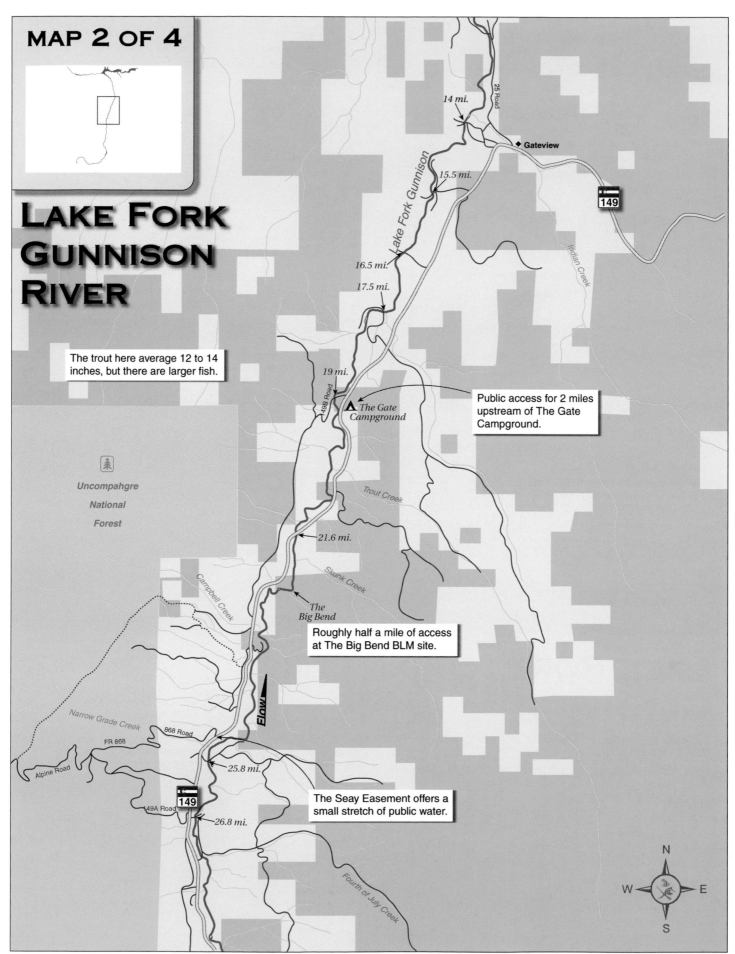

MAP 2 OF 4

LAKE FORK GUNNISON RIVER

The trout here average 12 to 14 inches, but there are larger fish.

Public access for 2 miles upstream of The Gate Campground.

Uncompahgre

National

Forest

Roughly half a mile of access at The Big Bend BLM site.

The Seay Easement offers a small stretch of public water.

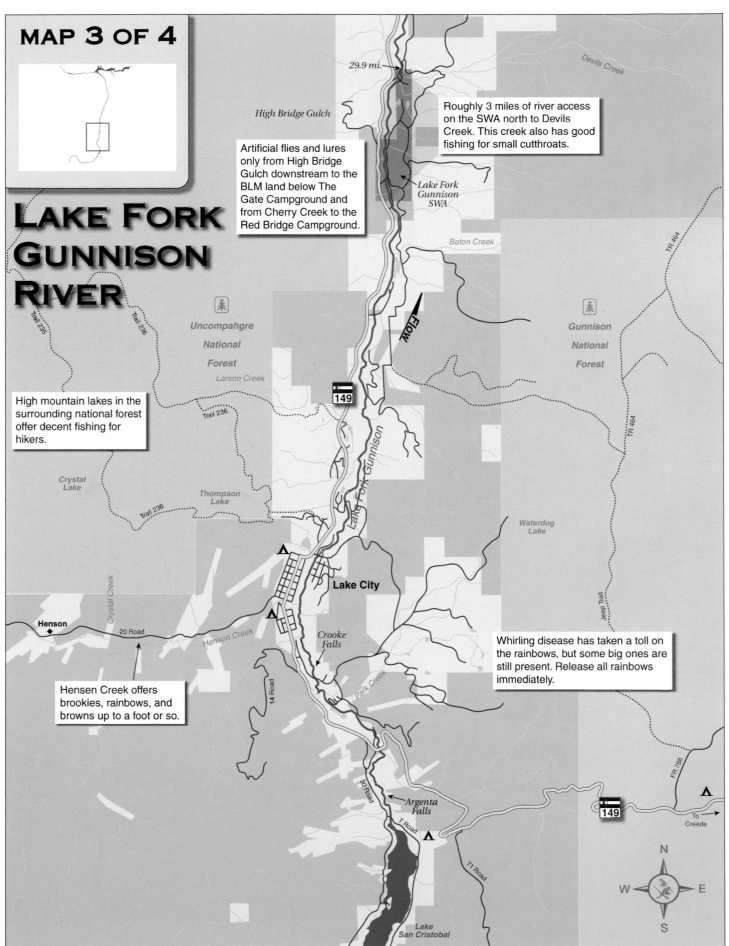

MAP 3 OF 4

LAKE FORK GUNNISON RIVER

29.9 mi.

High Bridge Gulch

Roughly 3 miles of river access on the SWA north to Devils Creek. This creek also has good fishing for small cutthroats.

Artificial flies and lures only from High Bridge Gulch downstream to the BLM land below The Gate Campground and from Cherry Creek to the Red Bridge Campground.

Lake Fork Gunnison SWA

Baton Creek

Devils Creek

TR 464

Flow

Trail 235

Trail 236

Uncompahgre National Forest

Larson Creek

Gunnison National Forest

High mountain lakes in the surrounding national forest offer decent fishing for hikers.

Trail 236

Lake Fork Gunnison

149

TR 464

Crystal Lake

Trail 236

Thompson Lake

Waterdog Lake

Crystal Creek

Jeep Trail

Lake City

Henson

20 Road

Henson Creek

Crooke Falls

Whirling disease has taken a toll on the rainbows, but some big ones are still present. Release all rainbows immediately.

Hensen Creek offers brookies, rainbows, and browns up to a foot or so.

14 Road

Park Creek

30 Road

Argenta Falls

149

To Creede

FR 788

T Road

71 Road

N
W   E
S

Lake San Cristobal

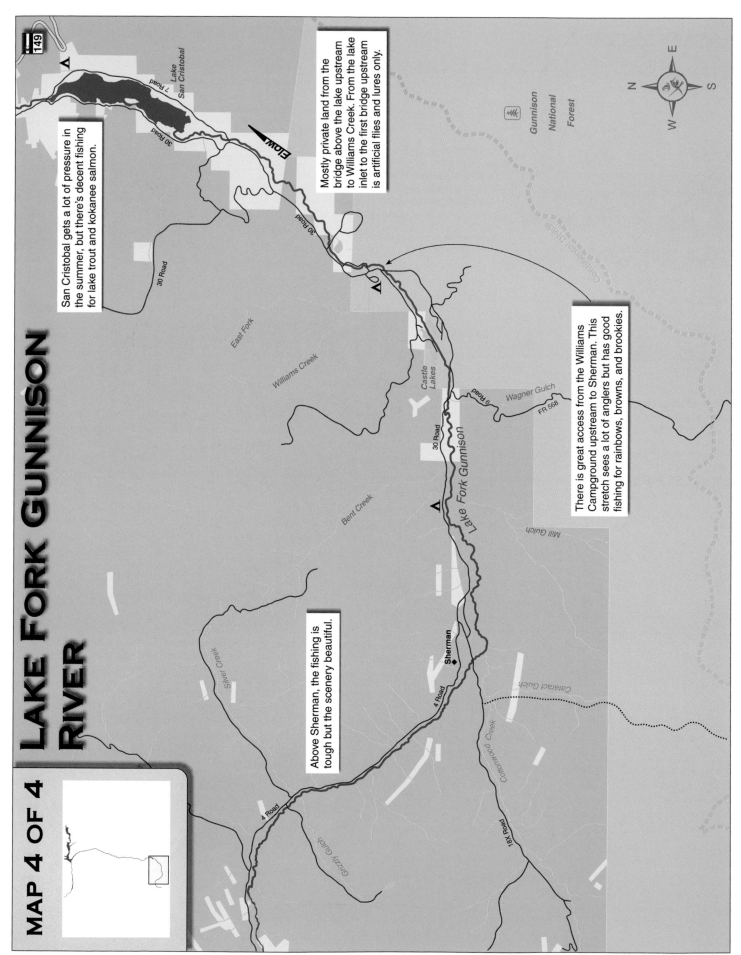

LAKE FORK GUNNISON RIVER

MAP 4 OF 4

San Cristobal gets a lot of pressure in the summer, but there's decent fishing for lake trout and kokanee salmon.

Mostly private land from the bridge above the lake upstream to Williams Creek. From the lake inlet to the first bridge upstream is artificial flies and lures only.

There is great access from the Williams Campground upstream to Sherman. This stretch sees a lot of anglers but has good fishing for rainbows, browns, and brookies.

Above Sherman, the fishing is tough but the scenery beautiful.

Gunnison National Forest

Continental Divide

Lake San Cristobal

East Fork

Williams Creek

Castle Lakes

Wagner Gulch

FR 568

9 Road

30 Road

7 Road

Bent Creek

Silver Creek

Lake Fork Gunnison

Mill Gulch

Sherman

Cataract Gulch

Cottonwood Creek

Grizzly Gulch

4 Road

18X Road

149

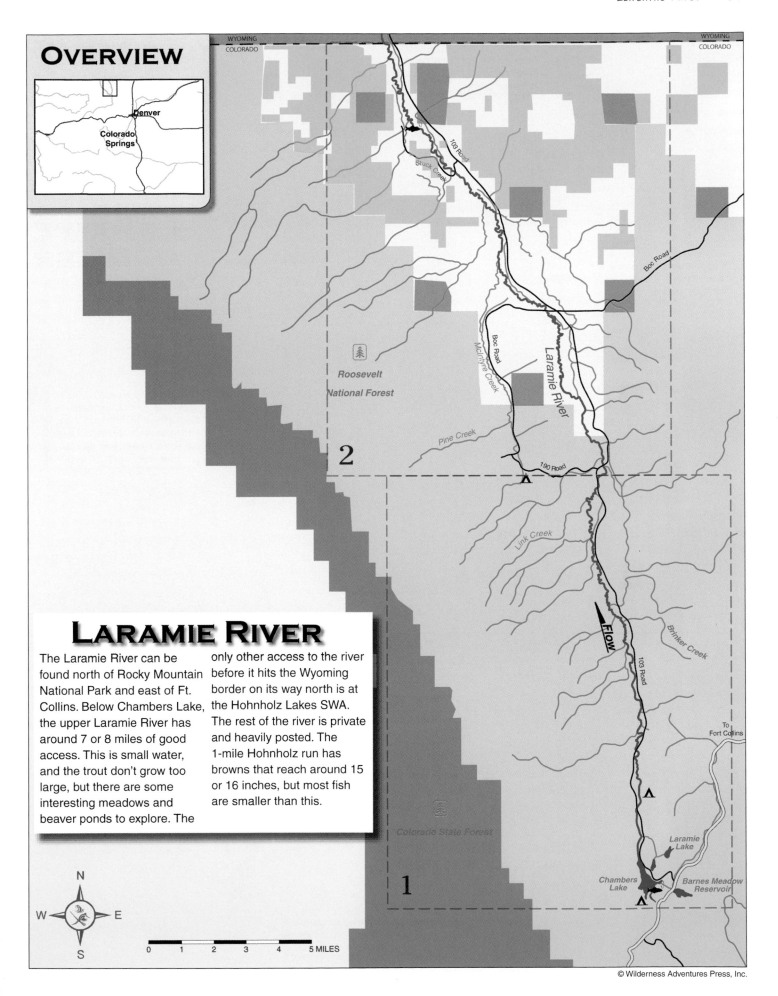

OVERVIEW

LARAMIE RIVER

The Laramie River can be found north of Rocky Mountain National Park and east of Ft. Collins. Below Chambers Lake, the upper Laramie River has around 7 or 8 miles of good access. This is small water, and the trout don't grow too large, but there are some interesting meadows and beaver ponds to explore. The only other access to the river before it hits the Wyoming border on its way north is at the Hohnholz Lakes SWA. The rest of the river is private and heavily posted. The 1-mile Hohnholz run has browns that reach around 15 or 16 inches, but most fish are smaller than this.

0 1 2 3 4 5 MILES

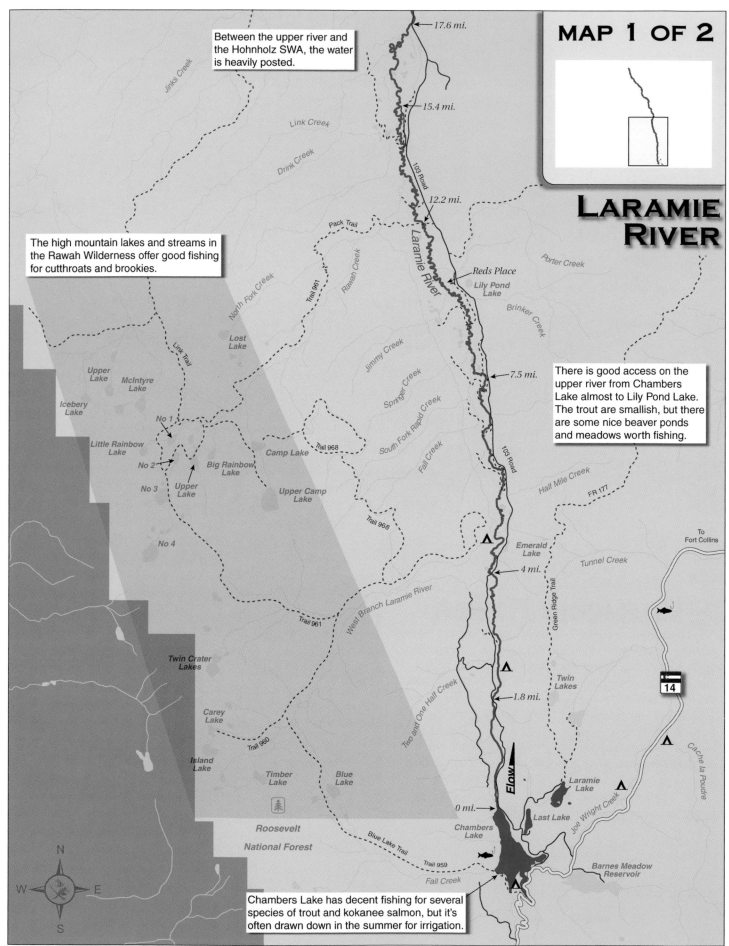

Between the upper river and the Hohnholz SWA, the water is heavily posted.

The high mountain lakes and streams in the Rawah Wilderness offer good fishing for cutthroats and brookies.

There is good access on the upper river from Chambers Lake almost to Lily Pond Lake. The trout are smallish, but there are some nice beaver ponds and meadows worth fishing.

Chambers Lake has decent fishing for several species of trout and kokanee salmon, but it's often drawn down in the summer for irrigation.

MAP 1 OF 2

LARAMIE RIVER

17.6 mi.

15.4 mi.

12.2 mi.

Reds Place

Lily Pond Lake

7.5 mi.

4 mi.

1.8 mi.

0 mi.

Jinks Creek

Link Creek

Drink Creek

Pack Trail

Laramie River

103 Road

Porter Creek

Brinker Creek

North Fork Creek

Rawah Creek

Trail 961

Jimmy Creek

Springer Creek

South Fork Rapid Creek

Fall Creek

Half Mile Creek

FR 177

Tunnel Creek

To Fort Collins

Link Trail

Lost Lake

Upper Lake

McIntyre Lake

Iceberg Lake

No 1

Little Rainbow Lake

No 2

Big Rainbow Lake

No 3

Upper Lake

Camp Lake

Trail 968

Upper Camp Lake

Trail 968

No 4

Emerald Lake

Green Ridge Trail

Twin Lakes

14

Twin Crater Lakes

West Branch Laramie River

Trail 961

Two and One Half Creek

Carey Lake

Island Lake

Trail 960

Timber Lake

Blue Lake

Flow

Laramie Lake

Last Lake

Joe Wright Creek

Cache la Poudre

Roosevelt National Forest

Blue Lake Trail

Trail 959

Chambers Lake

Barnes Meadow Reservoir

Fall Creek

N W E S

© Wilderness Adventures Press, Inc.

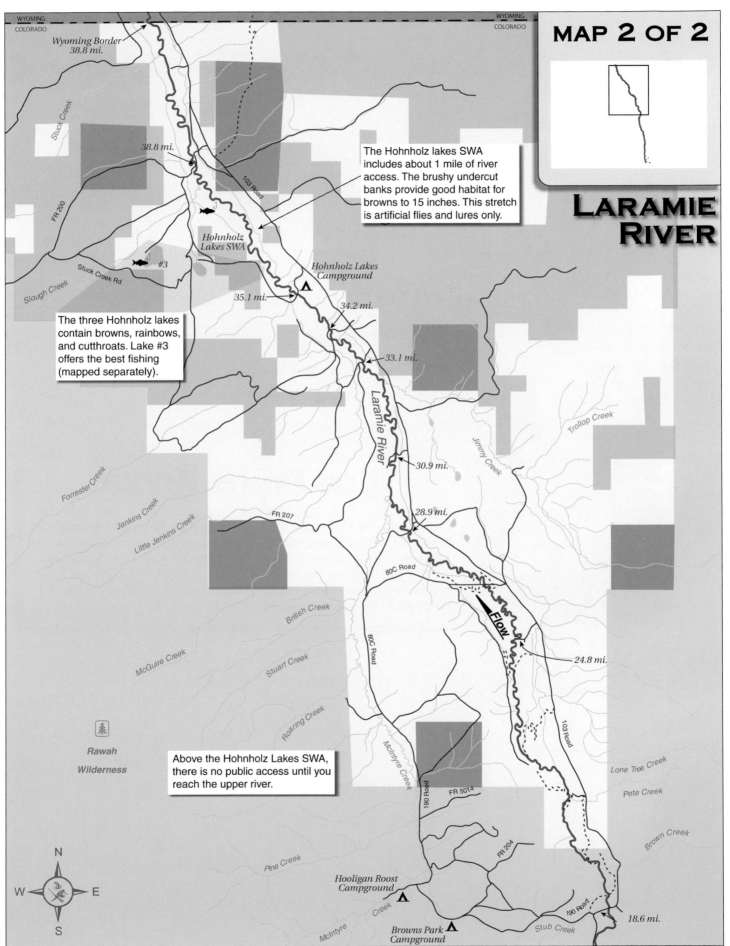

MAP 2 OF 2

LARAMIE RIVER

The Hohnholz lakes SWA includes about 1 mile of river access. The brushy undercut banks provide good habitat for browns to 15 inches. This stretch is artificial flies and lures only.

The three Hohnholz lakes contain browns, rainbows, and cutthroats. Lake #3 offers the best fishing (mapped separately).

Above the Hohnholz Lakes SWA, there is no public access until you reach the upper river.

WYOMING
COLORADO

Wyoming Border
38.8 mi.

38.8 mi.

103 Road

FR 200

Stuck Creek

Stuck Creek Rd

#3

Slough Creek

Hohnholz Lakes SWA

Hohnholz Lakes Campground

35.1 mi.

34.2 mi.

33.1 mi.

Laramie River

Trollop Creek

Jimmy Creek

30.9 mi.

28.9 mi.

Forrester Creek

Jenkins Creek

Little Jenkins Creek

FR 207

80C Road

80C Road

Flow

24.8 mi.

103 Road

British Creek

McGuire Creek

Stuart Creek

Roaring Creek

McIntyre Creek

Rawah Wilderness

190 Road

FR 5014

Lone Tree Creek

Pete Creek

FR 204

Brown Creek

N
W   E
S

Pine Creek

Hooligan Roost Campground

McIntyre Creek

Browns Park Campground

190 Road

Stub Creek

18.6 mi.

© Wilderness Adventures Press, Inc.

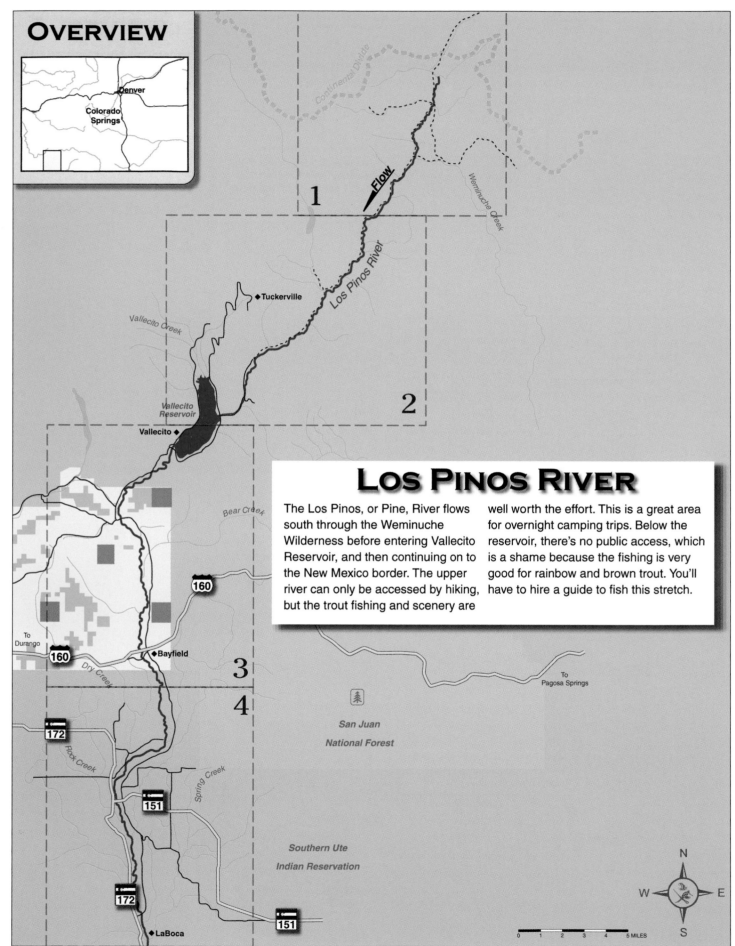

OVERVIEW

Denver

Colorado
Springs

Flow

1

Weminuche Creek

Continental Divide

◆Tuckerville

Los Pinos River

Vallecito Creek

2

Vallecito
Reservoir

Vallecito ◆

Bear Creek

160

To
Durango

160 ◆Bayfield

Dry Creek

3

4

172

Rock Creek

151

Spring Creek

San Juan

National Forest

To
Pagosa Springs

Southern Ute

Indian Reservation

172

◆LaBoca

151

0 1 2 3 4 5 MILES

N
W   E
S

LOS PINOS RIVER

The Los Pinos, or Pine, River flows south through the Weminuche Wilderness before entering Vallecito Reservoir, and then continuing on to the New Mexico border. The upper river can only be accessed by hiking, but the trout fishing and scenery are well worth the effort. This is a great area for overnight camping trips. Below the reservoir, there's no public access, which is a shame because the fishing is very good for rainbow and brown trout. You'll have to hire a guide to fish this stretch.

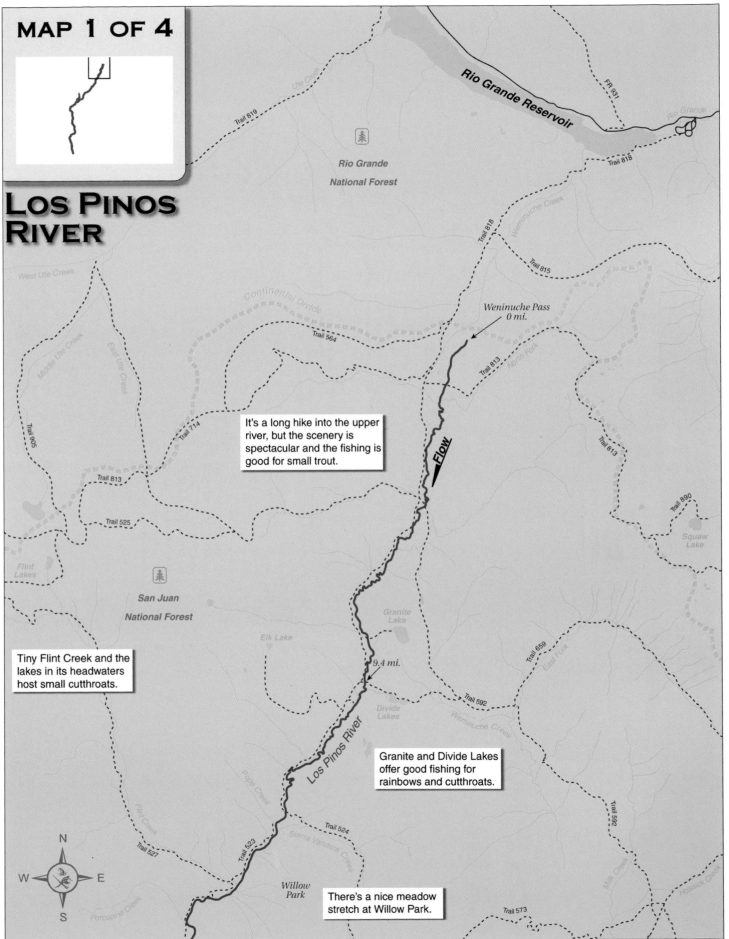

MAP 1 OF 4

LOS PINOS RIVER

Rio Grande Reservoir

Rio Grande National Forest

Ute Creek

Trail 819

FR 931

Rio Grande

Trail 818

Weninuche Creek

Trail 818

Trail 815

West Ute Creek

Continental Divide

Weninuche Pass
0 mi.

Trail 564

Trail 813

North Fork

Middle Ute Creek

East Ute Creek

Trail 813

Trail 714

It's a long hike into the upper river, but the scenery is spectacular and the fishing is good for small trout.

Flow

Trail 905

Trail 813

Trail 525

Trail 890

Squaw Lake

Flint Lakes

San Juan National Forest

Granite Lake

Elk Lake

Tiny Flint Creek and the lakes in its headwaters host small cutthroats.

9.4 mi.

Trail 659

East Fork

Divide Lakes

Trail 592

Weninuche Creek

Granite and Divide Lakes offer good fishing for rainbows and cutthroats.

Los Pinos River

Pope Creek

Flint Creek

Trail 523

Trail 524

Sierra Vandera Creek

Trail 592

Milk Creek

Trail 527

N
W E
S

Willow Park

There's a nice meadow stretch at Willow Park.

Trail 573

Porcupine Creek

Hossick Creek

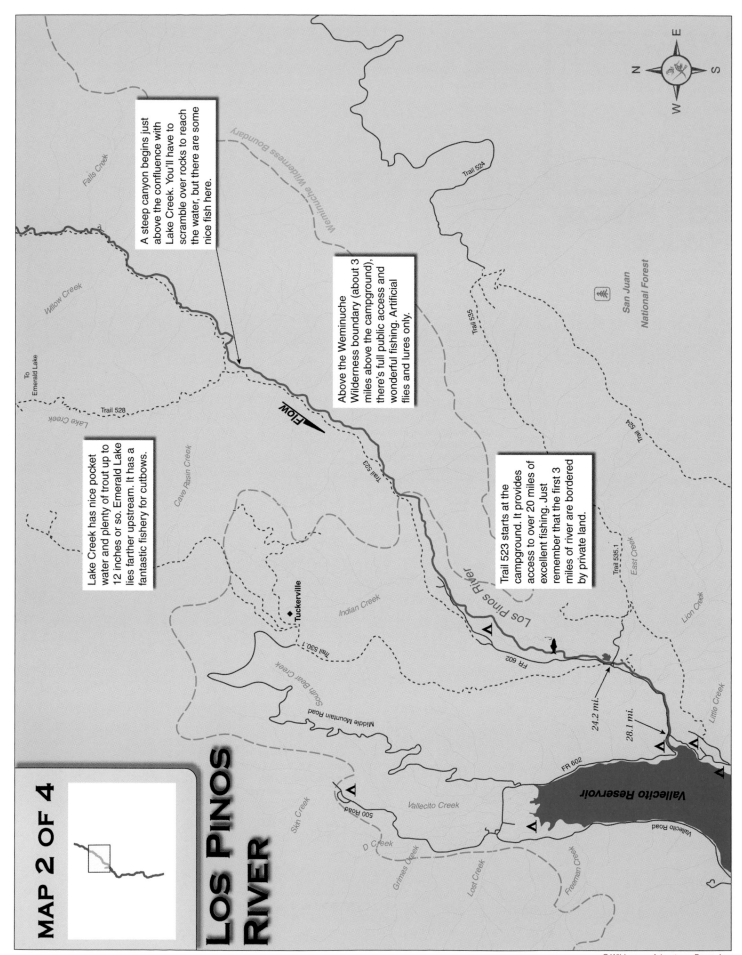

A steep canyon begins just above the confluence with Lake Creek. You'll have to scramble over rocks to reach the water, but there are some nice fish here.

Above the Weminuche Wilderness boundary (about 3 miles above the campground), there's full public access and wonderful fishing. Artificial flies and lures only.

Lake Creek has nice pocket water and plenty of trout up to 12 inches or so. Emerald Lake lies farther upstream. It has a fantastic fishery for cutbows.

Trail 523 starts at the campground. It provides access to over 20 miles of excellent fishing. Just remember that the first 3 miles of river are bordered by private land.

Flow

Los Pinos River

San Juan National Forest

Vallecito Reservoir

LOS PINOS RIVER

MAP 2 OF 4

© Wilderness Adventures Press, Inc.

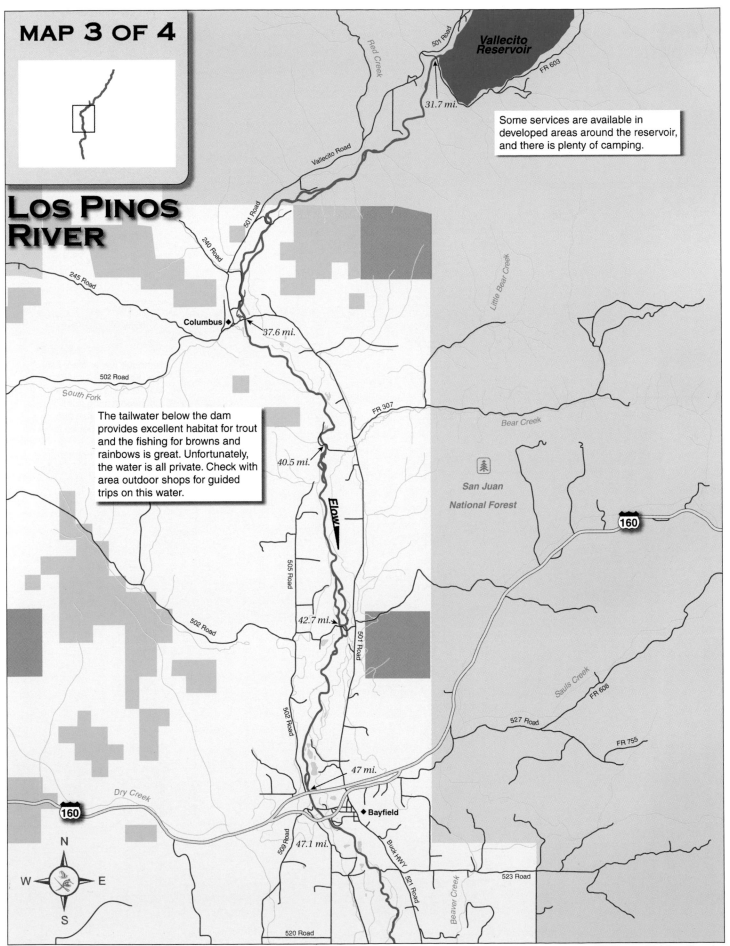

MAP 3 OF 4

LOS PINOS RIVER

Some services are available in developed areas around the reservoir, and there is plenty of camping.

The tailwater below the dam provides excellent habitat for trout and the fishing for browns and rainbows is great. Unfortunately, the water is all private. Check with area outdoor shops for guided trips on this water.

Vallecito Reservoir

Red Creek

501 Road

FR 603

31.7 mi.

Vallecito Road

501 Road

240 Road

245 Road

Columbus ◆

37.6 mi.

502 Road

South Fork

Little Bear Creek

FR 307

Bear Creek

San Juan National Forest

40.5 mi.

Flow

160

502 Road

505 Road

501 Road

42.7 mi.

Sauls Creek

FR 608

527 Road

FR 755

47 mi.

Dry Creek

160

508 Road

502 Road

◆ Bayfield

47.1 mi.

Buck HWY

521 Road

523 Road

Beaver Creek

520 Road

N W E S

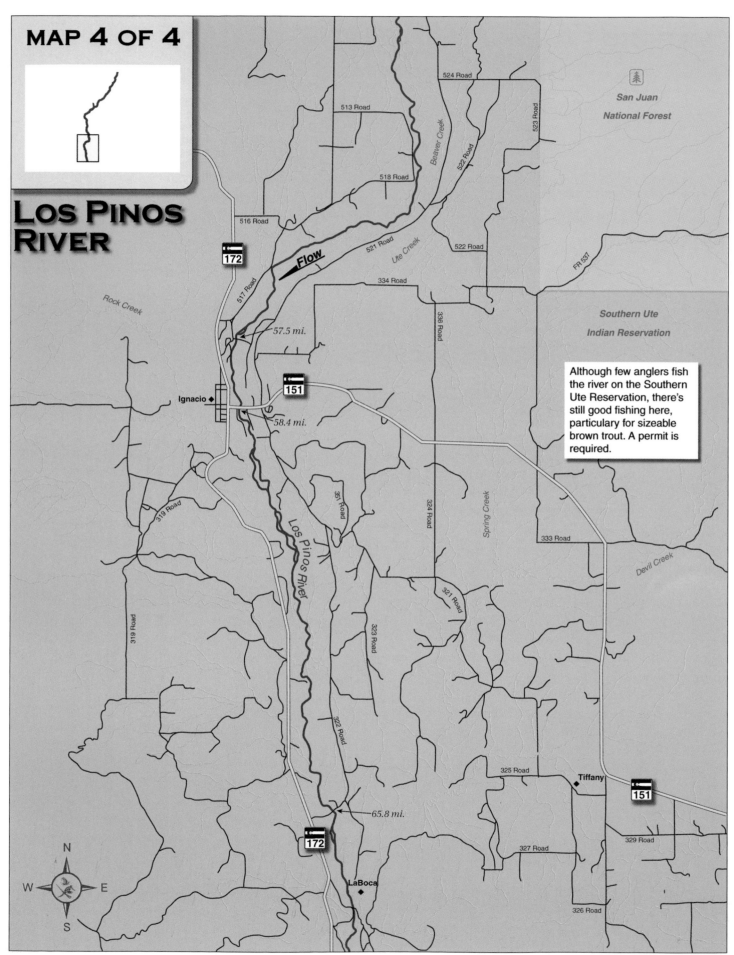

MAP 4 OF 4

LOS PINOS RIVER

172

← **Flow**

57.5 mi.

151

Ignacio ◆

58.4 mi.

Although few anglers fish the river on the Southern Ute Reservation, there's still good fishing here, particulary for sizeable brown trout. A permit is required.

524 Road

513 Road

518 Road

516 Road

521 Road

517 Road

Rock Creek

Beaver Creek

522 Road

523 Road

Ute Creek

334 Road

522 Road

FR 537

336 Road

San Juan National Forest

Southern Ute Indian Reservation

Spring Creek

333 Road

Devil Creek

319 Road

351 Road

324 Road

Los Pinos River

319 Road

321 Road

323 Road

322 Road

325 Road

Tiffany ◆

151

329 Road

65.8 mi.

327 Road

172

LaBoca ◆

326 Road

N
W E
S

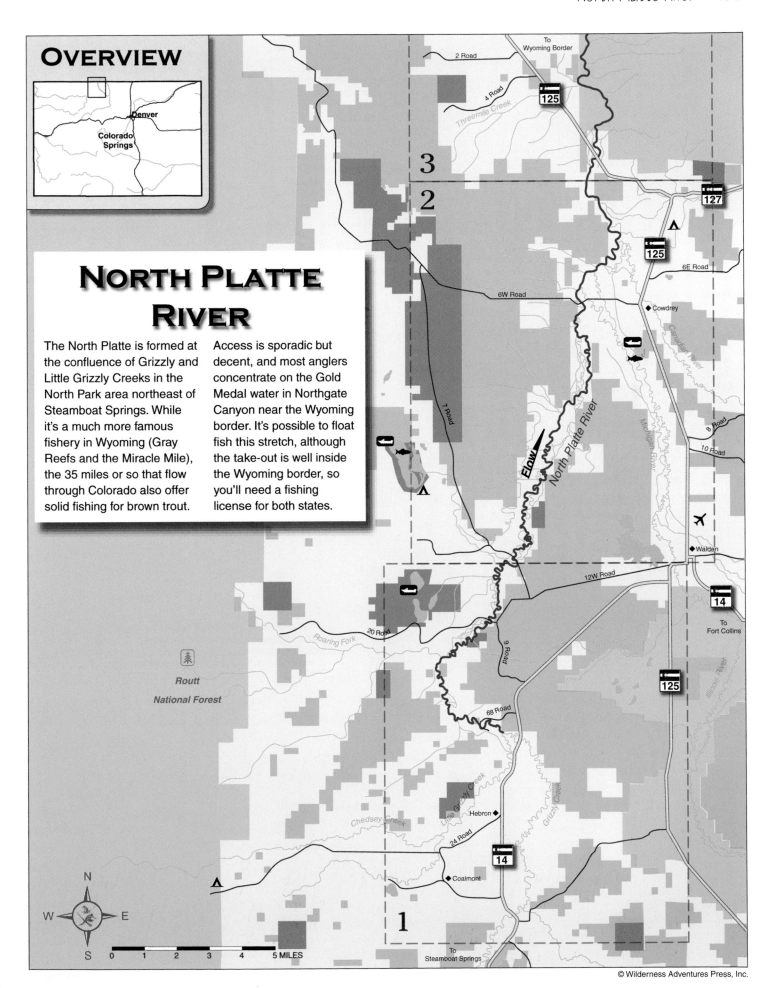

OVERVIEW

NORTH PLATTE RIVER

The North Platte is formed at the confluence of Grizzly and Little Grizzly Creeks in the North Park area northeast of Steamboat Springs. While it's a much more famous fishery in Wyoming (Gray Reefs and the Miracle Mile), the 35 miles or so that flow through Colorado also offer solid fishing for brown trout.

Access is sporadic but decent, and most anglers concentrate on the Gold Medal water in Northgate Canyon near the Wyoming border. It's possible to float fish this stretch, although the take-out is well inside the Wyoming border, so you'll need a fishing license for both states.

Denver
Colorado Springs

To Wyoming Border
2 Road
4 Road
Threemile Creek
125
127
125
6E Road
6W Road
Cowdrey
7 Road
Flow
North Platte River
Canadian River
Michigan River
8 Road
10 Road
Walden
125
12W Road
14
To Fort Collins
9 Road
20 Road
Roaring Fork
68 Road
125
Routt National Forest
Illinois River
Grizzly Creek
Chedsey Creek
Little Grizzly Creek
Hebron
24 Road
14
Coalmont
1
To Steamboat Springs

N
W E
S
0 1 2 3 4 5 MILES

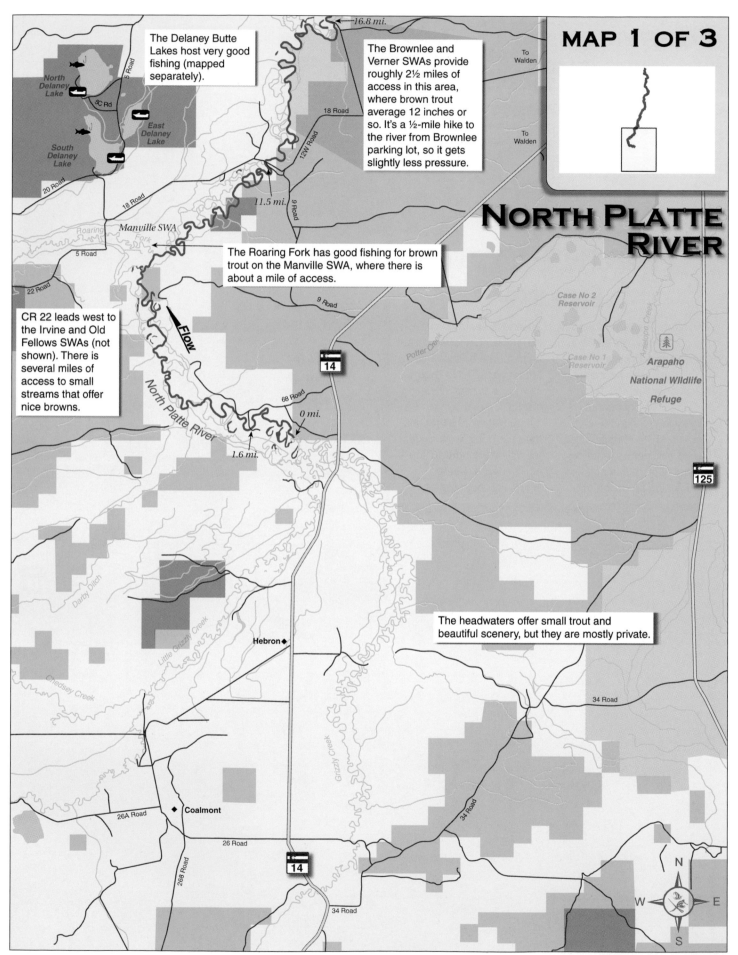

The Delaney Butte Lakes host very good fishing (mapped separately).

The Brownlee and Verner SWAs provide roughly 2½ miles of access in this area, where brown trout average 12 inches or so. It's a ½-mile hike to the river from Brownlee parking lot, so it gets slightly less pressure.

The Roaring Fork has good fishing for brown trout on the Manville SWA, where there is about a mile of access.

CR 22 leads west to the Irvine and Old Fellows SWAs (not shown). There is several miles of access to small streams that offer nice browns.

The headwaters offer small trout and beautiful scenery, but they are mostly private.

MAP 1 OF 3

NORTH PLATTE RIVER

To Walden

Arapaho National Wildlife Refuge

Case No 2 Reservoir

Case No 1 Reservoir

North Delaney Lake

East Delaney Lake

South Delaney Lake

Manville SWA

North Platte River

Hebron ◆

Coalmont ◆

← 16.8 mi.

11.5 mi.

0 mi.

1.6 mi.

© Wilderness Adventures Press, Inc.

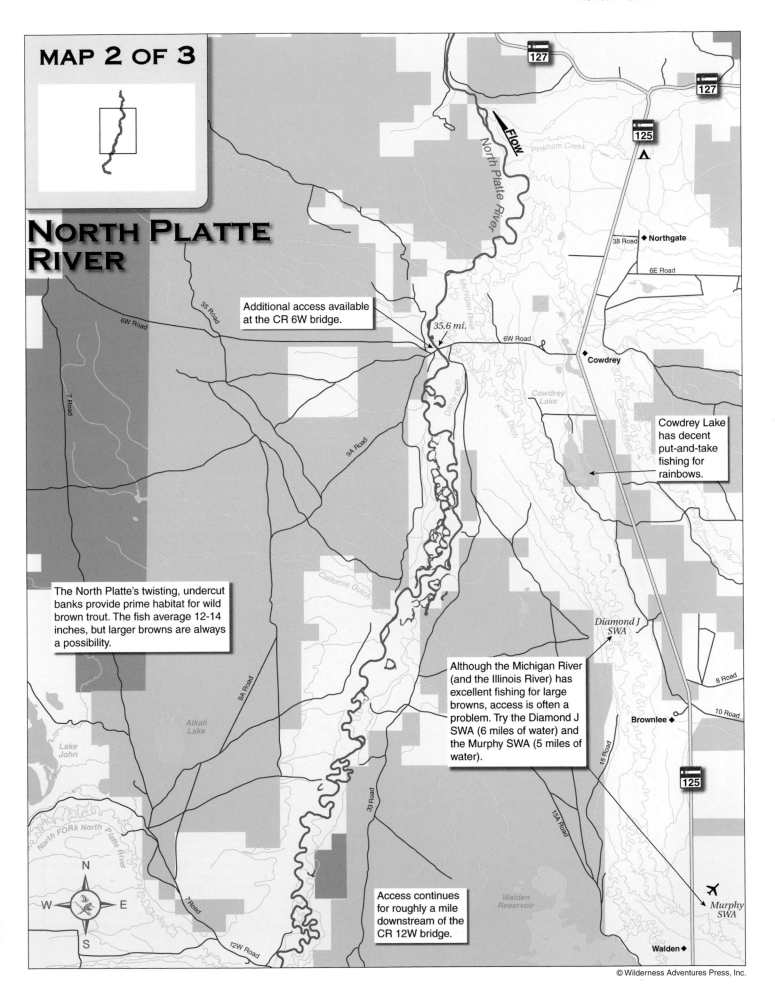

MAP 2 OF 3

NORTH PLATTE RIVER

Additional access available at the CR 6W bridge.

35.6 mi.

Cowdrey Lake has decent put-and-take fishing for rainbows.

The North Platte's twisting, undercut banks provide prime habitat for wild brown trout. The fish average 12-14 inches, but larger browns are always a possibility.

Although the Michigan River (and the Illinois River) has excellent fishing for large browns, access is often a problem. Try the Diamond J SWA (6 miles of water) and the Murphy SWA (5 miles of water).

Access continues for roughly a mile downstream of the CR 12W bridge.

© Wilderness Adventures Press, Inc.

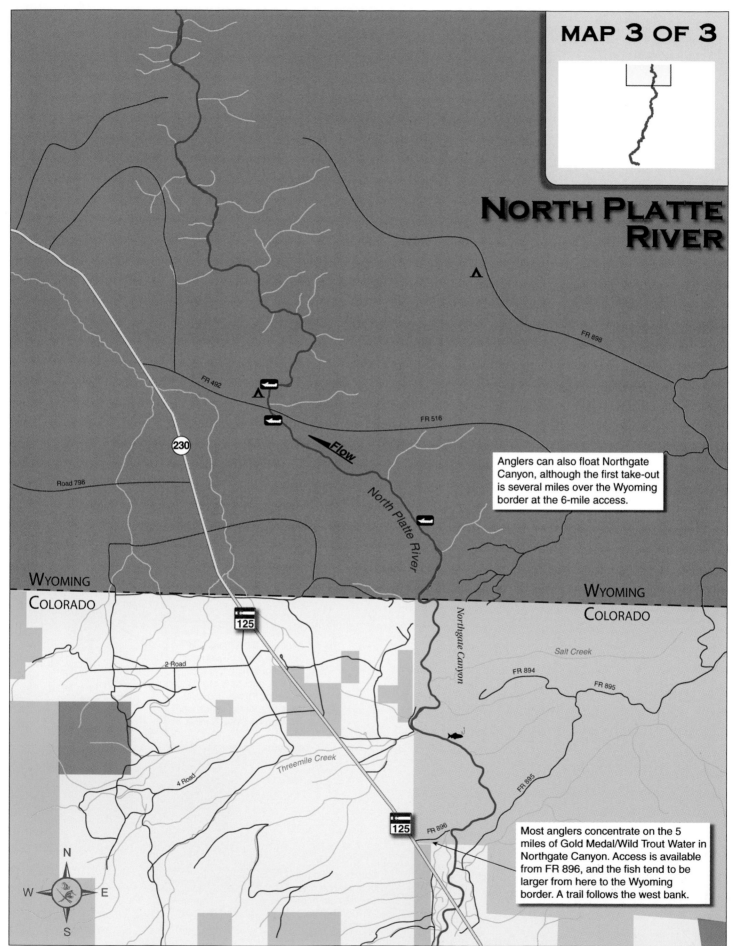

MAP 3 OF 3

NORTH PLATTE RIVER

FR 898

FR 492

FR 516

230

Road 798

Flow

North Platte River

Anglers can also float Northgate Canyon, although the first take-out is several miles over the Wyoming border at the 6-mile access.

WYOMING

COLORADO

WYOMING

COLORADO

Salt Creek

Northgate Canyon

FR 894

FR 895

125

2 Road

4 Road

Threemile Creek

FR 895

125

FR 896

Most anglers concentrate on the 5 miles of Gold Medal/Wild Trout Water in Northgate Canyon. Access is available from FR 896, and the fish tend to be larger from here to the Wyoming border. A trail follows the west bank.

N
W E
S

© Wilderness Adventures Press, Inc.

PIEDRA RIVER

The Piedra drains the southern slopes of the San Juans, continuing south to Navaho Reservoir at the New Mexico border. As there's little road access to the main stem, anglers willing to walk a bit can find solitude and great fishing for browns and rainbows up to 12 or 14 inches. The upper river also has good fishing, with brook and cutthroat trout becoming more prevalent. This is a great little river, and the angling hordes are usually kept at bay by the daunting hikes in to prime water. Pagosa Springs is close by and Durango is 40 minutes to the west.

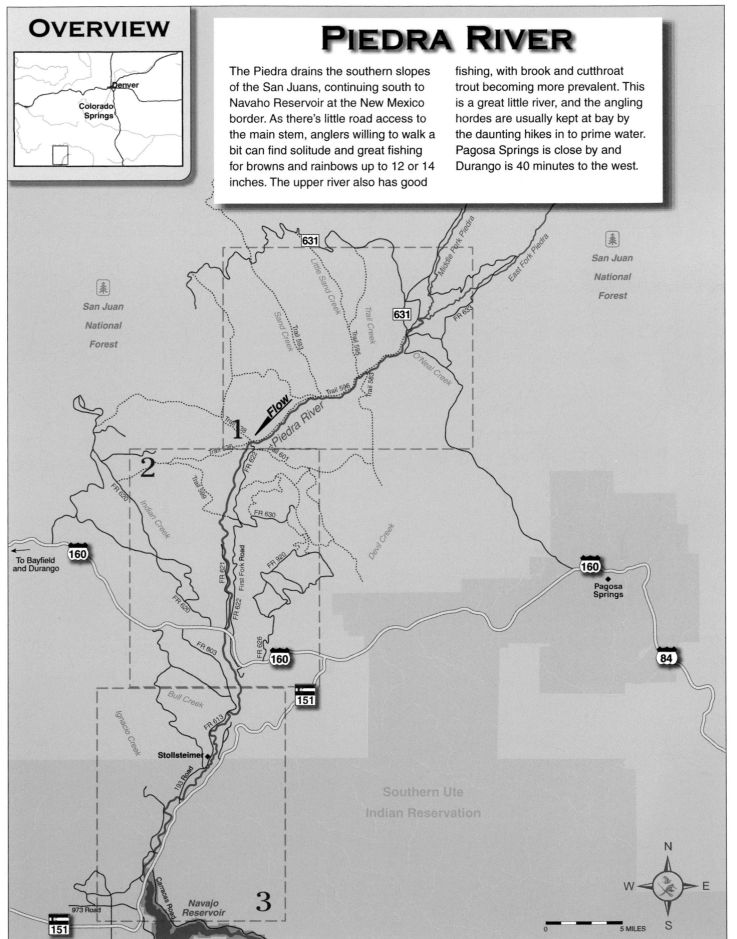

OVERVIEW

© Wilderness Adventures Press, Inc.

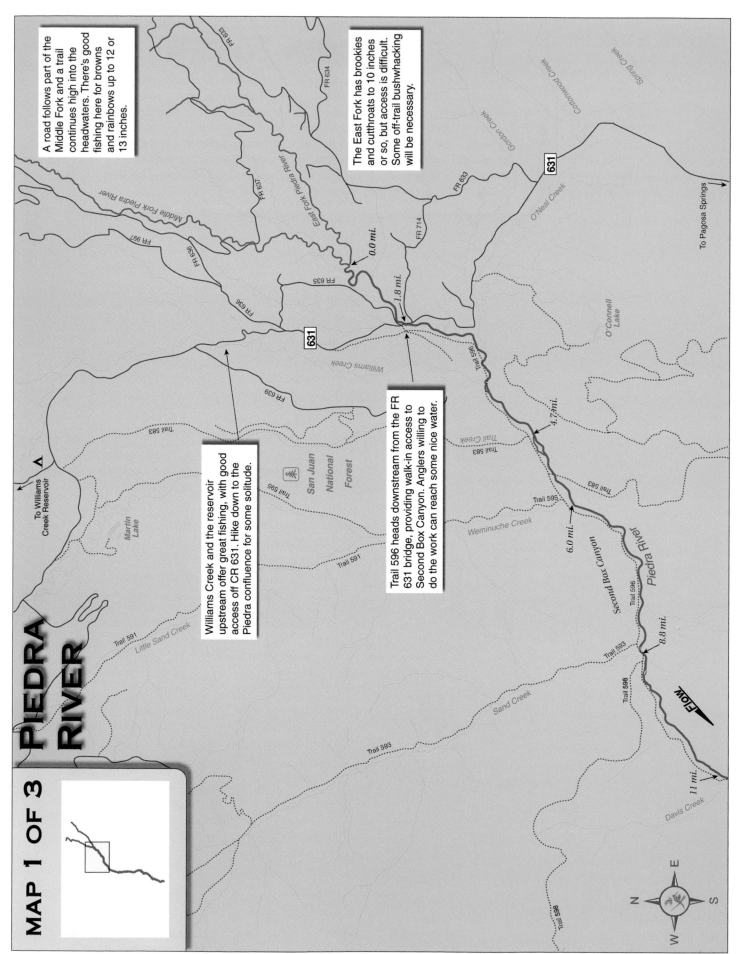

A road follows part of the Middle Fork and a trail continues high into the headwaters. There's good fishing here for browns and rainbows up to 12 or 13 inches.

The East Fork has brookies and cutthroats to 10 inches or so, but access is difficult. Some off-trail bushwhacking will be necessary.

Williams Creek and the reservoir upstream offer great fishing, with good access off CR 631. Hike down to the Piedra confluence for some solitude.

Trail 596 heads downstream from the FR 631 bridge, providing walk-in access to Second Box Canyon. Anglers willing to do the work can reach some nice water.

PIEDRA RIVER

MAP 1 OF 3

San Juan National Forest

To Williams Creek Reservoir

Martin Lake

O'Connell Lake

To Pagosa Springs

Middle Fork Piedra River

East Fork Piedra River

Williams Creek

Cottonwood Creek

Spring Creek

Gordon Creek

O'Neal Creek

Weminuche Creek

Trail Creek

Second Box Canyon

Piedra River

Little Sand Creek

Sand Creek

Davis Creek

FR 855

FR 634

FR 637

FR 997

FR 636

FR 635

FR 639

FR 714

FR 653

631

631

Trail 583

Trail 595

Trail 591

Trail 596

Trail 593

Trail 598

0.0 mi.

1.8 mi.

4.7 mi.

6.0 mi.

8.8 mi.

11 mi.

FLOW

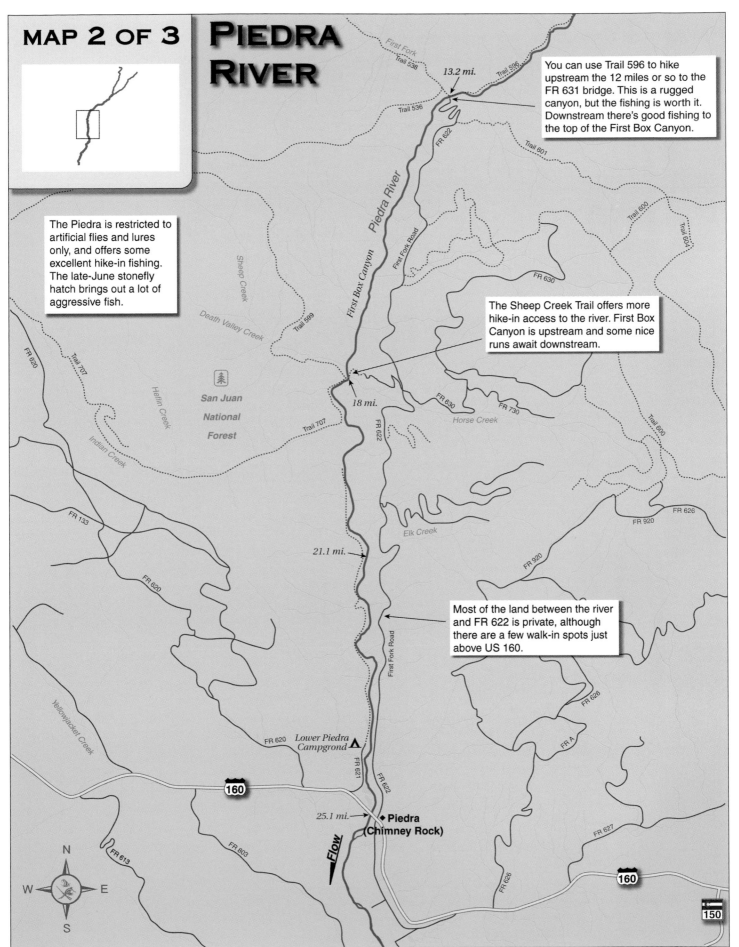

MAP 2 OF 3 PIEDRA RIVER

You can use Trail 596 to hike upstream the 12 miles or so to the FR 631 bridge. This is a rugged canyon, but the fishing is worth it. Downstream there's good fishing to the top of the First Box Canyon.

The Piedra is restricted to artificial flies and lures only, and offers some excellent hike-in fishing. The late-June stonefly hatch brings out a lot of aggressive fish.

The Sheep Creek Trail offers more hike-in access to the river. First Box Canyon is upstream and some nice runs await downstream.

Most of the land between the river and FR 622 is private, although there are a few walk-in spots just above US 160.

First Fork
Trail 538
Trail 596
13.2 mi.
Trail 536
Trail 601
FR 622
Trail 600
Piedra River
First Fork Road
Trail 604
FR 630
First Box Canyon
Sheep Creek
Trail 599
Death Valley Creek
18 mi.
FR 630
FR 730
Horse Creek
Trail 707
FR 622
Trail 600
FR 620
Trail 707
Heflin Creek
San Juan
National
Forest
Indian Creek
Elk Creek
FR 626
FR 920
FR 920
21.1 mi.
FR 133
FR 620
FR 626
FR A
Yellowjacket Creek
Lower Piedra
Campgrond
FR 620
FR 621
FR 622
160
25.1 mi.
Piedra
(Chimney Rock)
Flow
FR 803
FR 626
FR 627
FR 613
160
150

N
W   E
S

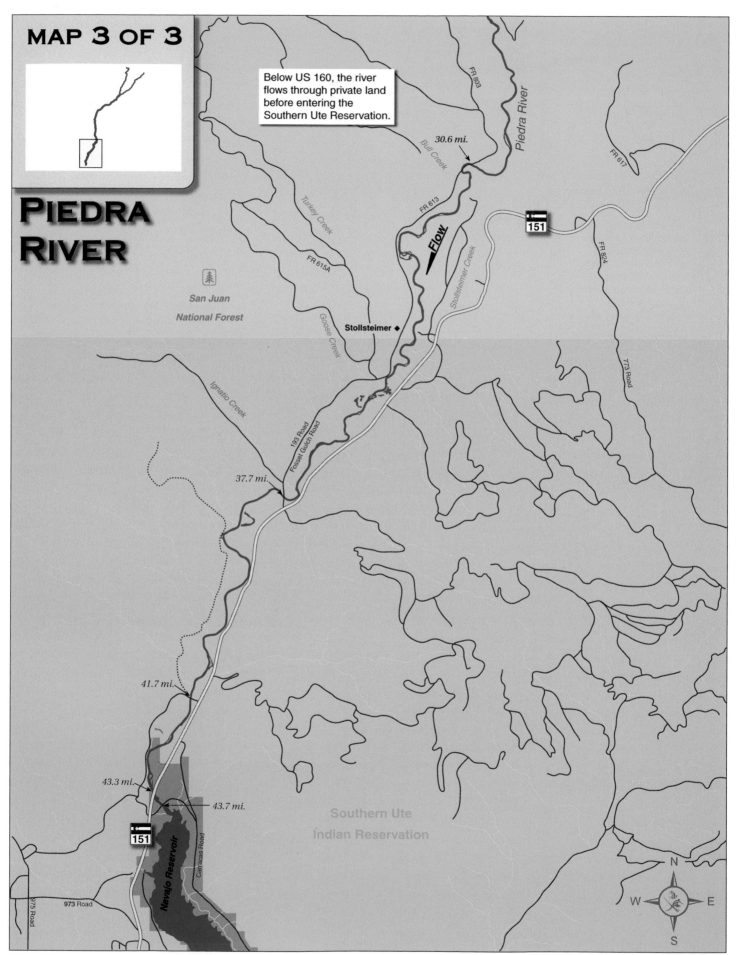

MAP 3 OF 3

PIEDRA RIVER

Below US 160, the river flows through private land before entering the Southern Ute Reservation.

Piedra River

FR 803

30.6 mi.

Bull Creek

FR 613

FR 617

Flow

151

FR 824

Turkey Creek

Stollsteimer Creek

FR 615A

773 Road

San Juan

National Forest

Goose Creek

Stollsteimer ◆

Ignatio Creek

193 Road

Fosset Gulch Road

37.7 mi.

41.7 mi.

43.3 mi.

43.7 mi.

Southern Ute
Indian Reservation

151

Carracas Road

Navajo Reservoir

975 Road

973 Road

N

W   E

S

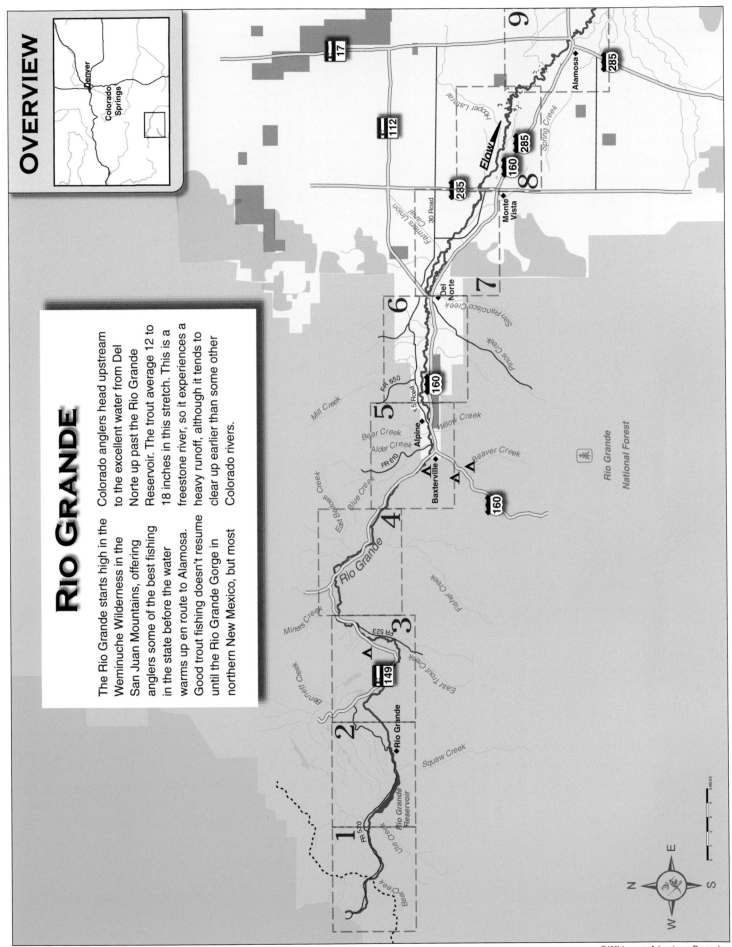

OVERVIEW

Denver

Colorado Springs

RIO GRANDE

The Rio Grande starts high in the Weminuche Wilderness in the San Juan Mountains, offering anglers some of the best fishing in the state before the water warms up en route to Alamosa. Good trout fishing doesn't resume until the Rio Grande Gorge in northern New Mexico, but most

Colorado anglers head upstream to the excellent water from Del Norte up past the Rio Grande Reservoir. The trout average 12 to 18 inches in this stretch. This is a freestone river, so it experiences a heavy runoff, although it tends to clear up earlier than some other Colorado rivers.

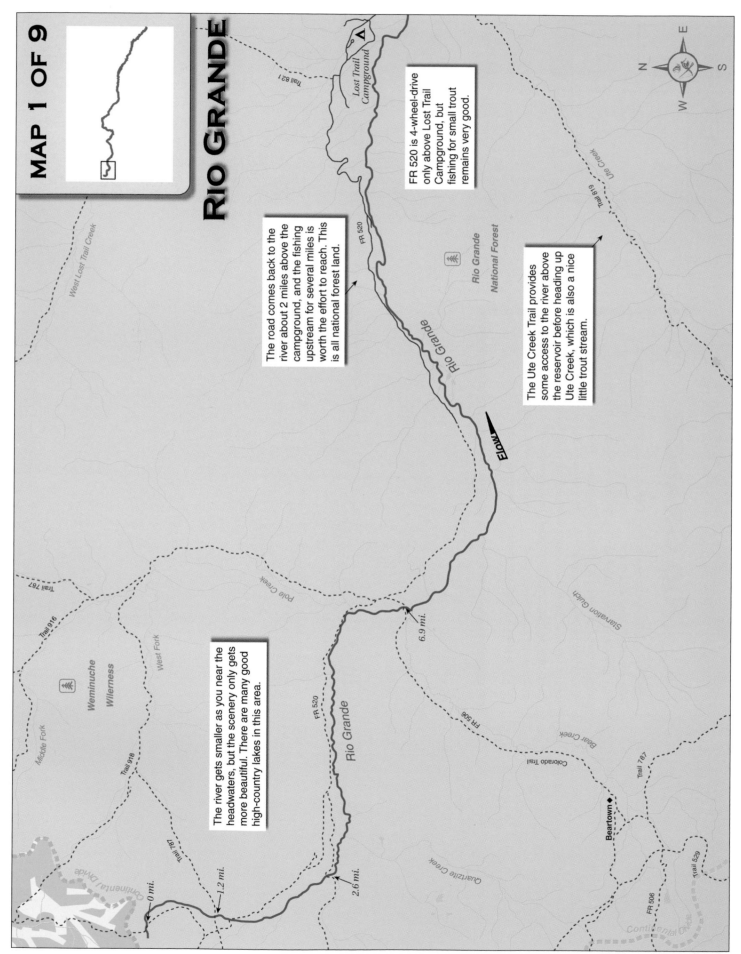

RIO GRANDE

MAP 1 OF 9

FR 520 is 4-wheel-drive only above Lost Trail Campground, but fishing for small trout remains very good.

The road comes back to the river about 2 miles above the campground, and the fishing upstream for several miles is worth the effort to reach. This is all national forest land.

The Ute Creek Trail provides some access to the river above the reservoir before heading up Ute Creek, which is also a nice little trout stream.

The river gets smaller as you near the headwaters, but the scenery only gets more beautiful. There are many good high-country lakes in this area.

Lost Trail Campground

Trail 821

FR 520

Rio Grande

Rio Grande National Forest

Ute Creek

Trail 819

FLOW

Stanaticn Gulch

West Lost Trail Creek

Trail 787

Trail 916

West Fork

Pole Creek

Weminuche Wilerness

Middle Fork

Trail 918

Trail 787

Continental Divide

0 mi.

1.2 mi.

2.6 mi.

FR 520

Rio Grande

6.9 mi.

FR 506

Quartzite Creek

Colorado Trail

Bear Creek

Trail 787

Beartown

FR 506

Trail 529

Continental Divide

N E S W

© Wilderness Adventures Press, Inc.

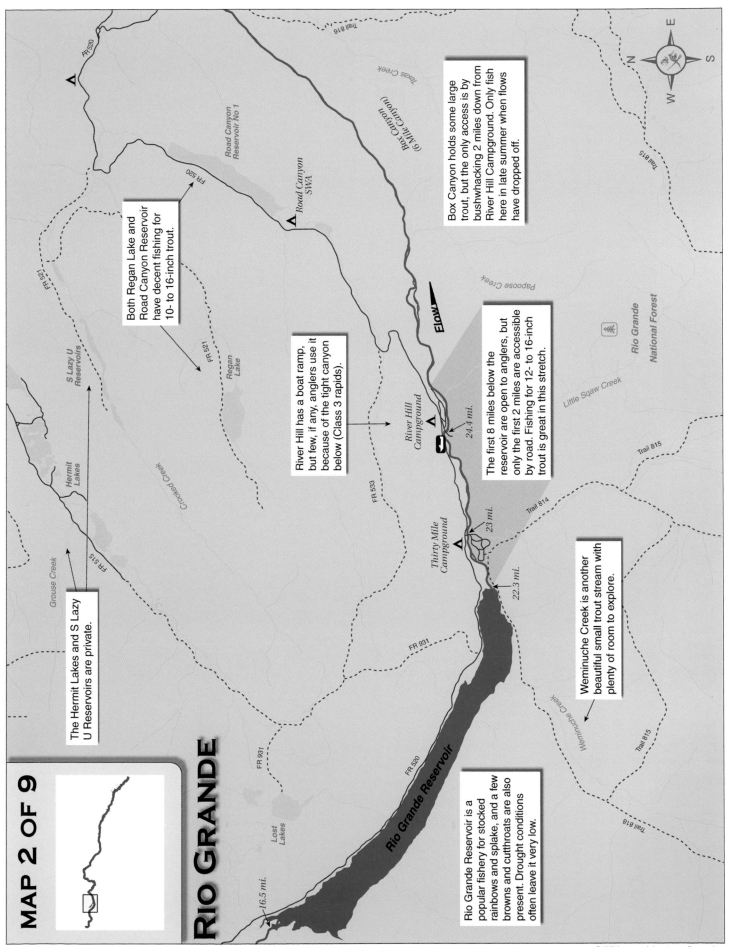

MAP 2 OF 9

RIO GRANDE

Both Regan Lake and Road Canyon Reservoir have decent fishing for 10- to 16-inch trout.

The Hermit Lakes and S Lazy U Reservoirs are private.

Box Canyon holds some large trout, but the only access is by bushwhacking 2 miles down from River Hill Campground. Only fish here in late summer when flows have dropped off.

River Hill has a boat ramp, but few, if any, anglers use it because of the tight canyon below (Class 3 rapids).

The first 8 miles below the reservoir are open to anglers, but only the first 2 miles are accessible by road. Fishing for 12- to 16-inch trout is great in this stretch.

Weminuche Creek is another beautiful small trout stream with plenty of room to explore.

Rio Grande Reservoir is a popular fishery for stocked rainbows and splake, and a few browns and cutthroats are also present. Drought conditions often leave it very low.

© Wilderness Adventures Press, Inc.

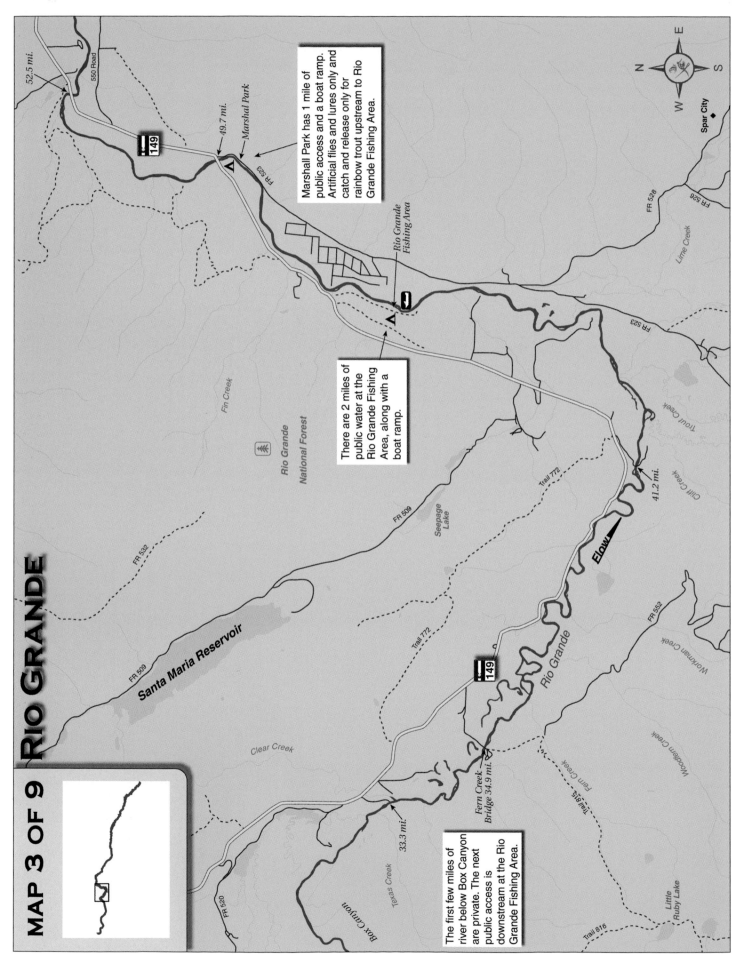

MAP 3 OF 9 RIO GRANDE

Marshall Park has 1 mile of public access and a boat ramp. Artificial flies and lures only and catch and release only for rainbow trout upstream to Rio Grande Fishing Area.

There are 2 miles of public water at the Rio Grande Fishing Area, along with a boat ramp.

The first few miles of river below Box Canyon are private. The next public access is downstream at the Rio Grande Fishing Area.

52.5 mi.

550 Road

49.7 mi.

Marshal Park

FR 523

Spar City

Rio Grande Fishing Area

FR 528

FR 526

Lime Creek

FR 523

Fin Creek

Rio Grande National Forest

FR 509

Seepage Lake

Trail 772

Flow

41.2 mi.

Cliff Creek

Trout Creek

FR 532

FR 509

Santa Maria Reservoir

Trail 772

149

Rio Grande

FR 552

Workman Creek

Clear Creek

Fern Creek Bridge 34.9 mi.

Woodenn Creek

33.3 mi.

Trail 915

Fern Creek

Texas Creek

Box Canyon

FR 520

Little Ruby Lake

Trail 816

© Wilderness Adventures Press, Inc.

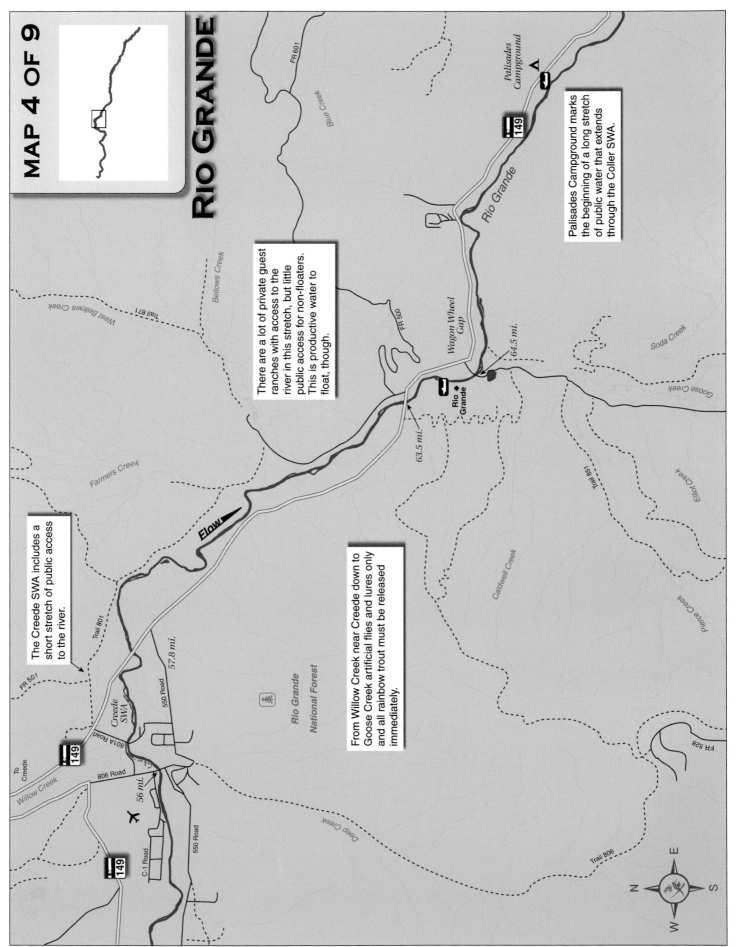

MAP 4 OF 9

RIO GRANDE

Palisades Campground marks the beginning of a long stretch of public water that extends through the Coller SWA.

There are a lot of private guest ranches with access to the river in this stretch, but little public access for non-floaters. This is productive water to float, though.

The Creede SWA includes a short stretch of public access to the river.

From Willow Creek near Creede down to Goose Creek artificial flies and lures only and all rainbow trout must be released immediately.

Rio Grande
National Forest

Flow

Palisades Campground

149

Rio Grande

Wagon Wheel Gap

64.5 mi.

63.5 mi.

FR 601

Blue Creek

FR 500

Bellows Creek

West Bellows Creek

Trail 871

Farmers Creek

FR 501

Trail 801

Creede SWA

To Creede

Willow Creek

149

806 Road

801A Road

550 Road

57.8 mi.

56 mi.

550 Road

C-1 Road

149

Deep Creek

Caldwell Creek

Trail 851

Soda Creek

Goose Creek

Elliott Creek

Pierce Creek

FR 828

Trail 806

N E S W

© Wilderness Adventures Press, Inc.

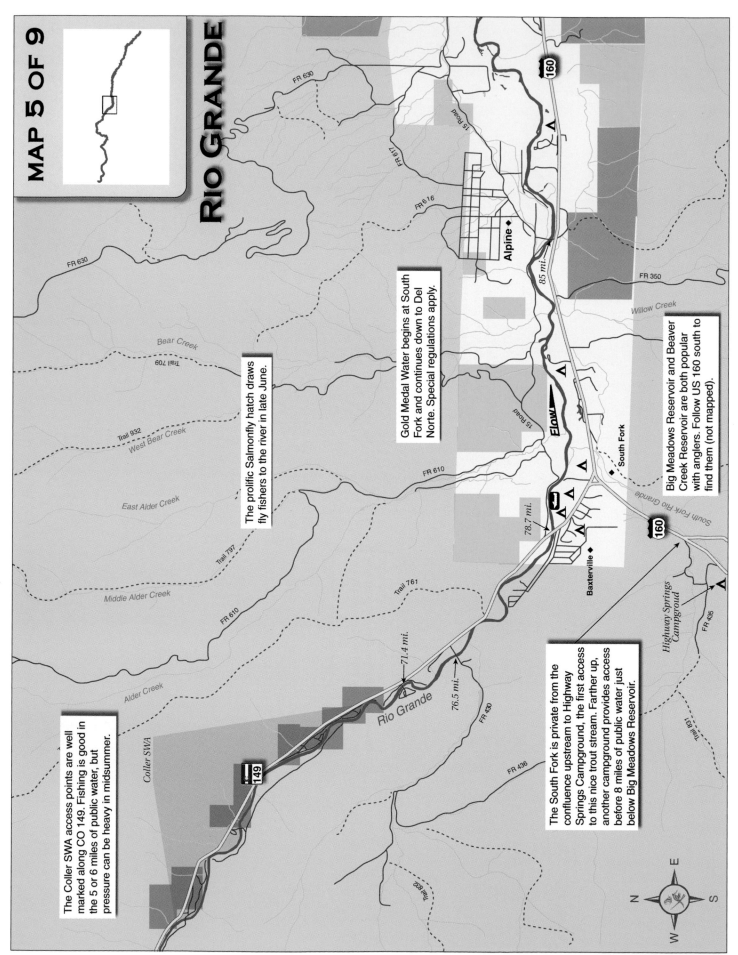

MAP 5 OF 9

RIO GRANDE

The Coller SWA access points are well marked along CO 149. Fishing is good in the 5 or 6 miles of public water, but pressure can be heavy in midsummer.

The prolific Salmonfly hatch draws fly fishers to the river in late June.

Gold Medal Water begins at South Fork and continues down to Del Norte. Special regulations apply.

Big Meadows Reservoir and Beaver Creek Reservoir are both popular with anglers. Follow US 160 south to find them (not mapped).

The South Fork is private from the confluence upstream to Highway Springs Campground, the first access to this nice trout stream. Farther up, another campground provides access before 8 miles of public water just below Big Meadows Reservoir.

© Wilderness Adventures Press, Inc.

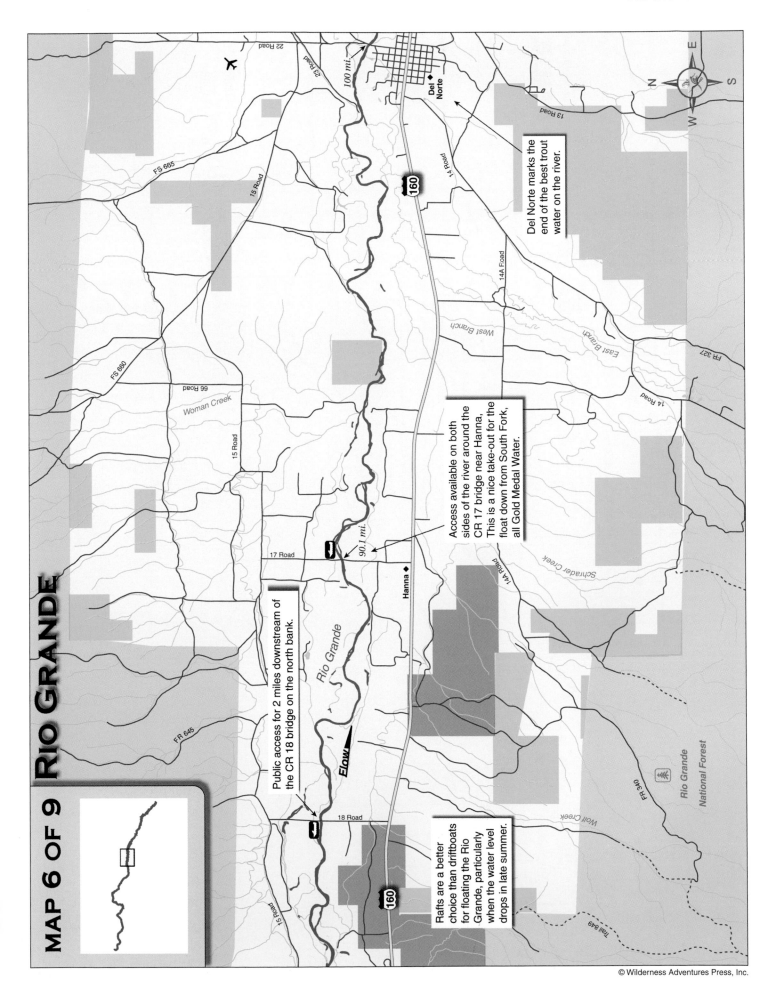

MAP 6 OF 9 RIO GRANDE

Del Norte marks the end of the best trout water on the river.

Access available on both sides of the river around the CR 17 bridge near Hanna. This is a nice take-out for the float down from South Fork, all Gold Medal Water.

Public access for 2 miles downstream of the CR 18 bridge on the north bank.

Rafts are a better choice than driftboats for floating the Rio Grande, particularly when the water level drops in late summer.

100 mi.

90.1 mi.

Del Norte

Hanna

Rio Grande

Woman Creek

Schrader Creek

Wolf Creek

Rio Grande National Forest

Flow

22 Road

23 Road

15 Road

FS 665

FS 660

66 Road

15 Road

FR 645

15 Road

17 Road

18 Road

14 Road

14A Road

13 Road

West Branch

East Branch

FR 327

14 Road

½ Road

FR 340

Trail 849

160

160

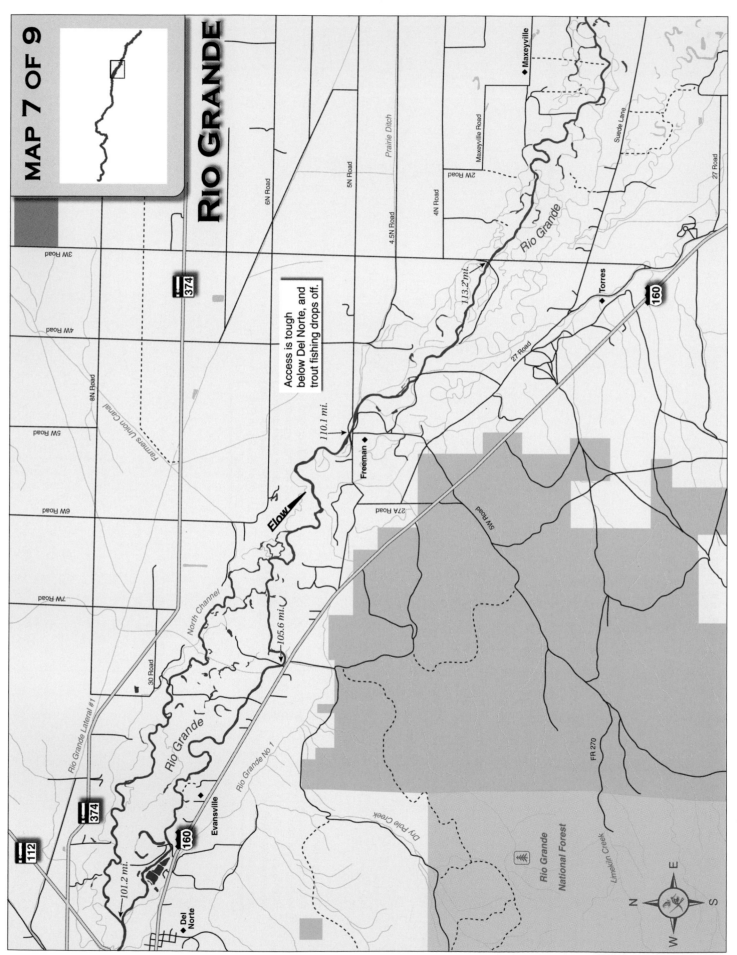

MAP 7 OF 9

RIO GRANDE

Access is tough below Del Norte, and trout fishing drops off.

113.2 mi.

110.1 mi.

105.6 mi.

101.2 mi.

Maxeyville

Torres

Freeman

Evansville

Del Norte

Rio Grande

Rio Grande National Forest

Flow

Farmers Union Canal

Prairie Ditch

North Channel

Rio Grande Lateral #1

Rio Grande No 1

Dry Pole Creek

Limekiln Creek

FR 270

Maxeyville Road

Suede Lane

Prairie Ditch

3W Road

4W Road

5W Road

6W Road

7W Road

8N Road

6N Road

5N Road

4.5N Road

4N Road

2W Road

27 Road

27A Road

5W Road

27 Road

30 Road

374

374

160

160

112

© Wilderness Adventures Press, Inc.

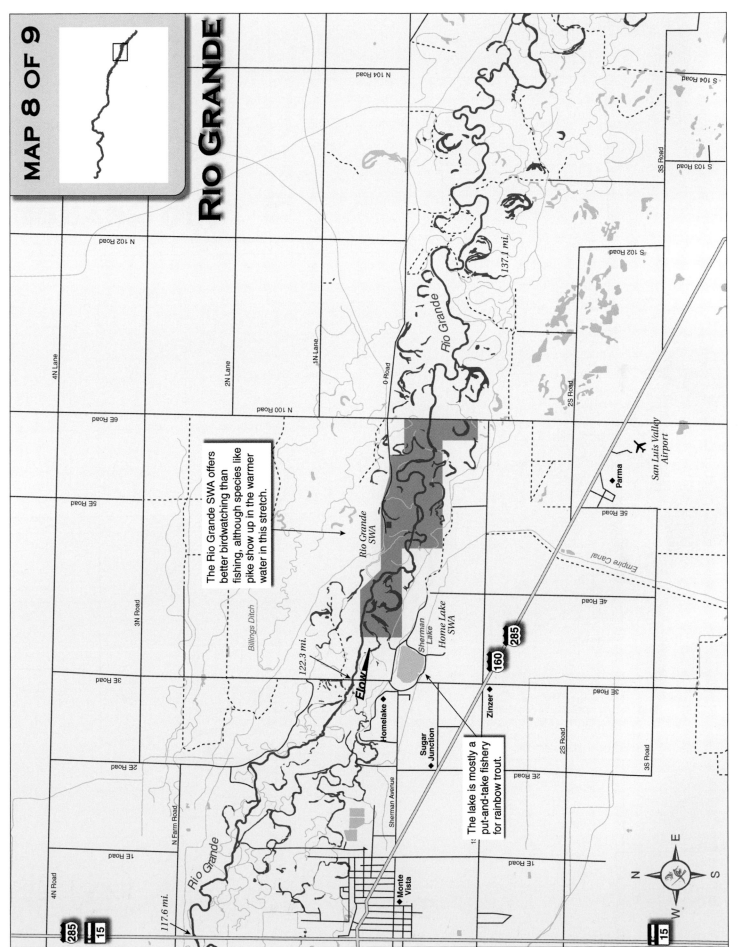

MAP 8 OF 9

RIO GRANDE

The Rio Grande SWA offers better birdwatching than fishing, although species like pike show up in the warmer water in this stretch.

The lake is mostly a put-and-take fishery for rainbow trout.

Rio Grande SWA

Sherman Lake

Home Lake SWA

San Luis Valley Airport

Parma

Billings Ditch

Flow

Homelake

Sugar Junction

Zinzer

Monte Vista

Sherman Avenue

Empire Canal

Rio Grande

137.1 mi.

122.3 mi.

117.6 mi.

285

15

160

285

15

285

15

N 104 Road

S 104 Road

S 103 Road

3S Road

N 102 Road

S 102 Road

4N Lane

2N Lane

1N Lane

0 Road

N 100 Road

6E Road

5E Road

5E Road

4E Road

2S Road

3S Road

3N Road

3E Road

3E Road

2E Road

2E Road

1E Road

1E Road

2E Road

N Farm Road

4N Road

© Wilderness Adventures Press, Inc.

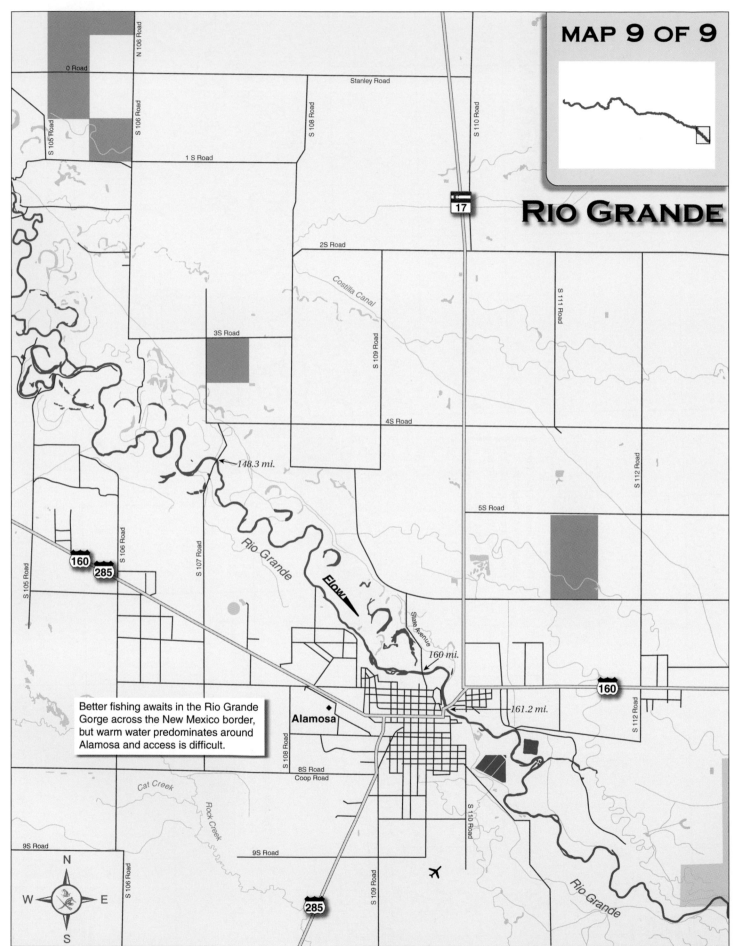

MAP **9** OF **9**

RIO GRANDE

Better fishing awaits in the Rio Grande Gorge across the New Mexico border, but warm water predominates around Alamosa and access is difficult.

Alamosa

© Wilderness Adventures Press, Inc.

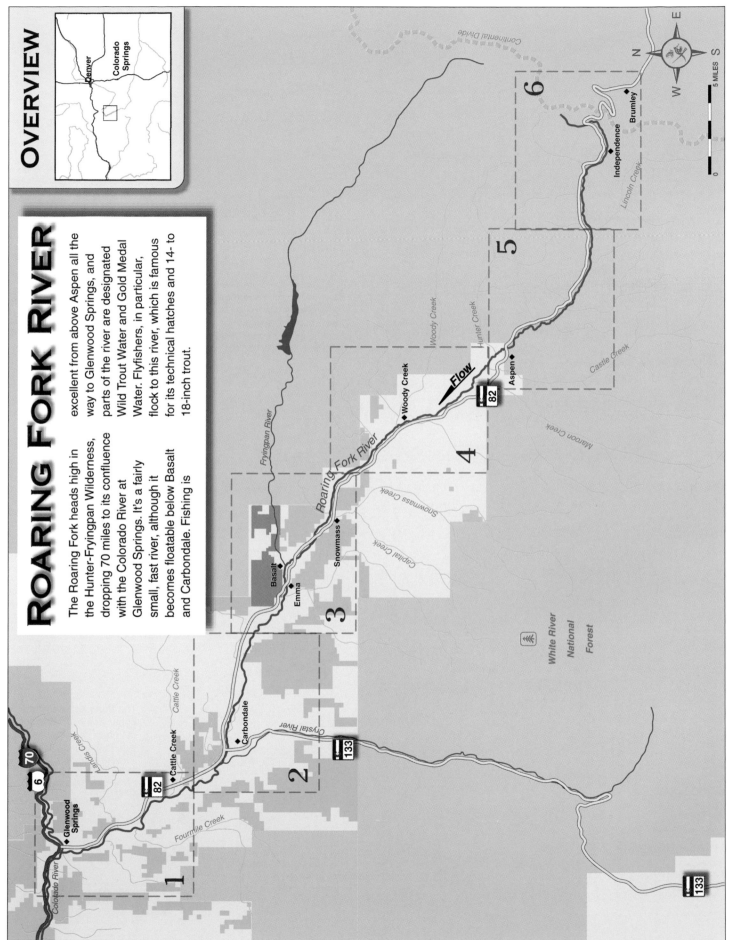

OVERVIEW

ROARING FORK RIVER

The Roaring Fork heads high in the Hunter-Fryingpan Wilderness, dropping 70 miles to its confluence with the Colorado River at Glenwood Springs. It's a fairly small, fast river, although it becomes floatable below Basalt and Carbondale. Fishing is excellent from above Aspen all the way to Glenwood Springs, and parts of the river are designated Wild Trout Water and Gold Medal Water. Flyfishers, in particular, flock to this river, which is famous for its technical hatches and 14- to 18-inch trout.

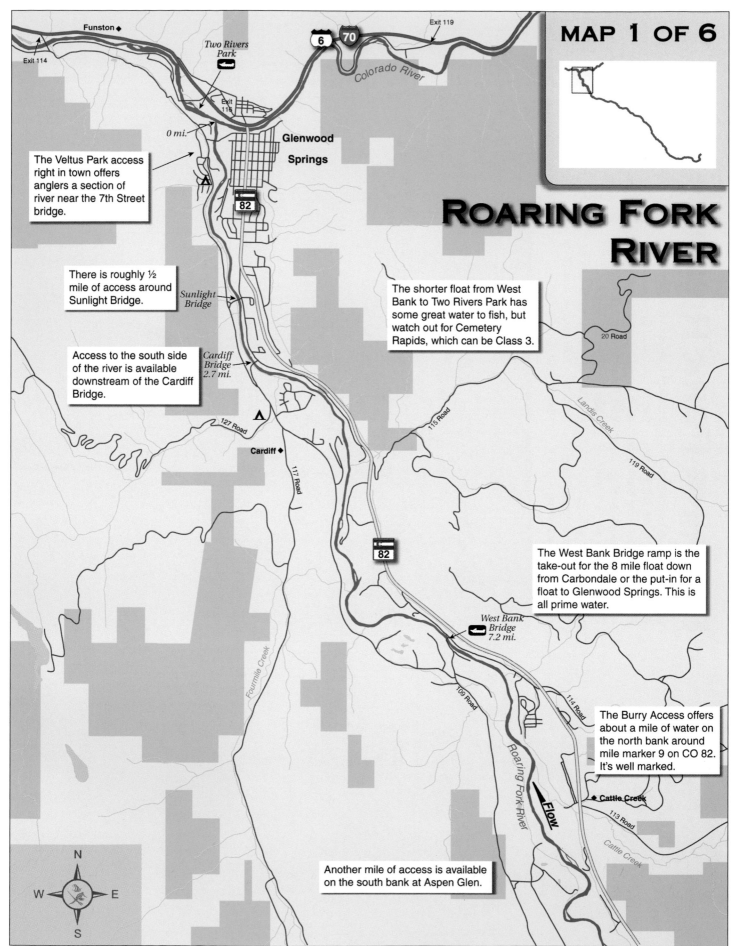

MAP 1 OF 6

Funston ◆

Exit 114

Two Rivers Park

Exit 119

Colorado River

Exit 116

0 mi.

Glenwood Springs

ROARING FORK RIVER

The Veltus Park access right in town offers anglers a section of river near the 7th Street bridge.

There is roughly ½ mile of access around Sunlight Bridge.

Sunlight Bridge

The shorter float from West Bank to Two Rivers Park has some great water to fish, but watch out for Cemetery Rapids, which can be Class 3.

20 Road

Access to the south side of the river is available downstream of the Cardiff Bridge.

Cardiff Bridge 2.7 mi.

Landis Creek

115 Road

127 Road

119 Road

Cardiff ◆

117 Road

The West Bank Bridge ramp is the take-out for the 8 mile float down from Carbondale or the put-in for a float to Glenwood Springs. This is all prime water.

West Bank Bridge 7.2 mi.

The Burry Access offers about a mile of water on the north bank around mile marker 9 on CO 82. It's well marked.

109 Road

114 Road

Fourmile Creek

Roaring Fork River

Flow

◆ Cattle Creek

113 Road

Cattle Creek

N
W   E
S

Another mile of access is available on the south bank at Aspen Glen.

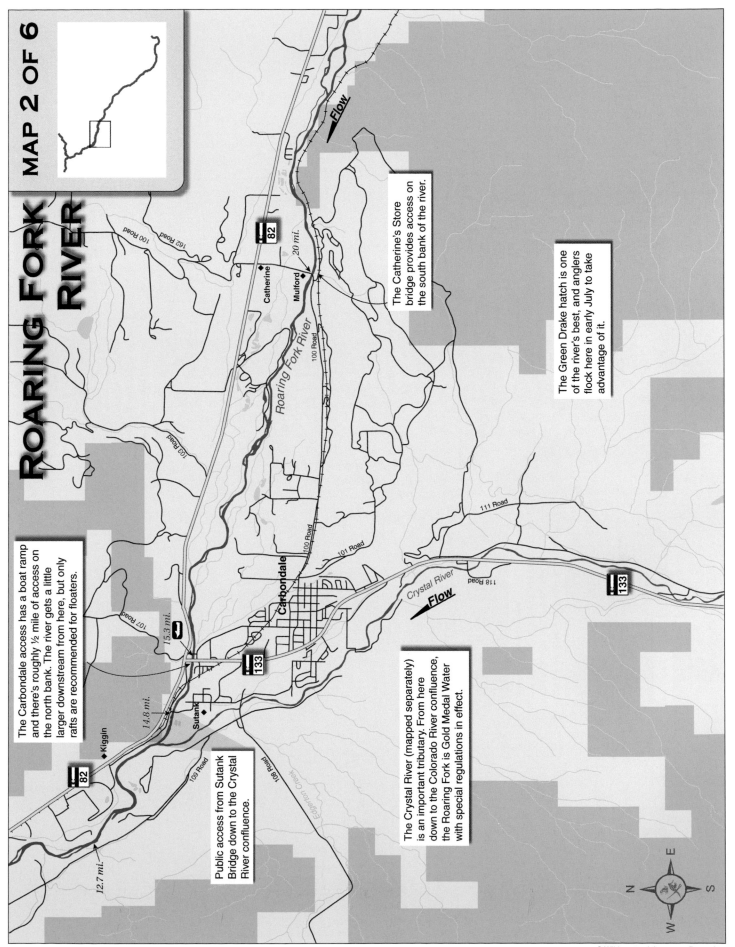

MAP 2 OF 6

ROARING FORK RIVER

The Carbondale access has a boat ramp and there's roughly ½ mile of access on the north bank. The river gets a little larger downstream from here, but only rafts are recommended for floaters.

Public access from Sutank Bridge down to the Crystal River confluence.

The Crystal River (mapped separately) is an important tributary. From here down to the Colorado River confluence, the Roaring Fork is Gold Medal Water with special regulations in effect.

The Catherine's Store bridge provides access on the south bank of the river.

The Green Drake hatch is one of the river's best, and anglers flock here in early July to take advantage of it.

Flow

20 mi.

Catherine

Mulford

Roaring Fork River

100 Road

100 Road

162 Road

103 Road

107 Road

15.3 mi.

14.8 mi.

Kiggin

12.7 mi.

82

Sutank

108 Road

109 Road

Edgerton Creek

Carbondale

133

133

1100 Road

101 Road

111 Road

118 Road

Crystal River

Flow

82

133

N

E

S

W

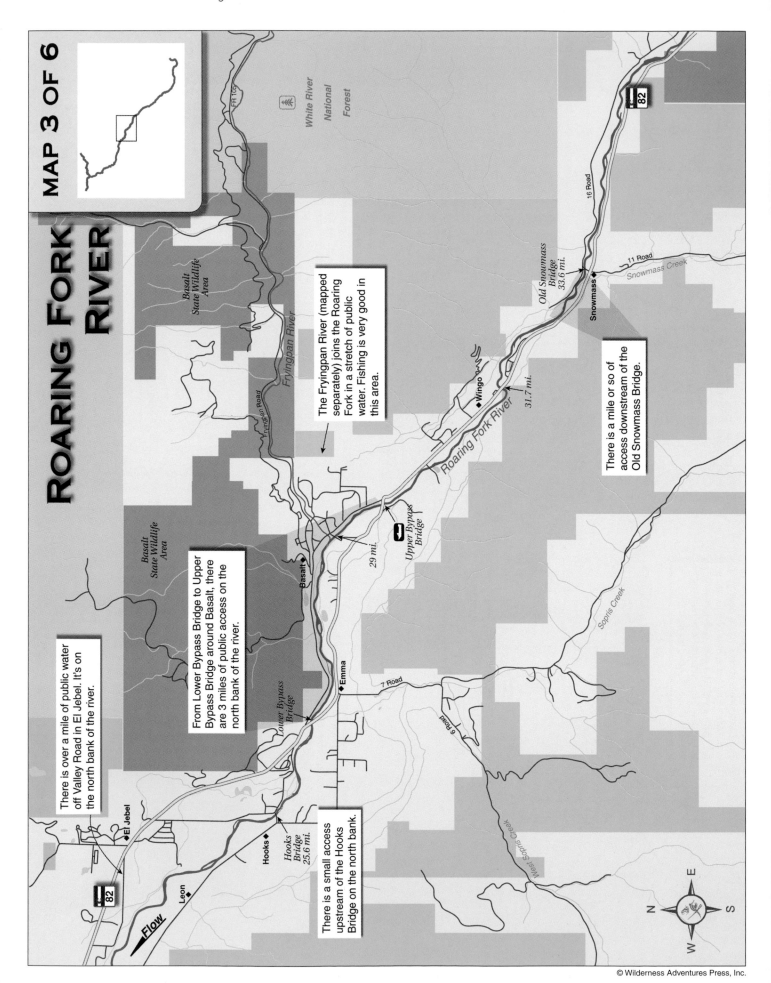

MAP 3 OF 6

ROARING FORK RIVER

White River National Forest

Basalt State Wildlife Area

Basalt State Wildlife Area

Fryingpan River

Fryingpan Road

FR 105

The Fryingpan River (mapped separately) joins the Roaring Fork in a stretch of public water. Fishing is very good in this area.

There is over a mile of public water off Valley Road in El Jebel. It's on the north bank of the river.

From Lower Bypass Bridge to Upper Bypass Bridge around Basalt, there are 3 miles of public access on the north bank of the river.

Basalt

Lower Bypass Bridge

Upper Bypass Bridge

29 mi.

31.7 mi.

Roaring Fork River

Wingo

Emma

7 Road

6 Road

Sopris Creek

Old Snowmass Bridge 33.6 mi.

16 Road

11 Road

Snowmass Creek

Snowmass

82

There is a mile or so of access downstream of the Old Snowmass Bridge.

There is a small access upstream of the Hooks Bridge on the north bank.

Hooks Bridge 25.6 mi.

Hooks

Leon

El Jebel

82

Flow

West Sopris Creek

N E S W

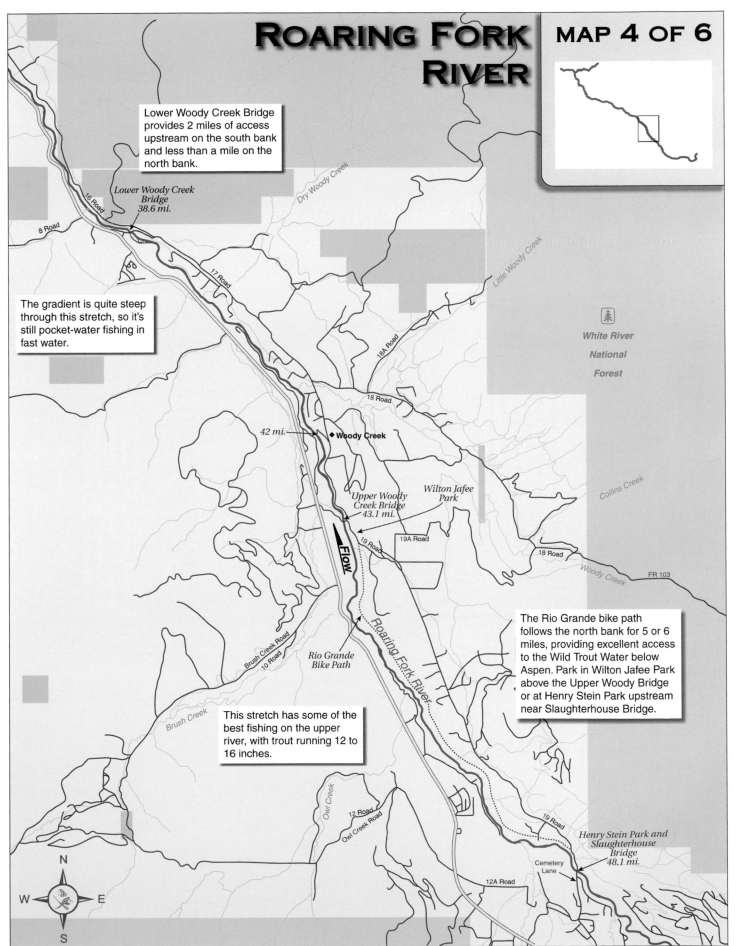

ROARING FORK RIVER

MAP 4 OF 6

Lower Woody Creek Bridge provides 2 miles of access upstream on the south bank and less than a mile on the north bank.

Lower Woody Creek Bridge
38.6 mi.

16 Road

8 Road

Dry Woody Creek

17 Road

The gradient is quite steep through this stretch, so it's still pocket-water fishing in fast water.

18A Road

Little Woody Creek

White River

National

Forest

18 Road

42 mi. ◆ **Woody Creek**

Collins Creek

Upper Woody Creek Bridge 43.1 mi.

Wilton Jafee Park

19A Road

19 Road

18 Road

Woody Creek

FR 103

Flow

Brush Creek Road
10 Road

Rio Grande Bike Path

Roaring Fork River

The Rio Grande bike path follows the north bank for 5 or 6 miles, providing excellent access to the Wild Trout Water below Aspen. Park in Wilton Jafee Park above the Upper Woody Bridge or at Henry Stein Park upstream near Slaughterhouse Bridge.

Brush Creek

This stretch has some of the best fishing on the upper river, with trout running 12 to 16 inches.

Owl Creek

12 Road

Owl Creek Road

19 Road

Henry Stein Park and Slaughterhouse Bridge 48.1 mi.

Cemetery Lane

12A Road

N
W E
S

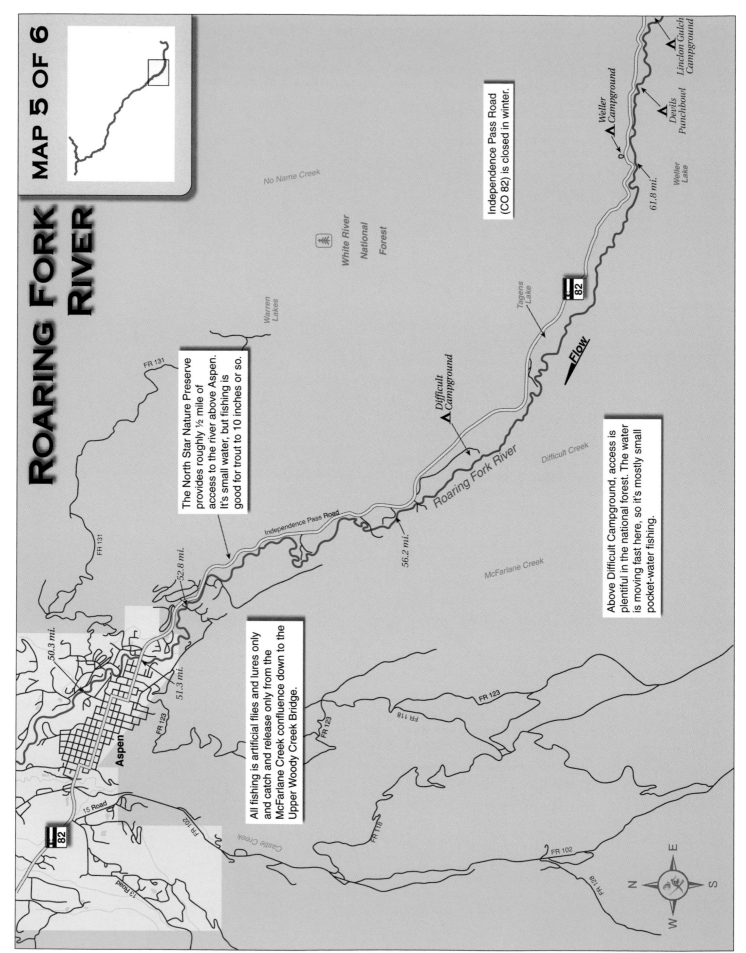

MAP 5 OF 6

ROARING FORK RIVER

No Name Creek

White River National Forest

Warren Lakes

FR 131

FR 131

Independence Pass Road (CO 82) is closed in winter.

Weller Campground

Devils Punchbowl

Lincoln Gulch Campground

0

61.8 mi.

Weller Lake

82

Tagens Lake

Flow

Difficult Campground

Roaring Fork River

Difficult Creek

McFarlane Creek

The North Star Nature Preserve provides roughly ½ mile of access to the river above Aspen. It's small water, but fishing is good for trout to 10 inches or so.

Independence Pass Road

56.2 mi.

52.8 mi.

51.3 mi.

50.3 mi.

Aspen

82

FR 123

FR 123

15 Road

FR 102

Castle Creek

13 Road

FR 123

FR 118

FR 118

FR 102

FR 128

All fishing is artificial flies and lures only and catch and release only from the McFarlane Creek confluence down to the Upper Woody Creek Bridge.

Above Difficult Campground, access is plentiful in the national forest. The water is moving fast here, so it's mostly small pocket-water fishing.

N E S W

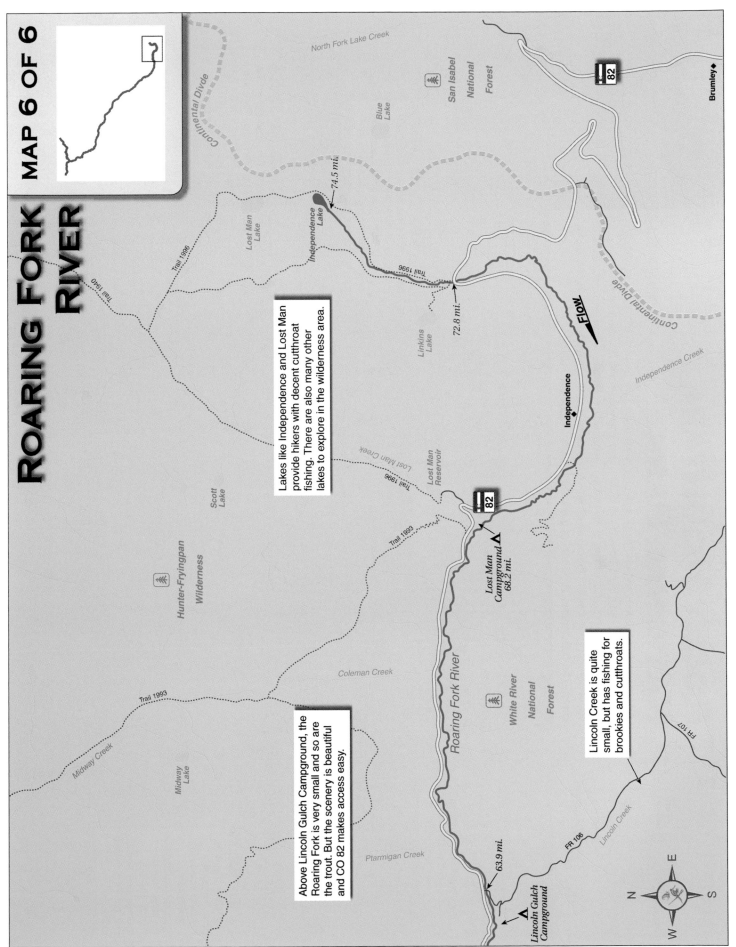

MAP 6 OF 6

ROARING FORK RIVER

Continental Divide

North Fork Lake Creek

San Isabel National Forest

Blue Lake

82

Brumley ◆

Lost Man Lake

74.5 mi.

Independence Lake

Trail 1996

Trail 1940

Trail 1996

72.8 mi.

Linkins Lake

FLOW

Continental Divide

Independence Creek

Lakes like Independence and Lost Man provide hikers with decent cutthroat fishing. There are also many other lakes to explore in the wilderness area.

Scott Lake

Hunter-Fryingpan Wilderness

Lost Man Creek

Trail 1996

Lost Man Reservoir

Independence ◆

Trail 1993

82

Lost Man Campground
68.2 mi.

Coleman Creek

White River National Forest

Trail 1993

Midway Creek

Midway Lake

Roaring Fork River

Above Lincoln Gulch Campground, the Roaring Fork is very small and so are the trout. But the scenery is beautiful and CO 82 makes access easy.

Ptarmigan Creek

63.9 mi.

Lincoln Creek is quite small, but has fishing for brookies and cutthroats.

FR 107

FR 106

Lincoln Creek

Lincoln Creek

Lincoln Gulch Campground

N W S E

© Wilderness Adventures Press, Inc.

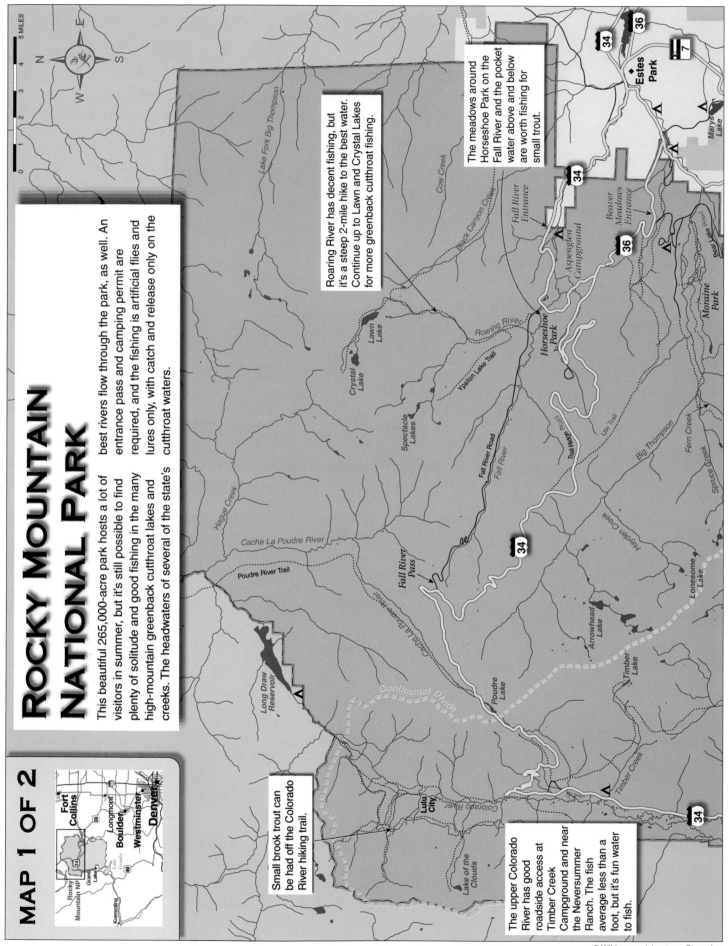

ROCKY MOUNTAIN NATIONAL PARK

This beautiful 265,000-acre park hosts a lot of visitors in summer, but it's still possible to find plenty of solitude and good fishing in the many high-mountain greenback cutthroat lakes and creeks. The headwaters of several of the state's best rivers flow through the park, as well. An entrance pass and camping permit are required, and the fishing is artificial flies and lures only, with catch and release only on the cutthroat waters.

MAP 1 OF 2

Roaring River has decent fishing, but it's a steep 2-mile hike to the best water. Continue up to Lawn and Crystal Lakes for more greenback cutthroat fishing.

The meadows around Horseshoe Park on the Fall River and the pocket water above and below are worth fishing for small trout.

Small brook trout can be had off the Colorado River hiking trail.

The upper Colorado River has good roadside access at Timber Creek Campground and near the Neversummer Ranch. The fish average less than a foot, but it's fun water to fish.

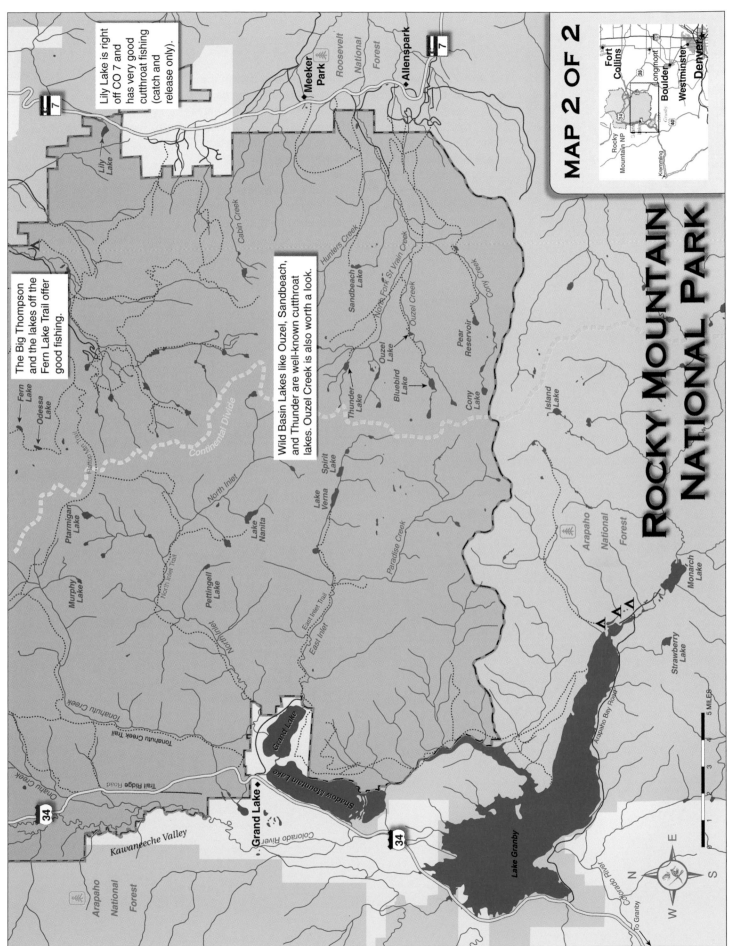

MAP 2 OF 2

ROCKY MOUNTAIN NATIONAL PARK

Lily Lake is right off CO 7 and has very good cutthroat fishing (catch and release only).

The Big Thompson and the lakes off the Fern Lake Trail offer good fishing.

Wild Basin Lakes like Ouzel, Sandbeach, and Thunder are well-known cutthroat lakes. Ouzel Creek is also worth a look.

© Wilderness Adventures Press, Inc.

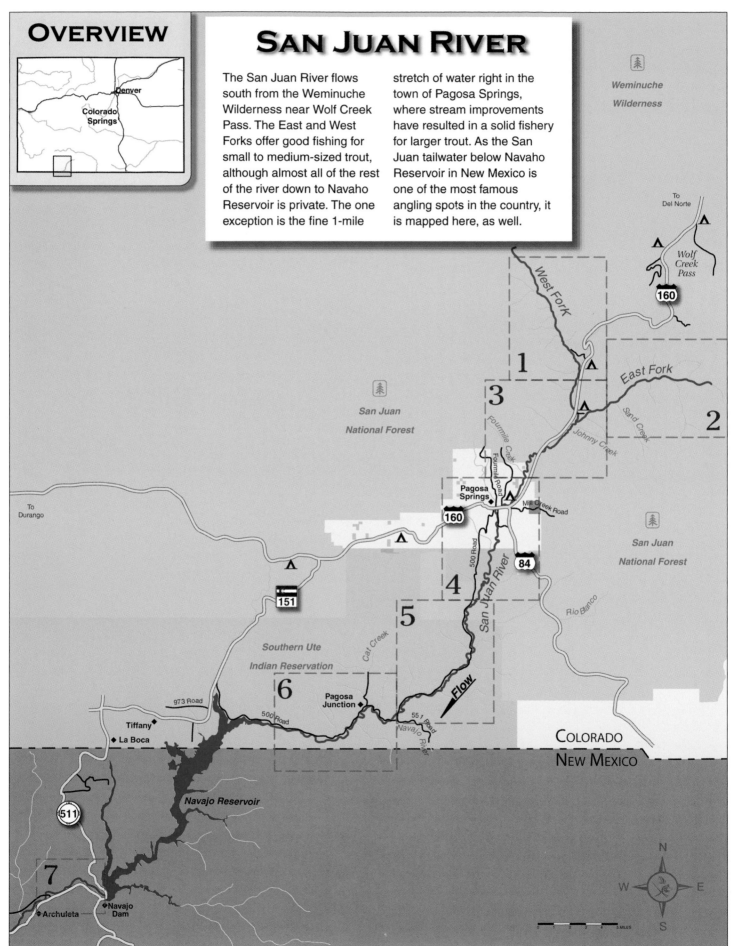

OVERVIEW

SAN JUAN RIVER

The San Juan River flows south from the Weminuche Wilderness near Wolf Creek Pass. The East and West Forks offer good fishing for small to medium-sized trout, although almost all of the rest of the river down to Navaho Reservoir is private. The one exception is the fine 1-mile stretch of water right in the town of Pagosa Springs, where stream improvements have resulted in a solid fishery for larger trout. As the San Juan tailwater below Navaho Reservoir in New Mexico is one of the most famous angling spots in the country, it is mapped here, as well.

Denver
Colorado Springs

Weminuche Wilderness

To Del Norte

Wolf Creek Pass

160

West Fork

East Fork

Sand Creek

1

3

2

San Juan

National Forest

Fourmile Creek

Fourmile Road

Johnny Creek

Pagosa Springs

160

Mill Creek Road

To Durango

San Juan

National Forest

500 Road

84

San Juan River

4

Rio Blanco

151

5

Cat Creek

Flow

Southern Ute

Indian Reservation

6

Pagosa Junction

55 1 Road

Navajo River

973 Road

500 Road

COLORADO

Tiffany

NEW MEXICO

La Boca

Navajo Reservoir

511

7

Archuleta

Navajo Dam

N
W   E
S

0 1 2 3   5 MILES

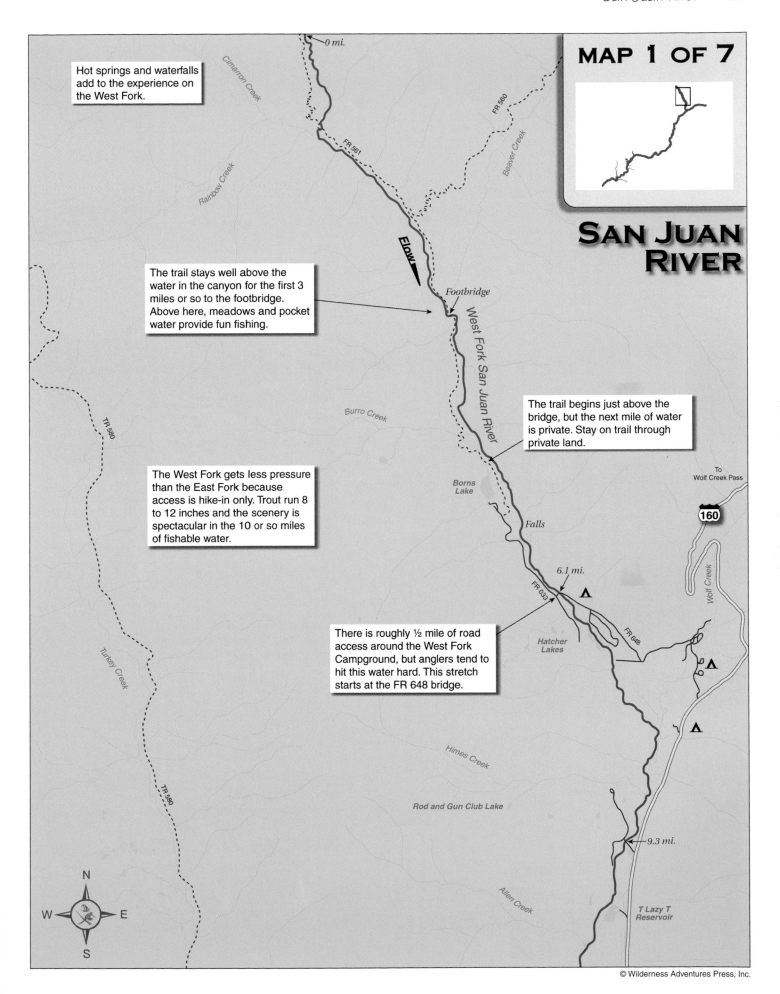

← 0 mi.

Hot springs and waterfalls add to the experience on the West Fork.

Cimarron Creek

FR 560

FR 561

Rainbow Creek

Beaver Creek

MAP 1 OF 7

SAN JUAN RIVER

Flow

Footbridge

The trail stays well above the water in the canyon for the first 3 miles or so to the footbridge. Above here, meadows and pocket water provide fun fishing.

West Fork San Juan River

Burro Creek

TR 580

The trail begins just above the bridge, but the next mile of water is private. Stay on trail through private land.

To Wolf Creek Pass

160

The West Fork gets less pressure than the East Fork because access is hike-in only. Trout run 8 to 12 inches and the scenery is spectacular in the 10 or so miles of fishable water.

Borns Lake

Falls

Wolf Creek

6.1 mi.

FR 033

Hatcher Lakes

FR 648

There is roughly ½ mile of road access around the West Fork Campground, but anglers tend to hit this water hard. This stretch starts at the FR 648 bridge.

Turkey Creek

Himes Creek

TR 590

Rod and Gun Club Lake

9.3 mi.

Allen Creek

T Lazy T Reservoir

N
W E
S

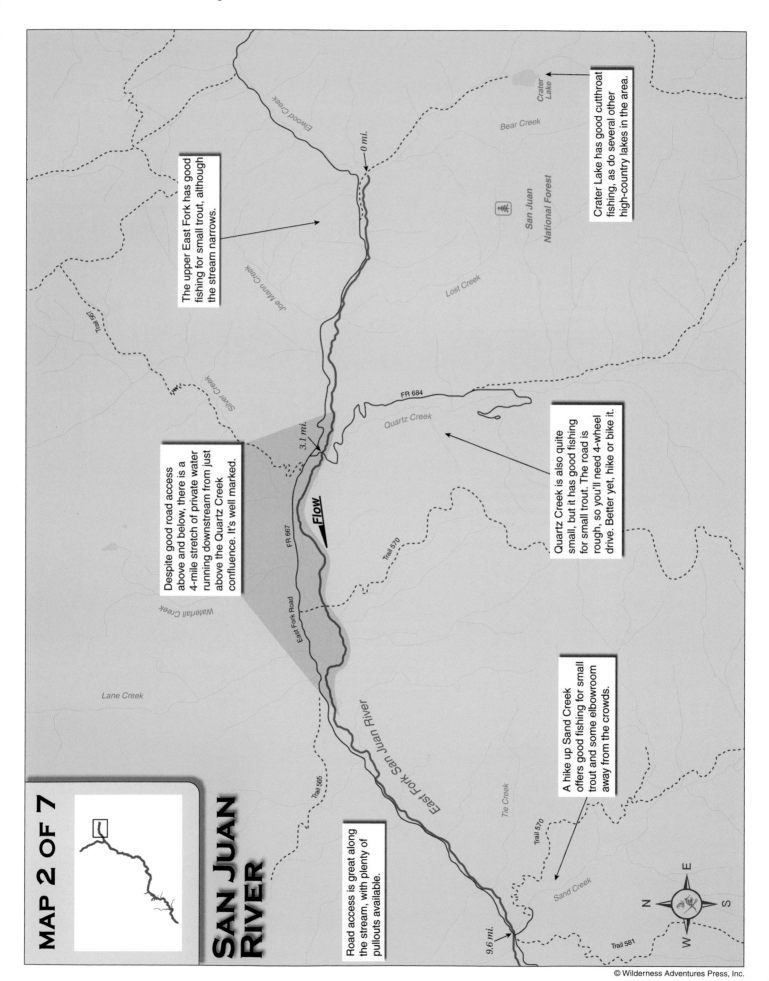

The upper East Fork has good fishing for small trout, although the stream narrows.

Crater Lake has good cutthroat fishing, as do several other high-country lakes in the area.

Quartz Creek is also quite small, but it has good fishing for small trout. The road is rough, so you'll need 4-wheel drive. Better yet, hike or bike it.

Despite good road access above and below, there is a 4-mile stretch of private water running downstream from just above the Quartz Creek confluence. It's well marked.

A hike up Sand Creek offers good fishing for small trout and some elbowroom away from the crowds.

Road access is great along the stream, with plenty of pullouts available.

MAP 2 OF 7

SAN JUAN RIVER

© Wilderness Adventures Press, Inc.

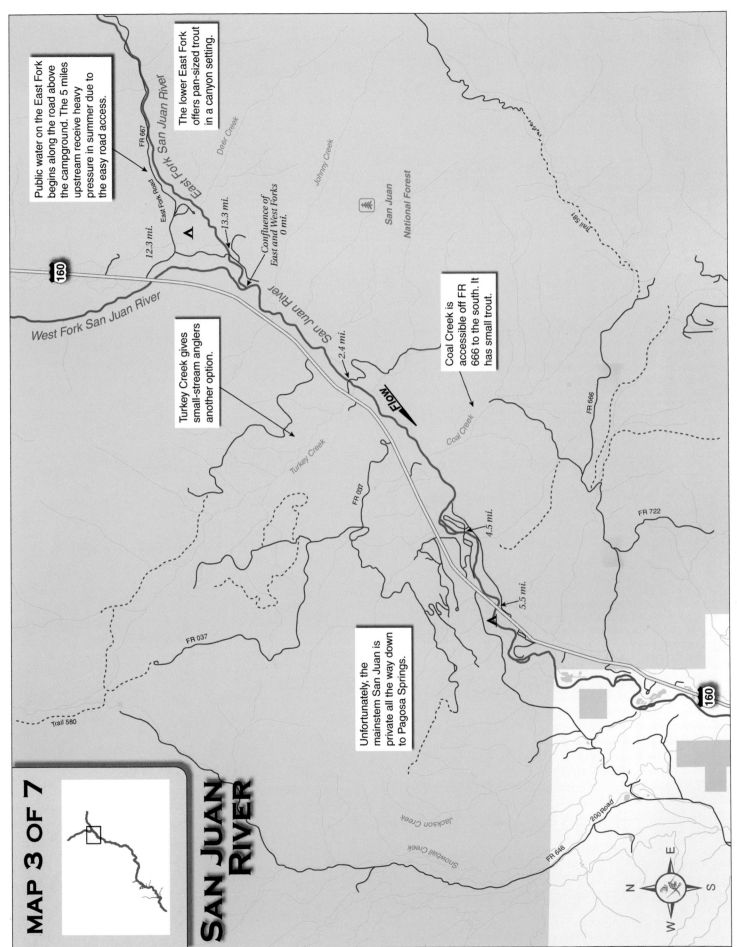

Public water on the East Fork begins along the road above the campground. The 5 miles upstream receive heavy pressure in summer due to the easy road access.

The lower East Fork offers pan-sized trout in a canyon setting.

East Fork San Juan River

FR 667

Deer Creek

Johnny Creek

San Juan National Forest

Trail 591

12.3 mi.

13.3 mi.

160

Confluence of East and West Forks 0 mi.

West Fork San Juan River

San Juan River

2.4 mi.

FLOW

Coal Creek is accessible off FR 666 to the south. It has small trout.

Coal Creek

FR 666

Turkey Creek gives small-stream anglers another option.

Turkey Creek

FR 037

FR 722

4.5 mi.

5.5 mi.

FR 037

Trail 580

Unfortunately, the mainstem San Juan is private all the way down to Pagosa Springs.

160

Jackson Creek

Snowball Creek

FR 646

200 Road

MAP 3 OF 7

SAN JUAN RIVER

N E S W

© Wilderness Adventures Press, Inc.

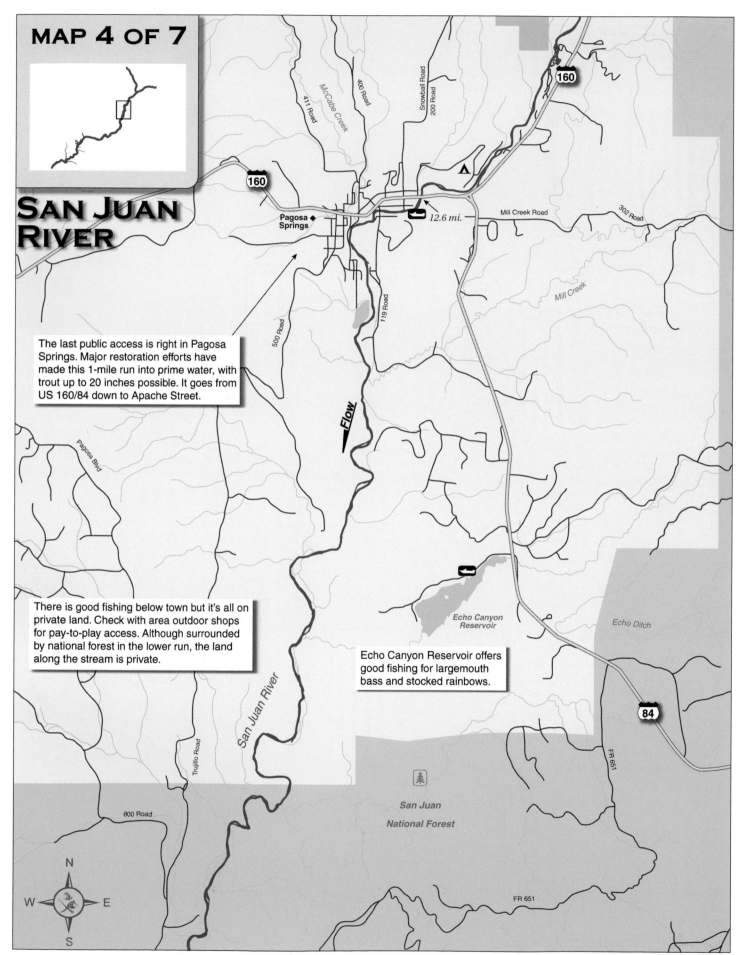

MAP **4** OF **7**

SAN JUAN RIVER

The last public access is right in Pagosa Springs. Major restoration efforts have made this 1-mile run into prime water, with trout up to 20 inches possible. It goes from US 160/84 down to Apache Street.

There is good fishing below town but it's all on private land. Check with area outdoor shops for pay-to-play access. Although surrounded by national forest in the lower run, the land along the stream is private.

Echo Canyon Reservoir offers good fishing for largemouth bass and stocked rainbows.

160

160

Pagosa Springs

12.6 mi.

Mill Creek Road

302 Road

Mill Creek

McCabe Creek

400 Road

411 Road

Snowball Road

200 Road

500 Road

719 Road

Flow

Echo Canyon Reservoir

Echo Ditch

84

FR 651

San Juan River

Trujillo Road

800 Road

San Juan National Forest

Pagosa Blvd

FR 651

N
W E
S

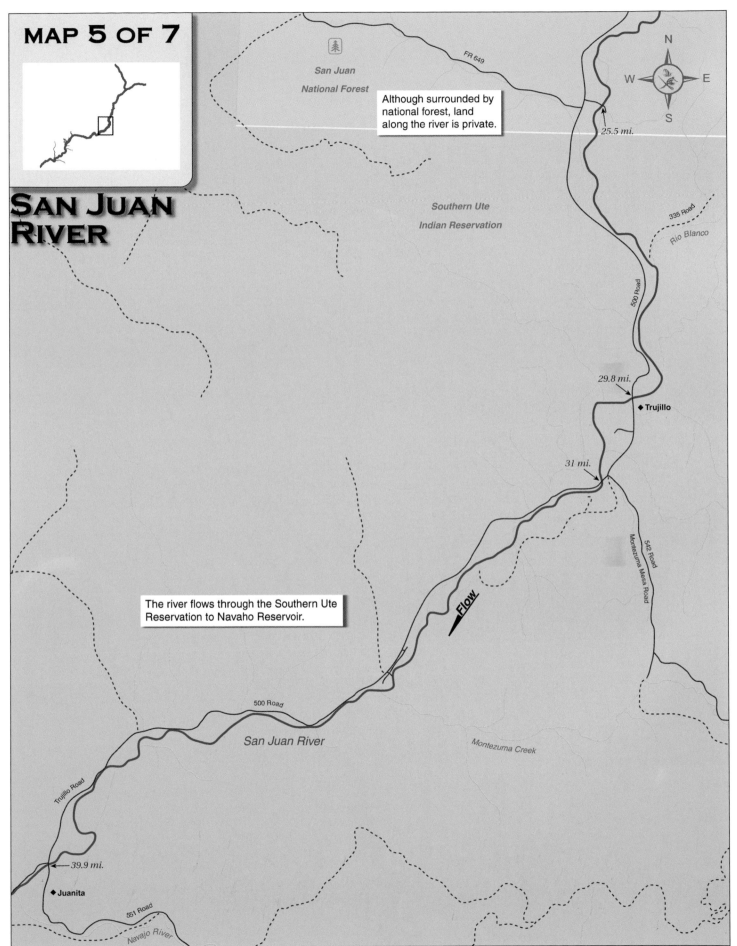

MAP 5 OF 7

SAN JUAN RIVER

San Juan
National Forest

FR 649

Although surrounded by
national forest, land
along the river is private.

25.5 mi.

Southern Ute
Indian Reservation

335 Road

Rio Blanco

500 Road

29.8 mi.

◆ Trujillo

31 mi.

542 Road

Montezuma Mesa Road

The river flows through the Southern Ute
Reservation to Navaho Reservoir.

Flow

500 Road

San Juan River

Montezuma Creek

Trujillo Road

39.9 mi.

◆ Juanita

551 Road

Navajo River

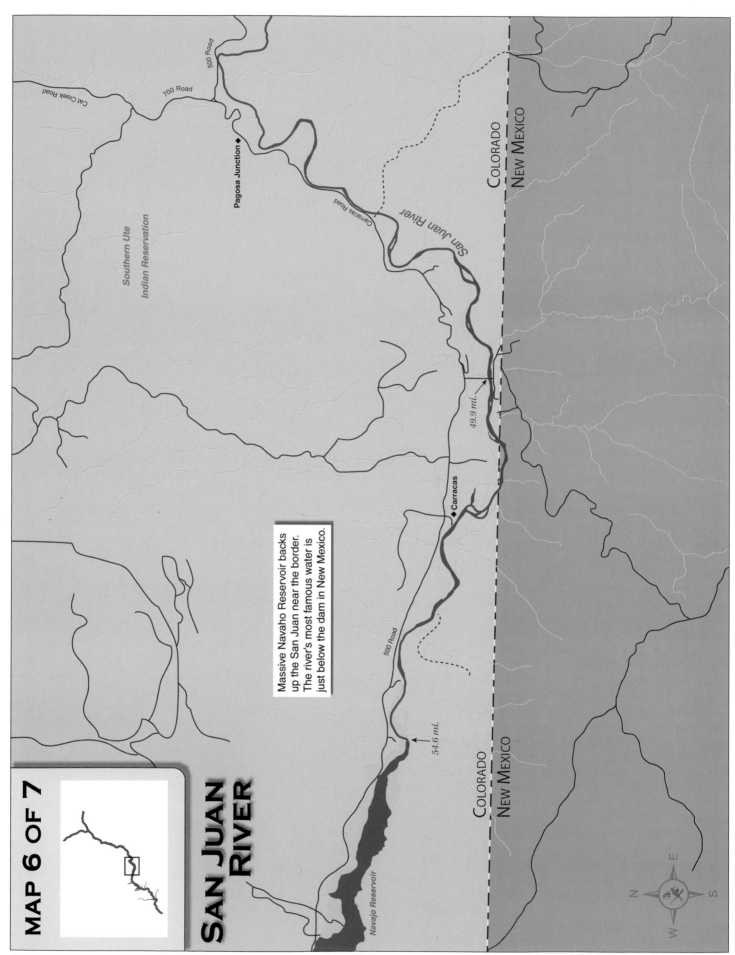

MAP 6 OF 7

SAN JUAN RIVER

Massive Navaho Reservoir backs up the San Juan near the border. The river's most famous water is just below the dam in New Mexico.

500 Road

700 Road

Cat Creek Road

◆ Pagosa Junction

Southern Ute
Indian Reservation

Carracas Road

San Juan River

COLORADO
NEW MEXICO

49.9 mi.

◆ Carracas

500 Road

54.6 mi.

COLORADO
NEW MEXICO

Navajo Reservoir

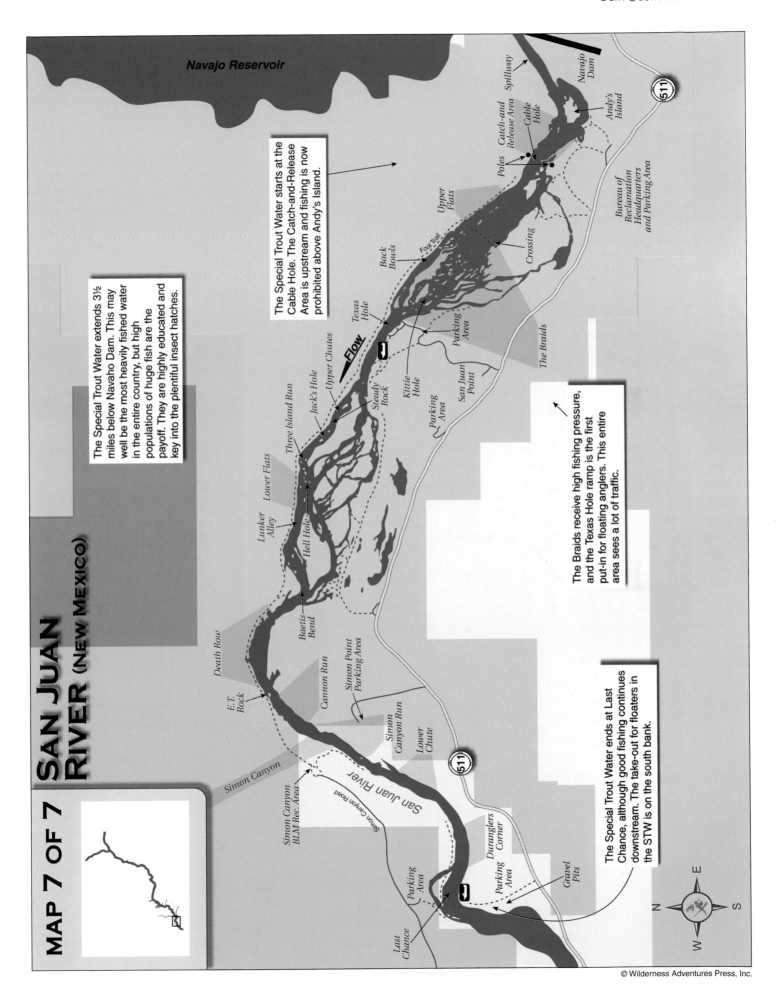

MAP 7 OF 7 SAN JUAN RIVER (NEW MEXICO)

The Special Trout Water extends 3½ miles below Navaho Dam. This may well be the most heavily fished water in the entire country, but high populations of huge fish are the payoff. They are highly educated and key into the plentiful insect hatches.

The Special Trout Water starts at the Cable Hole. The Catch-and-Release Area is upstream and fishing is now prohibited above Andy's Island.

The Braids receive high fishing pressure, and the Texas Hole ramp is the first put-in for floating anglers. This entire area sees a lot of traffic.

The Special Trout Water ends at Last Chance, although good fishing continues downstream. The take-out for floaters is the STW is on the south bank.

Navajo Reservoir

Navajo Dam

Spillway

Catch-and-Release Area

Cable Hole

Andy's Island

Poles

Bureau of Reclamation Headquarters and Parking Area

Upper Flats

Crossing

Back Bowls

Foot Trail

The Braids

Texas Hole

Parking Area

Flow

Upper Chutes

Jack's Hole

Steady Rock

Kittie Hole

Parking Area

San Juan Point

Three Island Run

Lower Flats

Lunker Alley

Hell Hole

Baetis Bend

Death Row

E.T. Rock

Cannon Run

Simon Point Parking Area

Simon Canyon Run

Lower Chute

Simon Canyon

Simon Canyon BLM Rec. Area

Simon Canyon Road

San Juan River

Duranglers Corner

Parking Area

Gravel Pits

Last Chance

Parking Area

511

511

N
E
W
S

© Wilderness Adventures Press, Inc.

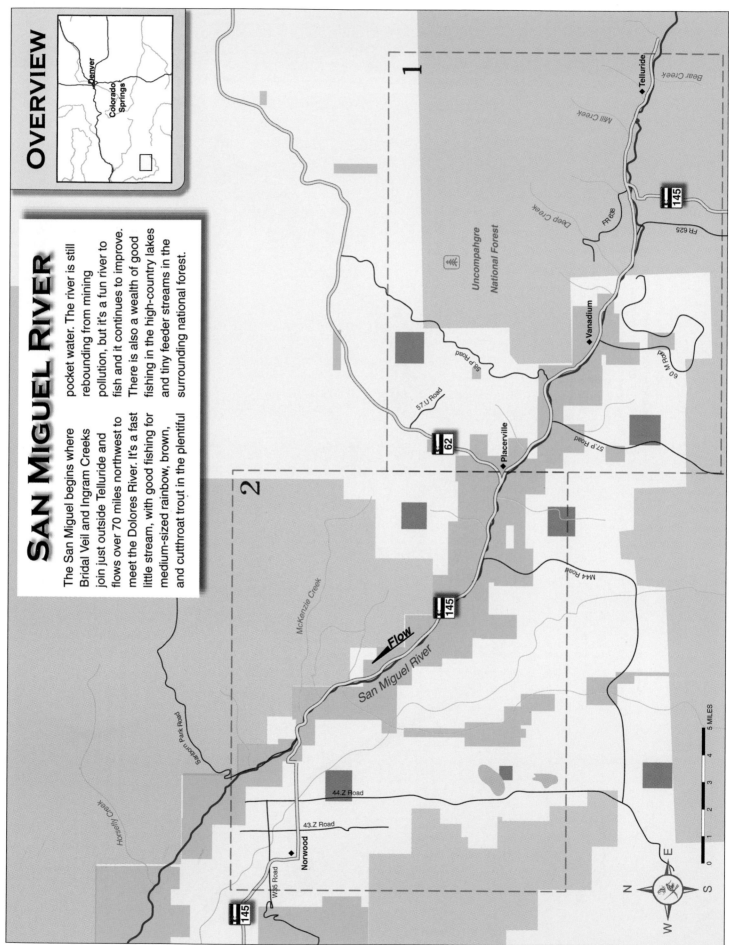

San Miguel River

The San Miguel begins where Bridal Veil and Ingram Creeks join just outside Telluride and flows over 70 miles northwest to meet the Dolores River. It's a fast little stream, with good fishing for medium-sized rainbow, brown, and cutthroat trout in the plentiful pocket water. The river is still rebounding from mining pollution, but it's a fun river to fish and it continues to improve. There is also a wealth of good fishing in the high-country lakes and tiny feeder streams in the surrounding national forest.

Overview

Denver
Colorado Springs

© Wilderness Adventures Press, Inc.

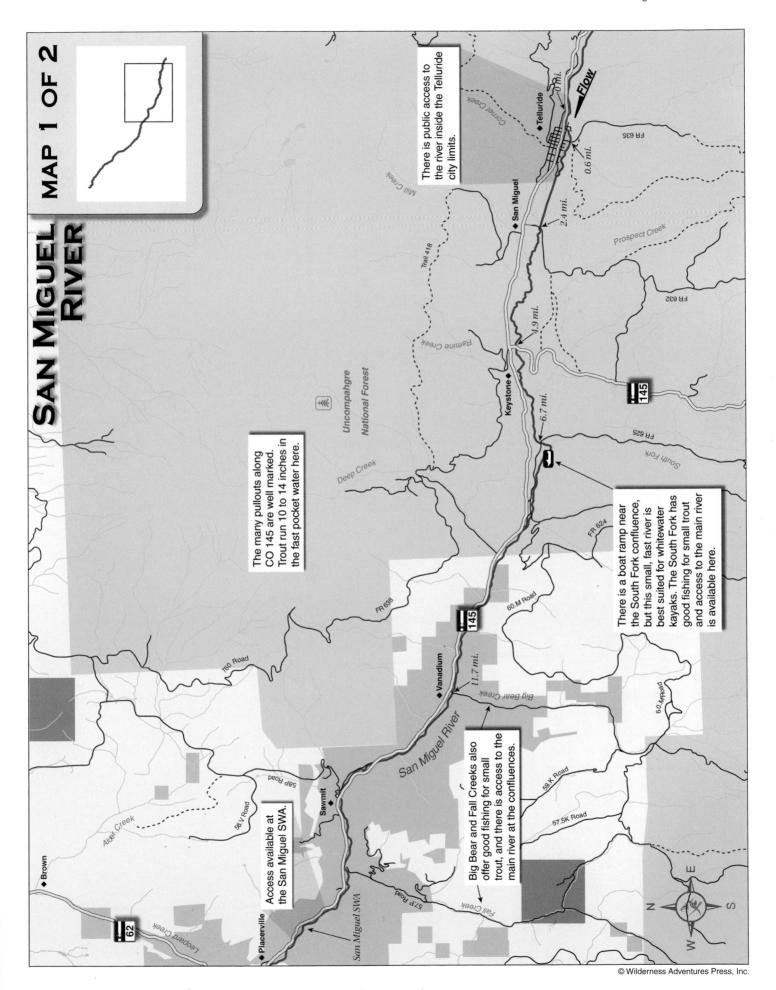

SAN MIGUEL RIVER

MAP 1 OF 2

There is public access to the river inside the Telluride city limits.

The many pullouts along CO 145 are well marked. Trout run 10 to 14 inches in the fast pocket water here.

There is a boat ramp near the South Fork confluence, but this small, fast river is best suited for whitewater kayaks. The South Fork has good fishing for small trout and access to the main river is available here.

Access available at the San Miguel SWA.

Big Bear and Fall Creeks also offer good fishing for small trout, and there is access to the main river at the confluences.

Uncompahgre National Forest

Flow

Telluride

San Miguel

Keystone

Vanadium

Sawmit

Brown

Placerville

San Miguel SWA

San Miguel River

Deep Creek

Mill Creek

Remine Creek

Prospect Creek

Comet Creek

Big Bear Creek

Fall Creek

Alder Creek

Leopard Creek

South Fork

Trail 418

FR 635

FR 632

FR 625

FR 624

FR 638

T60 Road

56 V Road

58P Road

57.P Road

57.5K Road

59.K Road

60.0.M Road

60.M Road

0 mi.
0.6 mi.
2.4 mi.
4.9 mi.
6.7 mi.
11.7 mi.

145
62

© Wilderness Adventures Press, Inc.

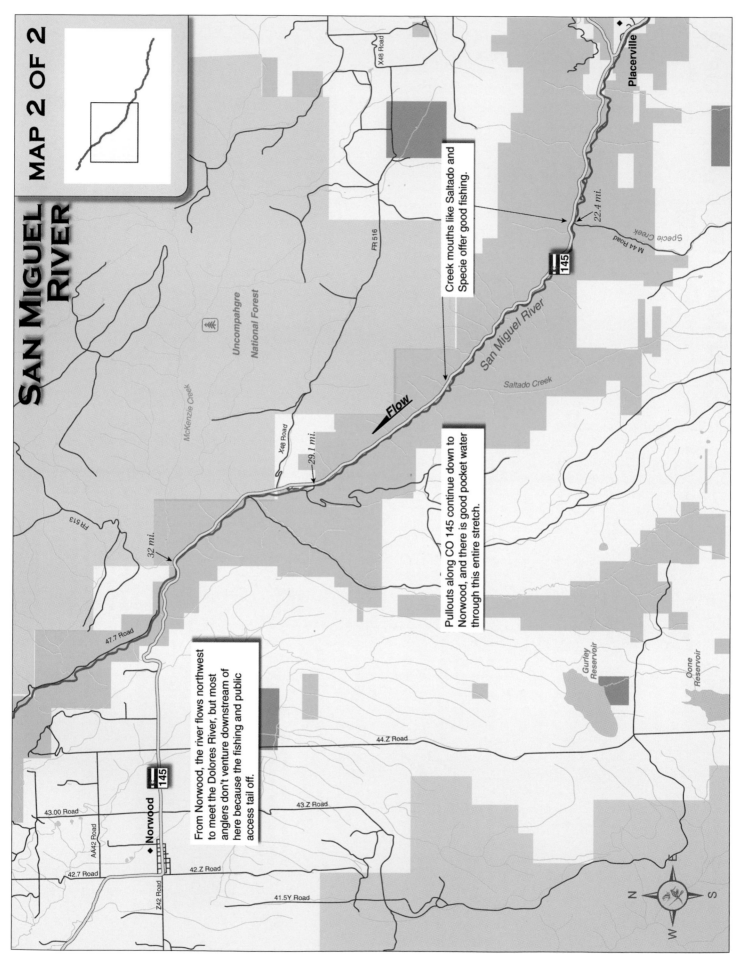

SAN MIGUEL RIVER

MAP 2 OF 2

Creek mouths like Saltado and Specie offer good fishing.

Pullouts along CO 145 continue down to Norwood, and there is good pocket water through this entire stretch.

From Norwood, the river flows northwest to meet the Dolores River, but most anglers don't venture downstream of here because the fishing and public access tail off.

22.4 mi.

29.1 mi.

32 mi.

Flow

San Miguel River

Uncompahgre National Forest

McKenzie Creek

Saltado Creek

Specie Creek

Placerville

Norwood

Gurley Reservoir

Oone Reservoir

X48 Road

FR 516

X48 Road

FR 513

M 44 Road

47.7 Road

44.Z Road

43.00 Road

AA42 Road

42.7 Road

Z42 Road

42.Z Road

41.5Y Road

43.Z Road

145

145

© Wilderness Adventures Press, Inc.

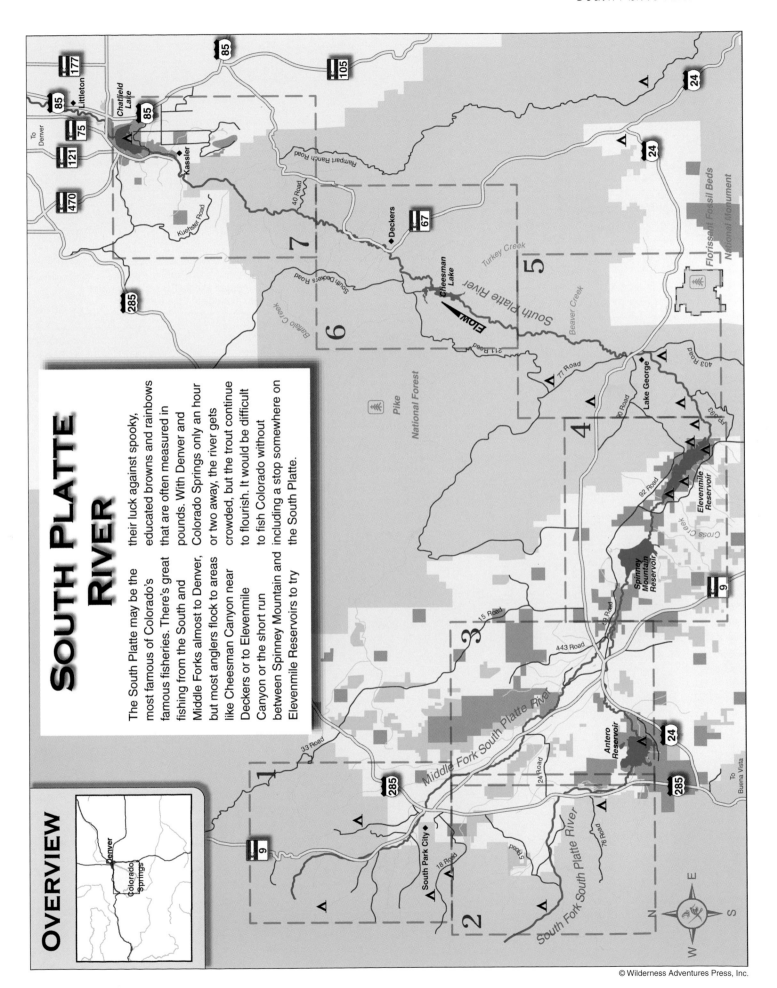

OVERVIEW

SOUTH PLATTE RIVER

The South Platte may be the most famous of Colorado's famous fisheries. There's great fishing from the South and Middle Forks almost to Denver, but most anglers flock to areas like Cheesman Canyon near Deckers or to Elevenmile Canyon or the short run between Spinney Mountain and Elevenmile Reservoirs to try their luck against spooky, educated browns and rainbows that are often measured in pounds. With Denver and Colorado Springs only an hour or two away, the river gets crowded, but the trout continue to flourish. It would be difficult to fish Colorado without including a stop somewhere on the South Platte.

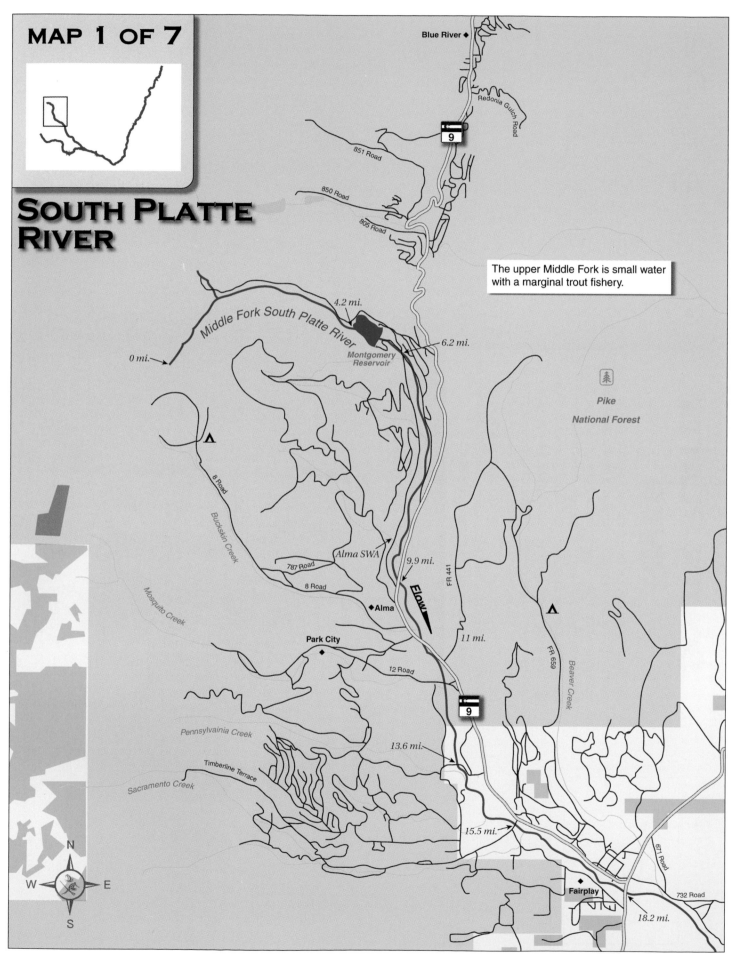

MAP 1 OF 7

SOUTH PLATTE RIVER

Blue River ◆

Redonia Gulch Road

9

851 Road

850 Road

805 Road

The upper Middle Fork is small water with a marginal trout fishery.

Middle Fork South Platte River

4.2 mi.

6.2 mi.

Montgomery Reservoir

0 mi.

Pike

National Forest

8 Road

Buckskin Creek

Alma SWA

9.9 mi.

787 Road

8 Road

FR 441

flow

Mosquito Creek

◆ Alma

11 mi.

Park City

◆

FR 659

Beaver Creek

12 Road

Pennsylvainia Creek

9

13.6 mi.

Timberline Terrace

Sacramento Creek

15.5 mi.

N
W E
S

Fairplay ◆

671 Road

732 Road

18.2 mi.

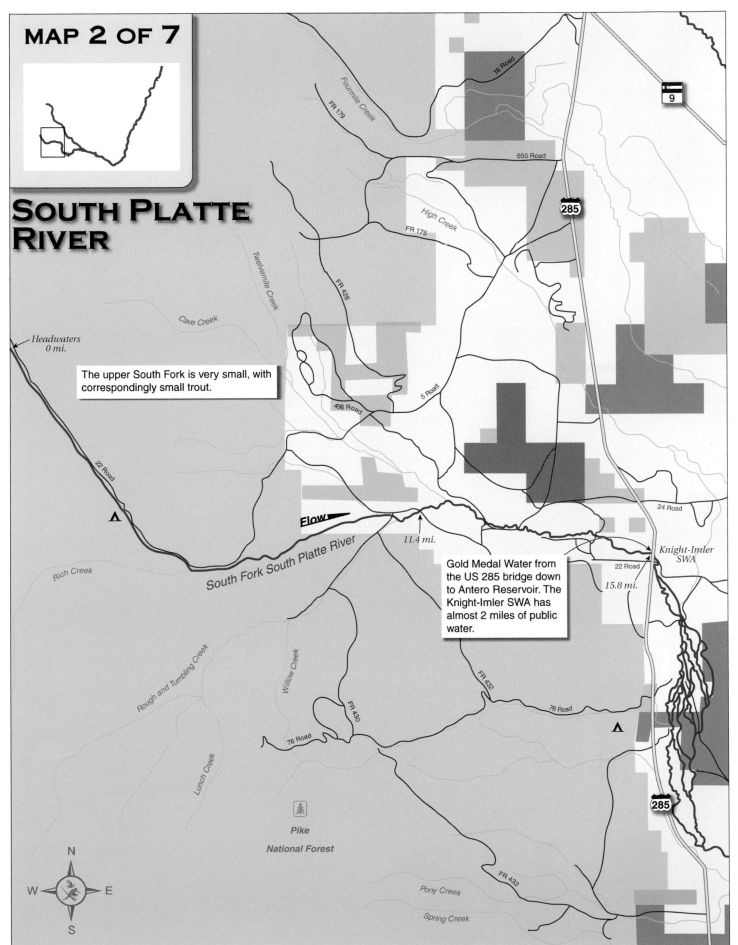

MAP 2 OF 7

SOUTH PLATTE RIVER

Headwaters
0 mi.

The upper South Fork is very small, with correspondingly small trout.

Flow

11.4 mi.

South Fork South Platte River

Gold Medal Water from the US 285 bridge down to Antero Reservoir. The Knight-Imler SWA has almost 2 miles of public water.

Knight-Imler SWA

15.8 mi.

Fourmile Creek

FR 179

18 Road

650 Road

High Creek

FR 175

Twelvemile Creek

Cave Creek

FR 426

5 Road

456 Road

22 Road

Rich Creek

Rough and Tumbling Creek

Willow Creek

FR 430

76 Road

Lunch Creek

FR 432

76 Road

24 Road

22 Road

Pike

National Forest

FR 433

Pony Creek

Spring Creek

N
W   E
S

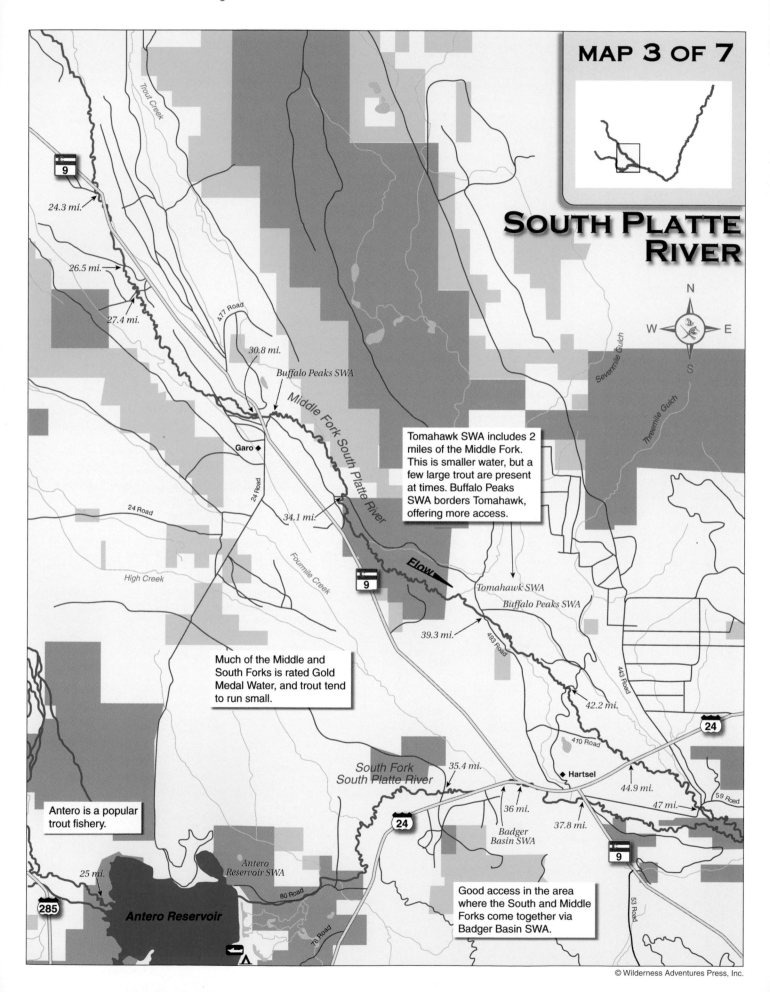

MAP 3 OF 7

SOUTH PLATTE RIVER

Trout Creek

9
24.3 mi.

26.5 mi.

27.4 mi.

30.8 mi.

Buffalo Peaks SWA

IX7 Road

Middle Fork South Platte River

Garo ◆

24 Road

24 Road

High Creek

Fourmile Creek

34.1 mi.

9

Flow

Sevenmile Gulch

Threemile Gulch

Tomahawk SWA includes 2 miles of the Middle Fork. This is smaller water, but a few large trout are present at times. Buffalo Peaks SWA borders Tomahawk, offering more access.

Tomahawk SWA

Buffalo Peaks SWA

39.3 mi.

493 Road

443 Road

42.2 mi.

Much of the Middle and South Forks is rated Gold Medal Water, and trout tend to run small.

24

410 Road

South Fork South Platte River

35.4 mi.

44.9 mi.

47 mi.

59 Road

Hartsel ◆

36 mi.

37.8 mi.

Antero is a popular trout fishery.

24

Badger Basin SWA

9

Antero Reservoir SWA

25 mi.

80 Road

285

Antero Reservoir

78 Road

Good access in the area where the South and Middle Forks come together via Badger Basin SWA.

53 Road

© Wilderness Adventures Press, Inc.

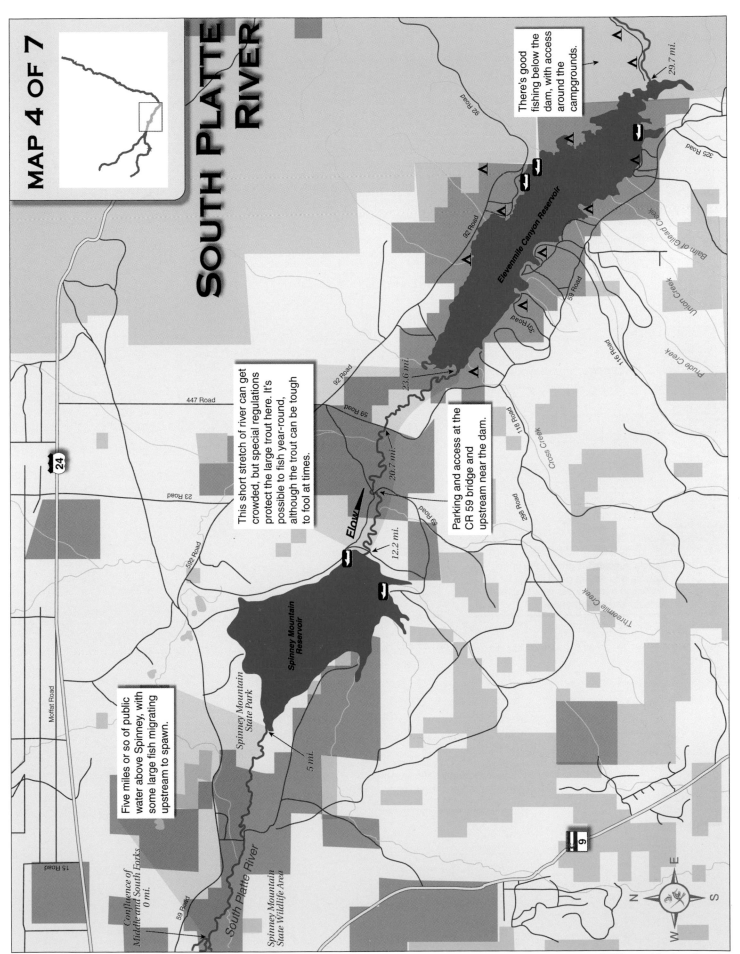

MAP 4 OF 7

SOUTH PLATTE RIVER

There's good fishing below the dam, with access around the campgrounds.

29.7 mi.

Elevenmile Canyon Reservoir

92 Road

325 Road

Balm of Gilead Creek

Union Creek

Prude Creek

59 Road

39 Road

116 Road

Cross Creek

Threemile Creek

23.6 mi.

This short stretch of river can get crowded, but special regulations protect the large trout here. It's possible to fish year-round, although the trout can be tough to fool at times.

447 Road

92 Road

59 Road

20.7 mi.

Elow

12.2 mi.

59 Road

Parking and access at the CR 59 bridge and upstream near the dam.

298 Road

11B Road

9

24

23 Road

592 Road

Spinney Mountain Reservoir

Spinney Mountain State Park

5 mi.

Moffat Road

15 Road

59 Road

Five miles or so of public water above Spinney, with some large fish migrating upstream to spawn.

Confluence of Middle and South Forks
0 mi.

South Platte River

Spinney Mountain State Wildlife Area

N
E
S
W

© Wilderness Adventures Press, Inc.

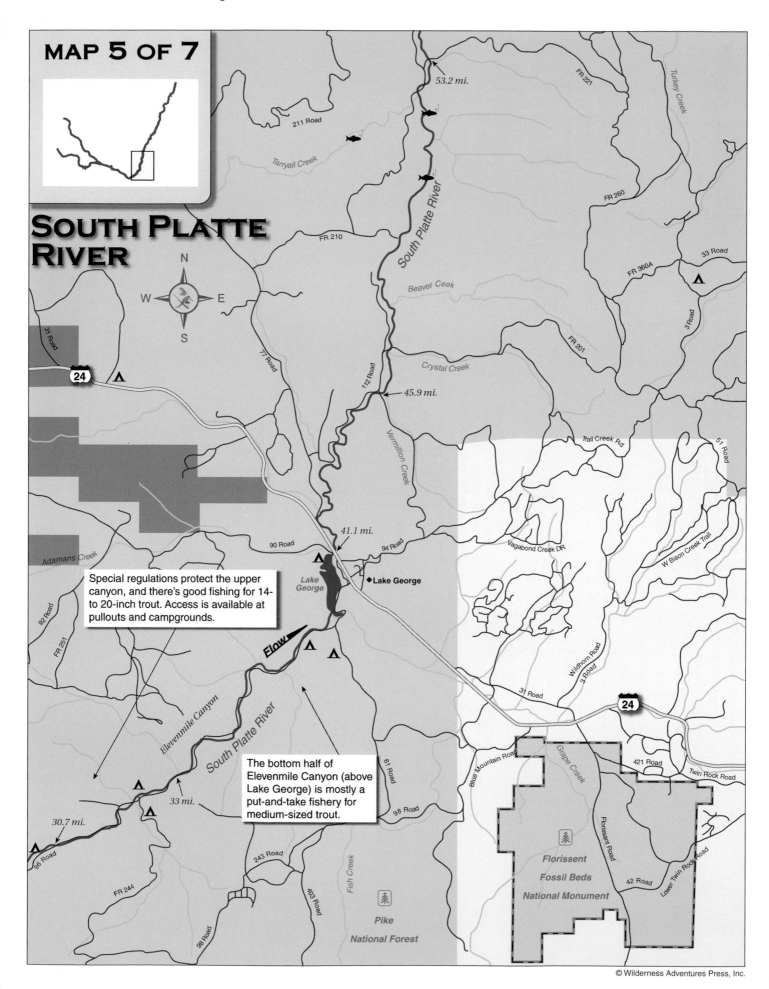

MAP 5 OF 7

SOUTH PLATTE RIVER

53.2 mi.

211 Road

Tarryall Creek

FR 221

Turkey Creek

FR 260

South Platte River

Beaver Ceek

FR 210

FR 360A

33 Road

FR 201

3 Road

77 Road

Crystal Creek

112 Road

45.9 mi.

31 Road

24

Vermillion Creek

94 Road

Trail Creek Rd

51 Road

90 Road

41.1 mi.

Lake George

◆ Lake George

Vagabond Creek DR

W Bison Creek Trail

Special regulations protect the upper canyon, and there's good fishing for 14- to 20-inch trout. Access is available at pullouts and campgrounds.

Adamans Creek

92 Road

FR 251

Flow

Wildhorn Road

3 Road

31 Road

24

Elevenmile Canyon

South Platte River

The bottom half of Elevenmile Canyon (above Lake George) is mostly a put-and-take fishery for medium-sized trout.

61 Road

Blue Mountain Road

Grape Creek

421 Road

Twin Rock Road

33 mi.

98 Road

30.7 mi.

96 Road

243 Road

Fish Creek

Florissant

FR 244

98 Road

403 Road

Fossil Beds

42 Road

Florissant Road

Lower Twin Rock Road

National Monument

Pike

National Forest

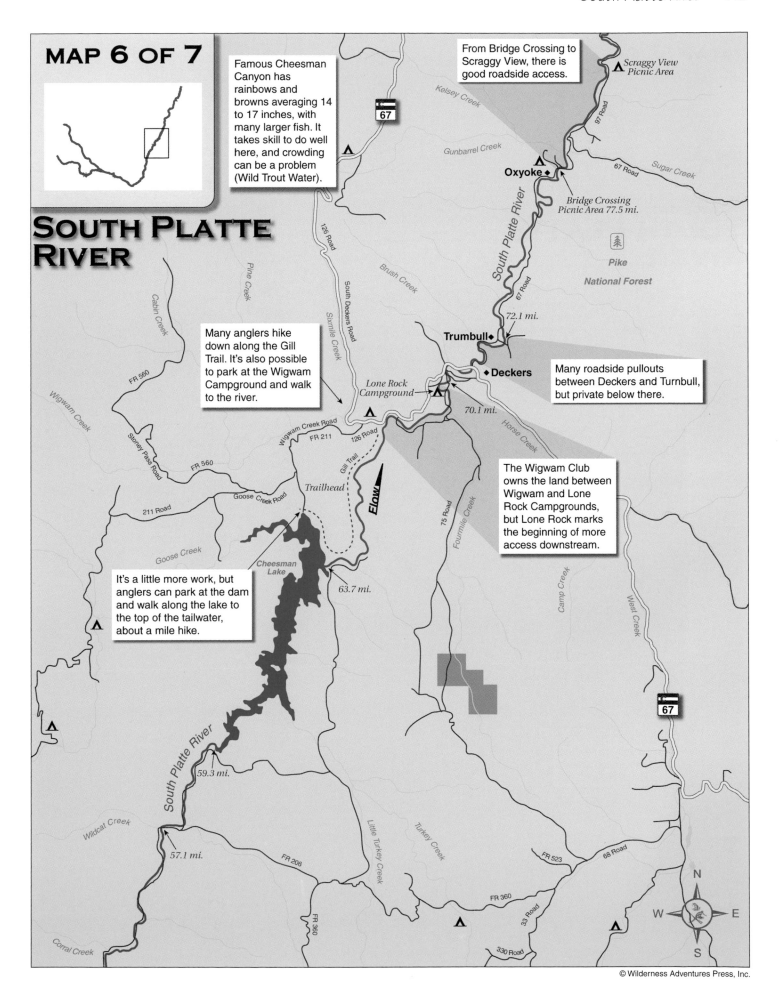

MAP 6 OF 7

SOUTH PLATTE RIVER

Famous Cheesman Canyon has rainbows and browns averaging 14 to 17 inches, with many larger fish. It takes skill to do well here, and crowding can be a problem (Wild Trout Water).

From Bridge Crossing to Scraggy View, there is good roadside access.

Many anglers hike down along the Gill Trail. It's also possible to park at the Wigwam Campground and walk to the river.

Many roadside pullouts between Deckers and Turnbull, but private below there.

The Wigwam Club owns the land between Wigwam and Lone Rock Campgrounds, but Lone Rock marks the beginning of more access downstream.

It's a little more work, but anglers can park at the dam and walk along the lake to the top of the tailwater, about a mile hike.

Scraggy View Picnic Area

Kelsey Creek

67

Gunbarrel Creek

97 Road

67 Road

Sugar Creek

Oxyoke ◆

Bridge Crossing Picnic Area 77.5 mi.

126 Road

Pine Creek

Brush Creek

South Deckers Road

Sixmile Creek

South Platte River

🌲

Pike National Forest

72.1 mi.

Trumbull ◆

Cabin Creek

Lone Rock Campground

◆ Deckers

70.1 mi.

Horse Creek

FR 560

Wigwam Creek

Wigwam Creek Road

FR 211

126 Road

Gill Trail

Flow

Stoney Pass Road

FR 560

Goose Creek Road

Trailhead

Camp Creek

West Creek

211 Road

Goose Creek

Cheesman Lake

63.7 mi.

75 Road

Fourmile Creek

67

South Platte River

59.3 mi.

Wildcat Creek

57.1 mi.

FR 206

Little Turkey Creek

Turkey Creek

FR 523

68 Road

FR 360

33 Road

Corral Creek

FR 360

330 Road

N
W E
S

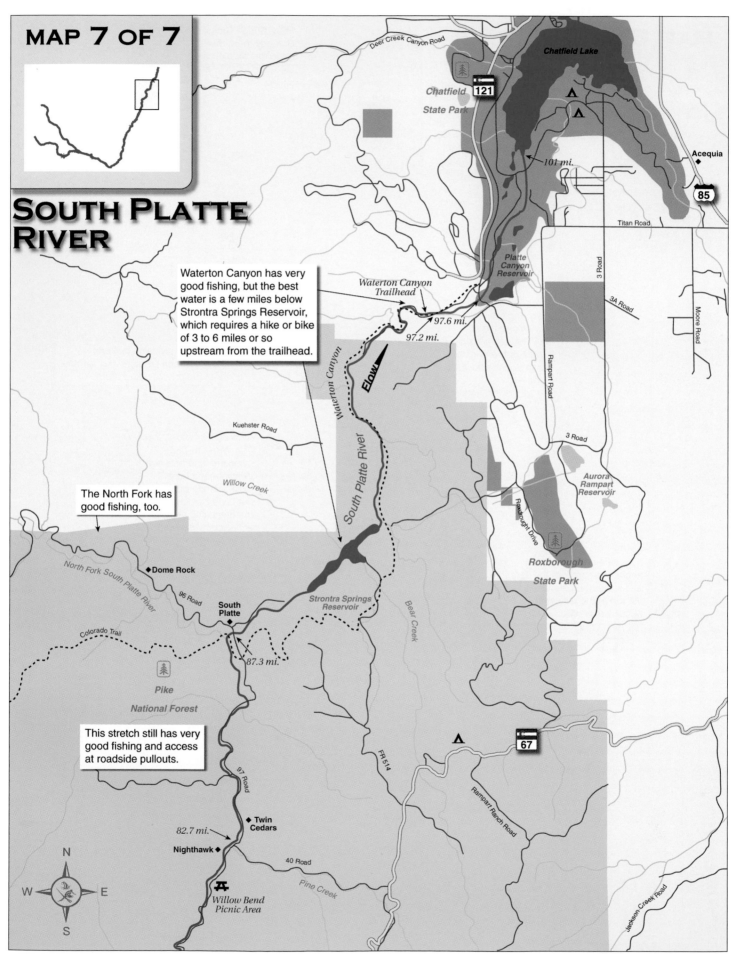

MAP **7** OF **7**

SOUTH PLATTE RIVER

Chatfield Lake

Acequia

Chatfield State Park

101 mi.

Titan Road

Waterton Canyon has very good fishing, but the best water is a few miles below Strontra Springs Reservoir, which requires a hike or bike of 3 to 6 miles or so upstream from the trailhead.

Waterton Canyon Trailhead

97.6 mi.

97.2 mi.

Platte Canyon Reservoir

3 Road

3A Road

Moore Road

Deer Creek Canyon Road

121

85

Flow

Waterton Canyon

Rampart Road

Kuehster Road

Willow Creek

South Platte River

3 Road

Aurora Rampart Reservoir

The North Fork has good fishing, too.

Roxborough State Park

Roxborough Drive

North Fork South Platte River

Dome Rock

96 Road

South Platte

Strontra Springs Reservoir

Bear Creek

Colorado Trail

87.3 mi.

Pike

National Forest

This stretch still has very good fishing and access at roadside pullouts.

67

FR 514

97 Road

Twin Cedars

82.7 mi.

Nighthawk

40 Road

Rampart Ranch Road

Jackson Creek Road

N

W   E

S

Willow Bend Picnic Area

Pine Creek

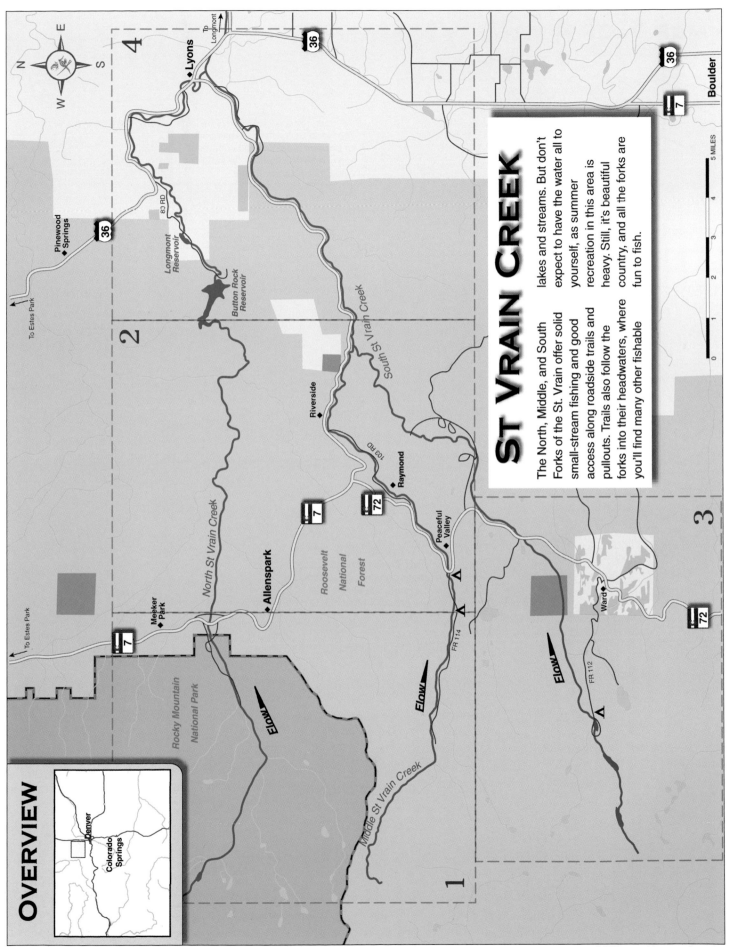

St Vrain Creek

The North, Middle, and South Forks of the St. Vrain offer solid small-stream fishing and good access along roadside trails and pullouts. Trails also follow the forks into their headwaters, where you'll find many other fishable lakes and streams. But don't expect to have the water all to yourself, as summer recreation in this area is heavy. Still, it's beautiful country, and all the forks are fun to fish.

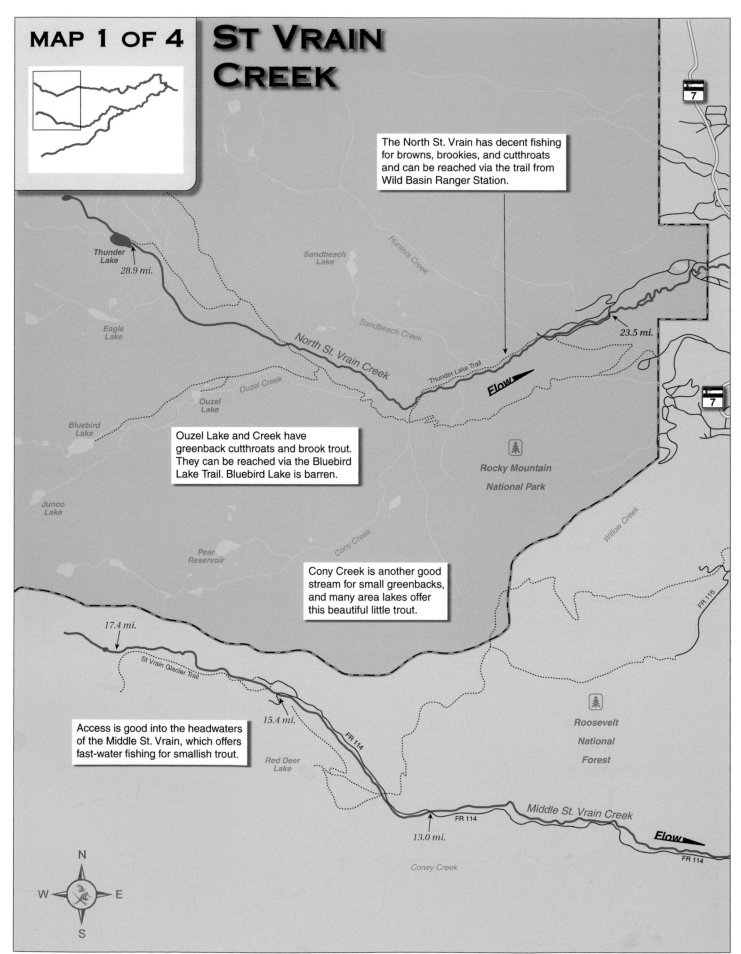

MAP 1 OF 4 ST VRAIN CREEK

The North St. Vrain has decent fishing for browns, brookies, and cutthroats and can be reached via the trail from Wild Basin Ranger Station.

Thunder Lake
28.9 mi.

Sandbeach Lake

Hunters Creek

North St. Vrain Creek

Eagle Lake

Sandbeach Creek

23.5 mi.

Ouzel Creek

Thunder Lake Trail

Flow

Ouzel Lake

Bluebird Lake

Ouzel Lake and Creek have greenback cutthroats and brook trout. They can be reached via the Bluebird Lake Trail. Bluebird Lake is barren.

Rocky Mountain

National Park

Willow Creek

Junco Lake

Cony Creek

Pear Reservoir

Cony Creek is another good stream for small greenbacks, and many area lakes offer this beautiful little trout.

FR 116

17.4 mi.

St Vrain Glacier Trail

15.4 mi.

FR 114

Roosevelt

Access is good into the headwaters of the Middle St. Vrain, which offers fast-water fishing for smallish trout.

Red Deer Lake

National

Forest

Middle St. Vrain Creek

FR 114

Flow

13.0 mi.

Coney Creek

FR 114

N
W E
S

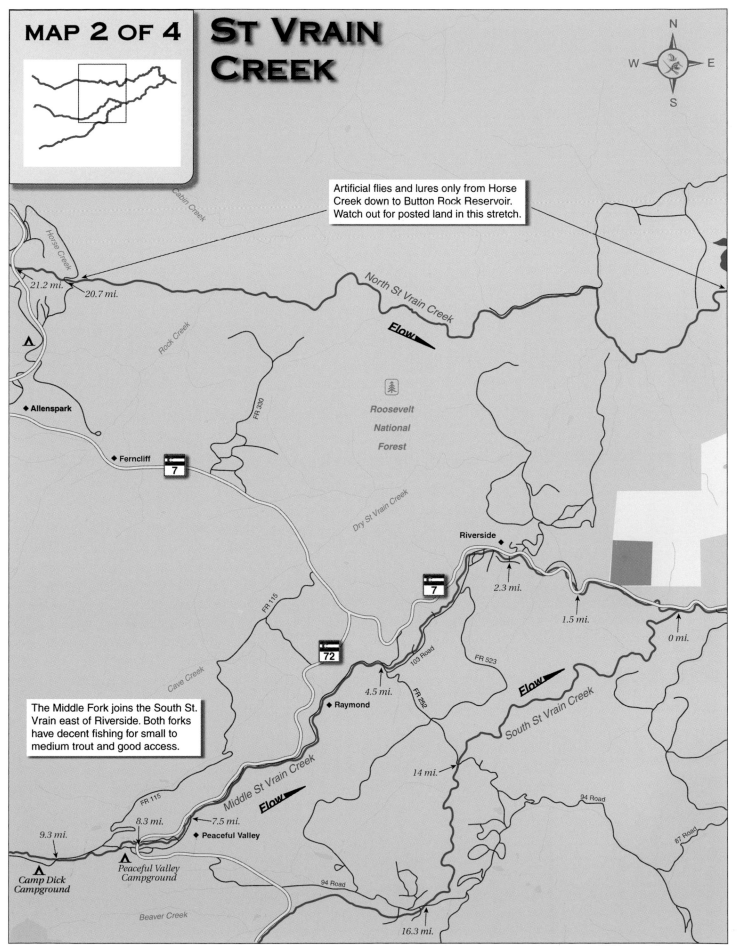

MAP 2 OF 4

ST VRAIN CREEK

Artificial flies and lures only from Horse Creek down to Button Rock Reservoir. Watch out for posted land in this stretch.

The Middle Fork joins the South St. Vrain east of Riverside. Both forks have decent fishing for small to medium trout and good access.

Cabin Creek

Horse Creek

North St Vrain Creek

Flow

21.2 mi.

20.7 mi.

Rock Creek

FR 330

Roosevelt

National

Forest

◆ Allenspark

◆ Ferncliff 7

Dry St Vrain Creek

Riverside ◆

2.3 mi.

7

1.5 mi.

0 mi.

FR 115

Cave Creek

72

4.5 mi.

103 Road

FR 523

FR 252

◆ Raymond

Flow

South St Vrain Creek

14 mi.

94 Road

Middle St Vrain Creek

Flow

87 Road

FR 115

8.3 mi.

7.5 mi.

9.3 mi.

◆ Peaceful Valley

Camp Dick Campground

Peaceful Valley Campground

94 Road

Beaver Creek

16.3 mi.

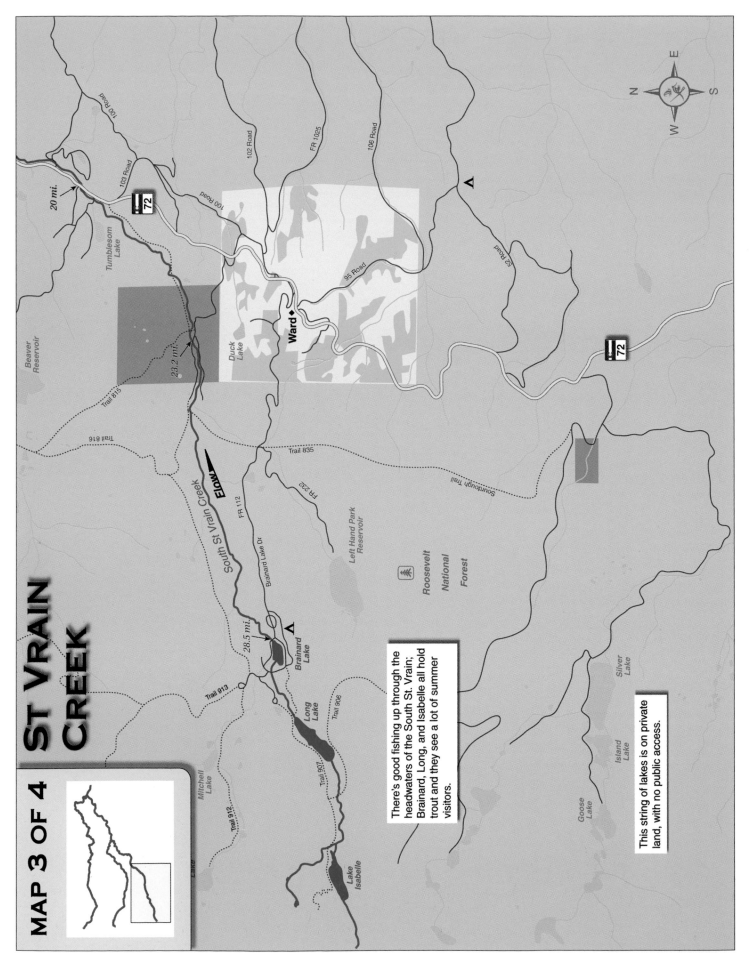

MAP 3 OF 4 | **ST VRAIN CREEK**

There's good fishing up through the headwaters of the South St. Vrain; Brainard, Long, and Isabelle all hold trout and they see a lot of summer visitors.

This string of lakes is on private land, with no public access.

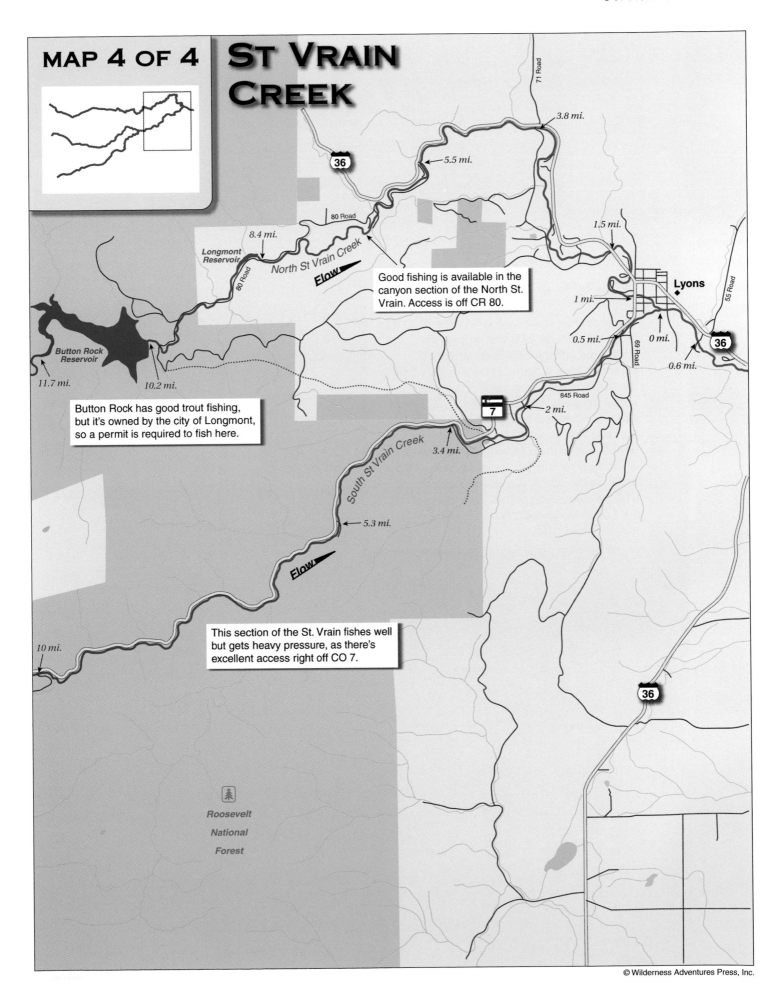

MAP 4 OF 4

ST VRAIN CREEK

71 Road

3.8 mi.

36

5.5 mi.

80 Road

8.4 mi.

Longmont Reservoir

80 Road

North St Vrain Creek

Flow

1.5 mi.

Lyons

55 Road

Good fishing is available in the canyon section of the North St. Vrain. Access is off CR 80.

1 mi.

Button Rock Reservoir

0.5 mi.

69 Road

0 mi.

36

11.7 mi.

10.2 mi.

0.6 mi.

Button Rock has good trout fishing, but it's owned by the city of Longmont, so a permit is required to fish here.

845 Road

7

2 mi.

South St Vrain Creek

3.4 mi.

5.3 mi.

Flow

This section of the St. Vrain fishes well but gets heavy pressure, as there's excellent access right off CO 7.

10 mi.

36

Roosevelt National Forest

© Wilderness Adventures Press, Inc.

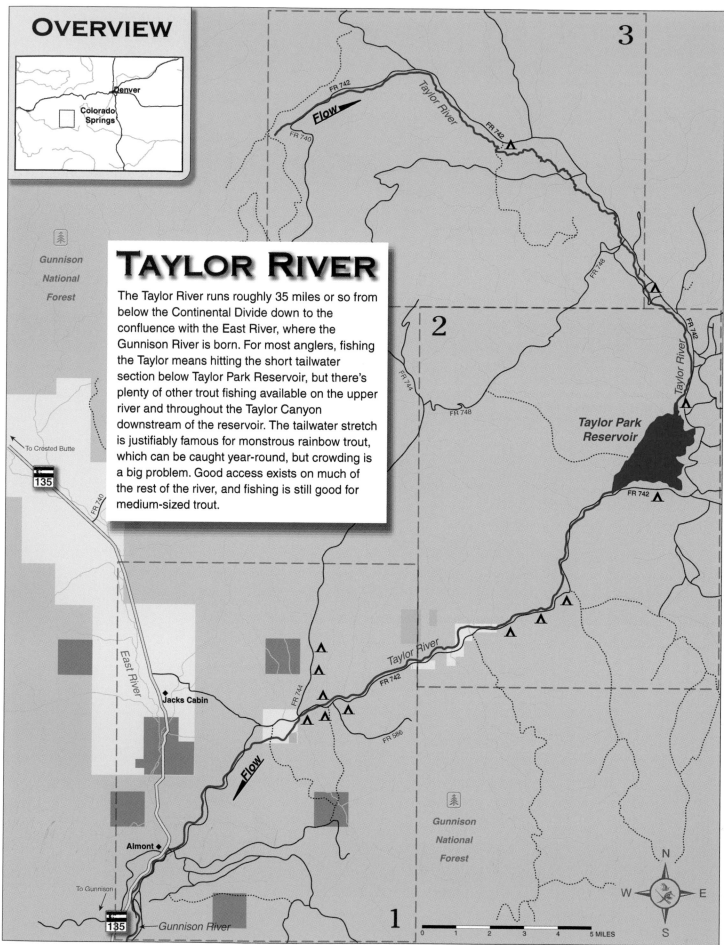

OVERVIEW

Denver
Colorado Springs

3

FR 742

Flow

FR 740

Taylor River

FR 742

Gunnison
National
Forest

FR 748

TAYLOR RIVER

The Taylor River runs roughly 35 miles or so from below the Continental Divide down to the confluence with the East River, where the Gunnison River is born. For most anglers, fishing the Taylor means hitting the short tailwater section below Taylor Park Reservoir, but there's plenty of other trout fishing available on the upper river and throughout the Taylor Canyon downstream of the reservoir. The tailwater stretch is justifiably famous for monstrous rainbow trout, which can be caught year-round, but crowding is a big problem. Good access exists on much of the rest of the river, and fishing is still good for medium-sized trout.

2

FR 744

FR 748

Taylor River

Taylor Park
Reservoir

To Crested Butte

135

FR 740

East River

Jacks Cabin

FR 744

Taylor River

FR 742

FR 586

FR 742

Flow

Almont ◆

Gunnison
National
Forest

To Gunnison

135

Gunnison River

1

0 1 2 3 4 5 MILES

N
W   E
S

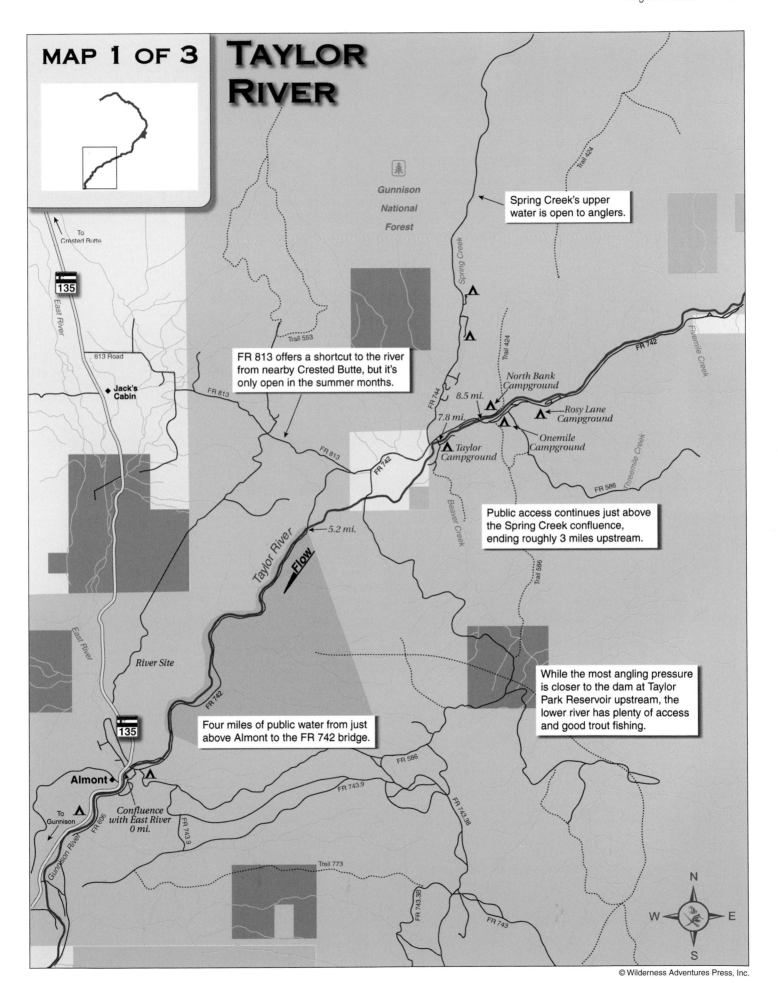

MAP 1 OF 3 **TAYLOR RIVER**

Gunnison National Forest

Spring Creek's upper water is open to anglers.

FR 813 offers a shortcut to the river from nearby Crested Butte, but it's only open in the summer months.

To Crested Butte

135

East River

813 Road

Jack's Cabin

FR 813

Trail 553

FR 813

FR 742

Spring Creek

Trail 424

Trail 424

FR 742

Fivemile Creek

North Bank Campground

8.5 mi.

FR 744

7.8 mi.

Rosy Lane Campground

Onemile Campground

Taylor Campground

Threemile Creek

FR 586

Public access continues just above the Spring Creek confluence, ending roughly 3 miles upstream.

Taylor River

5.2 mi.

Flow

Beaver Creek

Trail 586

While the most angling pressure is closer to the dam at Taylor Park Reservoir upstream, the lower river has plenty of access and good trout fishing.

River Site

East River

FR 742

135

Four miles of public water from just above Almont to the FR 742 bridge.

Almont

FR 586

FR 743.9

FR 743.38

To Gunnison

FR 606

Confluence with East River 0 mi.

FR 743.9

FR 743.38

Gunnison River

Trail 773

FR 743.38

FR 743

N
W E
S

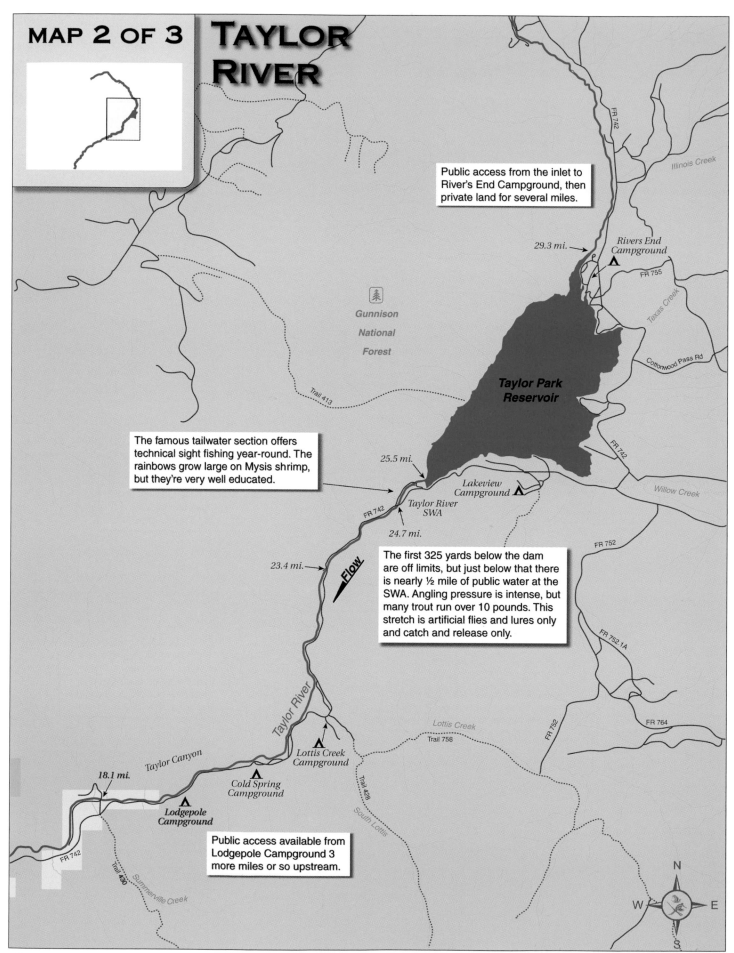

MAP 2 OF 3 TAYLOR RIVER

Public access from the inlet to River's End Campground, then private land for several miles.

Illinois Creek

FR 742

29.3 mi.

Rivers End Campground

FR 755

Texas Creek

Gunnison National Forest

Cottonwood Pass Rd

Taylor Park Reservoir

Trail 413

The famous tailwater section offers technical sight fishing year-round. The rainbows grow large on Mysis shrimp, but they're very well educated.

25.5 mi.

Lakeview Campground

FR 742

Willow Creek

FR 742

Taylor River SWA

24.7 mi.

FR 752

23.4 mi.

Flow

The first 325 yards below the dam are off limits, but just below that there is nearly ½ mile of public water at the SWA. Angling pressure is intense, but many trout run over 10 pounds. This stretch is artificial flies and lures only and catch and release only.

FR 752.1A

Taylor River

FR 752

Lottis Creek

FR 764

Trail 758

Lottis Creek Campground

Trail 428

Taylor Canyon

18.1 mi.

Cold Spring Campground

South Lottis

Lodgepole Campground

FR 742

Public access available from Lodgepole Campground 3 more miles or so upstream.

Trail 430

Summerville Creek

N

W E

S

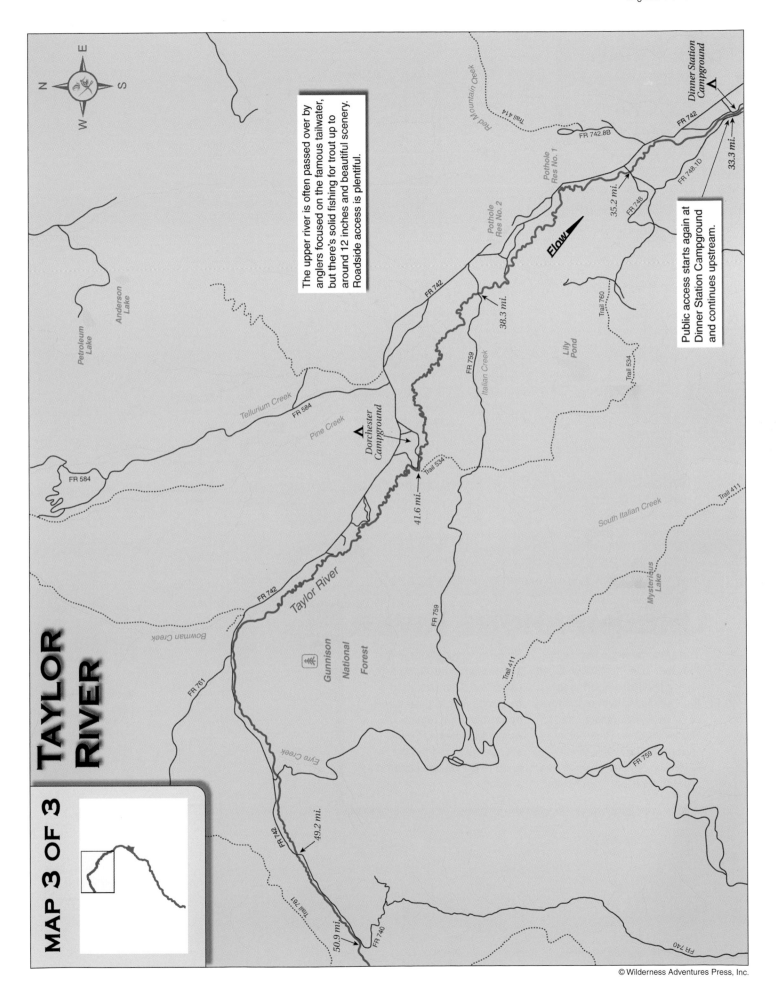

N E S W

MAP 3 OF 3

TAYLOR RIVER

Petroleum Lake

Anderson Lake

Tellurium Creek

FR 584

FR 584

Pine Creek

Bowman Creek

FR 742

Taylor River

FR 761

Eyre Creek

Trail 761

Gunnison National Forest

Dorchester Campground

41.6 mi.

49.2 mi.

50.9 mi.

FR 742

FR 740

FR 759

FR 759

FR 759

FR 742

FR 742

FR 748

FR 748.1D

FR 742.8B

Italian Creek

38.3 mi.

Trail 534

Trail 534

South Italian Creek

Trail 411

Trail 411

Lily Pond

Trail 760

Mysterious Lake

Trail 414

Red Mountain Creek

Pothole Res No. 1

Pothole Res No. 2

Flow

35.2 mi.

33.3 mi.

Dinner Station Campground

FR 740

The upper river is often passed over by anglers focused on the famous tailwater, but there's solid fishing for trout up to around 12 inches and beautiful scenery. Roadside access is plentiful.

Public access starts again at Dinner Station Campground and continues upstream.

© Wilderness Adventures Press, Inc.

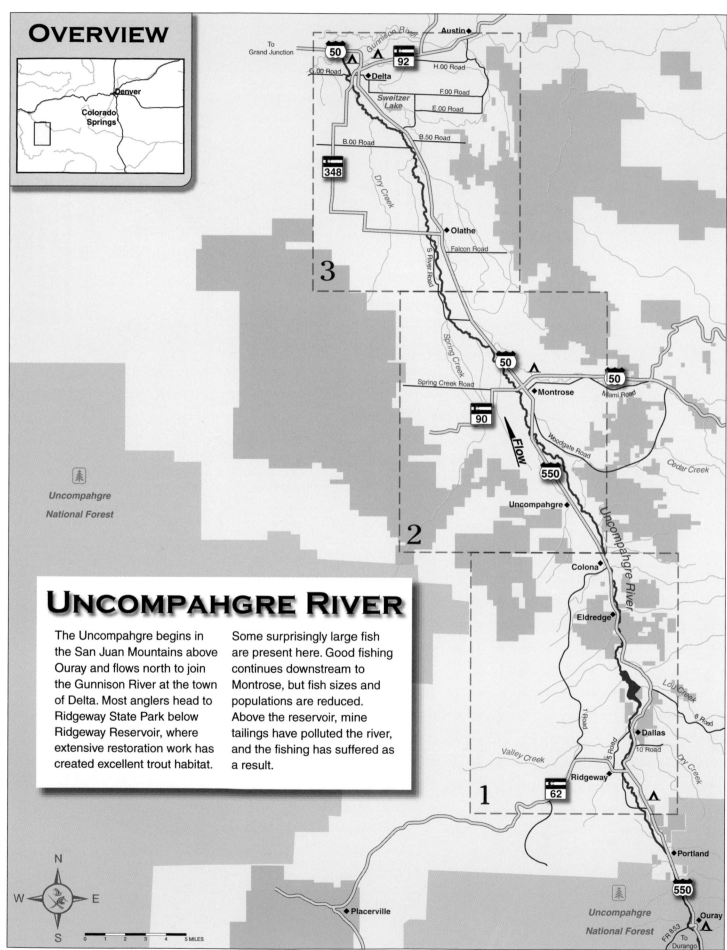

OVERVIEW

To Grand Junction

50

Gunnison River

Austin

92

G.00 Road

Delta

H.00 Road

Sweitzer Lake

F.00 Road

E.00 Road

B.00 Road

B.50 Road

348

Dry Creek

Olathe

Falcon Road

S. River Road

3

Spring Creek

50

Spring Creek Road

50

Montrose

Miami Road

90

Flow

Woodgate Road

Cedar Creek

550

Uncompahgre National Forest

Uncompahgre

2

Uncompahgre River

Colona

Eldredge

Loui Creek

1 Road

5 Road

Dallas

8 Road

10 Road

Dry Creek

Valley Creek

62

Ridgeway

1

Portland

550

Uncompahgre National Forest

Placerville

Ouray

FR 853

To Durango

UNCOMPAHGRE RIVER

The Uncompahgre begins in the San Juan Mountains above Ouray and flows north to join the Gunnison River at the town of Delta. Most anglers head to Ridgeway State Park below Ridgeway Reservoir, where extensive restoration work has created excellent trout habitat. Some surprisingly large fish are present here. Good fishing continues downstream to Montrose, but fish sizes and populations are reduced. Above the reservoir, mine tailings have polluted the river, and the fishing has suffered as a result.

N W E S

0 1 2 3 4 5 MILES

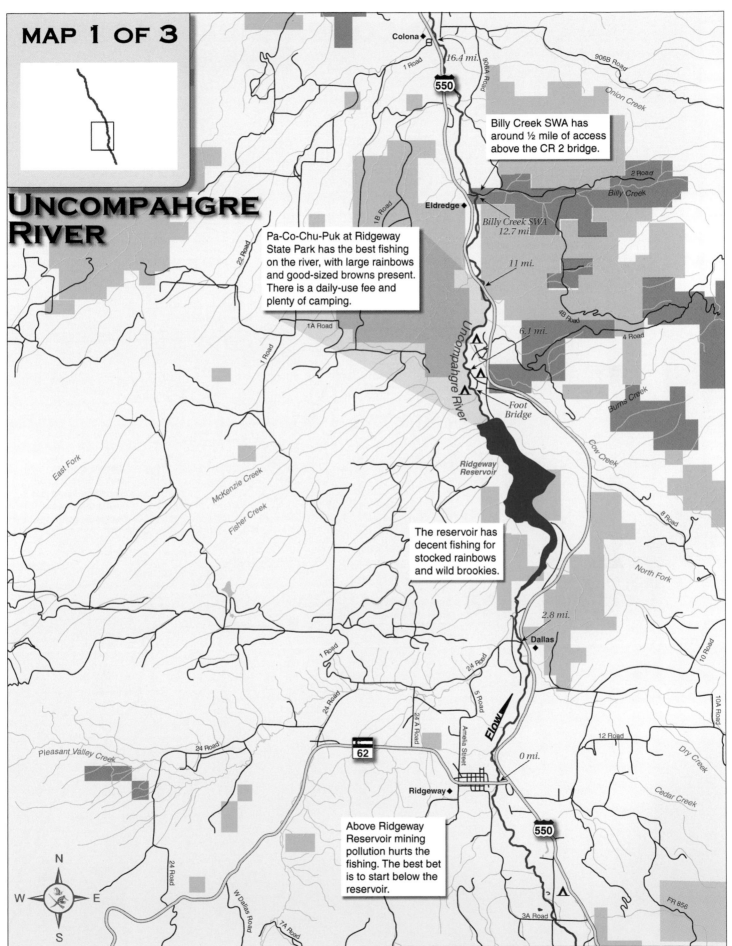

MAP 1 OF 3

UNCOMPAHGRE RIVER

Colona ◆

16.4 mi.

550

Billy Creek SWA has around ½ mile of access above the CR 2 bridge.

Eldredge ◆

Billy Creek SWA 12.7 mi.

11 mi.

Pa-Co-Chu-Puk at Ridgeway State Park has the best fishing on the river, with large rainbows and good-sized browns present. There is a daily-use fee and plenty of camping.

6.1 mi.

Foot Bridge

Ridgeway Reservoir

The reservoir has decent fishing for stocked rainbows and wild brookies.

Uncompahgre River

Burns Creek

Cow Creek

North Fork

2.8 mi.

Dallas ◆

East Fork

McKenzie Creek

Fisher Creek

62

Flow

0 mi.

Amelia Street

Pleasant Valley Creek

Ridgeway ◆

Above Ridgeway Reservoir mining pollution hurts the fishing. The best bet is to start below the reservoir.

550

Dry Creek

Cedar Creek

N
W E
S

© Wilderness Adventures Press, Inc.

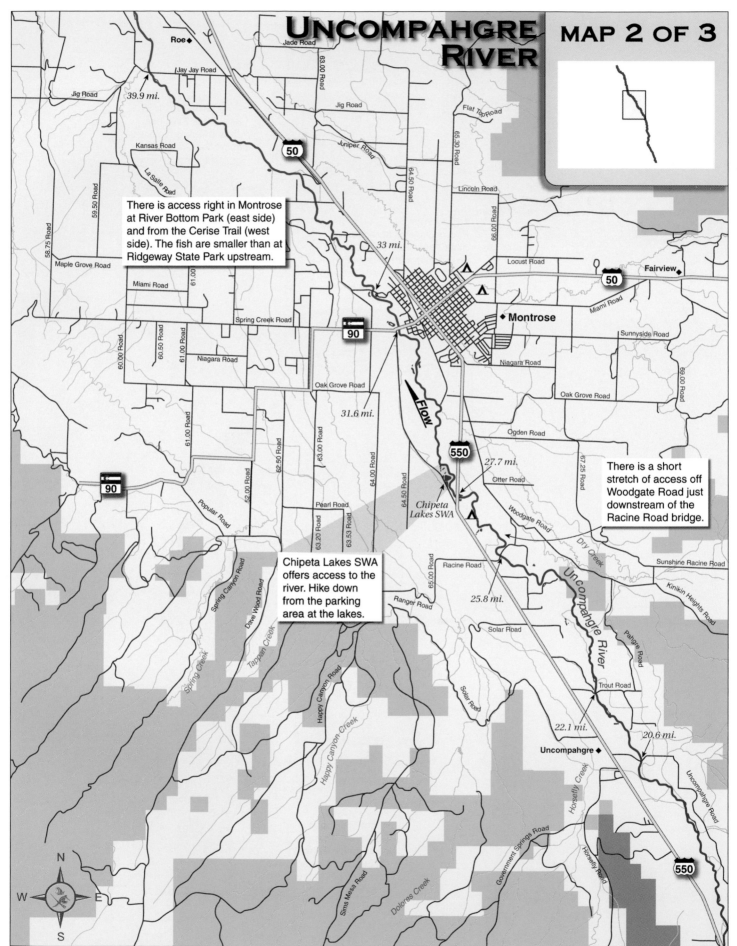

Roe ◆

Jade Road

Jig Road

Jay Jay Road

39.9 mi.

Jig Road

63.00 Road

Juniper Road

Flat Top Road

65.30 Road

Kansas Road

La Salle Road

59.50 Road

Lincoln Road

64.50 Road

58.75 Road

Maple Grove Road

66.00 Road

Locust Road

50

Fairview

There is access right in Montrose at River Bottom Park (east side) and from the Cerise Trail (west side). The fish are smaller than at Ridgeway State Park upstream.

33 mi.

Miami Road

61.00

Miami Road

◆ Montrose

Sunnyside Road

Spring Creek Road

90

Niagara Road

60.00 Road

60.50 Road

61.00 Road

Niagara Road

Oak Grove Road

69.00 Road

Oak Grove Road

31.6 mi.

Flow

Ogden Road

550

67.25 Road

61.00 Road

62.50 Road

63.00 Road

64.00 Road

27.7 mi.

Otter Road

There is a short stretch of access off Woodgate Road just downstream of the Racine Road bridge.

90

Popular Road

Pearl Road

64.50 Road

Chipeta Lakes SWA

Woodgate Road

Dry Creek

Sunshine Racine Road

Spring Canyon Road

Dave Wood Road

63.20 Road

63.53 Road

Chipeta Lakes SWA offers access to the river. Hike down from the parking area at the lakes.

65.00 Road

Racine Road

25.8 mi.

Kinikin Heights Road

Uncompahgre River

Palgre Road

Tappan Creek

Spring Creek

Ranger Road

Solar Road

Trout Road

22.1 mi.

20.6 mi.

Happy Canyon Road

Happy Canyon Creek

Solar Road

Uncompahgre ◆

Horsefly Creek

Uncompahgre Road

N W E S

Sins Mesa Road

Dolores Creek

Government Springs Road

Horsefly Road

550

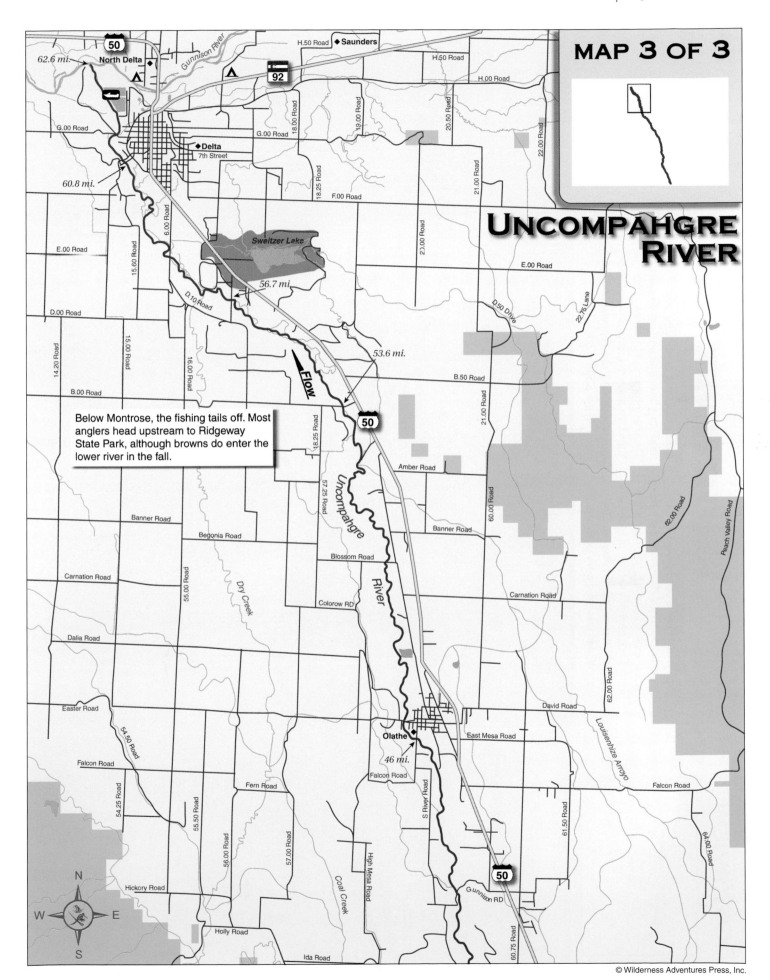

MAP 3 OF 3

UNCOMPAHGRE RIVER

Below Montrose, the fishing tails off. Most anglers head upstream to Ridgeway State Park, although browns do enter the lower river in the fall.

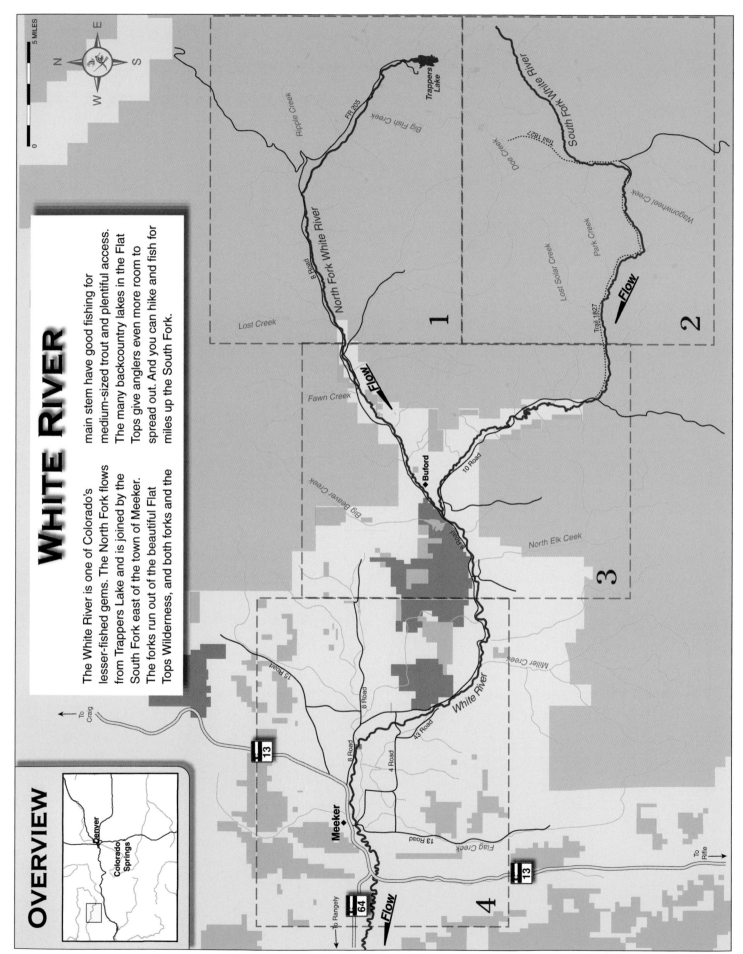

WHITE RIVER

The White River is one of Colorado's lesser-fished gems. The North Fork flows from Trappers Lake and is joined by the South Fork east of the town of Meeker. The forks run out of the beautiful Flat Tops Wilderness, and both forks and the main stem have good fishing for medium-sized trout and plentiful access. The many backcountry lakes in the Flat Tops give anglers even more room to spread out. And you can hike and fish for miles up the South Fork.

OVERVIEW

Denver

Colorado Springs

5 MILES

Trappers Lake

FR 205

Ripple Creek

Big Fish Creek

South Fork White River

Doe Creek

Trail 1827

Wagonwheel Creek

Park Creek

Lost Solar Creek

North Fork White River

8 Road

Flow

Flow

1

2

Lost Creek

Fawn Creek

Buford

10 Road

Big Beaver Creek

North Elk Ceek

8 Road

3

Miller Creek

White River

13 Road

6 Road

8 Road

43 Road

4 Road

To Craig

13

Meeker

13 Road

Flag Creek

13

To Rifle

To Rangely

64

Flow

4

© Wilderness Adventures Press, Inc.

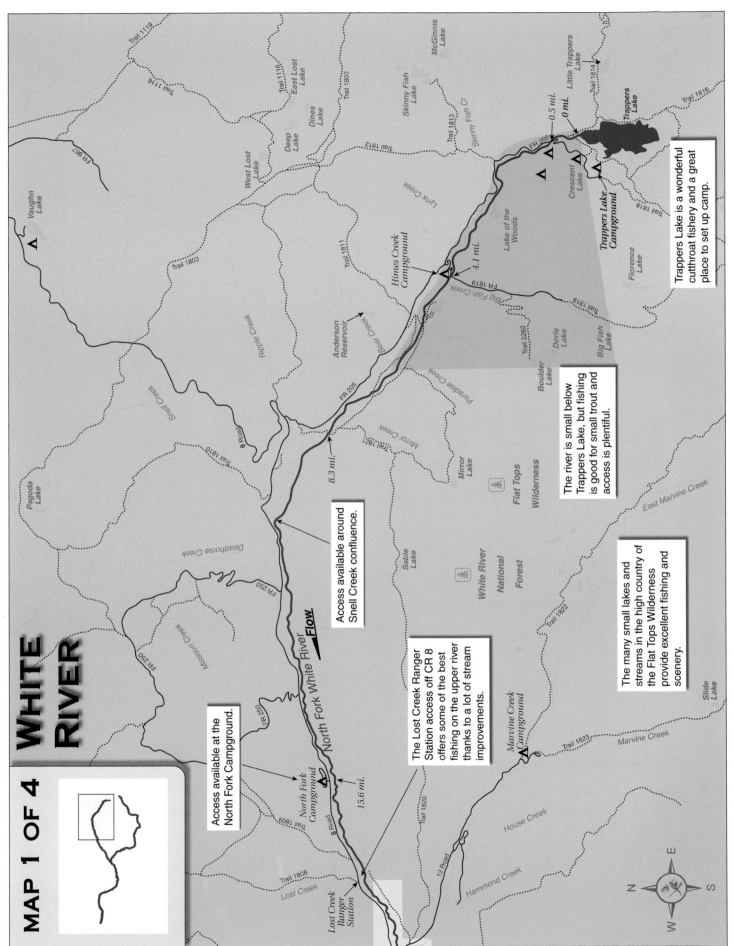

MAP 1 OF 4

WHITE RIVER

Trappers Lake is a wonderful cutthroat fishery and a great place to set up camp.

Trappers Lake Campground

0 mi.

0.5 mi.

Little Trappers Lake

Trappers Lake

McGinnis Lake

Skinny Fish Lake

Skinny Fish Cr

Crescent Lake

Florence Lake

The river is small below Trappers Lake, but fishing is good for small trout and access is plentiful.

Big Fish Creek

Doris Lake

Big Fish Lake

Boulder Lake

Lake of the Woods

Lynx Creek

Himes Creek Campground

4.1 mi.

The many small lakes and streams in the high country of the Flat Tops Wilderness provide excellent fishing and scenery.

East Marvine Creek

Slide Lake

Flat Tops Wilderness

Mirror Lake

White River National Forest

Sable Lake

Marvine Creek

Marvine Creek Campground

House Creek

Hammond Creek

Trail 1822

Trail 1823

Trail 1920

Anderson Reservoir

Bear Creek

Paradise Creek

Mirror Creek

Trail 1821

Trail 2262

Access available around Snell Creek confluence.

8.3 mi.

FR 205

8 Road

Trail 1810

Snell Creek

Ripple Creek

Trail 1811

Trail 1803

The Lost Creek Ranger Station access off CR 8 offers some of the best fishing on the upper river thanks to a lot of stream improvements.

FR 250

Deadhorse Creek

Missouri Creek

North Fork White River

Flow

Access available at the North Fork Campground.

North Fork Campground

15.6 mi.

8 Road

12 Road

Trail 1808

Lost Creek

Lost Creek Ranger Station

Pagoda Lake

Vaughn Lake

FR 967

West Lost Lake

Deep Lake

Dines Lake

East Lost Lake

Trail 1116

Trail 1118

Trail 1119

Trail 1803

Trail 1813

Trail 1812

Trail 1814

Trail 1816

Trail 1818

Trail 1819

N E W S

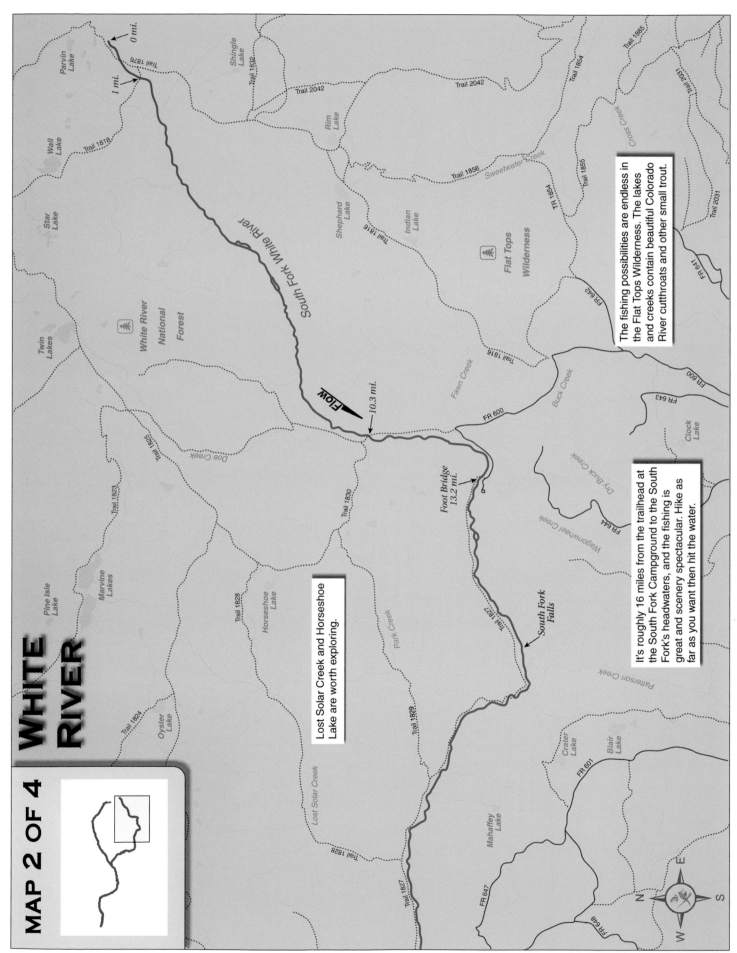

MAP 2 OF 4

WHITE RIVER

The fishing possibilities are endless in the Flat Tops Wilderness. The lakes and creeks contain beautiful Colorado River cutthroats and other small trout.

It's roughly 16 miles from the trailhead at the South Fork Campground to the South Fork's headwaters, and the fishing is great and scenery spectacular. Hike as far as you want then hit the water.

Lost Solar Creek and Horseshoe Lake are worth exploring.

South Fork White River

Flow

0 mi.

1 mi.

10.3 mi.

Foot Bridge 13.2 mi.

South Fork Falls

White River National Forest

Flat Tops Wilderness

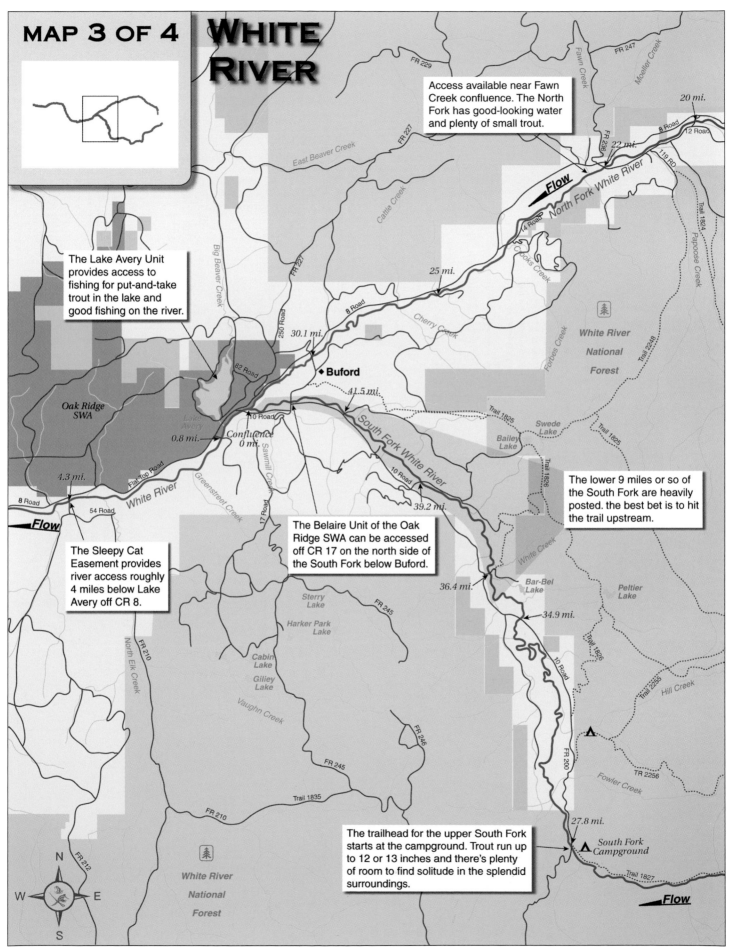

MAP 3 OF 4 WHITE RIVER

Access available near Fawn Creek confluence. The North Fork has good-looking water and plenty of small trout.

The Lake Avery Unit provides access to fishing for put-and-take trout in the lake and good fishing on the river.

The lower 9 miles or so of the South Fork are heavily posted. the best bet is to hit the trail upstream.

The Belaire Unit of the Oak Ridge SWA can be accessed off CR 17 on the north side of the South Fork below Buford.

The Sleepy Cat Easement provides river access roughly 4 miles below Lake Avery off CR 8.

The trailhead for the upper South Fork starts at the campground. Trout run up to 12 or 13 inches and there's plenty of room to find solitude in the splendid surroundings.

© Wilderness Adventures Press, Inc.

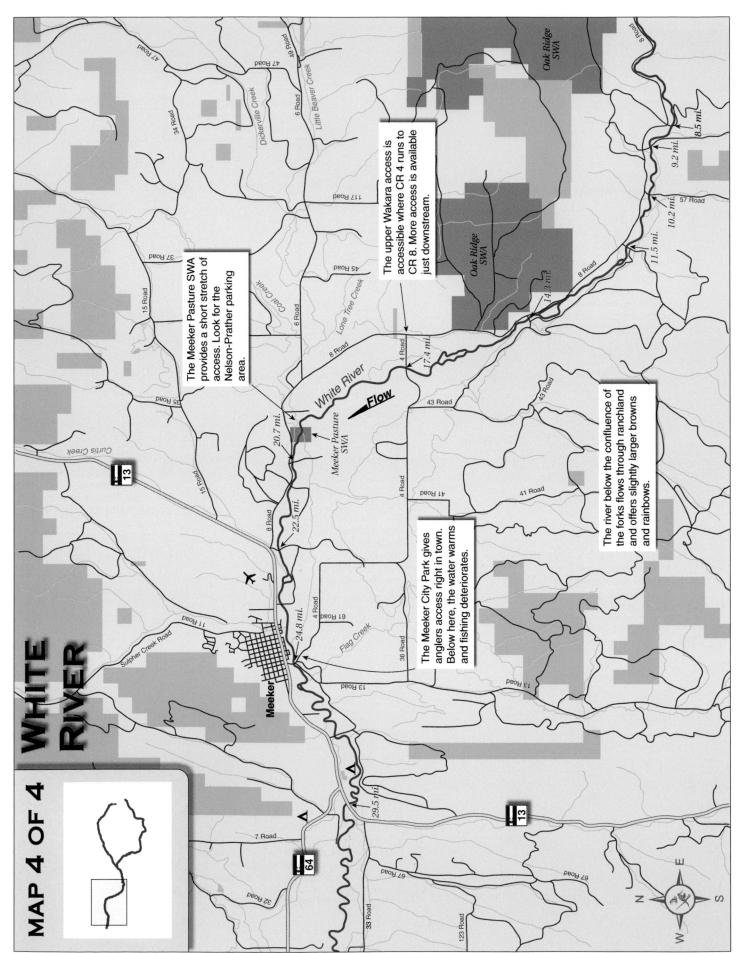

WHITE RIVER

MAP 4 OF 4

The Meeker Pasture SWA provides a short stretch of access. Look for the Nelson-Prather parking area.

The upper Wakara access is accessible where CR 4 runs to CR 8. More access is available just downstream.

The river below the confluence of the forks flows through ranchland and offers slightly larger browns and rainbows.

The Meeker City Park gives anglers access right in town. Below here, the water warms and fishing deteriorates.

© Wilderness Adventures Press, Inc.

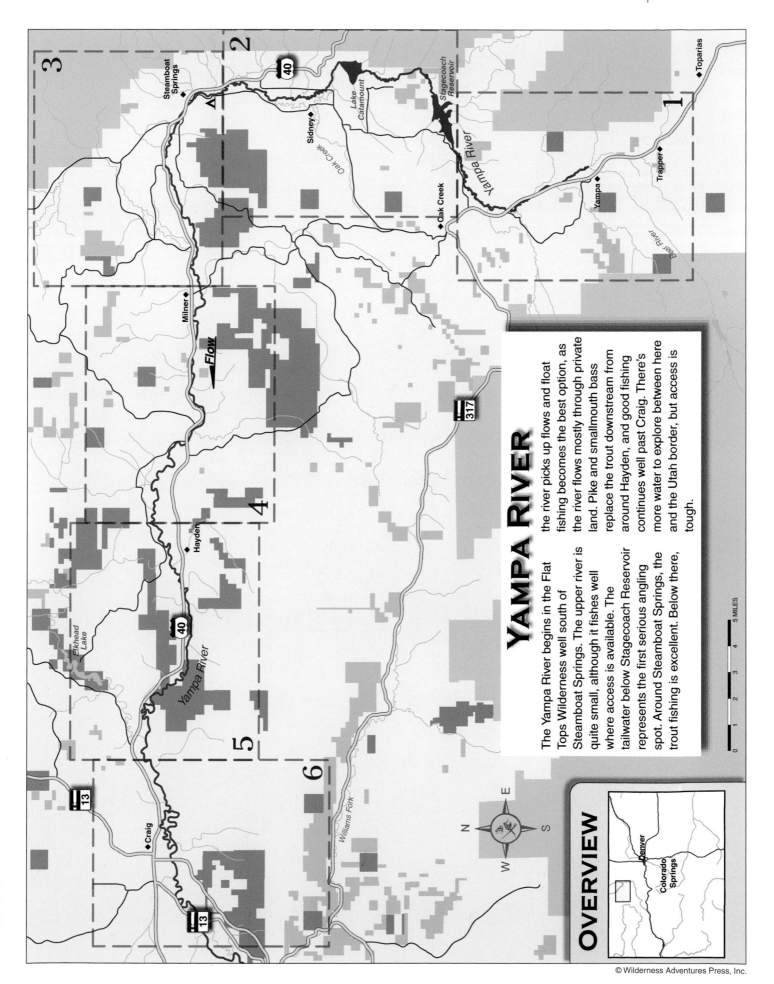

YAMPA RIVER

The Yampa River begins in the Flat Tops Wilderness well south of Steamboat Springs. The upper river is quite small, although it fishes well where access is available. The tailwater below Stagecoach Reservoir represents the first serious angling spot. Around Steamboat Springs, the trout fishing is excellent. Below there, the river picks up flows and float fishing becomes the best option, as the river flows mostly through private land. Pike and smallmouth bass replace the trout downstream from around Hayden, and good fishing continues well past Craig. There's more water to explore between here and the Utah border, but access is tough.

OVERVIEW

N E S W

5 MILES
0 1 2 3 4 5

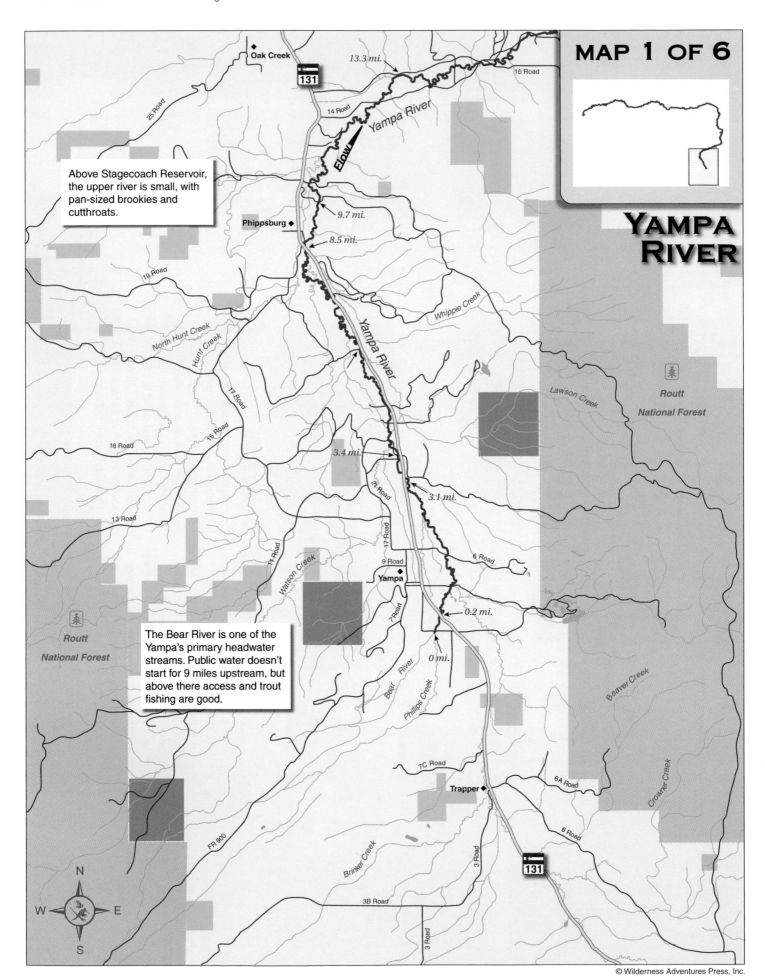

MAP 1 OF 6

YAMPA RIVER

Oak Creek

131

13.3 mi.

16 Road

14 Road

Yampa River

Flow

25 Road

Above Stagecoach Reservoir, the upper river is small, with pan-sized brookies and cutthroats.

9.7 mi.

Phippsburg

8.5 mi.

19 Road

Whipple Creek

North Hunt Creek

Hunt Creek

Yampa River

Lawson Creek

Routt National Forest

17 Road

16 Road

18 Road

3.4 mi.

21 Road

3.1 mi.

13 Road

17 Road

6 Road

14 Road

Watson Creek

9 Road

Yampa

Routt National Forest

The Bear River is one of the Yampa's primary headwater streams. Public water doesn't start for 9 miles upstream, but above there access and trout fishing are good.

0.2 mi.

Bear River

7 Road

0 mi.

Phillips Creek

Beaver Creek

Crowner Creek

7C Road

6A Road

Trapper

FR 900

6 Road

131

Brinker Creek

3 Road

3B Road

3 Road

N
W E
S

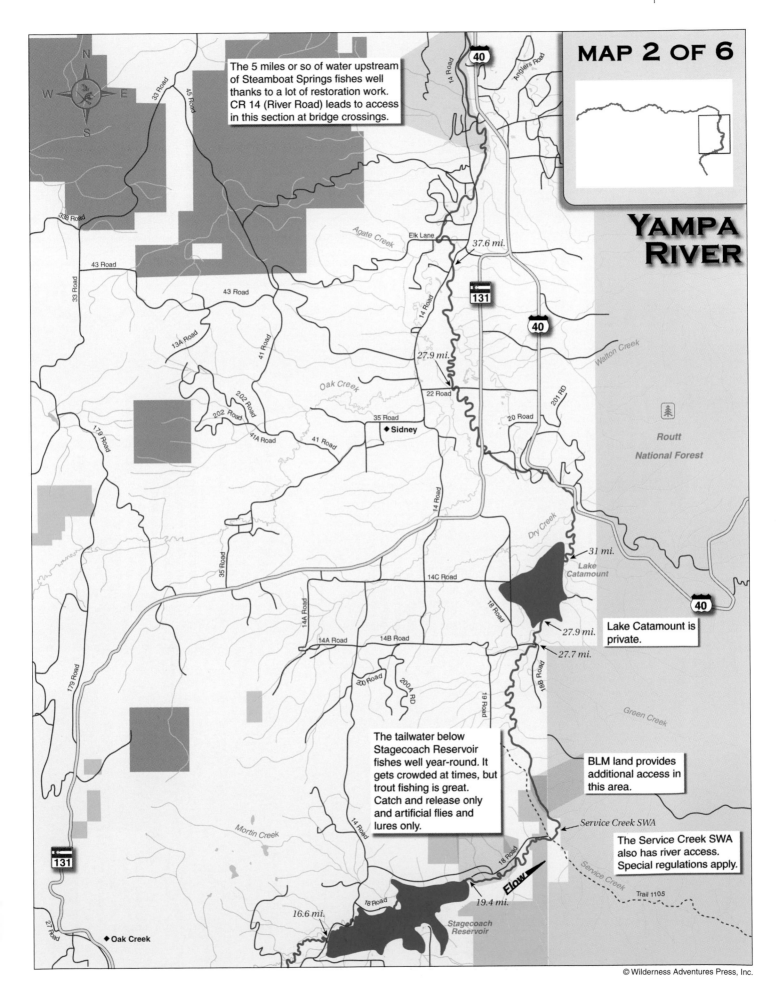

MAP 2 OF 6

YAMPA RIVER

The 5 miles or so of water upstream of Steamboat Springs fishes well thanks to a lot of restoration work. CR 14 (River Road) leads to access in this section at bridge crossings.

37.6 mi.

27.9 mi.

31 mi.

27.9 mi.

27.7 mi.

Routt National Forest

Lake Catamount is private.

The tailwater below Stagecoach Reservoir fishes well year-round. It gets crowded at times, but trout fishing is great. Catch and release only and artificial flies and lures only.

BLM land provides additional access in this area.

Service Creek SWA

The Service Creek SWA also has river access. Special regulations apply.

Flow

19.4 mi.

16.6 mi.

Stagecoach Reservoir

◆ Oak Creek

◆ Sidney

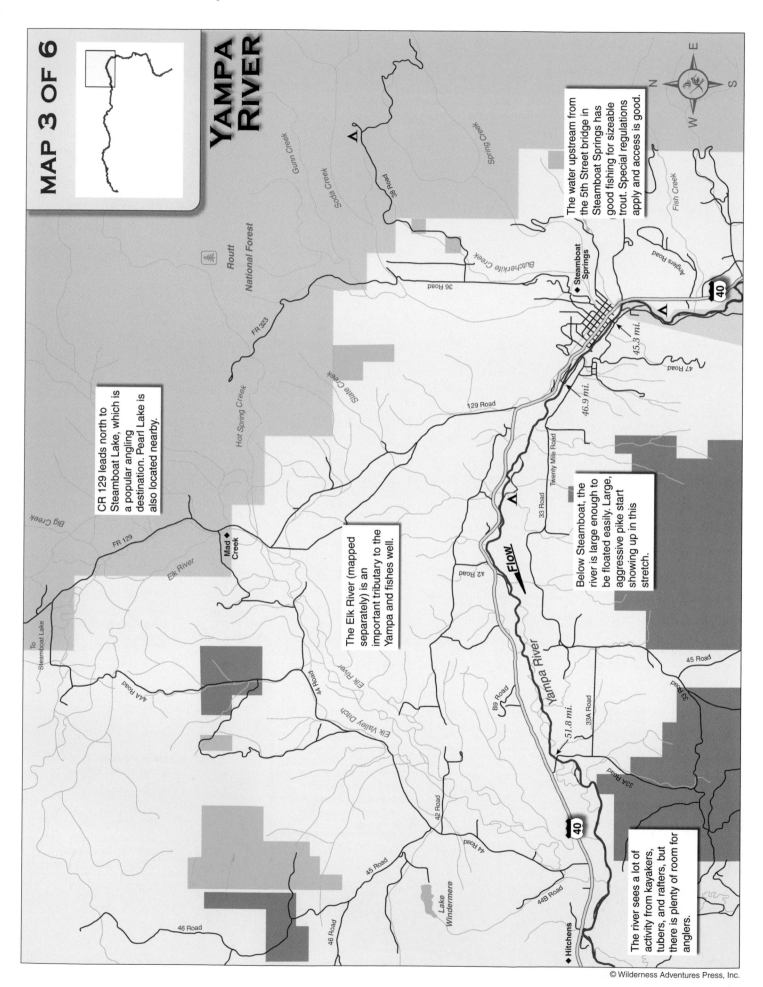

MAP 3 OF 6

YAMPA RIVER

The water upstream from the 5th Street bridge in Steamboat Springs has good fishing for sizeable trout. Special regulations apply and access is good.

CR 129 leads north to Steamboat Lake, which is a popular angling destination. Pearl Lake is also located nearby.

The Elk River (mapped separately) is an important tributary to the Yampa and fishes well.

Below Steamboat, the river is large enough to be floated easily. Large, aggressive pike start showing up in this stretch.

The river sees a lot of activity from kayakers, tubers, and rafters, but there is plenty of room for anglers.

Routt National Forest

Steamboat Springs

Yampa River

FLOW

45.3 mi.

46.9 mi.

51.8 mi.

Lake Windermere

Hitchens

Mad Creek

Gunn Creek

Soda Creek

Spring Creek

Fish Creek

Butcherkite Creek

Hot Spring Creek

Slate Creek

Big Creek

Elk River

Elk Valley Ditch

Steamboat Lake

To

38 Road

36 Road

47 Road

129 Road

Anglers Road

Twenty Mile Road

33 Road

42 Road

44 Road

45 Road

46 Road

44A Road

33A Road

33A Road

44B Road

B9 Road

FR 323

FR 129

40

40

© Wilderness Adventures Press, Inc.

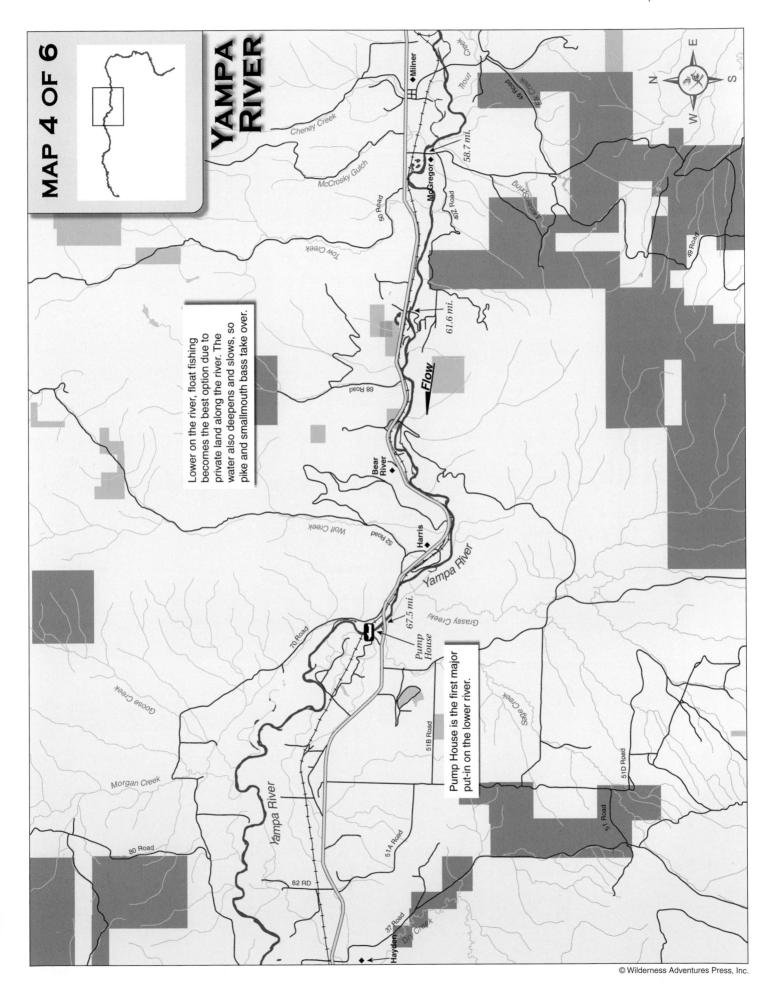

MAP 4 OF 6

YAMPA RIVER

Lower on the river, float fishing becomes the best option due to private land along the river. The water also deepens and slows, so pike and smallmouth bass take over.

Pump House is the first major put-in on the lower river.

Flow

58.7 mi.

61.6 mi.

67.5 mi.

Milner

McGregor ♦

Bear River ♦

Harris ♦

Pump House

Hayden ♦

Cheney Creek

McCrosky Gulch

Tow Creek

Trout Creek

Elk Creek

Milner Spring

49 Road

50 Road

40Z Road

68 Road

Wolf Creek

52 Road

Yampa River

Grassy Creek

Goose Creek

70 Road

80 Road

Morgan Creek

82 RD

37 Road

Dry Creek

51A Road

51B Road

Sage Creek

51 Road

51D Road

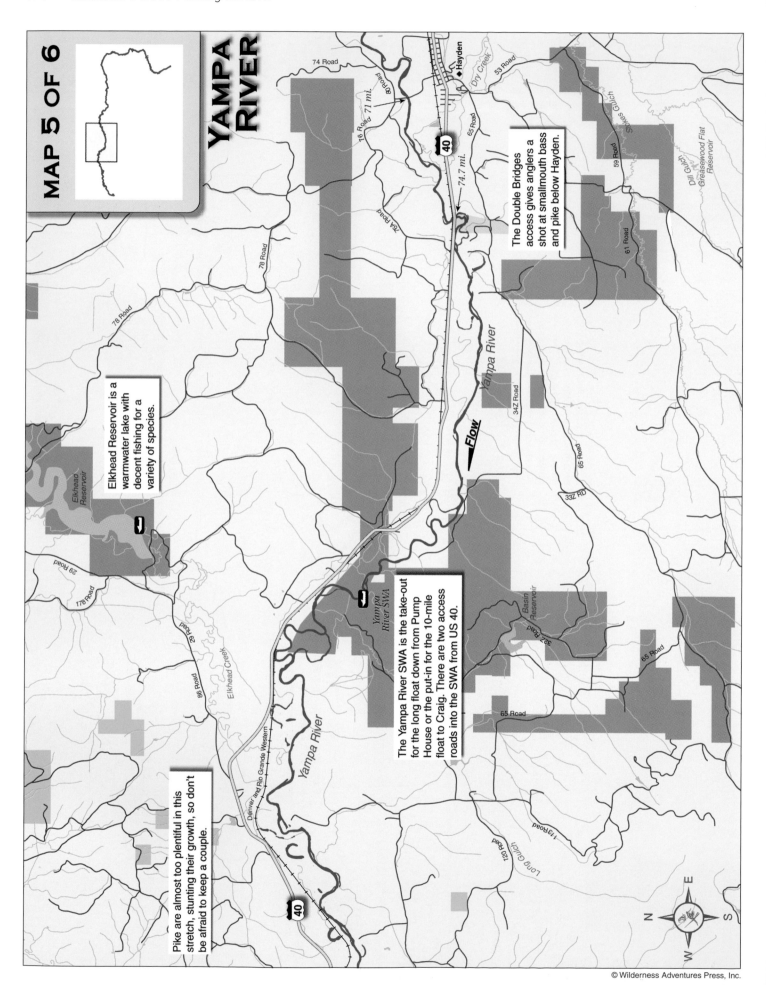

MAP 5 OF 6

YAMPA RIVER

Elkhead Reservoir is a warmwater lake with decent fishing for a variety of species.

Pike are almost too plentiful in this stretch, stunting their growth, so don't be afraid to keep a couple.

The Yampa River SWA is the take-out for the long float down from Pump House or the put-in for the 10-mile float to Craig. There are two access roads into the SWA from US 40.

The Double Bridges access gives anglers a shot at smallmouth bass and pike below Hayden.

Flow

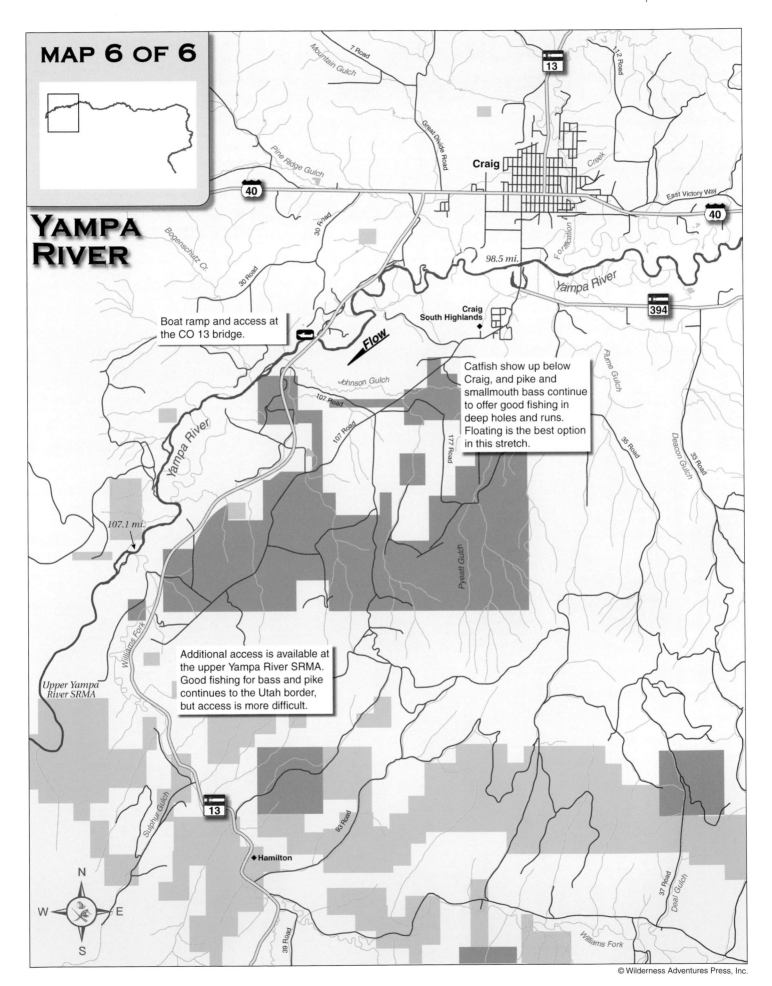

MAP **6** OF **6**

YAMPA RIVER

Boat ramp and access at the CO 13 bridge.

Flow

Catfish show up below Craig, and pike and smallmouth bass continue to offer good fishing in deep holes and runs. Floating is the best option in this stretch.

Additional access is available at the upper Yampa River SRMA. Good fishing for bass and pike continues to the Utah border, but access is more difficult.

Craig

Craig South Highlands

98.5 mi.

Yampa River

107.1 mi.

Yampa River

Upper Yampa River SRMA

Williams Fork

Hamilton

Mountain Gulch

7 Road

112 Road

Great Divide Road

Creek

East Victory Way

Pine Ridge Gulch

Bogenschutz Cr.

30 Road

30 Road

Formation

Johnson Gulch

107 Road

107 Road

177 Road

Flume Gulch

35 Road

Deacon Gulch

33 Road

Pyeatt Gulch

Sulphur Gulch

93 Road

37 Road

Deal Gulch

39 Road

Williams Fork

N W E S

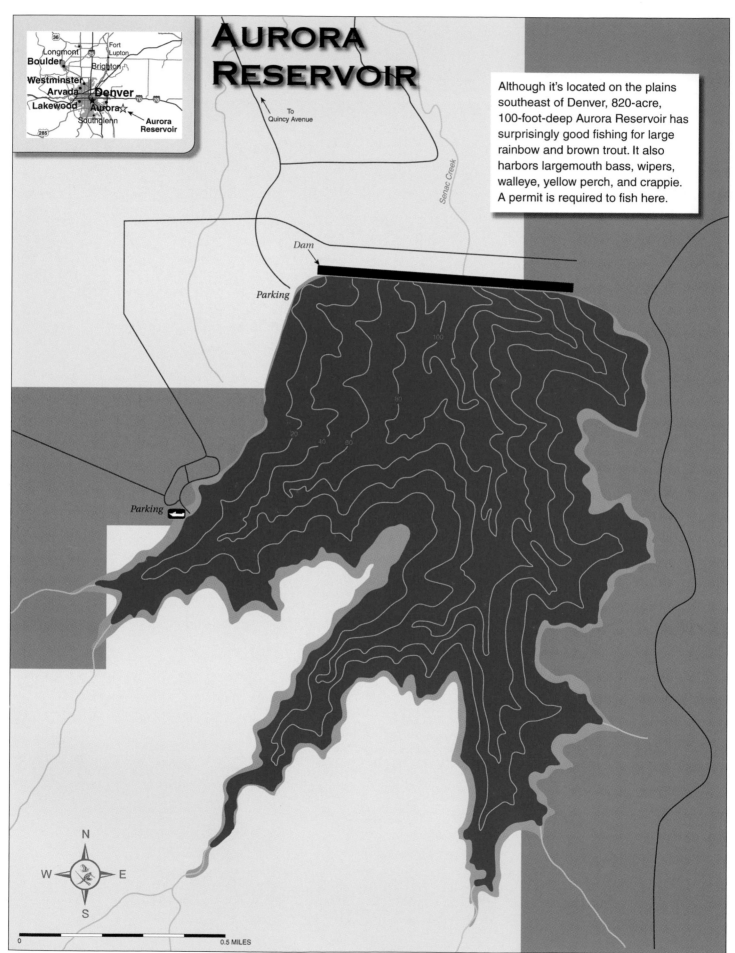

AURORA RESERVOIR

Although it's located on the plains southeast of Denver, 820-acre, 100-foot-deep Aurora Reservoir has surprisingly good fishing for large rainbow and brown trout. It also harbors largemouth bass, wipers, walleye, yellow perch, and crappie. A permit is required to fish here.

To Quincy Avenue

Senac Creek

Dam

Parking

Parking

100

80

20 40 60 80

N
W E
S

0   0.5 MILES

Longmont
Boulder
Fort Lupton
Brighton
Westminster
Arvada   Denver
Lakewood   Aurora
Southglenn   Aurora Reservoir

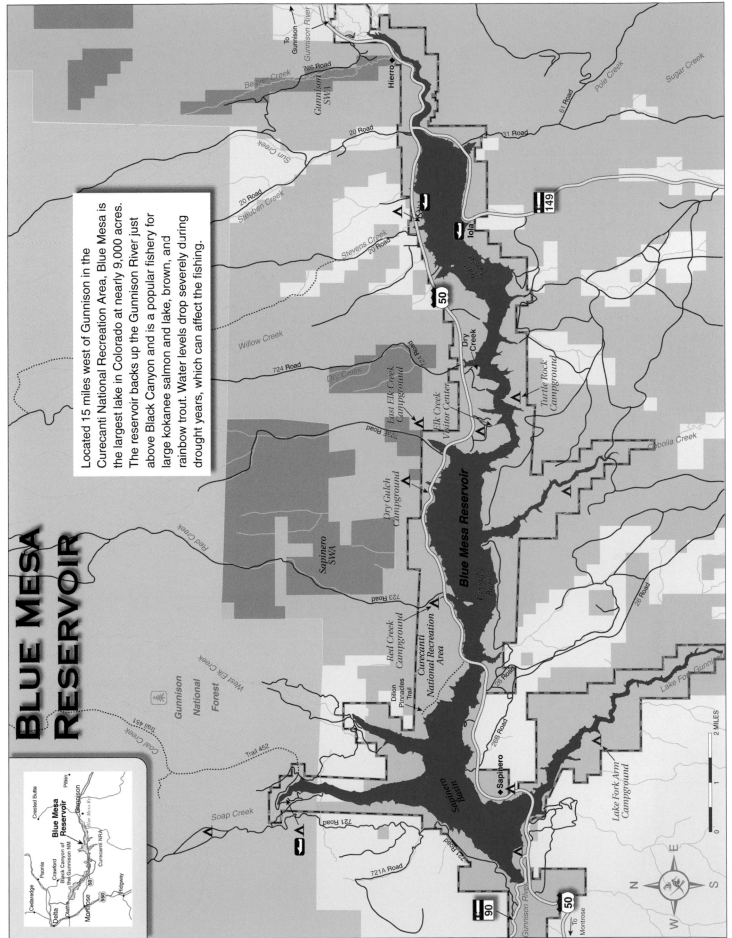

BLUE MESA RESERVOIR

Located 15 miles west of Gunnison in the Curecanti National Recreation Area, Blue Mesa is the largest lake in Colorado at nearly 9,000 acres. The reservoir backs up the Gunnison River just above Black Canyon and is a popular fishery for large kokanee salmon and lake, brown, and rainbow trout. Water levels drop severely during drought years, which can affect the fishing.

© Wilderness Adventures Press, Inc.

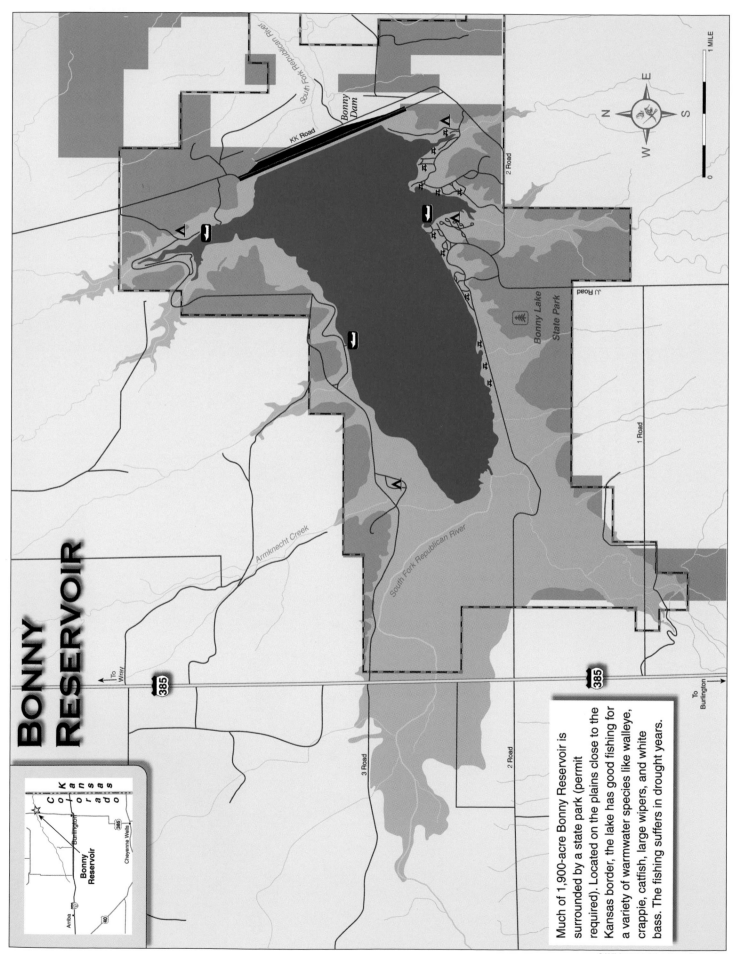

BONNY RESERVOIR

Much of 1,900-acre Bonny Reservoir is surrounded by a state park (permit required). Located on the plains close to the Kansas border, the lake has good fishing for a variety of warmwater species like walleye, crappie, catfish, large wipers, and white bass. The fishing suffers in drought years.

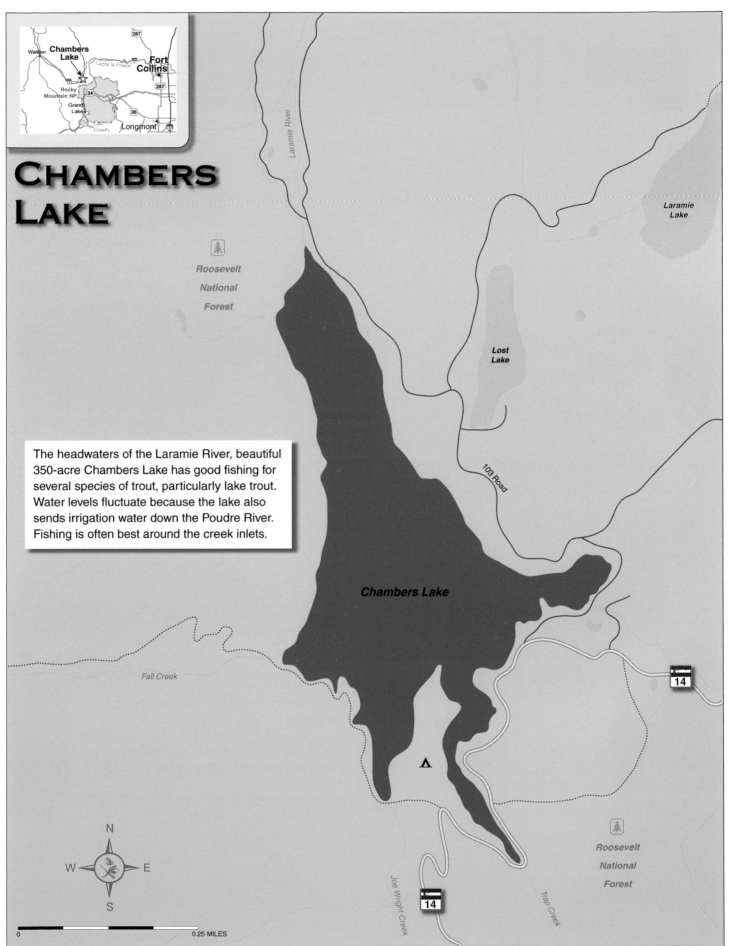

CHAMBERS LAKE

The headwaters of the Laramie River, beautiful 350-acre Chambers Lake has good fishing for several species of trout, particularly lake trout. Water levels fluctuate because the lake also sends irrigation water down the Poudre River. Fishing is often best around the creek inlets.

Chambers Lake

Laramie Lake

Lost Lake

Roosevelt National Forest

Roosevelt National Forest

103 Road

Fall Creek

Joe Wright Creek

Trap Creek

14

14

N W E S

0   0.25 MILES

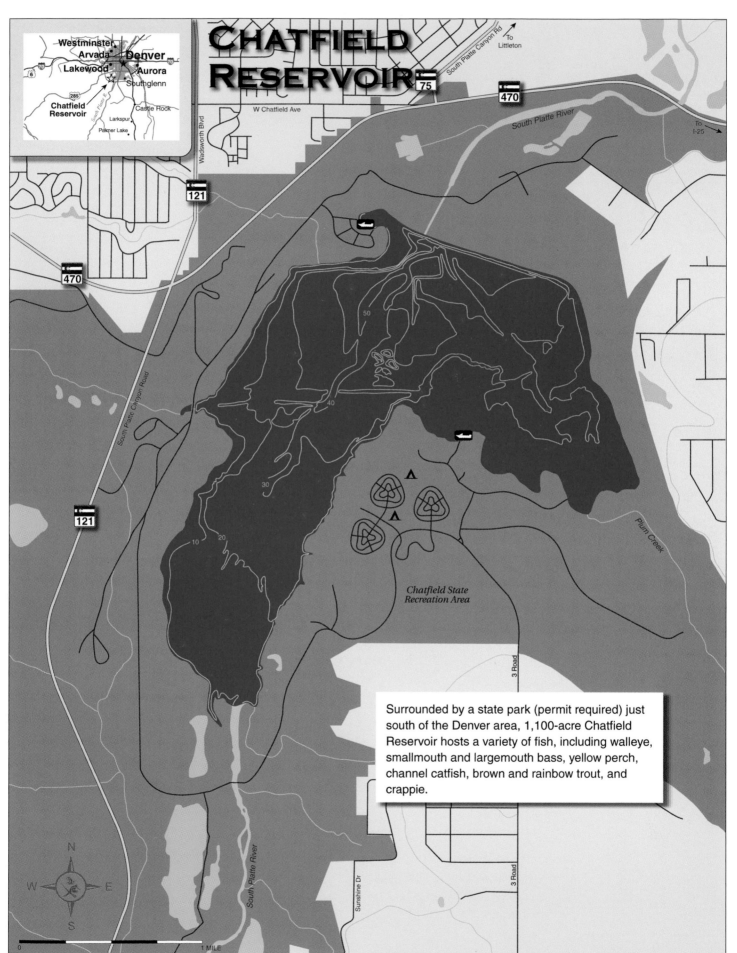

Surrounded by a state park (permit required) just south of the Denver area, 1,100-acre Chatfield Reservoir hosts a variety of fish, including walleye, smallmouth and largemouth bass, yellow perch, channel catfish, brown and rainbow trout, and crappie.

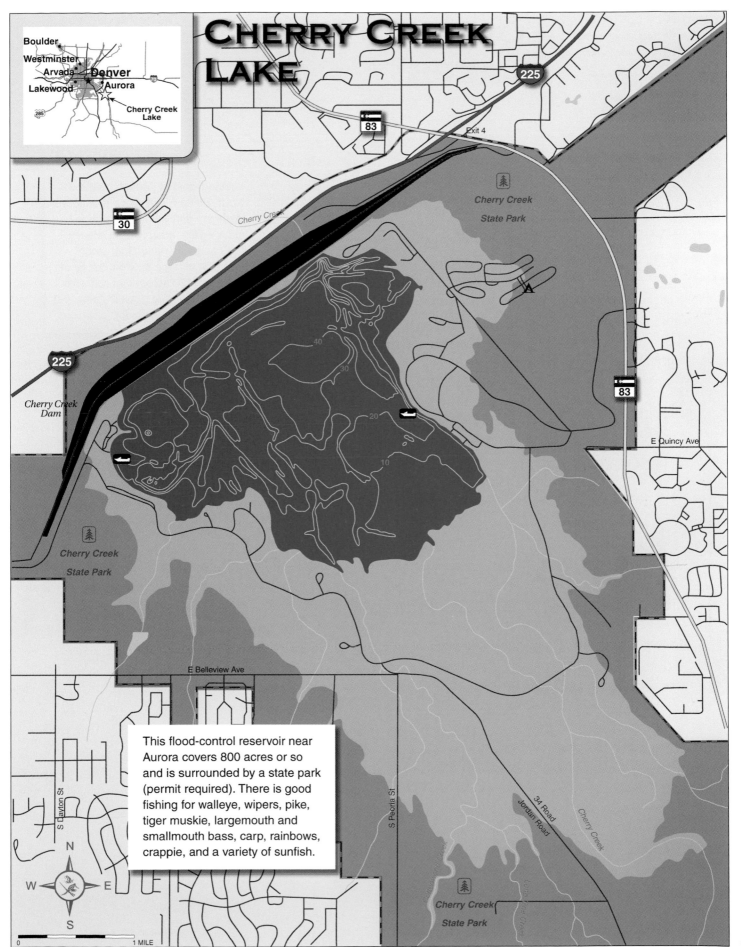

CHERRY CREEK LAKE

Boulder
Westminster
Arvada
Lakewood
Denver
Aurora
Cherry Creek Lake

Cherry Creek State Park

Cherry Creek

Exit 4

225

83

30

225

Cherry Creek Dam

83

E Quincy Ave

40

30

20

10

Cherry Creek State Park

E Belleview Ave

S Clayton St

S Peoria St

34 Road

Jordan Road

Cherry Creek

This flood-control reservoir near Aurora covers 800 acres or so and is surrounded by a state park (permit required). There is good fishing for walleye, wipers, pike, tiger muskie, largemouth and smallmouth bass, carp, rainbows, crappie, and a variety of sunfish.

N
W   E
S

0   1 MILE

Cherry Creek State Park

DELANEY BUTTE LAKES

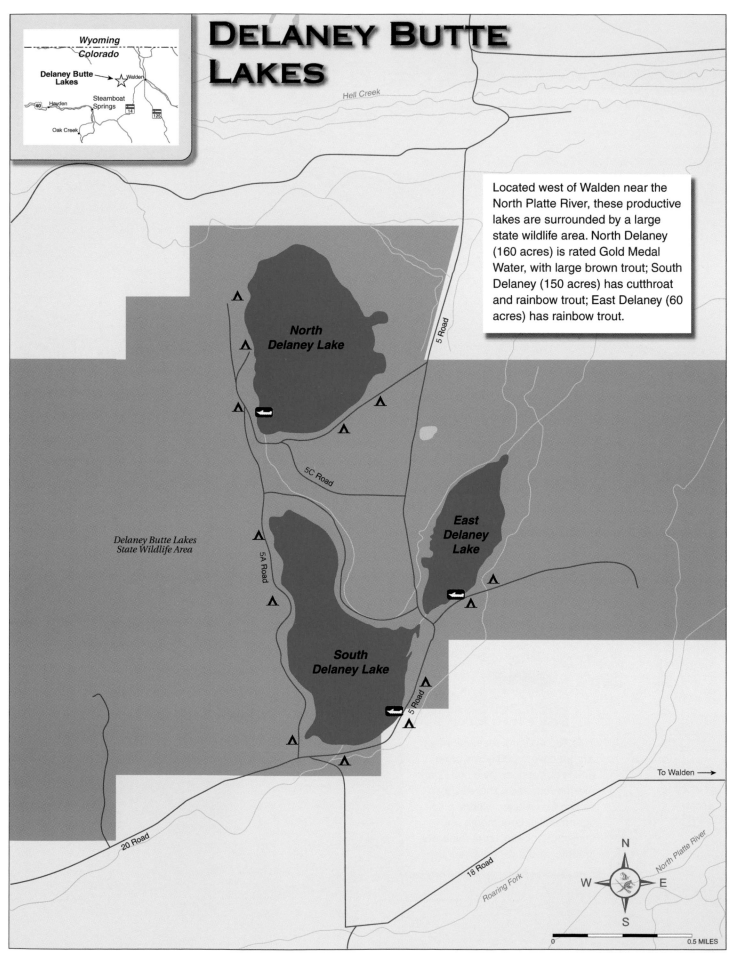

Wyoming
Colorado

Delaney Butte Lakes → Walden

Hayden
Steamboat Springs
Oak Creek

Hell Creek

Located west of Walden near the North Platte River, these productive lakes are surrounded by a large state wildlife area. North Delaney (160 acres) is rated Gold Medal Water, with large brown trout; South Delaney (150 acres) has cutthroat and rainbow trout; East Delaney (60 acres) has rainbow trout.

North Delaney Lake

5 Road

5C Road

East Delaney Lake

Delaney Butte Lakes State Wildlife Area

5A Road

South Delaney Lake

5 Road

To Walden →

20 Road

18 Road

Roaring Fork

North Platte River

N
W   E
S

0   0.5 MILES

© Wilderness Adventures Press, Inc.

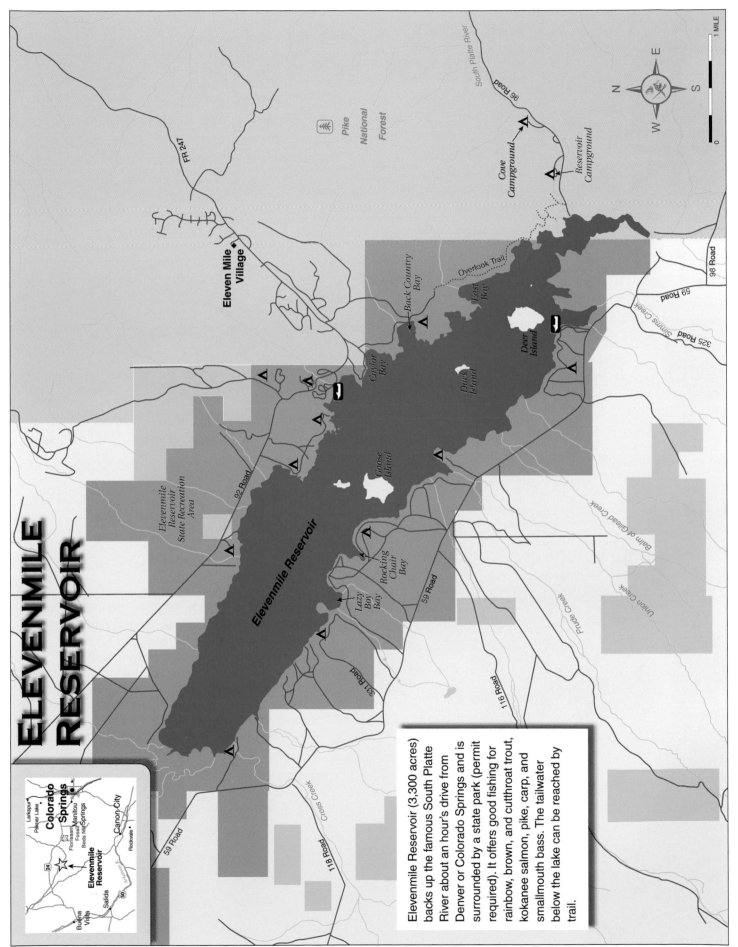

ELEVENMILE RESERVOIR

Pike National Forest

South Platte River

96 Road

Cove Campground

Reservoir Campground

N
W — E
S

1 MILE
0

FR 247

Eleven Mile Village

Back Country Bay

Overlook Trail

West Bay

98 Road

Deer Island

59 Road

325 Road

Simms Creek

Gaylor Bay

Duck Island

Goose Island

Elevenmile Reservoir State Recreation Area

92 Road

Rocking Chair Bay

Lazy Boy Bay

Balm of Gilead Creek

59 Road

Prude Creek

Union Creek

Elevenmile Reservoir

331 Road

116 Road

118 Road

Cross Creek

59 Road

Larkspur
Palmer Lake
Colorado Springs
Manitou Springs
Florissant Fossil Beds Nt'l Monument
24
Elevenmile Reservoir
Buena Vista
Salida
50
Canon City
Rockvale

Elevenmile Reservoir (3,300 acres) backs up the famous South Platte River about an hour's drive from Denver or Colorado Springs and is surrounded by a state park (permit required). It offers good fishing for rainbow, brown, and cutthroat trout, kokanee salmon, pike, carp, and smallmouth bass. The tailwater below the lake can be reached by trail.

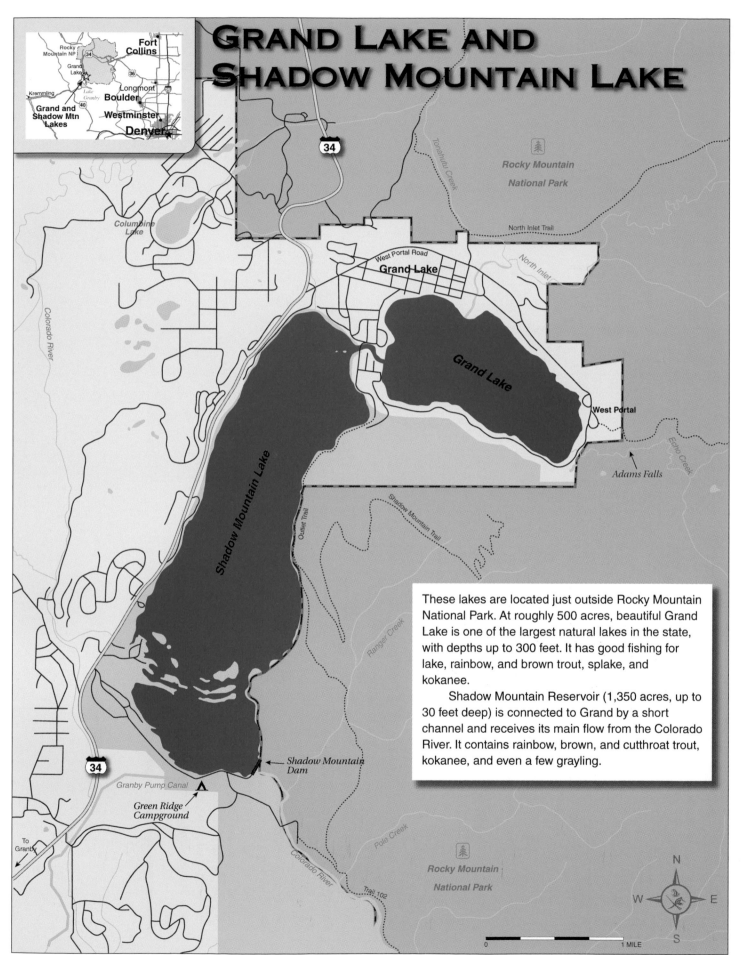

GRAND LAKE AND SHADOW MOUNTAIN LAKE

These lakes are located just outside Rocky Mountain National Park. At roughly 500 acres, beautiful Grand Lake is one of the largest natural lakes in the state, with depths up to 300 feet. It has good fishing for lake, rainbow, and brown trout, splake, and kokanee.

Shadow Mountain Reservoir (1,350 acres, up to 30 feet deep) is connected to Grand by a short channel and receives its main flow from the Colorado River. It contains rainbow, brown, and cutthroat trout, kokanee, and even a few grayling.

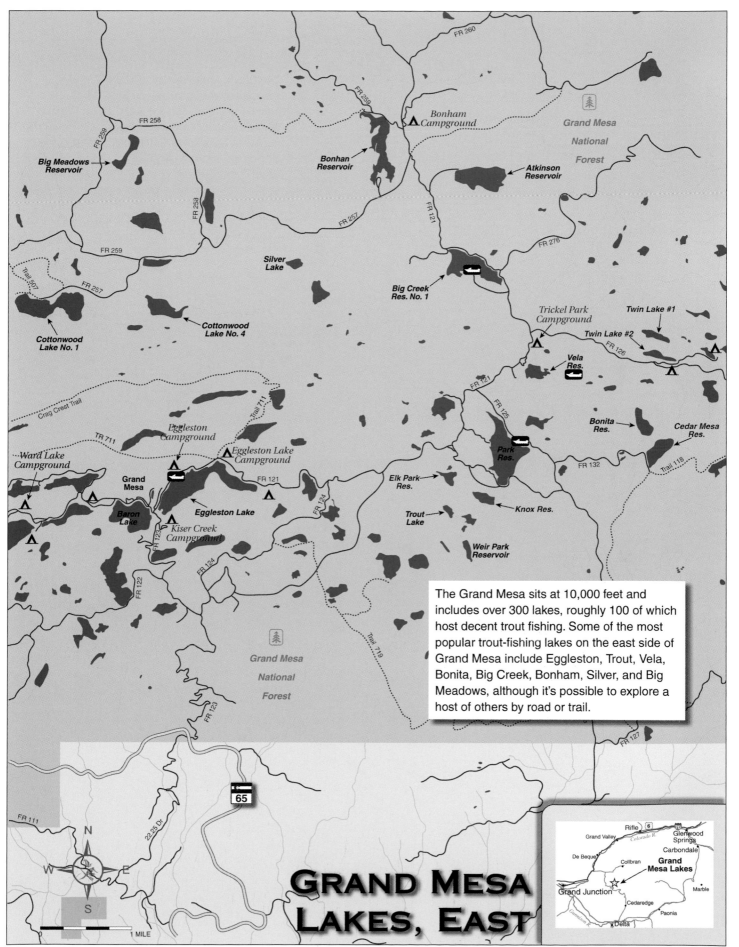

The Grand Mesa sits at 10,000 feet and includes over 300 lakes, roughly 100 of which host decent trout fishing. Some of the most popular trout-fishing lakes on the east side of Grand Mesa include Eggleston, Trout, Vela, Bonita, Big Creek, Bonham, Silver, and Big Meadows, although it's possible to explore a host of others by road or trail.

GRAND MESA LAKES, EAST

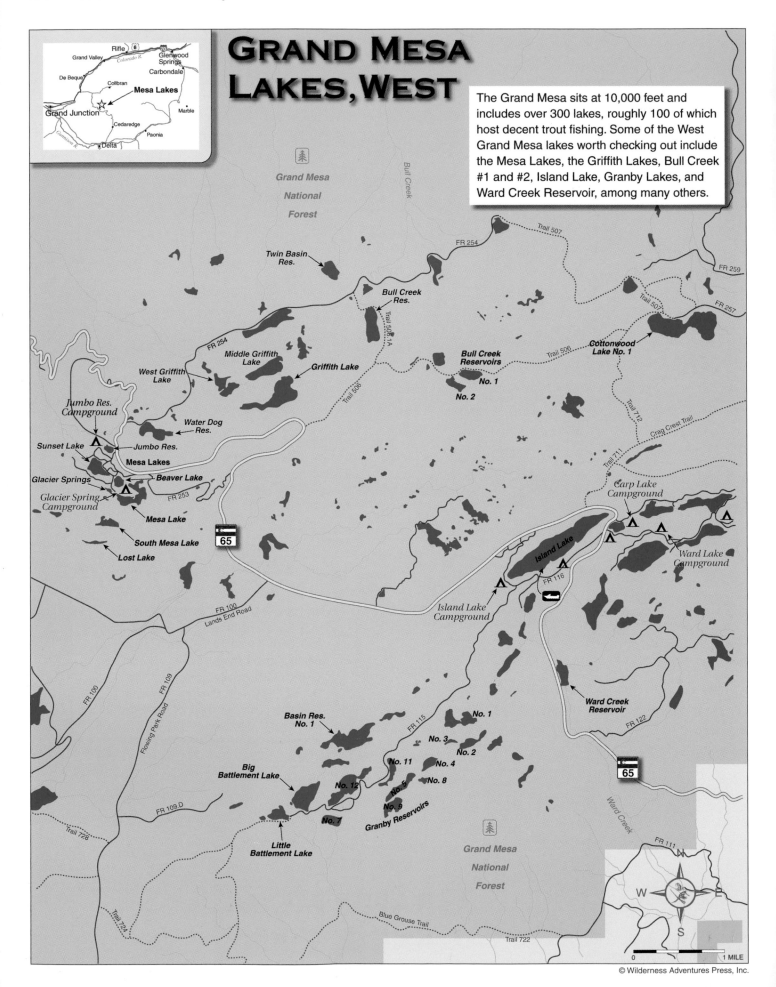

GRAND MESA LAKES, WEST

The Grand Mesa sits at 10,000 feet and includes over 300 lakes, roughly 100 of which host decent trout fishing. Some of the West Grand Mesa lakes worth checking out include the Mesa Lakes, the Griffith Lakes, Bull Creek #1 and #2, Island Lake, Granby Lakes, and Ward Creek Reservoir, among many others.

Grand Mesa
National
Forest

Rifle
Grand Valley
Grand Junction
De Beque
Collbran
Mesa Lakes
Glenwood Springs
Carbondale
Colorado R.
Marble
Cedaredge
Paonia
Delta
Gunnison R.

Bull Creek

Trail 507
FR 254
FR 259
FR 257
Trail 507

Twin Basin Res.

Bull Creek Res.

Trail 508.1A

FR 254
Middle Griffith Lake
West Griffith Lake
Griffith Lake
Trail 506

Bull Creek Reservoirs
No. 1
No. 2

Trail 506
Cottonwood Lake No. 1

Jumbo Res. Campground
Water Dog Res.
Trail 712
Crag Crest Trail
Trail 711

Sunset Lake
Jumbo Res.
Mesa Lakes
Glacier Springs
Beaver Lake
FR 253
Glacier Spring Campground
Mesa Lake
South Mesa Lake
Lost Lake

Carp Lake Campground
Ward Lake Campground
Island Lake
FR 116
Island Lake Campground

65

FR 100
Lands End Road

Ward Creek Reservoir
FR 122

FR 100
FR 109
Flowing Park Road

Basin Res. No. 1
FR 115
No. 1
No. 3
No. 2

Big Battlement Lake
No. 11
No. 4
No. 8
No. 12
No. 5
No. 9
No. 7
Granby Reservoirs

65

Ward Creek

FR 109.D

Trail 728
Little Battlement Lake

Grand Mesa
National
Forest

FR 111

N
W
E
S

Blue Grouse Trail

Trail 724
Trail 722

0   1 MILE

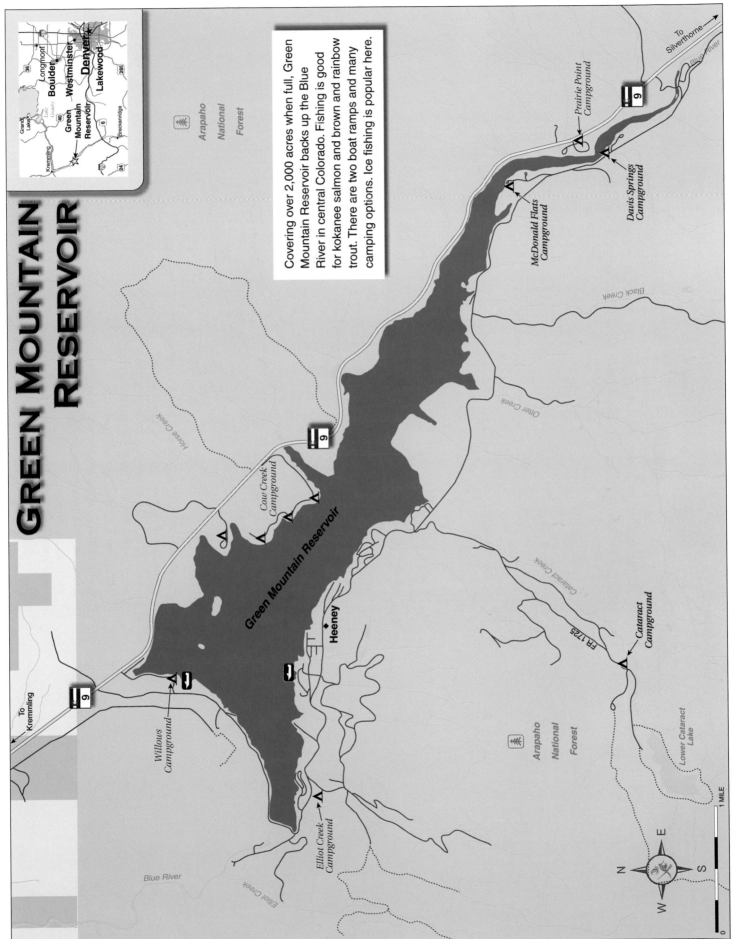

GREEN MOUNTAIN RESERVOIR

Covering over 2,000 acres when full, Green Mountain Reservoir backs up the Blue River in central Colorado. Fishing is good for kokanee salmon and brown and rainbow trout. There are two boat ramps and many camping options. Ice fishing is popular here.

Arapaho National Forest

To Silverthorne

Prairie Point Campground

Davis Springs Campground

McDonald Flats Campground

Black Creek

Otter Creek

Horse Creek

Cow Creek Campground

Green Mountain Reservoir

Cataract Creek

FR 1725

Cataract Campground

Heeney

Arapaho National Forest

Lower Cataract Lake

To Kremmling

Willows Campground

Elliot Creek Campground

Blue River

Elliot Creek

1 MILE

N E W S

© Wilderness Adventures Press, Inc.

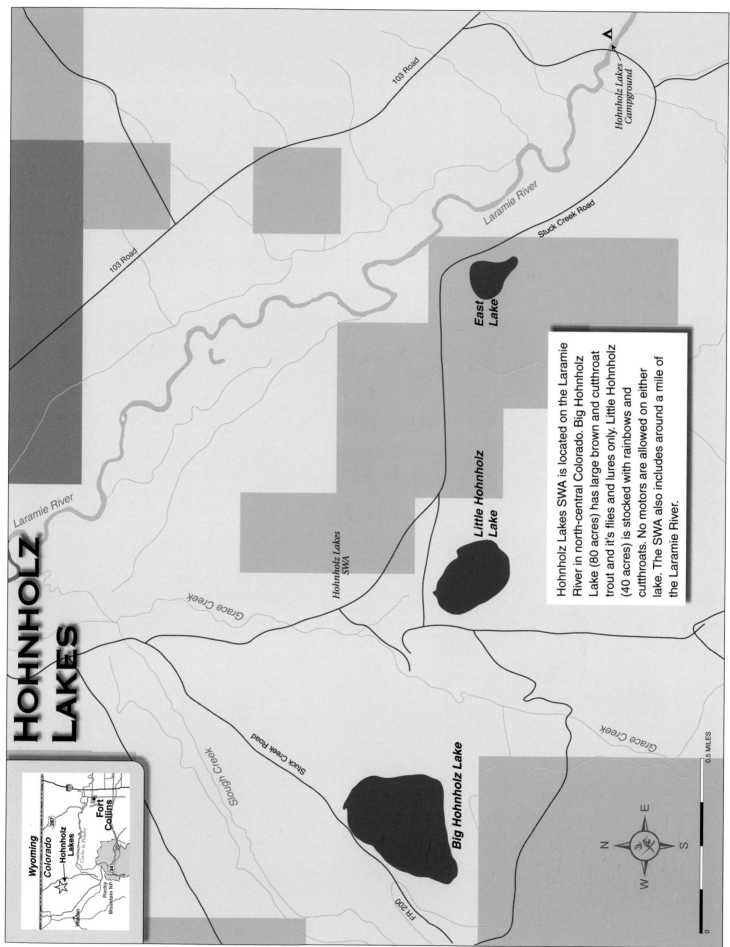

HOHNHOLZ LAKES

Hohnholz Lakes SWA is located on the Laramie River in north-central Colorado. Big Hohnholz Lake (80 acres) has large brown and cutthroat trout and it's flies and lures only. Little Hohnholz (40 acres) is stocked with rainbows and cutthroats. No motors are allowed on either lake. The SWA also includes around a mile of the Laramie River.

East Lake

Little Hohnholz Lake

Big Hohnholz Lake

Hohnholz Lakes SWA

Hohnholz Lakes Campground

103 Road

Laramie River

Stuck Creek Road

Grace Creek

Slough Creek

FR 200

0   0.5 MILES

Wyoming

Colorado

Hohnholz Lakes

Fort Collins

Rocky Mountain NP

Walden

Cache la Poudre

287

14

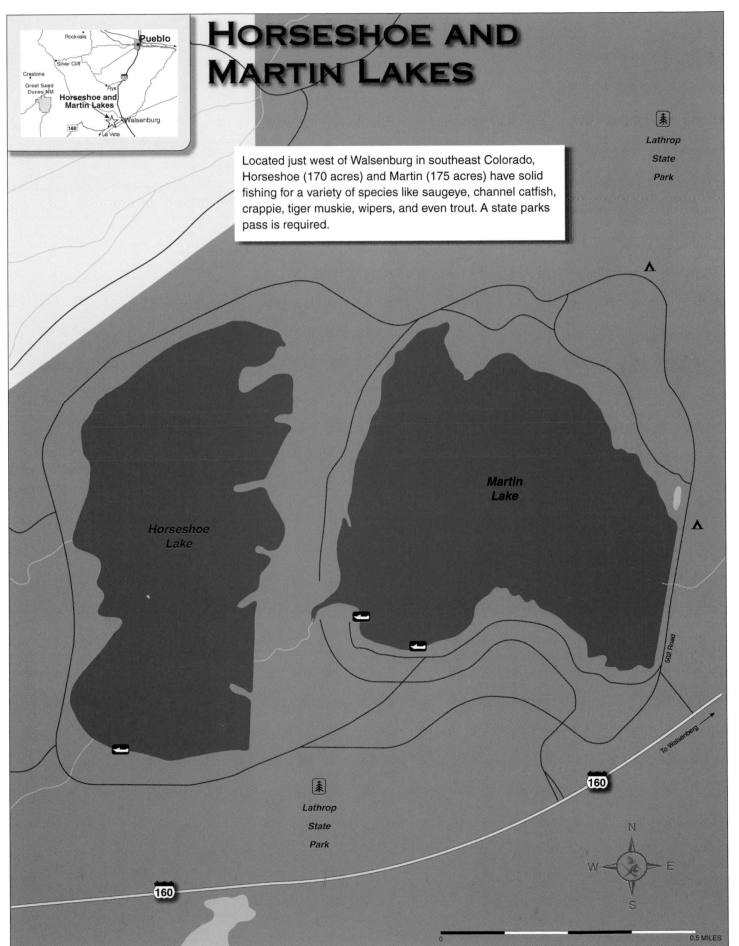

HORSESHOE AND MARTIN LAKES

Located just west of Walsenburg in southeast Colorado, Horseshoe (170 acres) and Martin (175 acres) have solid fishing for a variety of species like saugeye, channel catfish, crappie, tiger muskie, wipers, and even trout. A state parks pass is required.

Lathrop State Park

Martin Lake

Horseshoe Lake

Lathrop State Park

502 Road

To Walsenberg

160

160

N
W — E
S

0   0.5 MILES

© Wilderness Adventures Press, Inc.

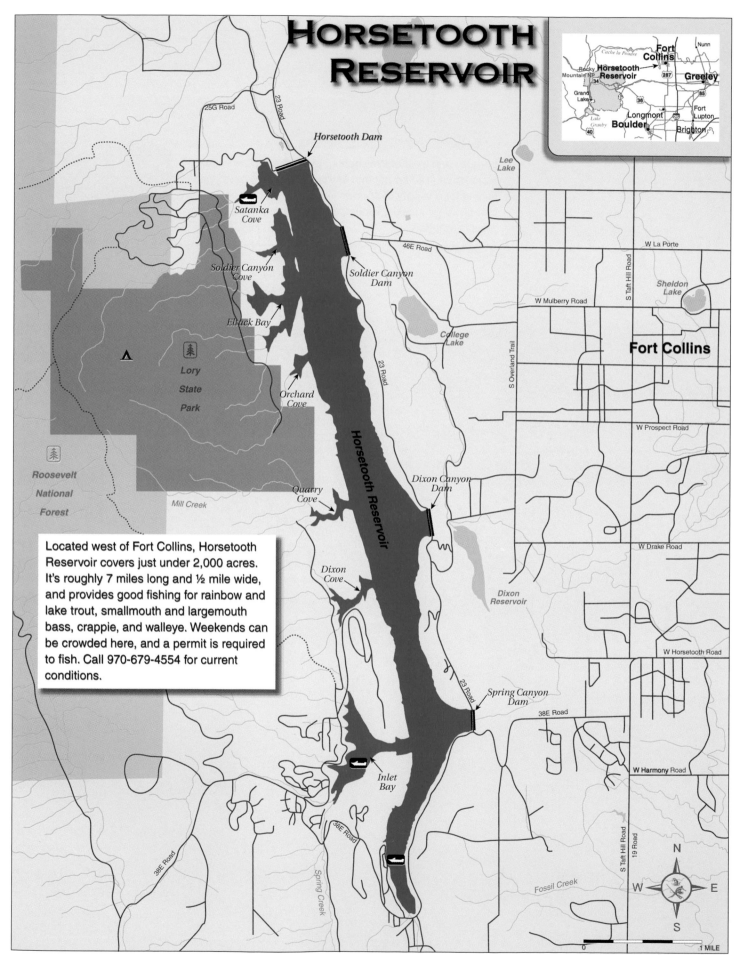

HORSETOOTH RESERVOIR

Horsetooth Dam

Satanka Cove

Soldier Canyon Cove

Soldier Canyon Dam

Eltuck Bay

Orchard Cove

Horsetooth Reservoir

Lory State Park

Roosevelt National Forest

Mill Creek

Quarry Cove

Dixon Canyon Dam

Dixon Cove

Dixon Reservoir

Lee Lake

College Lake

Sheldon Lake

Fort Collins

Spring Canyon Dam

Inlet Bay

Spring Creek

Fossil Creek

Located west of Fort Collins, Horsetooth Reservoir covers just under 2,000 acres. It's roughly 7 miles long and ½ mile wide, and provides good fishing for rainbow and lake trout, smallmouth and largemouth bass, crappie, and walleye. Weekends can be crowded here, and a permit is required to fish. Call 970-679-4554 for current conditions.

25G Road

23 Road

46E Road

W La Porte

W Mulberry Road

S Taft Hill Road

S Overland Trail

W Prospect Road

W Drake Road

W Horsetooth Road

38E Road

W Harmony Road

S Taft Hill Road

19 Road

Nunn
Fort Collins
Greeley
Cache la Poudre
Rocky Mountain NP
Horsetooth Reservoir
287
Grand Lake
34
36
Fort Lupton
85
Lake Granby
Longmont
Boulder
Brighton
40

1 MILE

0   1 MILE

N
W   E
S

© Wilderness Adventures Press, Inc.

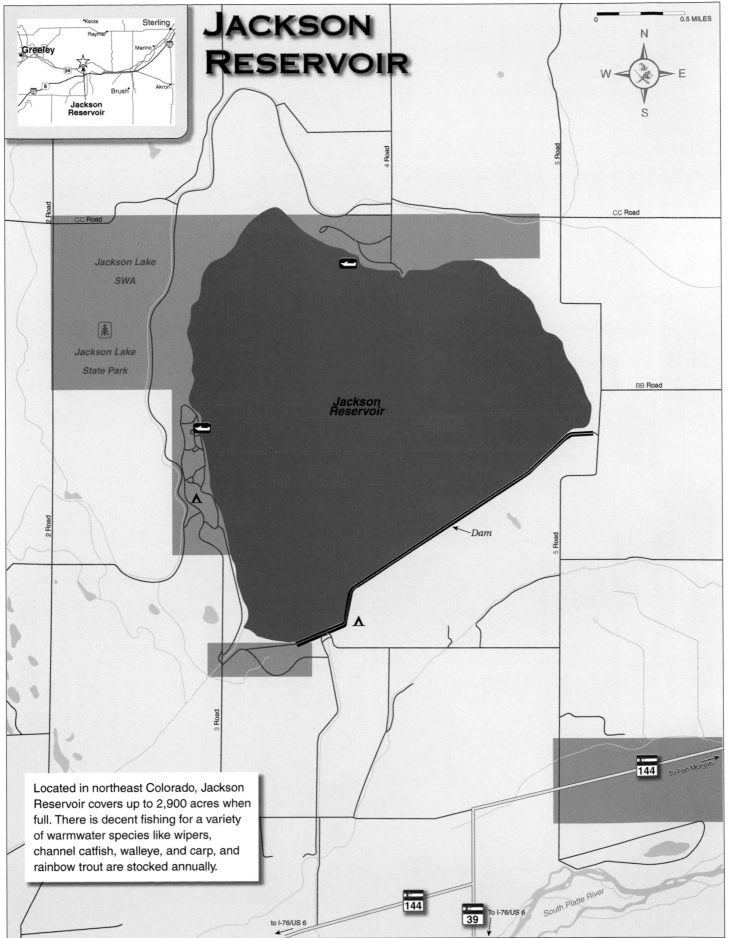

JACKSON RESERVOIR

Located in northeast Colorado, Jackson Reservoir covers up to 2,900 acres when full. There is decent fishing for a variety of warmwater species like wipers, channel catfish, walleye, and carp, and rainbow trout are stocked annually.

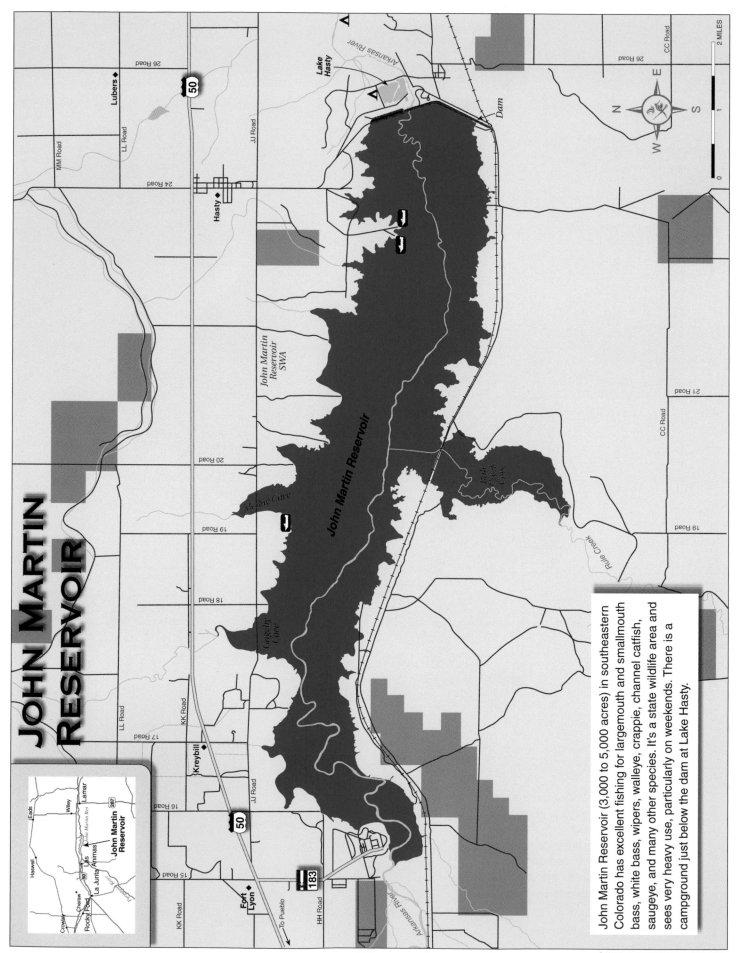

JOHN MARTIN RESERVOIR

John Martin Reservoir (3,000 to 5,000 acres) in southeastern Colorado has excellent fishing for largemouth and smallmouth bass, white bass, wipers, walleye, crappie, channel catfish, saugeye, and many other species. It's a state wildlife area and sees very heavy use, particularly on weekends. There is a campground just below the dam at Lake Hasty.

John Martin Reservoir SWA

John Martin Reservoir

Dam

Lake Hasty

Arkansas River

Rule Creek

Rule Ghost Creek

Alkaline Cove

Gageby Creek

Fort Lyon

Kreybill

Hasty

Lubers

50

50

183

26 Road

24 Road

21 Road

19 Road

18 Road

17 Road

16 Road

15 Road

20 Road

MM Road

LL Road

KK Road

JJ Road

HH Road

CC Road

To Pueblo

N

E

S

W

2 MILES

1

0

Eads

Haswell

Wiley

Lamar

287

Crowley

Cheraw

Rocky Ford

La Junta

Las Animas

John Martin Rex

John Martin Reservoir

Arkansas River

50

© Wilderness Adventures Press, Inc.

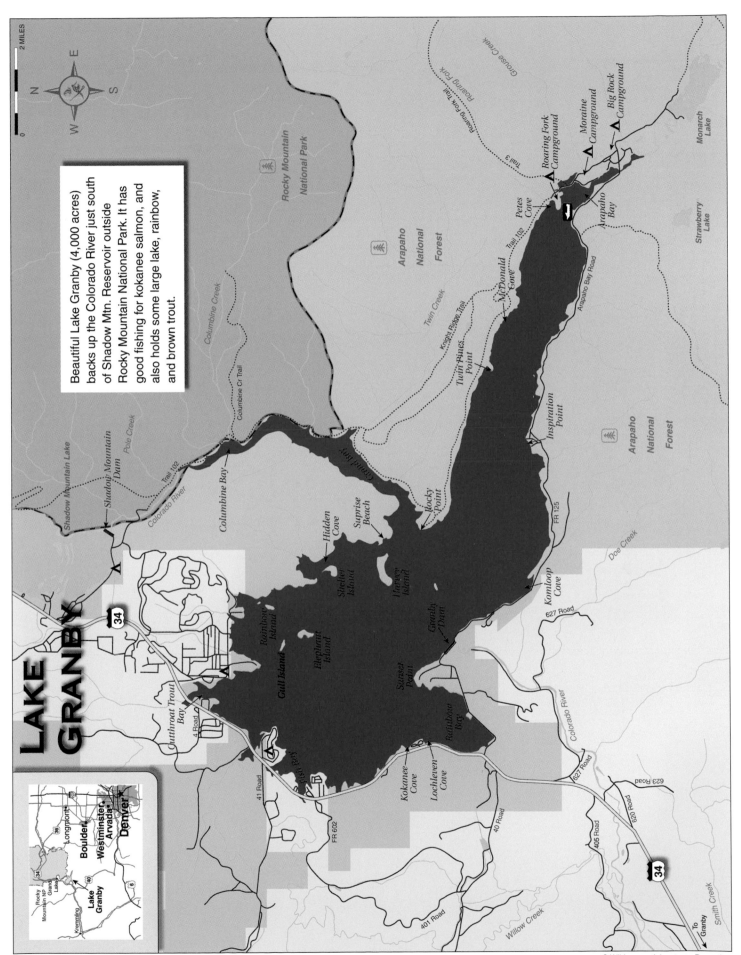

LAKE GRANBY

Beautiful Lake Granby (4,000 acres) backs up the Colorado River just south of Shadow Mtn. Reservoir outside Rocky Mountain National Park. It has good fishing for kokanee salmon, and also holds some large lake, rainbow, and brown trout.

2 MILES

N E S W

Rocky Mountain National Park

Arapaho National Forest

Monarch Lake

Strawberry Lake

Grouse Creek

Roaring Fork

Roaring Fork Trail

Trail 3

Roaring Fork Campground

Moraine Campground

Big Rock Campground

Petes Cove

Arapaho Bay

Arapaho Bay Road

McDonald Cove

Trail 102

Knight Ridge Trail

Twin Creek

Twin Pines Point

Inspiration Point

Arapaho National Forest

FR 125

Doe Creek

Komloop Cove

627 Road

Colorado River

Columbine Creek

Columbine Cr Trail

Pole Creek

Shadow Mountain Lake

Shadow Mountain Dam

Colorado River

Trail 102

Columbine Bay

Grand Bay

Hidden Cove

Suprise Beach

Rocky Point

Shelter Island

Harvey Island

Granby Dam

Rainbow Island

Elephant Island

Gull Island

Sunset Point

Rainbow Bay

Kokanee Cove

Lochleven Cove

Fish Bay

Cutthroat Trout Bay

4 Road

41 Road

FR 602

401 Road

40 Road

405 Road

623 Road

620 Road

627 Road

Willow Creek

Smith Creek

To Granby

34

34

Rocky Mountain NP

Grand Lake

Lake Granby

Kremmling

Longmont

Boulder

Westminster

Arvada

Denver

40

36

34

6

85

© Wilderness Adventures Press, Inc.

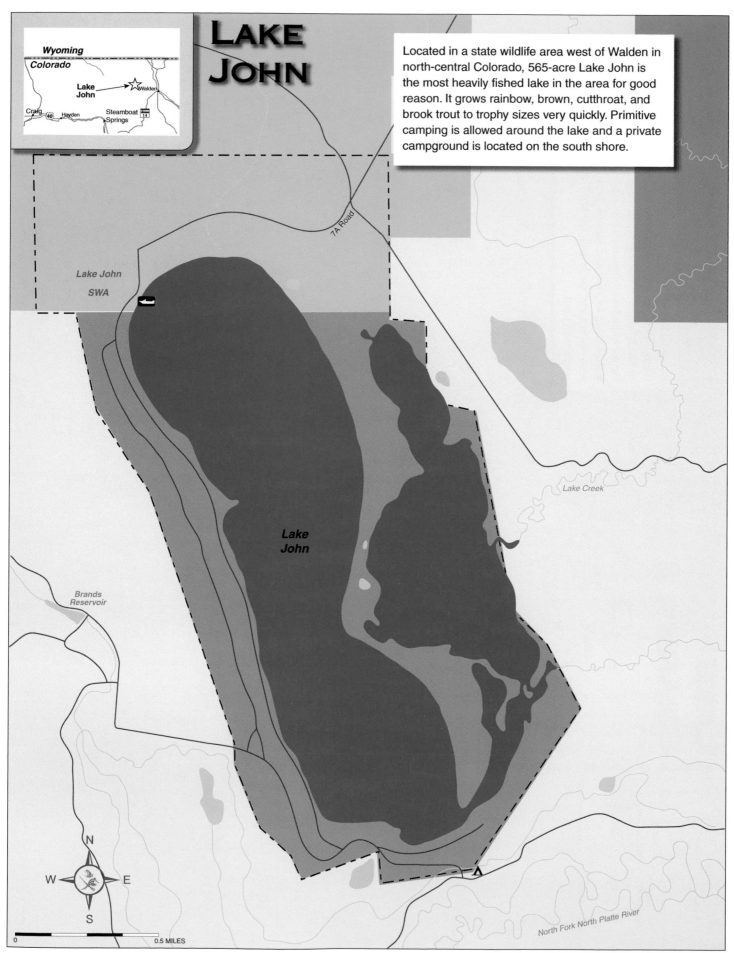

LAKE JOHN

Wyoming
Colorado

Lake John

Craig · 40 · Hayden · Steamboat Springs · 14 · Walden

Located in a state wildlife area west of Walden in north-central Colorado, 565-acre Lake John is the most heavily fished lake in the area for good reason. It grows rainbow, brown, cutthroat, and brook trout to trophy sizes very quickly. Primitive camping is allowed around the lake and a private campground is located on the south shore.

7A Road

Lake John SWA

Lake Creek

Lake John

Brands Reservoir

N
W E
S

0   0.5 MILES

North Fork North Platte River

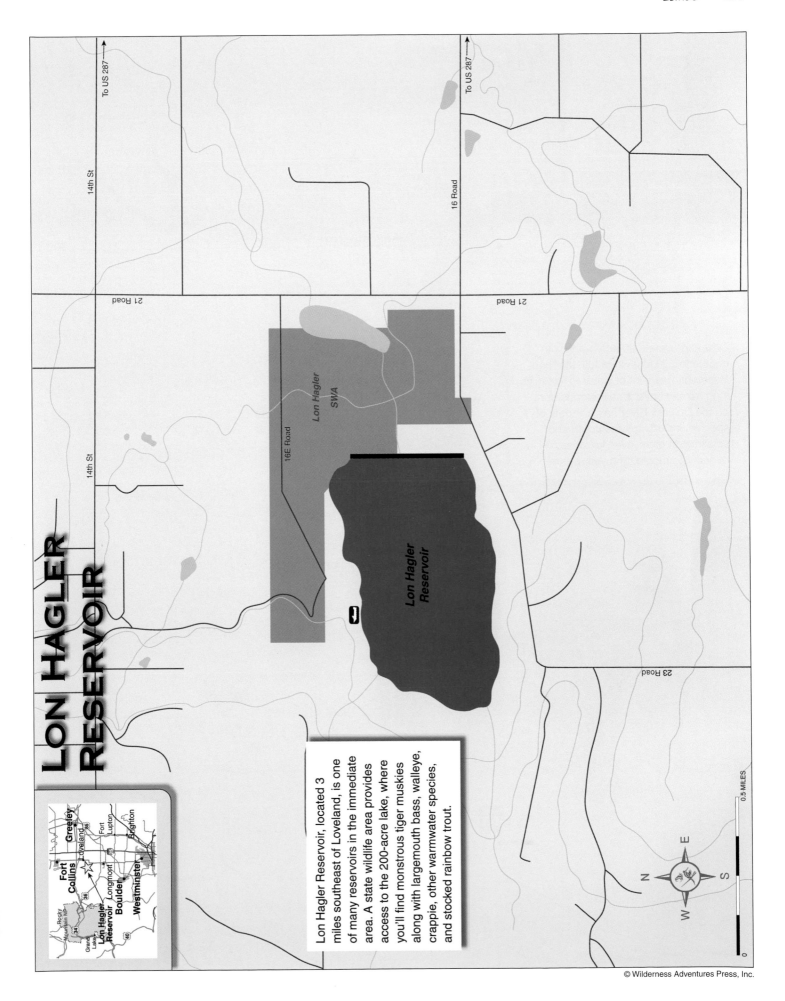

LON HAGLER RESERVOIR

Lon Hagler Reservoir, located 3 miles southeast of Loveland, is one of many reservoirs in the immediate area. A state wildlife area provides access to the 200-acre lake, where you'll find monstrous tiger muskies along with largemouth bass, walleye, crappie, other warmwater species, and stocked rainbow trout.

Lon Hagler SWA

Lon Hagler Reservoir

16E Road

14th St

21 Road

16 Road

23 Road

To US 287

0.5 MILES

N W E S

Fort Collins
Greeley
Loveland
Fort Lupton
Brighton
Longmont
Boulder
Westminster
Lon Hagler Reservoir
Rocky Mountain NP
Grand Lakes

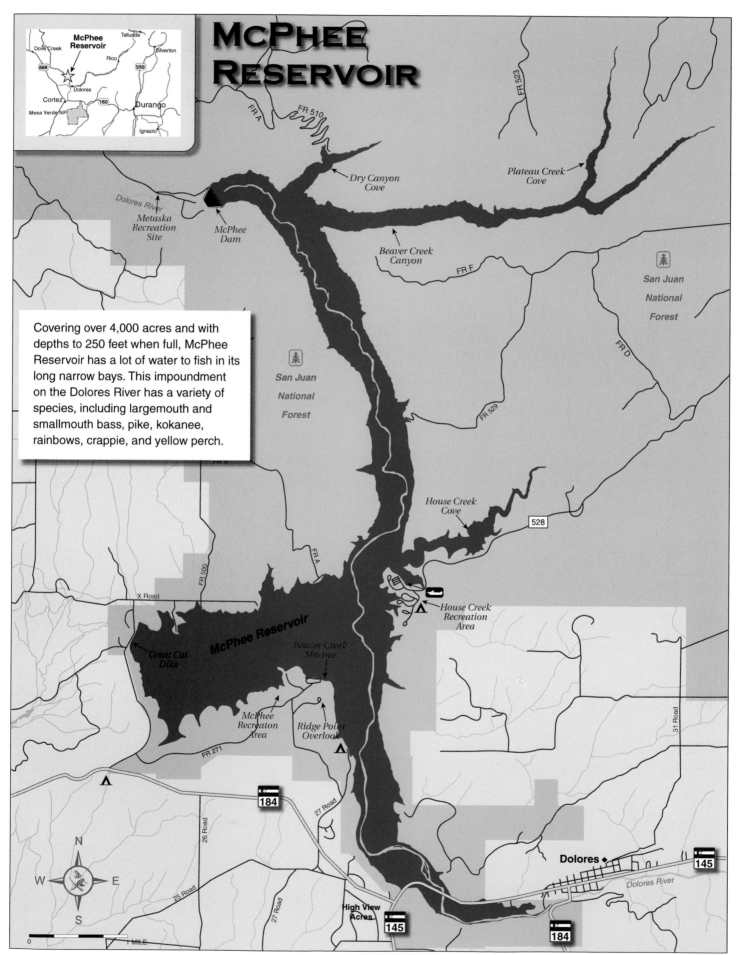

MCPHEE RESERVOIR

Covering over 4,000 acres and with depths to 250 feet when full, McPhee Reservoir has a lot of water to fish in its long narrow bays. This impoundment on the Dolores River has a variety of species, including largemouth and smallmouth bass, pike, kokanee, rainbows, crappie, and yellow perch.

Dry Canyon Cove

Plateau Creek Cove

Beaver Creek Canyon

San Juan National Forest

Dolores River

Metaska Recreation Site

McPhee Dam

San Juan National Forest

House Creek Cove

House Creek Recreation Area

McPhee Reservoir

Great Cut Dike

Beaver Creek Marina

McPhee Recreaton Area

Ridge Point Overlook

Dolores

Dolores River

High View Acres

FR 523
FR A
FR 510
FR F
FR D
FR 529
FR X
FR A
FR 500
X Road
FR 271
26 Road
25 Road
27 Road
27 Road
31 Road
528
184
145
145
184

N
W   E
S

0   1 MILE

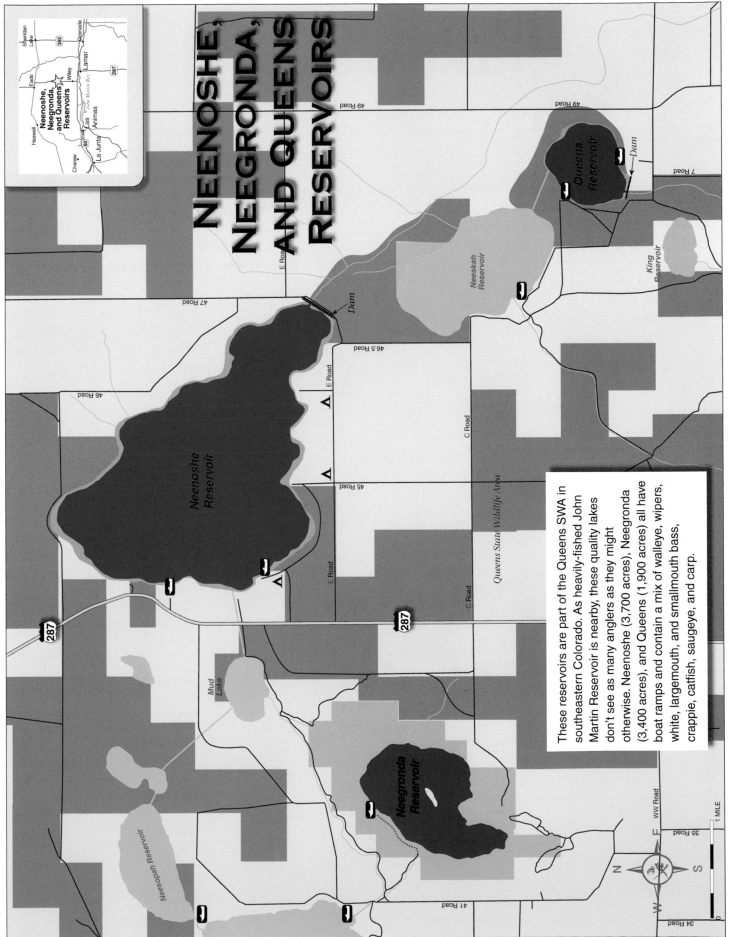

NEENOSHE, NEEGRONDA, AND QUEENS RESERVOIRS

Queens Reservoir

Dam

Neeskah Reservoir

King Reservoir

Dam

Neenoshe Reservoir

49 Road

49 Road

7 Road

47 Road

46.5 Road

46 Road

E Road

E Road

C Road

45 Road

Queens State Wildlife Area

C Road

E Road

287

Mud Lake

Neesopah Reservoir

Neegronda Reservoir

41 Road

35 Road

34 Road

WW Road

F

N

S

W

E

1 MILE

These reservoirs are part of the Queens SWA in southeastern Colorado. As heavily-fished John Martin Reservoir is nearby, these quality lakes don't see as many anglers as they might otherwise. Neenoshe (3,700 acres), Neegronda (3,400 acres), and Queens (1,900 acres) all have boat ramps and contain a mix of walleye, wipers, white, largemouth, and smallmouth bass, crappie, catfish, saugeye, and carp.

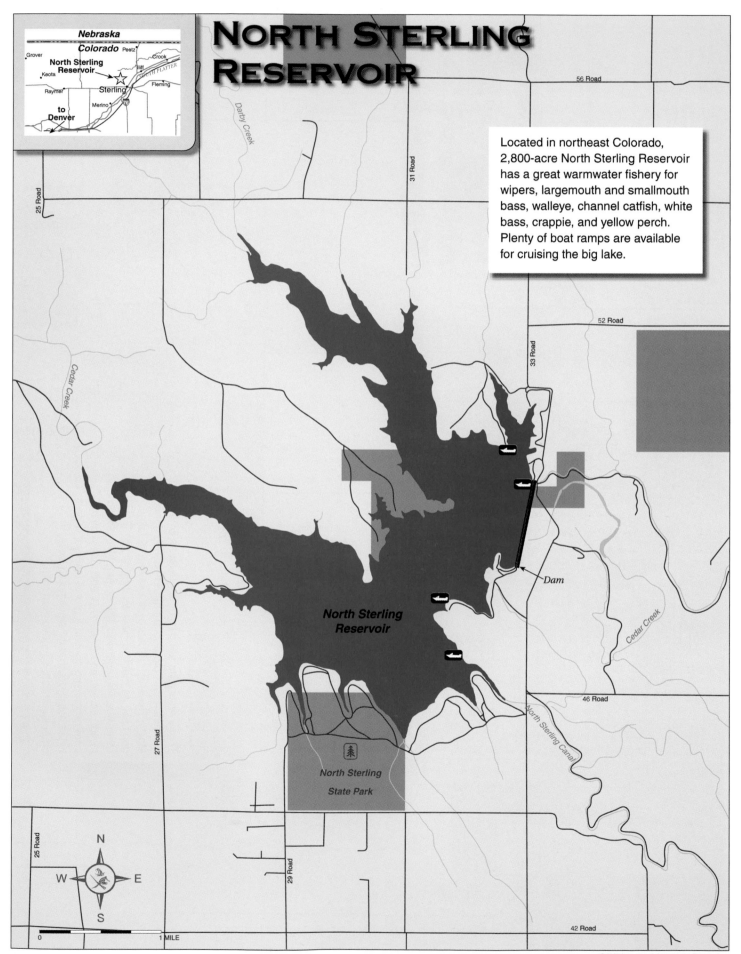

NORTH STERLING RESERVOIR

Located in northeast Colorado, 2,800-acre North Sterling Reservoir has a great warmwater fishery for wipers, largemouth and smallmouth bass, walleye, channel catfish, white bass, crappie, and yellow perch. Plenty of boat ramps are available for cruising the big lake.

North Sterling Reservoir

North Sterling State Park

Dam

0   1 MILE

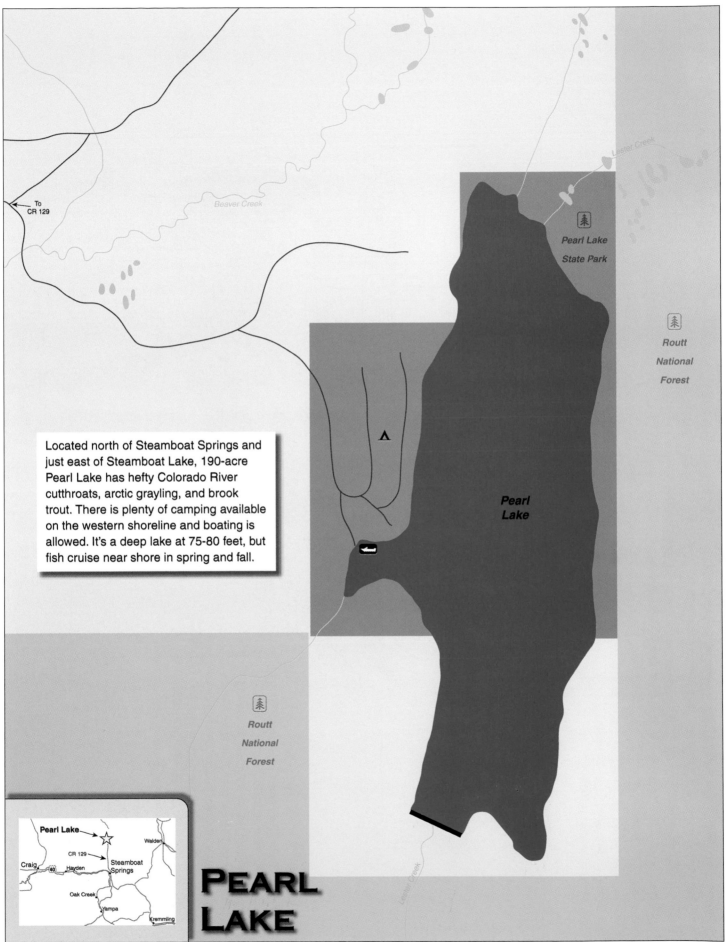

Beaver Creek

To
CR 129

Lester Creek

Pearl Lake
State Park

Routt

National

Forest

Pearl
Lake

Located north of Steamboat Springs and just east of Steamboat Lake, 190-acre Pearl Lake has hefty Colorado River cutthroats, arctic grayling, and brook trout. There is plenty of camping available on the western shoreline and boating is allowed. It's a deep lake at 75-80 feet, but fish cruise near shore in spring and fall.

Routt

National

Forest

Lester Creek

Pearl Lake

Walden

CR 129

Craig 40 Hayden Steamboat
Springs

Oak Creek

Yampa

Kremmling

PEARL
LAKE

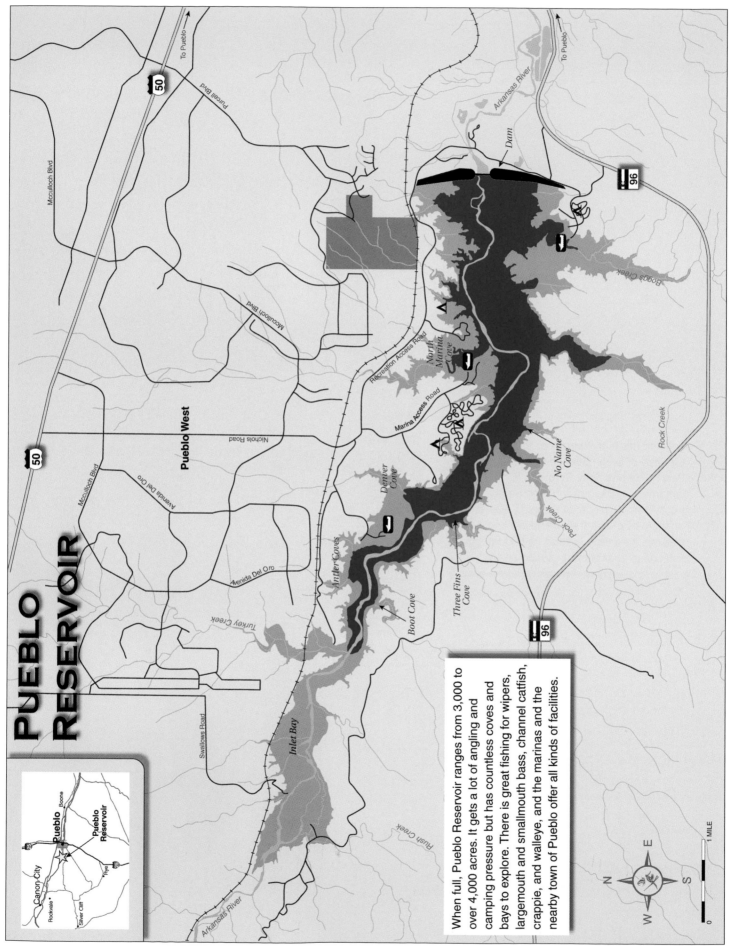

PUEBLO RESERVOIR

When full, Pueblo Reservoir ranges from 3,000 to over 4,000 acres. It gets a lot of angling and camping pressure but has countless coves and bays to explore. There is great fishing for wipers, largemouth and smallmouth bass, channel catfish, crappie, and walleye, and the marinas and the nearby town of Pueblo offer all kinds of facilities.

1 MILE

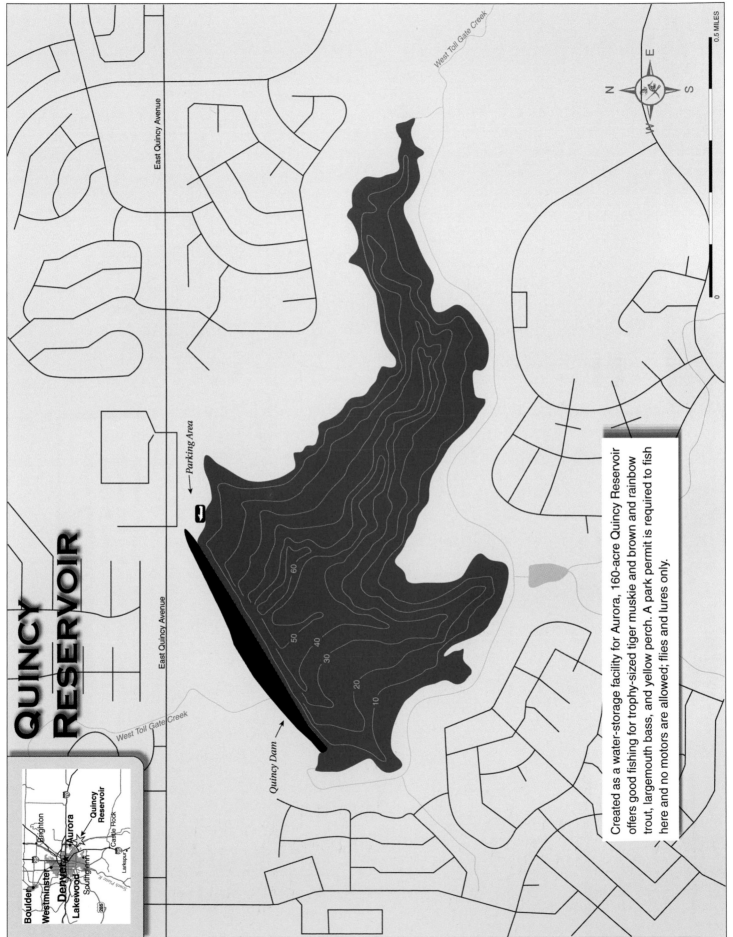

QUINCY RESERVOIR

Parking Area

Quincy Dam

East Quincy Avenue

West Toll Gate Creek

West Gate Creek

60

50

40

30

20

10

Created as a water-storage facility for Aurora, 160-acre Quincy Reservoir offers good fishing for trophy-sized tiger muskie and brown and rainbow trout, largemouth bass, and yellow perch. A park permit is required to fish here and no motors are allowed; flies and lures only.

Boulder
Westminster
Denver
Lakewood
Brighton
Aurora
Quincy Reservoir
Southglenn
Castle Rock
Larkspur

0.5 MILES

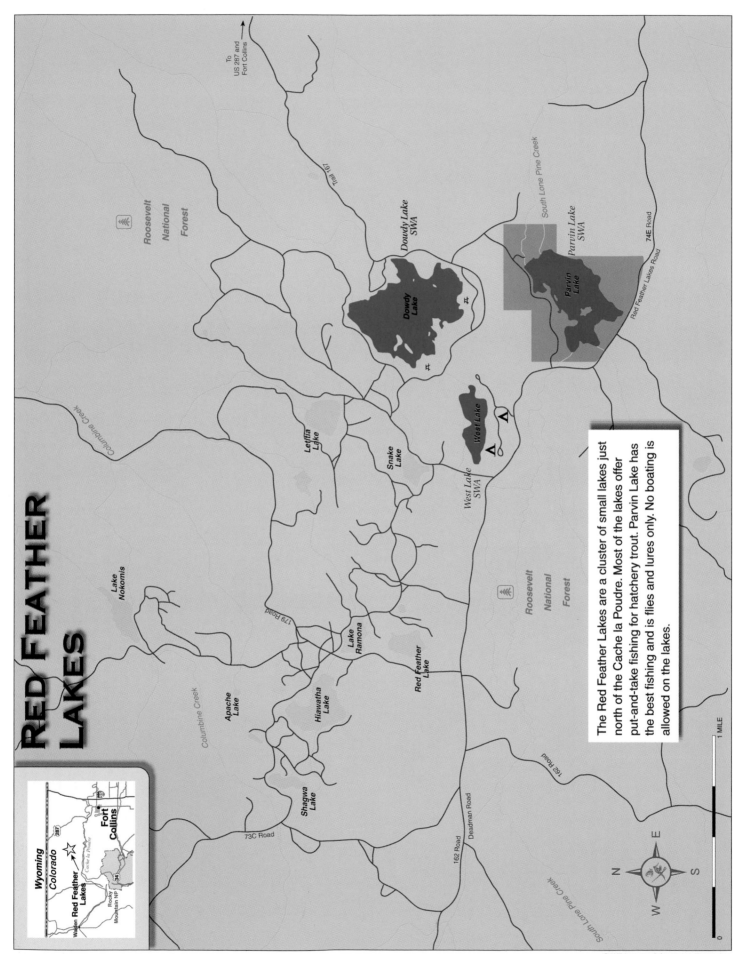

RED FEATHER LAKES

The Red Feather Lakes are a cluster of small lakes just north of the Cache la Poudre. Most of the lakes offer put-and-take fishing for hatchery trout. Parvin Lake has the best fishing and is flies and lures only. No boating is allowed on the lakes.

Roosevelt National Forest

Dowdy Lake SWA

Dowdy Lake

Parvin Lake SWA

Parvin Lake

South Lone Pine Creek

74E Road

Red Feather Lakes Road

Trail 167

To US 287 and Fort Collins

Columbine Creek

Letffia Lake

Snake Lake

West Lake

West Lake SWA

Lake Nokomis

179 Road

Lake Ramona

Red Feather Lake

Roosevelt National Forest

Columbine Creek

Apache Lake

Hiawatha Lake

Shagwa Lake

73C Road

162 Road

Deadman Road

182 Road

South Lone Pine Creek

Wyoming
Colorado
Fort Collins
Cache la Poudre
Red Feather Lakes
Walden
Rocky Mountain NP

1 MILE
0

N E S W

© Wilderness Adventures Press, Inc.

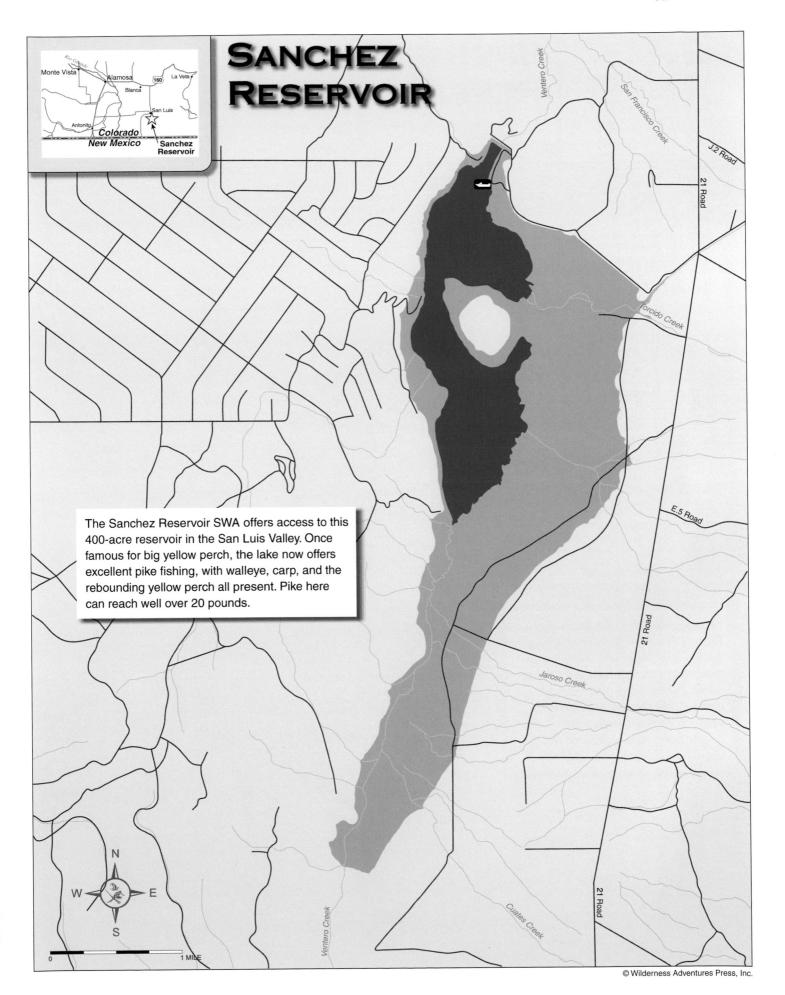

SANCHEZ RESERVOIR

The Sanchez Reservoir SWA offers access to this 400-acre reservoir in the San Luis Valley. Once famous for big yellow perch, the lake now offers excellent pike fishing, with walleye, carp, and the rebounding yellow perch all present. Pike here can reach well over 20 pounds.

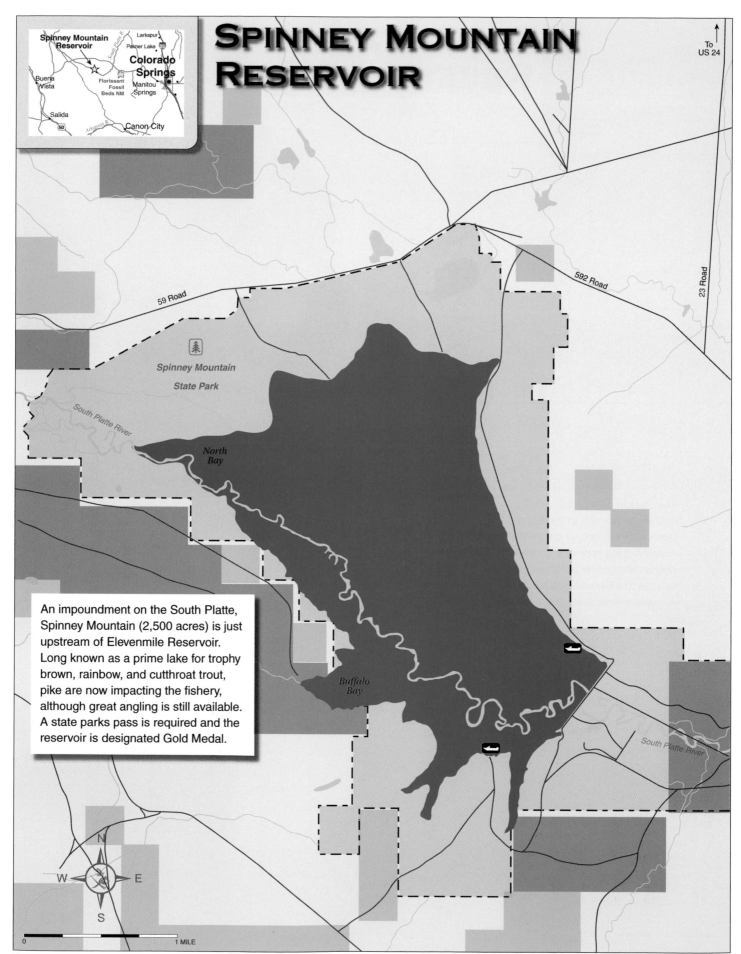

SPINNEY MOUNTAIN RESERVOIR

Spinney Mountain Reservoir

Larkspur
Palmer Lake

Colorado Springs

Buena Vista

Florissant Fossil Beds NM

Manitou Springs

Salida

Arkansas R.

Canon City

To US 24

592 Road

23 Road

59 Road

Spinney Mountain

State Park

South Platte River

North Bay

An impoundment on the South Platte, Spinney Mountain (2,500 acres) is just upstream of Elevenmile Reservoir. Long known as a prime lake for trophy brown, rainbow, and cutthroat trout, pike are now impacting the fishery, although great angling is still available. A state parks pass is required and the reservoir is designated Gold Medal.

Buffalo Bay

South Platte River

N
W   E
S

0   1 MILE

© Wilderness Adventures Press, Inc.

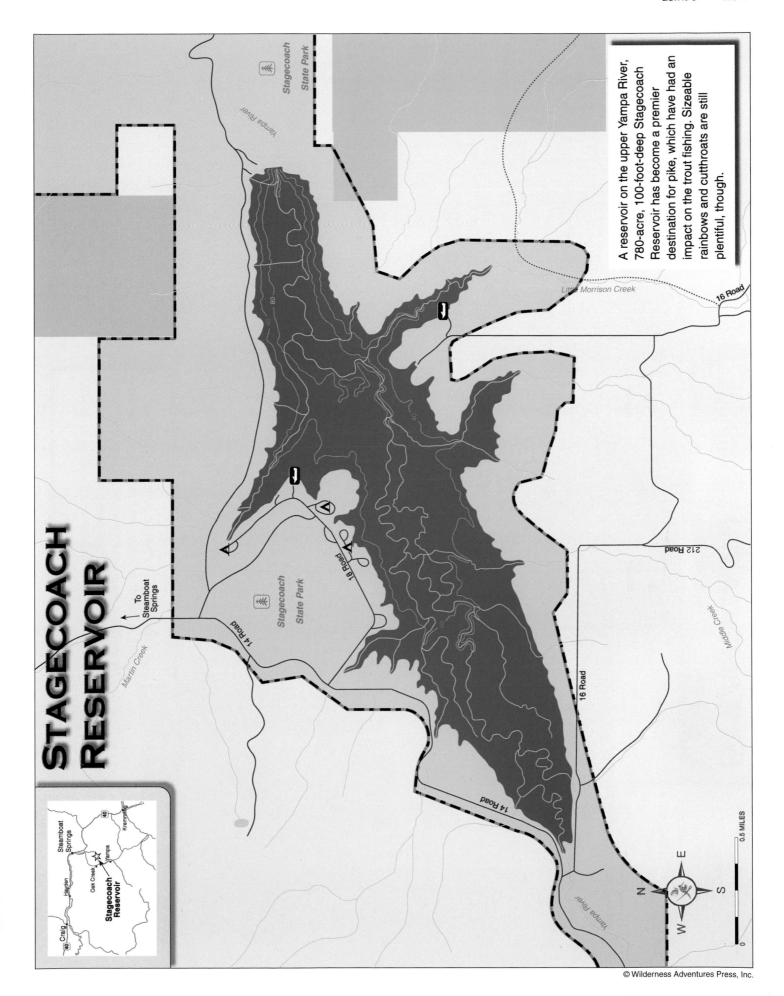

STAGECOACH RESERVOIR

A reservoir on the upper Yampa River, 780-acre, 100-foot-deep Stagecoach Reservoir has become a premier destination for pike, which have had an impact on the trout fishing. Sizeable rainbows and cutthroats are still plentiful, though.

Stagecoach State Park

Yampa River

Little Morrison Creek

16 Road

212 Road

16 Road

Middle Creek

80

40

40

18 Road

Stagecoach State Park

14 Road

To Steamboat Springs

Martin Creek

14 Road

Yampa River

N
E
S
W

0.5 MILES

Steamboat Springs

Hayden

Craig

Oak Creek

Yampa

Kremmling

Stagecoach Reservoir

© Wilderness Adventures Press, Inc.

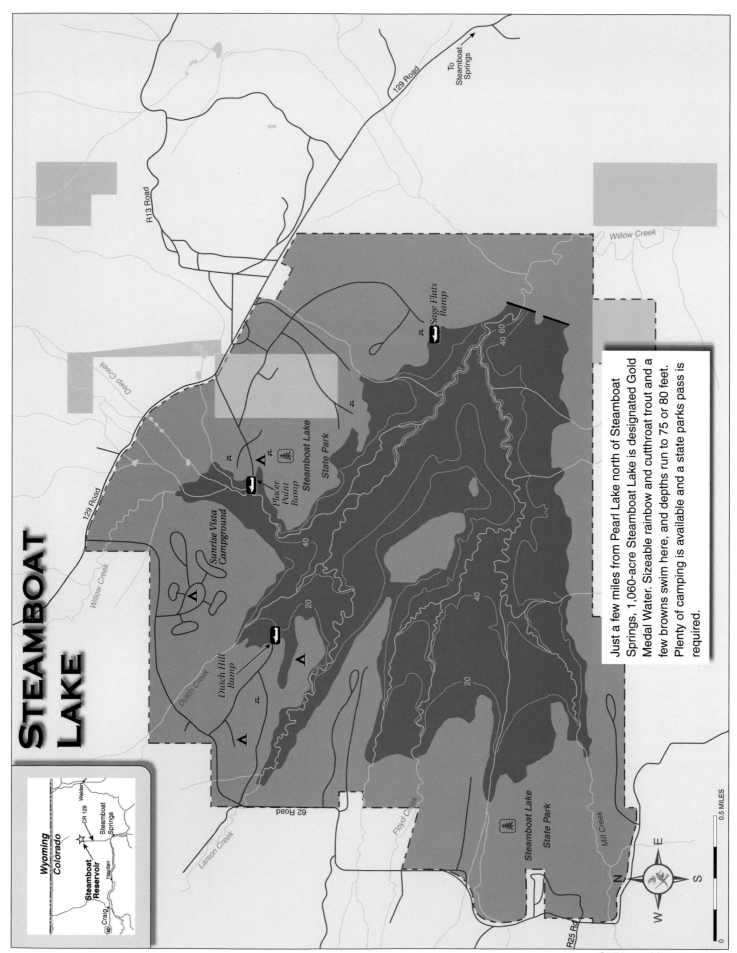

STEAMBOAT LAKE

Just a few miles from Pearl Lake north of Steamboat Springs, 1,060-acre Steamboat Lake is designated Gold Medal Water. Sizeable rainbow and cutthroat trout and a few browns swim here, and depths run to 75 or 80 feet. Plenty of camping is available and a state parks pass is required.

Sage Flats Ramp

Steamboat Lake State Park

Placer Point Ramp

Sunrise Vista Campground

Dutch Hill Ramp

129 Road

Willow Creek

Deep Creek

To Steamboat Springs

R13 Road

Dutch Creek

62 Road

Larson Creek

Floyd Creek

Mill Creek

R25 Rd

Willow Creek

40 60

40

20

20

40

Wyoming
Colorado

Walden

CR 129

Steamboat Springs

Steamboat Reservoir

Hayden

Craig

N
W E
S

0   0.5 MILES

© Wilderness Adventures Press, Inc.

TAYLOR PARK RESERVOIR

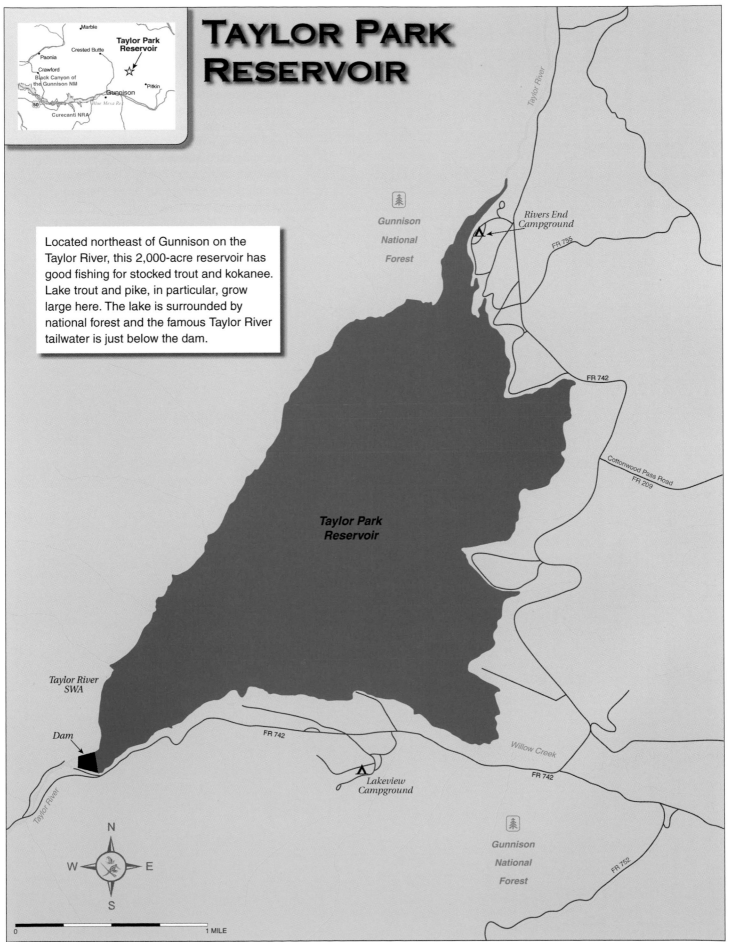

Marble
Taylor Park Reservoir
Crested Butte
Paonia
Crawford
Black Canyon of
the Gunnison NM
Gunnison
Pitkin
50
Blue Mesa Res.
Curecanti NRA

Located northeast of Gunnison on the Taylor River, this 2,000-acre reservoir has good fishing for stocked trout and kokanee. Lake trout and pike, in particular, grow large here. The lake is surrounded by national forest and the famous Taylor River tailwater is just below the dam.

Taylor River

Gunnison
National
Forest

Rivers End Campground

FR 755

FR 742

Cottonwood Pass Road
FR 209

Taylor Park
Reservoir

Taylor River
SWA

Dam

FR 742

Willow Creek

FR 742

Lakeview
Campground

Taylor River

Gunnison
National
Forest

FR 752

N
W   E
S

0   1 MILE

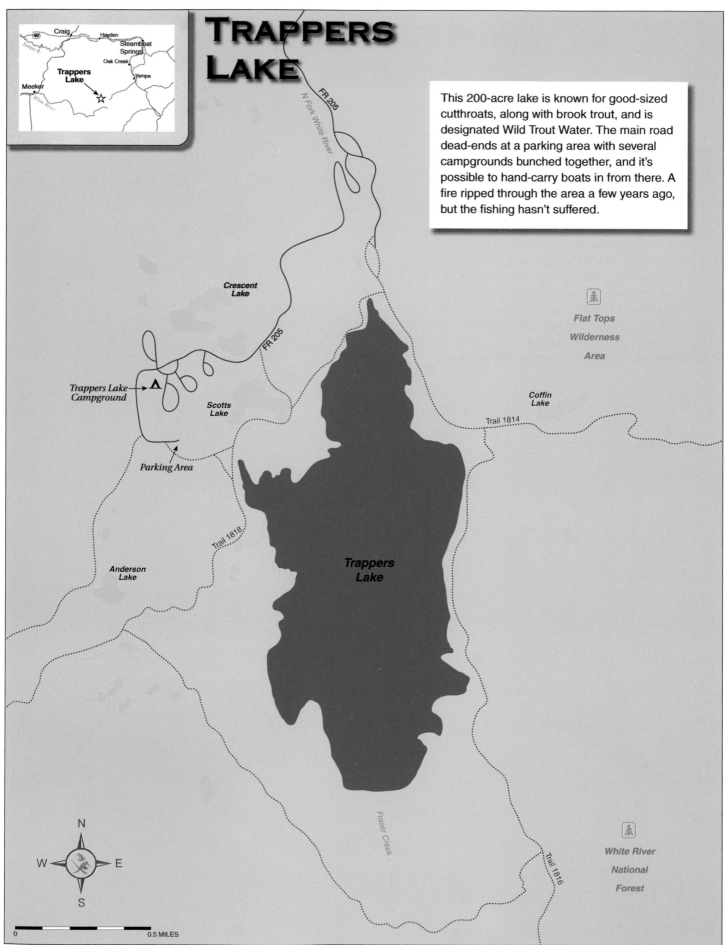

TRAPPERS LAKE

Craig
Hayden
Steamboat Springs
Oak Creek
Yampa
Trappers Lake
Meeker
White River
Yampa R.
40

This 200-acre lake is known for good-sized cutthroats, along with brook trout, and is designated Wild Trout Water. The main road dead-ends at a parking area with several campgrounds bunched together, and it's possible to hand-carry boats in from there. A fire ripped through the area a few years ago, but the fishing hasn't suffered.

FR 205

N Fork White River

Crescent Lake

FR 205

Flat Tops
Wilderness
Area

Trappers Lake Campground

Scotts Lake

Coffin Lake

Trail 1814

Parking Area

Trail 1818

Trappers Lake

Anderson Lake

Fraser Creek

White River
National
Forest

Trail 1816

N
W   E
S

0   0.5 MILES

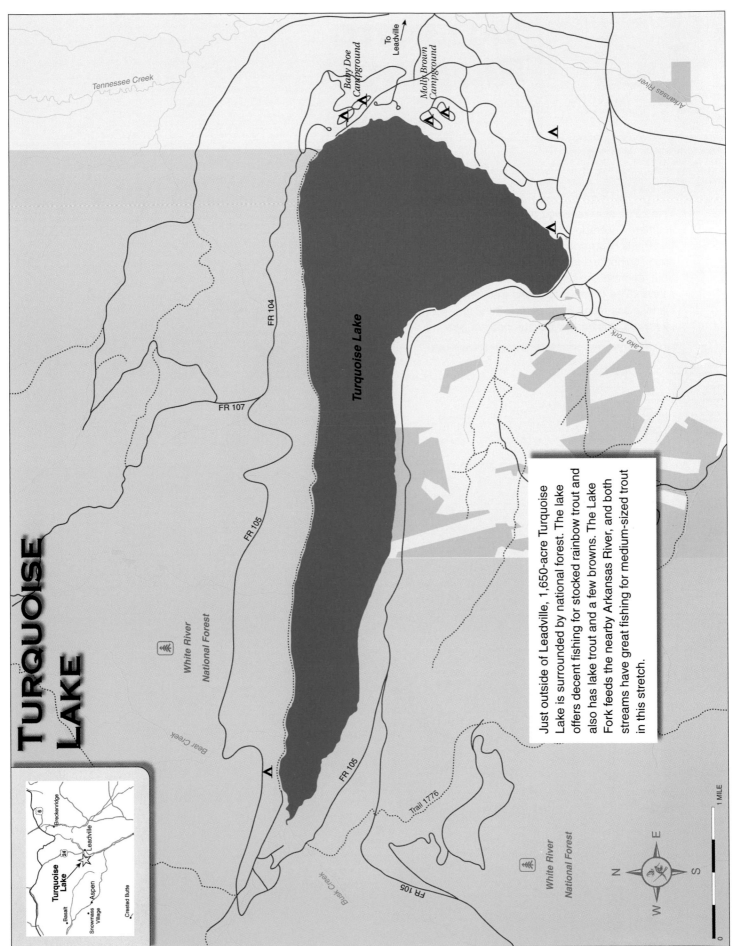

TURQUOISE LAKE

Tennessee Creek

Baby Doe Campground

Molly Brown Campground

To Leadville

Arkansas River

Turquoise Lake

FR 104

FR 107

FR 105

Lake Fork

White River National Forest

Bear Creek

FR 105

Trail 1776

Bisk Creek

FR 105

White River National Forest

Just outside of Leadville, 1,650-acre Turquoise Lake is surrounded by national forest. The lake offers decent fishing for stocked rainbow trout and also has lake trout and a few browns. The Lake Fork feeds the nearby Arkansas River, and both streams have great fishing for medium-sized trout in this stretch.

Breckenridge

Leadville

Turquoise Lake

Basalt

Aspen

Snowmass Village

Crested Butte

N W E S

1 MILE

0

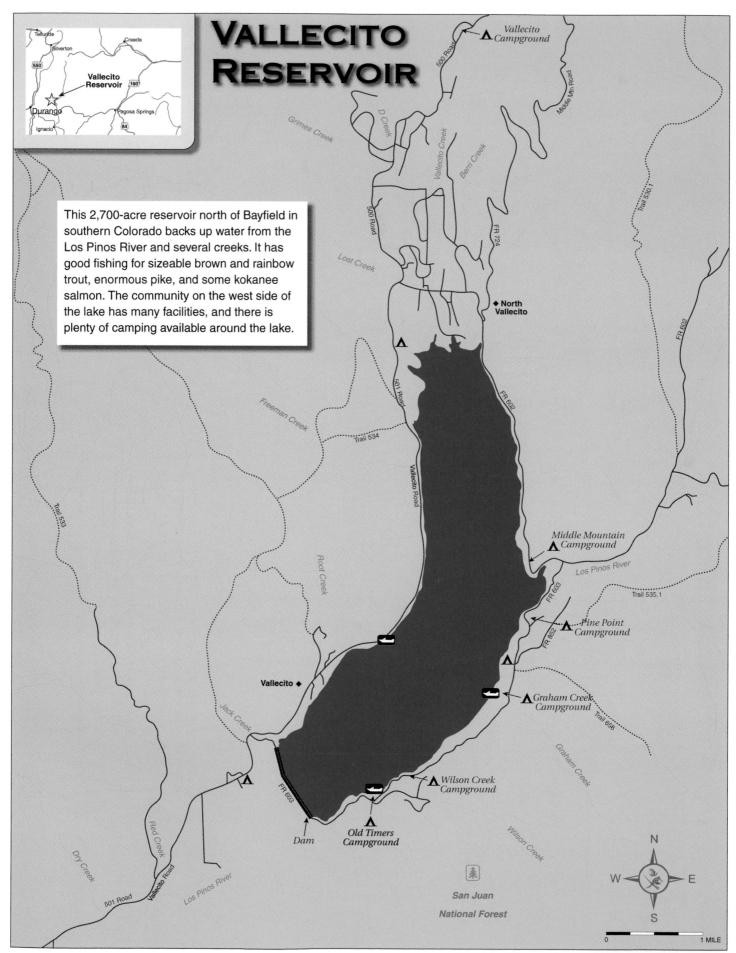

VALLECITO RESERVOIR

This 2,700-acre reservoir north of Bayfield in southern Colorado backs up water from the Los Pinos River and several creeks. It has good fishing for sizeable brown and rainbow trout, enormous pike, and some kokanee salmon. The community on the west side of the lake has many facilities, and there is plenty of camping available around the lake.

Telluride
Silverton
Creede
550
Vallecito Reservoir
160
Durango
Ignacio
Pagosa Springs
84

Vallecito Campground
500 Road
Grimes Creek
D Creek
Vallecito Creek
Berri Creek
Middle Mtn Road
Trail 530.1
500 Road
FR 724
Lost Creek
North Vallecito
FR 692
Freeman Creek
501 Road
FR 602
Trail 534
Vallecito Road
Trail 533
Root Creek
Middle Mountain Campground
Los Pinos River
Trail 535.1
FR 603
Pine Point Campground
FR 852
Vallecito
Graham Creek Campground
Trail 656
Jack Creek
Wilson Creek Campground
Graham Creek
FR 603
Dam
Old Timers Campground
Wilson Creek
Red Creek
Dry Creek
Los Pinos River
501 Road
Vallecito Road
San Juan
National Forest

N
W E
S

0   1 MILE

© Wilderness Adventures Press, Inc.

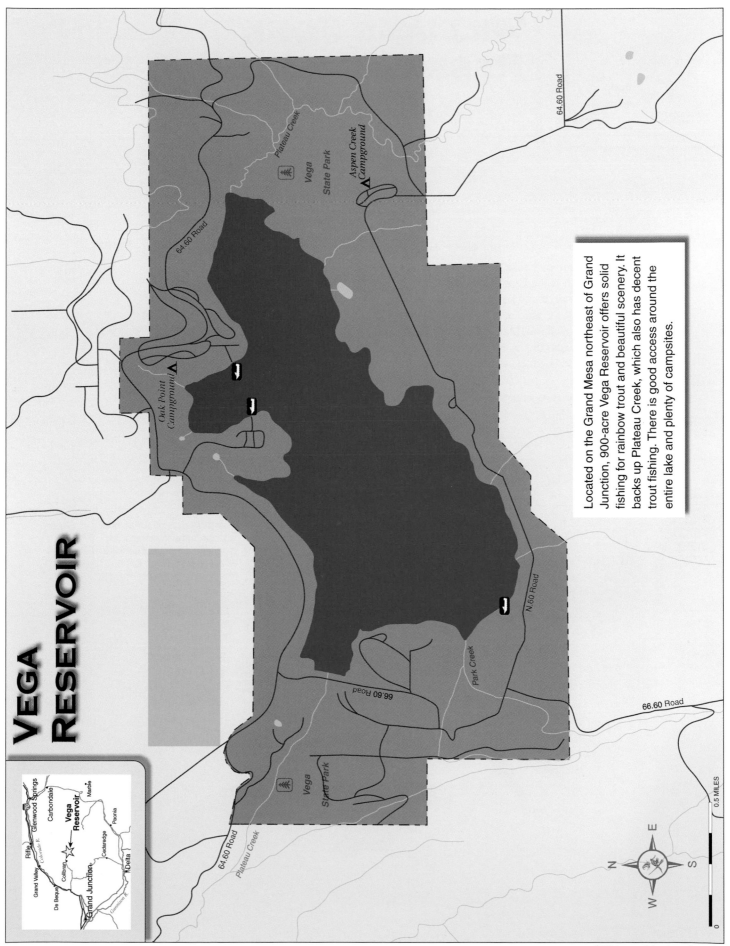

VEGA RESERVOIR

Located on the Grand Mesa northeast of Grand Junction, 900-acre Vega Reservoir offers solid fishing for rainbow trout and beautiful scenery. It backs up Plateau Creek, which also has decent trout fishing. There is good access around the entire lake and plenty of campsites.

Oak Point Campground

Aspen Creek Campground

Vega State Park

Plateau Creek

Park Creek

64.60 Road

66.60 Road

N.60 Road

Grand Valley
Rifle
De Beque
Glenwood Springs
Carbondale
Colorado R.
Collbran
Marble
Vega Reservoir
Grand Junction
Cedaredge
Paonia
Delta
Gunnison R.

N
E
S
W

0   0.5 MILES

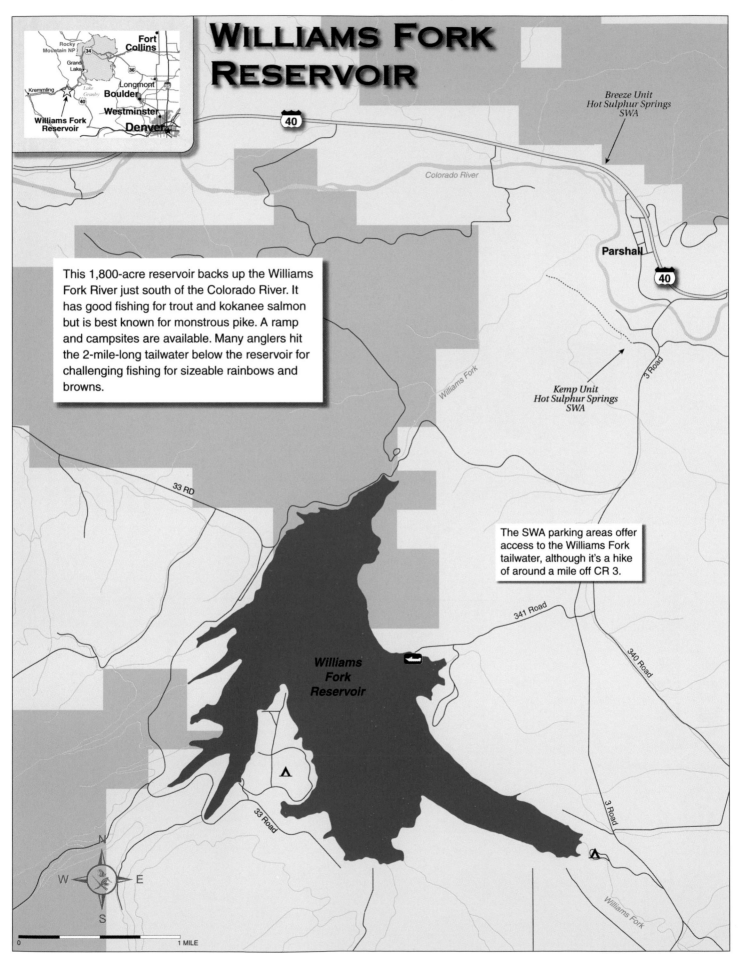

WILLIAMS FORK RESERVOIR

This 1,800-acre reservoir backs up the Williams Fork River just south of the Colorado River. It has good fishing for trout and kokanee salmon but is best known for monstrous pike. A ramp and campsites are available. Many anglers hit the 2-mile-long tailwater below the reservoir for challenging fishing for sizeable rainbows and browns.

The SWA parking areas offer access to the Williams Fork tailwater, although it's a hike of around a mile off CR 3.

Williams Fork Reservoir

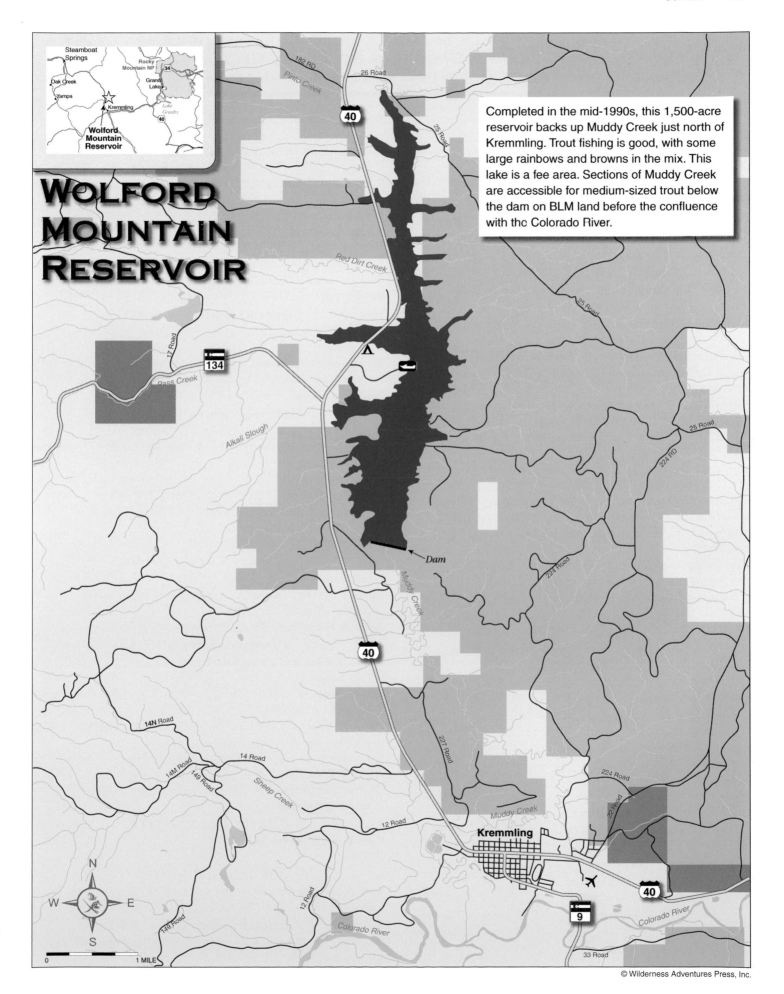

WOLFORD MOUNTAIN RESERVOIR

Completed in the mid-1990s, this 1,500-acre reservoir backs up Muddy Creek just north of Kremmling. Trout fishing is good, with some large rainbows and browns in the mix. This lake is a fee area. Sections of Muddy Creek are accessible for medium-sized trout below the dam on BLM land before the confluence with the Colorado River.

Dam

Kremmling

0   1 MILE

N
W   E
S

FLY & TACKLE SHOPS, GUIDES & SPORTING GOODS BY CITY (AREA CODES LISTED WITH CITY NAME)

ALAMOSA - 719

Alamosa Sporting Goods, 1114 Main / 589-3006

Kristi Mountain Sports, Villa Mall / West Highway 160 / 589-9759

Spencer Sporting Goods, 616 Main / 589-4361

ALMONT - 970

Three Rivers Resort, 130 Country Road / Almont 81210 / 641-1303

ANTONITO - 719

Cottonwood Meadows Fly Shop, 34591 Highway 17 / 376-5660

Fox Creek Store, 26573 Hwy 17 / Antonito 81120 / 376-5881

ASPEN - 970

Elkstream Outfitters Inc., 6400 Highway 82 / 928-8380, 800-287-9656 / Fax: 945-5455

Aspen Outfitting Company, 315 East Dean Avenue / 925-3406

Aspen Flyfishing at Aspen Sports, 303 East Durant Avenue / 920-6886

Aspen Taylor Creek At Aspen Sports, 408 E. Cooper St. Mall / Aspen 81611 / 970-925-6331

Aspen Trout Guides Inc., 614 East Durant Avenue / 920-1050, 925-7875

Highlands Outfitting, 4102 Railhead Lodge / 0133 Prospector Road / Aspen 81611 / 920-9080

Mark Justin Outdoor, 217 S Galena / Aspen 81611 / 925-1046

Mountains and Streams, 424 E. Cooper Street / 925 -5580

Oxbow Outfitters Co., 623 East Durant Avenue / 925-1505, 800-421-1505

Western Sports, 555 East Durant / 963-0696

The Outfitters, Snowmass Village Mall / 923-5959

Pomeroy Sports, 614 E. Durante Ave. / Aspen 81611 / 970-925-7875

AVON - 970

Fly Fishing Outfitters, 1060 West Beaver Creek Blvd. / Avon 81620 / 476-3474, 800 595-8090

Dixon Outfitters, 142 Beaver Creek P1 / Avon 81620 / 949-1985

Gorsuch Outfitters, 0097 Main, Unit E102 / 926-0900

BASALT - 970

Fryingpan Anglers, 123 Emma Road, Suite 100 / 927-3441 / email: anglers@rof.net / Web page: wwwexpo.flyshop.com/frypan

Taylor Creek Fly Shop Inc., City Market Shopping Center / 927-4374

Frying Pan River Ranch, 32042 Frying Pan River Road / Meredith

BAYFIELD - 970

Streamside Lodge Fly Shop at Wit's End Guest Ranch & Resort, Inc., 254 Cr 500 / Bayfield, CO 81122 / 800-236-9483, 884-7203

BERTHOUD - 970

Bennett's Inc., 121 Bunyan Ave / Berthoud 80513 / 532-2213

BOULDER - 303

Front Range Anglers, 629-B South Broadway / 80303 / 494-1375

Boulder Outdoor Center, 2510 47th / 444-8420, 800-364-9376

Bucking Brown Trout Company, 26 East 1st Street / Nederland 80466 / 258-3225 / email: buckingb@earthnet.net

Kinsley and Company, 1155 13th Street / 442-6204, 800-442-7420

McGuckin Hardware, 2525 Arapahoe Avenue / 443-1822

Mountain Sports, 821 Pearl Street / 443-6770

The Orvis Shop, 1155 13th St. / 442-6204, 800-442-7420

Rocky Mountain Anglers, 1904 Araphoe Avenue / 447-2400

Rocky Mountain Outfitters, 1738 Pearl / 444-9080

Southcreek Ltd., 415 Main Street / Lyons 80540 / 823-6402

BRECKENRIDGE - 970

Blue River Anglers, 209 N Main / Breckenridge 80424 / 453-9171

Breckenridge Outfitters, 100 North Main Suite 206 / 453-4135 / web site: www.breck.net/breckout / Email: breckout@colorado.net

Mountain Angler, 311 S Main / Box 467 / 453-4665

BUENA VISTA - 719

Arkanglers, 545 US Highway 24 N / 395-1796

Arkansas River Fly Shop, 545 N Hwy 24 / 395-1796 / www.arkanglers.com

Between the Lines, 17920-YS Highway 285, Nathrop / 539-2067

Good Brothers Inc., 320 Charles Street / 395-9348

Hi-Rocky Gift and Sport Store, 111 Cottonwood Avenue / 395-2258

The Trailhead, 707 Highway 24 North / 395-8001

CANON CITY - 719

Royal Gorge Anglers, 1210 Royal Gorge Boulevard / 269-3474

Bubba's Sporting Goods, 723 Main Street / 275-4626

Capricorn Sports, 275-4351

Jimmy's Sport Shop, 311 Main Street / 275-3685

CARBONDALE - 970

Alpine Angling and Adventure Travel, 981 Cowen / 963-9245 / web site: www.rfanglers.com

Inland Drifters, 0928 Highway 133 / 963-7438 / Web site: wwwinlanddrifters.com

Western Sports, 400 East Valley Road / 963-3030 / email: wsport@rof.net / Web page: www.wsports.com

Troutfitters of Aspen, 0038 Stagecoach Circle / 963-0696

AAA Float Anglers, 0848 Roaring Fork Road 106 / 963-3354

Capital Peak Outfitters, 0554 Valley Road / 963-0211

River Adventures Inc., 963-4660

CASTLE ROCK - 303

Plum Creek Anglers, 981 N Park St / Castle Rock 80104 / 814-0868

CENTENNIAL - 303

River & Stream Co., Southglenn Mall / 6911 S University Blvd / Centennial, CO 80122 / 794-7864

COLORADO SPRINGS - 719

Blue River Anglers, 209 Main St., Breckenridge / 453-9171

Peak Fly Shop, 5666 North Academy Boulevard / 80918 / 260-1415

Anglers Covey, 917 West Colorado Avenue / 471-2984, 800-753-4746

Broadmoor Sporting Classics, P.O. Box 1439 / 80901 / 577-5832

Colorado Springs Angler, 3609-19B Austin Bluffs Pkwy 1531-5413

Pikes Peak Angler, 119 North Tejon / 636-3348

Roth Angling, 144-4 Crystal Park Road, Manitou Springs / 80829 / 685-0316

Colorado Fishing Adventures, 6421 Pulpit Rock Drive, 80918 / 598-5787

Flies and Lies, 8570 South Highway 67 / Deckers 80135 / 647-2237

General Fishing Tackle, 3201 North El Paso / 634-3348

Sports Hut, 719 Dale, Fountain / 382-7646

Tackle Shack, 430 West Fillmore / 635-1359

Tricos, 535 Lionstone Drive / 574-5480

All American Sports, 3690 North Academy Boulevard / 574-4400

Blick's Sporting Goods, 119 North Tejon / 636-3348

Great Outdoors Sporting Goods, 520 E. Midland Ave, Woodland Park / 687-0401

Grand West Outfitters, 3250 North Academy Boulevard / 596-3031

Mountain Chalet, 226 North Tejon / 633-0732

CREEDE - 719

Rod and Reel Fly Shop, 101 Creede Avenue / 658-2955

The Ramble House, 116 Creede Avenue / 658-2482 / email: rambhse@rmi.net

San Juan Sports, 658-2359

Rio Grande Angler, 13 South Main St. / Creede 81130 / 658-2255

CRESTED BUTTE - 970

Dragonfly Anglers, 307 Elk Avenue, P.O. Box 1116 / 349-1228

Alpine Outside, 315 6th Street / 349-5011

Harmel's Fly Shop, P.O. Box 399, Almont / 800-235-3402

Troutfitter Sports, 114 Elk Avenue, P.O. Box 2779 / 349-1323

The Alpineer, 419 6th Street / 349-6286

The Colorado Boarder, 32 Crested Mountain Lane / 349-9828

Efflin Sports, 10 Crested Butte Way / 349-6121

Gene Taylor's Sports, 19 Emmons Rd / 349-5386

DE BEQUE - 970

High Lonesome Lodge, 0275 222 Road P.O. Box 88 / De Beque 81630 / 283-9420

DELTA - 970

Gunnison River Pleasure Park, Highway 92 at the confluence of the North Fork of the Gunnison with the Gunnison / 907-2810 Lane, Lazear 81420 / 872-2525

The Sports Network, 252 Main Street / 874-7811

DENVER AREA - 303

All Pro Fish'n Sport, 6221 South Santa Fe Drive / Littleton 80120 / 795-3474

Alpine Angler, 2390 South Chambers Road / Aurora / 873-6997

Anglers All, 5211 Santa Fe Drive / Littleton 80120 / 794-1104

Angler Art & Gifts, 201 Fillmore St., Ste D /Denver

Bear Creek Fly Fishing Company, Box 267 / Idledale 80453 / 697-7352

Blue Quill Anglers, 1532 Bergan Parkway / Evergreen 80439 / 674-4700

Boxwood Gulch Ranch, 838-2465 / Owner: Dan Mauritz / email: boxwood@flyfishers.com

Colorado Angler Fly Shop, 1457 Nelson / Lakewood 80215 / 232-8298 / web site: www.coloradoangler.com / email: RioDS@aol.com

Colorado Sports & Tackle, 5385 Quebec St / Commerce City / 80022 / 287-2111

The Complete Angler, 9616 East Arapahoe Road / Englewood / 858-8436

The Denver Angler, 5455 West 38th Avenue / Denver 80212 / 403-4512

Diamond B Ranch, 569-2130 /970-225-2034

Discount Fishing Tackle Inc., 2645 South Santa Fe Drive / 698-2550

Discount Fishing Tackle Inc., 5550 Wadsworth Bypass / Arvada 80002 / 4000 South Parker Road / Aurora 80015

Duck Creek Sporting Goods, 400 S Boulder Rd / Lafayette 80026 / 665-8845

The Flyfisher Ltd., 120 Madison Street / Denver 80206 / 322-5014 / Orvis

The Executive Angler, 535 16th St, / Denver 80202 / 825-0616

Two Guys Fly Shop, 705 S. Public Rd / Lafayette 80026 / 665-4229 / Fax: 665-4229

Flyfishing Services, Inc., 7925 West Layton #523 / Littleton / 979-3077

Flyfitters Inc., 8168 South Holly / Littleton 80122 / 850-7933

Galyan's, 31 West Flatiron Circle / Broomfield 80020 / 720-887-0900

Marty's Fly For All, 18898 East Saratoga Circle / Aurora / Owner: Marty Bartholomew / 690-6967

Master Angler, 8754 Cloverleaf Circle / Parker 80134 / 680-1004, 888-808-1004

Orvis Englewood, 9619 B East Country Line Road / Englewood / 768-9600

Outdoor Sports Supply, 822 E 19th Ave / Denver 80218 / 861-1218

Plum Creek Anglers, 11 Wilcox / Castle Rock 80104 / 814-0858

River and Stream Co., 6911 S University Blvd / Littleton / 794-7864

Rocky Mountain Angling Club, Creekside Suite 102, 6099 South Quebec / Englewood 80111 / 739-1993, 800-524-1814

Royal Stevens Ltd., 1610 East Girard Place Unit #1 / Englewood 80110 / 788-0433

Sportsman's Warehouse, 14140 East Ellsworth Ave. / Aurora 80012 / 720-858-1800

St. Vrain Angler, 8951 Harlan Street, Westminster / 412-1111

South Platte Angler, 10714 Highway 285 / Conifer / 838-8687

The Trout Fisher Inc., 2020 South Parker Road / Denver 80231 / 369-7970

Trout's Flyfishing, 1069 Old South Gaylord Street / Denver 80209 / 733-1434

The Gone Fishing Company, P.O. Box 440322 / 680-2430

Riverside Anglers at the Riverside Hotel / 499-9614

The Hatch Fly Shop, 480 Sioux Trail Unit #50 / Pine Junction 80430 / 816-0487

Uncle Milty's Tackle Box, 4811 South Broadway / Englewood / 789-3775

Alpenglow Mountain Sport Inc., 885 Lupine / Golden / 277-0133

Bait and Bullet Shop, 59 South 1 Avenue / Brighton / 659-3286

Colorado Sport and Tackle, 5385 Quebec / Commerce City / 287-2111

Jumbo Sports, 7848 County Line Road / Littleton / 792-3374

Grand West Outfitters, 801 Broadway / 825-0300

High Country Bass'n Shop, 1126 South Sheridan Boulevard / 934-4156

Taylor Creek Angling, 223 Milwaukee / Denver 81621 / 927-4374

Western Flies, 8365 Eaton Way / Arvada 80003

DURANGO - 970

Colorado Trails Ranch, 12161 County Road / 240 Durango 81301

Durango Sporting Goods (Gardenswartz), 780 Main Ave / Durango 81301

Durango Fly Goods, 139 East 5th Street / 259-0999 / Orvis endorsed

Duranglers Flies and Supplies, 801-B Main Avenue / 385-4081

Anasazi Anglers Inc., 607 Sunnyside Drive / 385-4665 / email: angler@rmii.com

Don Oliver Fishing Guide, 15 Oak Valley Drive / 382-0364

Outfitter Sporting Goods, 341 Railroad Avenue / 882-7740

River Drifters Fly Shop and West Fork Outfitters, P.O. Box 300, Dolores 81323 / 882-7959, 888-882-8001

Animas Sporting Goods, 1444 Main Avenue / 247-3898

Clayton's Goods for the Woods, Durango Mall / 247-5725

Backcountry Experience, 780 Main Avenue / 247-5830

Durango Sporting Goods, 863 Main Avenue / 259-6696

Gardenswartz Sporting Goods, 863 Main Avenue / 247-2660

EAGLE - 970

Eagle River Anglers, 1011/z Loren Lane / 328-2323

Monarch River Guides, 4199 Trough Road / Bond 80423 / 653-4210

Eagle Pharmacy, 301 Broadway / 328-6875

The Sports Recycler, 34510-A6 Highway 6 / Edwards 81632 / 926-3867

EDWARDS - 970

Gorsuch Outfitters, 0097 Main Street Unit E102 / Edwards 81632 / 926-0900

ESTES PARK - 970

Estes Angler, 338 West Riverside Drive / 586-2110, 800-586-2110

Colorado Wilderness Sports, 358 East Elkhorn Avenue / 586-6548

Rocky Mountain Adventures Inc., 1360 Big Thompson Avenue / 586-6191

Coast to Coast/Ben Franklin Stores, 461 East Wonderview Avenue / 586-3496

Outdoor World, 156 East Elkhorn Avenue / 586-2114

Scott's Sporting Goods, 870 Moraine Avenue / 586-2877

EVERGREEN - 303

The Hatch Fly Shop, 32214 Ellingwood Trail #210 / 674-0482

FORT COLLINS - 970

St. Peters Fly Shop, 202 Remington Street / 498-8968

Rocky Mountain Adventures, 1117 North Highway 287 / 493-4005

Elkhorn Outfitters Fishing Adventures, 484-6272

Rocky Ridge Sporting and Conservation Club, 633 Gait Circle / 221-4868

Longs Drug Store #226, 743 S Lemay Ave / Fort Collins 80524 / 482-3503

Discount Fishing Tackle, 1793 S College Ave / 472-1911

Outdoor World, 1611 S College Ave / 221-5166

FRISCO - 970

Antlers Sport, 900 Summit Blvd / Frisco 80443-5060 / 668-3152

GLENWOOD SPRINGS - 970

Roaring Fork Anglers, 2114 Grand Avenue / 945-0180 / URL:www.rfanglers.com

Elkstream Outfitters Inc., 6400 Highway 82 / 928-8380, 800-287-9656 / Fax: 945-5455

Colorado Canoe and Kayak, 910 Grand / 928-9949

Relay Sports, 715 Grand Avenue / 928-0936

Summit Canyon Mountaineering, 732 Grand Ave / Glenwood Sprgs 81601 / 945-6994

Timberline Sporting Goods, 101 East 3rd / Rifle 81650 / 800-625-4868

GRANBY - 970

Nelson Fly and Tackle, 72149 Highway 40, P.O. Box 336 / Tabernash 80478 / 726-8558

Devil's Thumb Ranch Resort, P.O. Box 750 / Tabernash 80478 / 800-933-4339 / web site: rkymtnhi.com/devthumb

Fletcher's Sporting Goods, 217 West Agate Avenue / 887-3747

GRAND JUNCTION - 970

Big Creek Fly Shop, 549 Main St / Grand Junction 81501 / 241-6095

Western Anglers, 2454 Highway 6 and 50 #103 / 244-8658

B & H Sports, 599 Northgate Drive / 245-6605

Gene Taylor's Sporting Goods, 445 West Gunnison Avenue / 242-8165

Eddy Sport, 580 32 Rd Unit E / Grand Junction 81504 / 434-4811

The Fishermans Guild, 251 Beacon Court Unit 8 / 241-7661

Sportsman's Warehouse, Grand Junction 12464 US Highway 6 & 50 / 243-8100

GREELEY - 970

Garretson Sport Center, 3817 W 10th / Greeley 80634 / 353-8068

Stone Creek, Ltd., 2645-6th Avenue / Greeley 80634-8906 / 330-7476

GUNNISON - 970

High Mountain Outdoors, 115 South Wisconsin / 641-4243 or 800-793-4243

Adventure Experiences, Inc., #2 Illinois, CR 742 / Almont / 641-4708, 641-0507

Three Rivers Fly Shop, Willowfly Anglers / P.O. Box 339 / Almont / 641-1303

Tenderfoot Rafting and Outdoor Adventures, 300 East Tomichi Avenue / 641-2200

Gene Taylor's Sporting Goods, 201 West Tomichi Avenue / 641-1845

Traders Rendezvous, 516 West Tomichi Avenue / 641-5077

Hot Sulphur Springs - 970

Riverside Angler, located in the Ute Trail and Riverside Motels / 725-0025

Dave Parri's Outfitting, P.O. Box 254 / 725-3531

Kremmling - 970

Elktrout Lodge, 1853 CR 33, P.O. Box 614 / 724-3343 / Web site: www.elktrout.com

Dan's Fly Shop, Box 220 / Lake City 82135 / 944-2281

Chuck McGuire Fly Fishing, P.O. Box 1244 / 724-3811

Fishin' Hole Sporting Goods, Highway 40 / 724-9407

Motion Sports, 208 Eagle Avenue / 724-9067

Sportsman Quick Stop, 200 Park Center Avenue / 724-9523

Lake City - 970

Dan's Fly Shop, P.O. Box 220 / 944-2281 / Owner: Dan Hall / web site:xmission.com/-gastown/flyfishing / Email: lampert@gunnison.com

The General Store, Box 143 Highway 149 / 944-2513

The Sportsman, Box 340 Highway 149 / 944-2526

The Tackle Box, 144 South Gunnison Avenue / 944-2306

Timberline Craftsman, 227 Silver St / Delta / 944-2334

Town Square Mini-Mart and Tackle Shop, 944-2236

Back Country Navigator, 811 N Hwy 149 / 944-6277

Lazear - 970

Gunnison River Pleasure Park, 970-2810 Lane / Lazear 81420 / 872-2525

Leadville - 719

Bill's Sport Shop Inc., 225 Harrison Avenue / 486-0739

Buckhorn Sporting Goods, 616 Harrison Avenue / 486-3111

Otto's Hardware and General Mercantile, 1902 Poplar / 486-2220

Longmont - 303

St. Vrain Angler, 418 Main Street / Longmont 80501 / 651-6061

Loveland - 970

Bob's Fly Tying Specialties, 406 South Lincoln Avenue / 667-1107 / Web site: www.inetmkt.com/bobs / email: bob@streamside.com

Butte House Fly Shop, 4412 West Eisenhower Boulevard / 667-9772

Brown's Corner Sporting Goods, 1310 East Eisenhower Boulevard / 663-4913

Great Western Fly Fishing Co., 2180 W Eisenhower Blvd. / Loveland / 461-0701 / www.greatwesternflyfishing.com

Sportsman's Warehouse, 1675 Rocky Mountain Ave / 461-5000

Lyons - 303

Lyons Angler, 415 Main St / Lyons 80520 / 823-5888

Meeker - 970

Buffalo Horn Ranch, 13825 County Road #7 / Meeker 81641 / 878-5450

Cherokee Outfitters, P.O. Box 537 / 878-5750

Elk Creek Lodge, Llc P.O. Box 130 / Meeker 81641 / 878-5454

Wyatt's Sport Center, 223 West Market / 878-4428

Rocky Mountain Archery Pro Shop, 654 Main / 878-4300

Lone Tom Outfitting, 12888 RBC 8 / 878-5122

Marvine Outfitters, P.O. Box 130 / 878-4320

Downing's Hardware, 624 Market / 878-4608

Rio Blanco Ranch Company, 3050 Trappers Lake Road / Meeker 81641 / 878-3444

Montrose - 970

Bear Dance River Guides & Outfitters, 31329 Highway 550 / Montrose 81401 / 626-2140

Cimarron Creek, 317 East Main Street / 249-0408

Gunnison River Expeditions, 19500 Highway 550 / 249-4441

Montrose Sporting Goods, 245 West Main Street / 249-9292

Bennett's Tackle, 121 Bunyan Avenue / Berthoud 80513 / 532-2213

Morrison - 303

Morrison Angler, 103/ Bear Creek Ave / Morrison 80465 / 697-3835

Nederland - 303

Bucking Brown Trout Co, 26 East First Street / P.O. Box 3116 / Nederland 80466 / 258-3225

Pagosa Springs - 970

Back Country Angler, 350 Pagosa Street / 264-4202

Colorado Fishing Adventures, 264-4168 / 731-4141

Let It Fly, 1501 West Hwy 160, #2 / 264-3189 / Fax 264-3190

Ski and Bow Rack Inc., East end of Pagosa Springs / 264-2370

Lake Capote, 17 miles west of Pagosa on Highway 160 / 731-5256 / Private fishing

Pagosa Clay and Trout Ranch, 731-9830

Pagosa Sports, 432 Pagosa Street / 264-5811

Pagosa Springs Hardware, 543 San Juan Street / 264-4353

Pine Junction - 303

The Hatch Fly Shop, 480 Sioux Trail Unit 50 / Pine Junction 80470 / 816-0487

Pueblo - 719

Angler's Choice, 503 Avacado / Pueble 81005 1564-2671

Flying Feather Trout Flies, 15 Heatherwood Ct / Pueblo 81001

Pueblo Sporting Goods, 703 W 9th St #2 / 543-7755

Sports Hut, 332 South McCulloch Boulevard / 547-2848

T and M Sporting Goods, 2023 Lakeview Avenue / 564-0790

Salida - 970

Arkanglers, 7500 W Highway 50 / Full service fly shop / 719-539-4223

Arkansas River Fly Shop, 7500 US Highway 50 / 539-3474

Triple J Trout Ranch / 539-3094

Homestead Sports Center, 11238 West Highway 50 / Poncha Springs / 539-7507

Salida Sporting Goods, 511 East Highway 50 / 539-6221

American Outdoor Sports, 645 East Rainbow Boulevard / 530-0725

G and G Sporting Goods, East Highway 50 / 539-4303

Good Brothers Inc., 116 South F Street / 539-7777

Headwaters Outdoor Equipment, 228 North F Street / 539-4506

Silverthorne - 970

Arapahoe Anglers, 191 Blue River Pkwy / P.O. Box 2540 / 262-2878, 888-876-8818 / email: aanglers@csn.net / Web site: www.fishcolorado.com

Cutthroat Outfitters, 400 Blue River Parkway / 262-2878

Columbine Outfitters, 247 Summit Place Shopping Ctr / Silverthorne 80498 / 262-0966

Gold Medal Fly Shop, 1130 Blue River Parkway, Silverthorne 80498 / 468-8961

Summit Guides, Keystone Village, P.O. Box 2489 / 468-8945

Antler's, 908 North Summit Boulevard / Frisco 80443 / 668-3152

Eddie Bear's Sporting Good Store, 591 Blue River Pkwy / 468-9320

Wilderness Sports, 266 Summit Plaza / 468-5687

South Fork - 719

The Powder Connection Ski and Gift Shop, 31101 Highway 160 / 873-5644

Rainbow Grocery & Sporting, 30359 W Highway Us 160 / South Fork 81154 / 873-5545

Steamboat Springs - 970

Blue Sky West, 435 Lincoln Ave / Steamboat Springs 80477 / 879-8033

Bucking Rainbow Outfitters, 402 Lincoln Avenue, 775616 / 879-8747 / Orvis

Buggywhip's, P.O. Box 770477 / 879-8033, 800-759-0343

Guided Fly Fishing, P.O. Box 880632 / 879-7238

Steamboat Fishing Company Inc., P.O. Box 776250, 635 Lincoln Avenue / 879-6552

Straightline, P.O. Box 4887 / 744 Lincoln Avenue / 879-7568, 800-354-5463

Back Door Sport Ltd., 811 Yampa / 879-6249

Good Time Sports, 730 Lincoln Avenue / 879-7818

Inside Edge Sports, 1835 Central Park Plaza / 879-1250

Lahaina Ski and Sport, Gondola Square / 879-2323

Shop and Hop Food Store, 35775 East US Highway 40 / 879-2489

Sportstalker, 2305 Mt. Werner Circle / 879-0371

Colorado River Guides, P.O. Box 711 / Oak Creek 80467 / 736-2406, 800-938-7238

Spiro's Trading Post, 107 Main / Oak Creek 80467 / 736-2443

Steamboat Fishing CO., 635 Lincoln / Steamboat Springs 80477 / 879-6552

Tabernash - 970

Nelson Fly & Tackle Shop, 72149 Hwy 40 / Tabernash 80478 / 726-8558

Telluride - 970

Telluride Anglers, 121 West Colorado, P.O. Box 3554 / 728-0773

Telluride Sports, 150 West Colorado / 728-4477, 800-828-7547

Telluride Outside, 1982 West Highway 145, P.O. Box 685 / 728-3895, 800-831-6230

The Telluride Mountaineer, 219 East Colorado / 728-6736

Paragon Ski and Sport, 213 West Colorado / 728-4525

Boarding House, 320 West Colorado / 728-0882

Freewheelin', 101 East Colorado / 728-4734

Screamin' Doggies, 750 West Pacific / 728-6970

Olympic Sports, 150 W Colorado Ave / Telluride 81435 / 728-4477

Thornton - 303

Sportsman's Warehouse, Thornton, 11 West 84th Ave / Thornton 80260

Vail - 970

American Trout, P.O. Box 1588, Frisco / 668-0331

Gorsuch Outfitters, 263 East Gore Creek Drive / 476-2294 / email: flyfish@vail.net

Fly Fishing Outfitters Inc., Box 2861 / 476-3474, 800-595-8090 / email: fish@vail.net

Gore Creek Fly Fisherman Inc., 183 East Gore Creek Drive / 476-3296, 800-369-3044

Mount Royal Anglers, 204 Main Street, Frisco / 668-4771

Vail Rod and Gun Club, Box 1848 / 476-3639

Walden - 970

Flies Only Tackle Shop, Box 37 / Cowdrey 80434 / 723-8248 or Box 968 / Walden 80480 / 723-4741

Corkle's Little Market, 1 mile north of Walden / 723-8211 / Fishing supplies & licenses

North Park Anglers, 524 Main Street / Box 548 / Walden 80480 / 723-4215 / www.northparkanglers.com

Sportsman Supply, 400 Main / 723-4343

Walden Hardware, 467 Main / 723-4655

Woodland Park - 719

Grizzly Outdoors, 210 West Midland Avenue / 687-6464

Great Outdoors Sporting Goods, 520 West Midland Avenue / 687-0401

New Mexico

Duranglers Flies and Supplies, 1003 Hwy 511 / Navajo Dam, NM 87419 / 505-632-5952

Rizuto's San Juan River Lodge, P.O. Box 6309 / Navajo Dam, NM 87419 / 505-632-3893 or 505-632-1411

Wildreness Adventures Press, Inc.
45 Buckskin Road
Belgrade, Montana 59714
www.wildadv.com